Jefferson's America

Jefferson's America

1760–1815

Norman K. Risjord

MADISON HOUSE

Madison 1991

This work is based on an earlier book published by the same author under the title *Forging the American Republic, 1760–1815*.

Printed in the United States of America on acid-free paper.

LIBRARY OF CONGRESS CATALOGING-IN-PUBLICATION DATA

Risjord, Norman K.
Jefferson's America, 1760–1815 / Norman K. Risjord. — 1st ed.
p. cm.
"Based on an earlier book published by the same author under the title Forging the American republic, 1760–1815"—T.p. verso.
Includes bibliographical references and index.
ISBN 0–945612–24–9. — ISBN 0–945612–25–7 (pbk.)
1. United States—History—Colonial period, ca. 1600–1775.
2. United States—History—Revolution, 1775–1783. 3. United States—History—1783–1815. I. Title.
E195.R58 1991
973—dc20 91–21533
CIP

Designed by William Kasdorf.
Typeset and produced by Impressions, Madison, Wisconsin.
Printed by Edwards Brothers, Inc.

Published by Madison House Publishers, Inc.
Post Office Box 3100, Madison, Wisconsin, 53704–0100

FIRST EDITION

For Connie,
who puts my books
into braille.

Contents

Preface *ix*
Maps *x*

INTRODUCTION: *The American Landscape in 1760* *1*

1 *England's Atlantic Community* *27*

The Atlantic Economy *28*
The Urban Experience *34*
The Educational Interchange *36*
The Artistic Community *43*
Dawn of Enlightenment *46*
Religious Awakenings *49*
British America in 1763 *54*

2 *The Imperial Challenge, 1763–1774* *56*

Writs of Assistance *58*
The Parson's Cause *60*
Parliament Takes a Hand *61*
The Stamp Act *63*
A New Challenge: Townshend Taxes *70*
"The Bloody Business on King Street" *74*
An Internal Distraction: The Regulators *76*
Controversy Over the Wilderness *78*
Sam Adams: Lonely Rebel *81*
Orchestrated Violence: The Tea Parties *83*

3 *Triumph of Independence* *88*

The Continental Congress *88*
The Road to Concord Bridge *92*

Siege of Boston *94*
"Common Sense" *96*
The Revolution as Civil War *100*
An Island Versus a Continent *103*
From Long Island to Trenton *105*
Contest for the Fourteenth Colony *109*
The Hinge of Fate *111*
A World War *116*
Winter at Valley Forge *119*
Stalemate in the North *120*
Campaign in the South *123*
The Road to Yorktown *126*
The Peacemakers *127*

4 *From Many, One* *132*

Thirteen Republics *133*
Articles of Confederation *137*
Organizing the West *141*
Demobilization and Depression *145*
The Fight Over Paper Money *149*
"A Little Rebellion . . ." *152*
Toward a Stronger Union *154*
The Federal Convention *158*
The Great Debate *164*

5 *The Search for National Identity* *174*

A Bourgeois Republic *175*
African Americans: Slave and Free *177*
Liberty's Daughters Become the Republic's Mothers *180*
Reform with Caution *183*
Toward a National Economy *188*
Religion: Institutionalizing Faith *193*
The Pursuit of Science *195*
An American Style in Literature and the Arts *197*
The Search for National Identity *205*

6 *The Federal Experiment* *208*

Launching the Vessel of State *208*
The Bill of Rights *211*
Public Finance: Hamilton vs. Madison *211*
The Politics of Neutrality *216*
Western Lands and Border Warfare *218*
The Whiskey Rebellion *223*
Jay's Treaty *225*

Washington's Farewell *227*
The Troubles of John Adams *230*
Federalist Repression *232*
The Politics of Peace *234*
"The Revolution of 1800" *236*
The Experiment Confirmed *239*

7 *Jefferson's "Empire for Liberty"* *241*
"A Wise and Frugal Government . . ." *241*
Gallatin at the Treasury *245*
Assault on the Courts *247*
National Honor and National Interest *251*
The Rising Empire *253*
Exploring Louisiana *256*
The West Florida Controversy *258*
The Conspiracy of Aaron Burr *261*
Neutral Rights *264*
The Embargo Experiment *264*
The Road to War *270*

8 *"Mr. Madison's War"* *274*
"The Greatest Indian" *277*
The Coming of War *281*
Snatching Defeat from the Jaws of Victory: 1812 *283*
Victories at Sea *285*
Recovery of the West: 1813 *287*
Politics and War: The East in 1813 *289*
Jackson and Horseshoe Bend *289*
The Campaign of 1814 *290*
From Lake Champlain to New Orleans *293*
The Peace of Christmas Eve *295*
The Hartford Convention *297*
Changing of the Guard *298*

Some Suggested Readings *300*
The American Landscape in 1760 *300*
England's Atlantic Community *301*
The Imperial Challenge, 1763–1774 *302*
Triumph of Independence, 1774–1783 *303*
From Many, One *304*
The Search for National Identity *305*
The Federal Experiment *306*
Jefferson's "Empire for Liberty" *307*
"Mr. Madison's War" *308*

Index *309*

Maps

Boston, 1775 *93*

Campaigns in New York and New Jersey, 1776–1777 *106*

Invasion of Canada, 1775–1776 *110*

Campaigns of 1777 *113*

Southern Campaigns, 1778–1781 *124*

United States, 1783 *130*

Popular Vote on the Constitution *167*

The Old Northwest *222*

The Louisiana Purchase *256*

West Florida Controversy *259*

Niagara Campaigns *283*

War in the West *288*

Jackson's Route to New Orleans *295*

Preface

THIS IS THE STORY OF THE BIRTH OF A NATION. But it is more than that because the nation's founders consciously experimented with a new form of government that had never before been tried on a large geographical scale—a republic with a representative system that was based on the consent of the governed. Such an experiment was a logical outgrowth of the Revolution itself, for the overthrow of imperial authority left Americans without a monarch and with little desire to find one. Moreover, both colonial inheritance and the methods which Revolutionary leaders used to mobilize popular support dictated that the new system be based on representative institutions.

Independence created as many difficulties as it solved. Still to be determined was the viability of the fragile union among the thirteen states, the stability and integrity of the republic they created, as well as the size and character of the popular base on which it rested. In resolving these issues Americans had a number of advantages from the beginning. They possessed, for instance, a common language, literature, and law. With the exception of the African American minority there was substantial ethnic homogeneity. Americans, as a result, seemed more concerned with their mutual interests than with their differences. As their political institutions matured they searched self-consciously for symbols of national identity, and they found them everywhere—in Noah Webster's "blue-backed speller," in the Bunker Hill monument, in the Fourth of July, in the Roman forums that graced Washington, D.C.

By no means was this process of nation-building completed by the War of 1812. Even so, that event is a symbolic end for the Revolutionary generation. Although the conflict brought little to boast of militarily, except for the Battle of New Orleans, it nevertheless produced a sense of national unity and silenced long-held fears that the republic might collapse at any moment. By 1815 the United States seemed to have forged a place of respect among western nations, and its people greeted the future with new-found confidence. In the succeeding years, it seemed only fitting that the Revolutionary generation, represented by Presidents Madison and Monroe, should relinquish the reins of power to a new generation of leaders—a generation that could be as willful as Andrew Jackson, as foresighted as John Quincy Adams, as insistent as John C. Calhoun, or as smooth as Henry Clay. It was a new game after 1815, and another story.

In the spring of 1989, Professor Peter H. Wood, whom I had not previously met, stopped me in a corridor during a meeting of the Organization of American Historians and asked me to consider revising my book *Forging the American Republic, 1760–1815,* which I wrote some twenty years ago. Professor Wood volunteered that he thought it still one of the best books in the field of the American Revolution and early national period. I was immensely flattered, especially in view of Professor Wood's distinction in the field of early American history. I agreed to give it some thought.

The revisions proved to be quite substantial, for there have been many important contributions in the field of early American history in the past twenty years. We now have a greater understanding of the culture of American cities in the eighteenth and early nineteenth centuries, and of the politics of artisans and shopkeepers. Important work has been done on the impact of the Revolution on women, African Americans, and Native Americans. And these are only a few examples of the wealth of recent historical writing. Because the book is aimed at the general reader, I have not included footnotes. But the text itself will reveal my indebtedness to Merrill Peterson, Gary Nash, Mary Beth Norton, Peter Onuf, Joyce Appleby, Sean Wilentz, Noble Cunningham, and Forrest McDonald, as well as many others. I also wish again to thank Michael L. Czechanski, who created the original maps.

In order to give the tale a more human dimension I have added anecdotal material from the life of Thomas Jefferson. He, after all, is a recurrent figure in the story, almost from beginning to end. In addition, he either instigated or wholeheartedly participated in the major forces of the age—liberal-democratic reform, the philosophy of free enterprise, westward expansion, and the definition of human and national rights, at home and abroad. These currents, in turn, shaped the nation's destiny for the remainder of the nineteenth century. The result is certainly not a biography of Jefferson; it is instead a history of America in Jefferson's time. The title *Jefferson's America,* suggested by my wife Connie, announces that theme.

Norman K. Risjord
Madison, Wisconsin

Jefferson's America

INTRODUCTION

The American Landscape in 1760

British North America in 1760 was a thin line of settlement stretching from the coast of Newfoundland to the sea islands of Georgia. In the century and a half since the founding of Jamestown, the white population had penetrated no more than150 miles inland from the sea. It was still little more than a European outpost, economically and culturally dependent on the motherland. Yet time had wrought an American temperament, an American way of looking at the world. The physical separation from Europe represented by three thousand miles of Atlantic generated a feeling of independent identity, a nascent national consciousness. A host of other influences—the wilderness environment, the intermingling of ethnic strains (English, Scottish, French, German, Dutch, Scandinavian)—fostered this feeling of self-conscious identity.

"What is an American, this new man?" asked the French visitor St. Jean de Crevecoeur. Except for some imaginative characterizations and fascinating prototypes, he never really found out. American society, as most visitors discovered, was too heterogeneous, individualistic, and scattered to be susceptible to much generalization. To describe it in universal terms would lose the infinite variety and color that attended life in the mid-eighteenth century. Let us, then, try to answer Crevecoeur's question by accompanying a mythical yet very curious Englishman, who arrived in the American colonies—let us say at Newport, Rhode Island—in the autumn of 1760. He has timed his journey well, for the great imperial contest with France is drawing to a close. In September of that year, the French governor-general of Canada surrendered to Lord Jeffrey Amherst, bringing to an end the French dominion in North America. Fighting continued in the West Indies; indeed, the British even seized Cuba from Spain. But the American settlements at last found peace, and the North Atlantic was almost a British lake. Our traveler himself never existed, but the journal of his travels through the American settlements is a composite of numerous travel diaries kept by both Americans and Europeans in the middle decades of the eighteenth century.

SEPTEMBER 15, 1760. This day we entered the harbor of Newport, in the colony of Rhode Island, after a passage of nearly four weeks from Bristol, England. This city is hardly a major seaport even by American standards—it numbers no more than 7,500 inhabitants—but in wartime it is a thriving center of privateering. Privateering is a type of warfare at which Americans are particularly adept, due to their ability to construct fast, sleek vessels and their penchant for making money even during national emergencies. A privateer is a privately-owned armed vessel which preys on enemy commerce for profit, under official sanction. In fact, the sloop on which I traveled had just had a successful cruise in the Bay of Biscay before putting into Bristol for repairs. It offered quick passage to America, so I seized the opportunity.

The harbor of Newport is part of a collection of river estuaries known as Narragansett Bay. The city itself sits on Rhode Island, the geographical feature from which the entire colony derives its name. The island, about twelve miles long and less than half that in width, is an open garden of farms. Newport is nestled between some lovely low-lying hills and the water's edge, and it has much of the appearance of an English country town. The houses are generally of wood frame, and nearly everyone has a substantial yard and garden. It lacks a cluttered, urban appearance because the streets are broad and few buildings rise above three stories. But it is not a rustic village, either. The streets are paved and lighted at night. The brick Colony House, where the government resides, is a most handsome building, but even better is the Redwood Library. Designed by Peter Harrison, an English architect who moved to the colonies some years ago, the library is modeled on a Grecian temple with four Doric columns in front supporting a massive portico.

Rhode Island's government is republican in form and democratic in spirit. The governor, the council, and the lower house of the assembly are all elected annually by the freeholders, and these officials carry on the public business with almost no interference from authorities in London. The democratic spirit also extends to religion, where any species of worship (including none at all) is tolerated. This attitude dates from the very beginnings of the colony, for many of the early settlers were dissenters and heretics ejected from Massachusetts. As a measure of this religious diversity, Newport possesses three Baptist and two Congregational churches, a Quaker meetinghouse, a Moravian meetinghouse, an Anglican church, and a Jewish synagogue.

The people of Newport, like other Yankees, have the reputation of being sharp traders almost completely devoted to the pursuit of gain, but I found them pleasant and courteous. Indeed, I was allowed to spend only one night in a public house before being invited to lodge with a physician whom I had met some years earlier in Edinburgh. The good doctor gave me a tour of the city and introduced me to its social life. We spent one evening at the theater and another dancing with some very enjoyable young ladies. I was even invited to a session of the Friday Night Club, a group that specializes in conversation, wine, and exquisite food. Newport is reputed to have the best fish market in the world, and the dining club maintained the town's integrity with a repast that included steamed lobsters, oysters, clams, and several different kinds of fish. In the past few years, the city has become a favorite summer retreat for the planters of Carolina and Georgia; perhaps that helps explain its gaiety, its variety of amusements, and its solicitous treatment of visitors.

THE ROADS BETWEEN THIS CITY AND BOSTON, I am told, are unreliable. All through America, road maintenance is in the hands of local authorities—town officials in New England, county courts elsewhere—hence the quality varies from poor to wretched, depending on the wealth of the locality and the diligence of the officials. I therefore abandoned my early notion of purchasing a carriage and instead resolved to travel by horseback. In this respect, my choice of Rhode Island for a landfall in America was a happy one, for the colony is renowned for its fine horses. Indeed, they sell large numbers of horses to planters in the West Indies.

Setting off on September 20, I rode northward across the island and then took a ferry over to the village of Bristol. From there a rather indifferent, rock-strewn road led northward into Massachusetts. It is surprising how little of Rhode Island seems to be cultivated; perhaps the soil is too stony. What little comes under the till is usually planted in maize, or Indian corn; the remainder is pasture and hayfields. Dairying is thus a major industry, and the colony's cheese is almost as famous as its horses.

The sky at this time of year is filled with enormous flights of migratory (or passenger) pigeons. At times they nearly blot out the sun, and the horizon is never entirely free of them. In the evening they settle into large trees, sometimes in such numbers as to break the branches. Once at roost they are almost impossible to arouse, and people can knock them down with long poles. At the ordinary, which is distinguished from an inn by having meals at pre-set hours, a mode that is less expensive for the traveler and more profitable for the innkeeper, where I spent the night, roast pigeon was the main item on the bill of fare, and it was excellent. The tavern keeper informed me that the poorer sort subsist on them almost entirely during their flight.

Boston still considers itself the intellectual center of the colonies, though it has been outdistanced by Philadelphia and New York in population and commerce. By a census taken in this year the city numbers 15,631. It extends for about two miles along the seaward side of a peninsula formed by the Charles River as it curves into Boston Bay. On the western edge of town is a lovely tree-lined mall overlooking the common pasture, and beyond that are several hills on one of which stands a beacon that is used to alarm the neighborhood of impending attack. Across the river is a fairly sizable village called Charlestown. Being unacquainted in Boston, I sought out an inn that could furnish supper for me and a stable for my horse. I then obtained lodging at a nearby house since inns are inclined to be noisy and expensive.

Boston has more of an urban appearance than Newport. Buildings are jammed together, and the streets, though paved with stones, are narrow and irregular, having been erected haphazardly as the city expanded. The center of the city is now a scene of blackened desolation. Last March the worst fire in its history consumed some four hundred buildings. On the other hand, the calamity will allow the city to renovate itself, and officials promise a close supervision of the reconstruction. The new buildings will also be in brick which is more durable and less expensive than wood. Lumber for construction purposes has to be brought by ship all the way from Maine, and it costs five times as much as brick. Even firewood is scarce and expensive in this place because the forests of eastern Massachusetts have been nearly exhausted by a century of cutting. Public inspectors closely supervise its sale to protect the populace from the sharp practices of country wood peddlers.

Though Boston is much like English cities in appearance, I found its citizenry quite different. In England a person is born to a social class and, barring an extreme turn in the wheel of fortune, he never leaves it. Americans generally make a similar distinction between gentlemen (though they have no heritable titles), the "middling sort," and the "lower orders," but no individual feels confined to his station in life. Indeed, they seem engaged in a mad scramble to "get ahead." The best families, whose pedigrees date from the beginnings of the colony, can be identified by their fine dress, elegant houses, genteel manners, and education; but for the rest of the people social differences seem to be largely a matter of money. Perhaps that is why they pursue wealth so avidly. It brings more than material rewards—it is the key to social status and political influence.

Curious to see how the poorest people fared, I visited the Boston Alms House. Built in the 1730s, it is a substantial brick edifice which houses the indigent and the homeless at public expense. The place was terrible, crowded with refugees from the Indian wars and sick soldiers being maintained at the expense of the province, though I was informed that in normal times there is ample room for the local poor. The able-bodied are expected to perform assigned tasks, but this labor is never sufficient to defray the cost of maintaining them. One of the overseers of the poor indicated that the workhouse would cost the city more than £2,000 this year. In addition, the city paid local physicians to provide free medical services to paupers. In times of peace the various forms of poor relief were the largest items in the city's outlay of expenses. Conditions in the Alms House were far from pleasant, but on the whole they seemed no worse than in similar establishments in England. In order to control expenditures on poor relief Boston, like other towns in New England, "warned" persons with no visible means of support to leave the town. This system was especially applied to new arrivals, many of whom doubtless had been "warned out" of some other Massachusetts town. Where such unfortunates finally come to light no one seems to know.

The streets of Boston are a source of constant entertainment, but walking them is neither safe nor soothing. The passing show offers infinite variety—chimney sweeps, wood peddlers, merchants, ladies, ministers, soldiers, and sailors. But it is also a bedlam of noise—women hawk mussels and fish in strident tones; wagoners shout, curse, and crack their whips; iron-rimmed carriage wheels rumble over cobblestones; cattle bawl as they are led to the slaughterhouse. Some years ago the General Court prohibited vehicles from passing by the State House during its sessions because representatives could not hear the proceedings. That rule was generally ignored, so now iron chains are put across King Street whenever the legislature convenes.

After a week in Boston I departed for the west country, determined to see some of the interior of this vast continent. From the summit of Beacon Hill one can see the distance of a day's ride, and it is a pleasant scene indeed. The countryside is quite open, a patchwork of green pastures and fields of ripening grain. Among the gentle hills are the spires of churches that betray the village communities which are the heart of New England society. However, I first had to negotiate the Charles River which is nearly a mile wide at this point.

Crossing rivers in this country presents about the same hazard for travelers as highwaymen do in Europe. Bridges are rare because the people lack the technology and finances to span large rivers, and they are considered unnecessary for small or shallow streams that can be waded. Ferry boats vary greatly in size and quality, but even the best of them are frail contraptions. Broad and flat-bottomed, without keels, they are either pushed across the river with poles or pulled by ropes. They are worrisome in fair weather, and in foul they are to be avoided altogether. In the course of our passage across the Charles a late-summer storm arose, and a clap of thunder frightened the wagon team that shared the vessel with me. The horses lurched to one side, the loaded wagon slipped on the leaning deck, and in an instant the boat capsized. Fortunately, we were by then only fifty feet from shore, and I emerged wet but unharmed. The unfortunate peddler, however, lost a good part of his merchandise, especially the salt and spices. A brief interval at an inn with a hot rum toddy while my clothing dried, and I was ready to resume my journey.

Just above the ferry crossing the river curved westward, and the road paralleled it to Cambridge, a village of perhaps a hundred houses. Harvard College, located here, is the oldest in the colonies, dating its founding to the year 1636. The college was initially intended to train Congregational ministers, but in recent years it has become more secular, attracting the sons of the gentry from all over New England. Its three classroom buildings are arranged in an open quadrangle. In appearance they remind one of the many public buildings erected in London after the Great Fire of 1666. It is a restrained baroque that found its best expression in the churches of Christopher Wren. Old Harvard, oldest of the buildings (1677), houses the college library. The largest library in America, it contains about 4,000 volumes, most of them on theological subjects.

West of Cambridge the road winds past woodlots and fields enclosed by stone fences. For some miles the road is quite crowded with wagons carrying firewood and the fall harvest of pumpkins and squash to the Boston market. Thereafter the traffic thins, the road deteriorates, villages and farms seem more scattered. Gigantic rocks break up the landscape, the soil seems thin and stony, the farms barely able to sustain themselves. It is evident that the inhabitants are unused to strangers, for they display an extraordinary curiosity. The saddle-weary traveler is plied with questions, ranging from the state of his own family and business to the condition of the world. Until all questions are satisfactorily answered and each member of the family has conferred and compared the results, it is nearly impossible to obtain food or drink. Friends in the city warned me of this trait and suggested a scheme devised by the famed Dr. Franklin. Whenever he stopped at a rural tavern the doctor summoned the master and mistress, the children, manservants, maidservants, and stable-boys and told the assembly:

> Worthy people, I am ____ of Philadelphia, by trade a ____ and a bachelor; I have some relations at Boston, to whom I am going to make a visit. My stay will be short, and I shall then return and follow my business, as a prudent man ought to do. This is all I know of myself, and all I can possibly inform you of; I beg therefore that you will have pity on me and my horse, and give us both some refreshment.

Farm families in remote areas of New England—and in the middle and southern colonies as well—survive by producing nearly all of their needs on the farm. They grow their own food, spin, weave, and sew their own clothing; they even fashion their own furniture and wagons. The little cash they need—to purchase such things as salt and kitchen pots—they obtain by selling a bit of surplus crop. Those with ready access to the forest sell firewood or make shingles and barrel staves. Potash, made from wood ashes and water and used in making soap, also has a ready market.

Life in the hinterland is harsh, and every family member has to bear his or her share of the work. Nor is there much prospect of getting ahead in the world. Even if the family, by great effort, were able to push back the forest and bring new land under cultivation, they would be little better off. They would have more grain to sell, but freight costs would consume most of the profit. Curiously, they seemed to accept their condition. The families with whom I spent evenings were suspicious of the wealthy and hostile to change. My reports of agricultural advances in England, such as crop rotation and the use of fertilizers, simply drew blank stares.

The Connecticut River valley, by contrast, is a land of deep, rich soil and prosperous farms. Country homes of wealthy "river barons" dot the landscape, and the social structure seems more like that of the Boston vicinity. Gone too is the feeling of rural isolation, for the river provides easy communication with the seacoast. West of the Connecticut River the land rises sharply into the Berkshire hills, graced with a lovely shower of autumn colors. This whole region, including parts of Vermont and Connecticut, is a major center of iron mining. It is called the Salisbury district, after the town in northwestern Connecticut where beds of ore were discovered about thirty years ago. The ore is dug from open pits and carried in wagons to furnaces. These are located near a wood supply, for they burn huge quantities of charcoal. The ore is dumped in at the top of these brick cones, and melted iron flows out from the bottom into sand molds. The stream of iron and its short tributaries look a bit like a nursing sow; hence the bars are called "pig" iron. Since this form of iron is highly carbonized and very brittle, it is almost useless. Further heating and much hammering by smiths is necessary before it can be fashioned into implements. A few forges for producing wrought iron have appeared in this area, but most pig iron is shipped to England for further treatment. Indeed, it is one of New England's most important exports.

ANOTHER DAY'S RIDE BROUGHT ME OUT OF THE HILLS and into the valley of the Hudson River. It is like crossing the frontier into another country, for the Dutch influence is everywhere evident, though New York has been a British colony for nearly a century. Even the farmhouses look as if they had been transplanted from the Netherlands or Saxony. Each has a framework of squared logs, which form the outline of the house and support the roof. The space between the rafters is filled with unfired bricks, mere lumps of clay, and these are covered with clapboards to prevent weathering. On the interior both bricks and rafters are painted with whitewash.

Since all traffic here goes southward along the Hudson, the road from Massachusetts was little more than a trail through the woods, and the absence of inns forced me to spend another night at a farmhouse. The Dutch family was accommodating, once I made clear my ability to pay, but their distaste for things English was everywhere evident. They spoke Dutch among themselves, and the few volumes displayed on a bookshelf were in Dutch. Dinner was cooked in a huge fireplace, which occupied one entire wall. Unlike fireplaces in New England, which are recessed in the wall, this one projected into the room. The hearth was part of the floor, and the chimney was suspended above the fire on ingeniously balanced rafters. It was thus open on three sides, and the entire family could gather round it on a frosty evening. Supper was a porridge made of boiled corn meal and milk, all carefully measured so not an ounce was left uneaten.

The city of Albany stretches along the west bank of the Hudson. Its main street runs for more than a mile along the river, the space between it and the water being occupied by gardens. In the center of town is a steep hill on which sits a rather dilapidated fort. The older houses are built in the Continental style, with stepped gables facing the street; some even have roofs of red tile imported from Holland. Each has its own garden and well, and on each side of the front steps (or "stoop" as the Dutch call it) are planted trees and shrubs. Every family has a cow, which is kept in the common pasture at the edge of town. In the evening the cattle go home of their own accord, meandering down the grassy street with their bells tinkling, to be milked under the master's tree. One is hard-put to decide whether Albany is really a city, or merely a heavily populated farm. I stayed at an ordinary, where supper consisted of pancakes made of mashed pumpkin and cornmeal.

After a day in Albany I boarded a sloop for the passage downriver to the city of New York. There are no roads between New York and Albany worthy of the name, since nearly all traffic goes by river. Sailing by day and anchoring at night, the 160-mile trip required four days. After the river slips through the Hudson Highlands it becomes very broad and sluggish. Indeed, at some times of the day, the incoming tide is stronger than the river current, and with a south wind a vessel has no choice but to anchor. I soon tired of this slow progress, and shortly after we passed the Spuyten Duyvil Creek, which separates Manhattan from the mainland, I put ashore to make the rest of the journey by horseback. Two hours' ride through well-groomed farmland brought me to Greenwich, a village of perhaps a dozen houses where I stopped for dinner at a very fine establishment called the Glass House. From there it was only another mile or so to the outskirts of New York.

The city of New York sits on the southern extremity of Manhattan Island, extending two miles up the East River and about half that distance up the Hudson. The city is blessed with the finest natural harbor on the seaboard, and the Hudson River offers a gateway to the interior. These natural advantages make it the fastest-growing city in the colonies. It has lately passed Boston in size, and it is probable that it will soon equal or even surpass Philadelphia. In appearance, however, it still resembles an overgrown Dutch village. The streets are narrow and irregular, except for Broadway, which extends northward from the Battery along the height of land between the two rivers. They have only recently begun to pave the streets (with money raised by lottery), and in some of the newer areas the stumps of old pine trees remain an obstacle to traffic. In the older part of town the houses are built in the Dutch fashion with gable ends fronting the street. Most are four or five stories high and built of brick; roofs are commonly tile or pine shingles. There is not the rivalry between English and Dutch that exists at Albany, but the social gap between the two is still apparent. One striking feature of the population is the number of Africans, both slave and free; they make up a sixth of the population. Every household of substance has one or more black servants, and free blacks are extensively employed as artisans, carpenters, shipbuilders, and fishermen.

New York has more first-class taverns and public houses than any city I have seen, except, of course, London. I took private lodgings, as usual, to ensure a peaceful night, but then explored the culinary delights of the city. Robert Todd's tavern on Broad Street provided a splendidly prepared leg of mutton, and after dinner the clientele, most of them royal officials, entertained me with political gossip. The following day I walked the city and then dined at the Horse and Cart, a place frequented by New Englanders. The food was less expensive and the company more sober.

TWO DAYS OF FREEZING DRIZZLE DAMPENED MY STAY in New York and served to remind me of the approach of winter. I thus decided to resume my journey in the hope of reaching Philadelphia before the roads became impassable, and travel more a task than a treat. The ferry across the harbor to Staten Island was a seaworthy schooner, much like the vessel I had taken south from Albany. On the nine-mile journey I was entertained by flocks of diving ducks, which the ship captain called "bluebills."

Staten Island is a pretty garden of small, close-packed farms. Every farm has an apple orchard, and now that the grain harvest is finished everyone is busy pressing cider. Oysters and clams abound on the beaches and rivers of this island, and fried or steamed they appear on every table. Large quantities of oysters are pickled in spices and vinegar and then exported to Europe or the West Indies. Clamshells have an additional value because they can be made into wampum, which is the main currency among the Indians. I paused to observe the process at one small factory on the island. Small oval-shaped pieces are cut from the shells; those taken from the center are purple, the rest are white. The pieces are then polished, drilled, and strung like beads. Purple, being scarcer, is regarded as the most valuable.

Another clumsy and half-rotten scow carried me to the New Jersey shore at Perth Amboy, a small but charming town of about a hundred houses. Located at the mouth of the Raritan River, this town could serve as the port for the whole province, but its trade, in fact, is inconsiderable. This half of New Jersey is dependent commercially upon New York City, as the western half is dominated by Philadelphia. The colony is divided socially, as well as economically. The eastern part was settled largely by the Dutch, New Englanders, and some Scots; hence it is predominantly Presbyterian. West Jersey was originally settled as a Quaker refuge, though the Quakers have since been outnumbered by English, German, and Irish immigrants.

The assembly and supreme court alternate between Amboy and Burlington on the Delaware River; until recently the colony was administered by the governor of New York—more often than not (so Jerseymen complain) as an afterthought.

After a night's rest, I resumed my journey westward up the Raritan River. The river here passes through steep banks of red sandstone, and it is navigable for shallow draft boats for fifteen or twenty miles inland. I passed a number of boats loaded with barrels of flour and stacks of lumber destined for New York. Toward mid-morning I forded the river (the tide was out and the ferry aground) and rode into New Brunswick, a village of about the same size and appearance as Amboy. The churches—two Dutch Reformed, one Anglican, and one Presbyterian—indicate the composition of the population. About half the inhabitants are Dutch, who moved here from Albany and still keep very much to themselves.

At Brunswick the main road turns southwest toward Princeton and Trenton. I decided instead to continue due west along the Raritan, since I wished to cross the Delaware near the Moravian villages of Bethlehem and Easton. The road along the river continued adequately for a while, since the soil is quite sandy, but when I rode up into the uplands between the two river valleys it all but vanished. Even so, the terrain was not difficult, and from the westernmost branch of the Raritan it was only a few miles to the Musconetcony, which led down to the Delaware. Without inns or signposts, however, I was forced to rely for accommodations and directions upon poor, grimy, inarticulate farmers. Nor was there any ferry on the Delaware at this point, and I had to intercept a passing riverboat to secure passage across. I shall think long and hard before I again decide to depart from the main-traveled roads in this country.

BETHLEHEM IS A SMALL RELIGIOUS COMMUNITY located just above the forks of the Delaware on the Lehigh River. It was founded by Moravians, a pious, industrious people who came to Pennsylvania to escape persecution in Germany. Their religious heritage goes back to the Bohemian scholar, John Hus, who led a protest against the corruption of the Roman Church a hundred years before Martin Luther. Hus and his followers in Bohemia and Moravia lived their daily lives by the simple injunctions of the Sermon on the Mount, avoiding excessive ceremony, ritual, and fine-spun doctrine. Such Christian charity was intolerable to both Church and Empire in Medieval Europe, and the sect was persecuted relentlessly. The Moravians scattered across central Europe in small bands, but they retained an intense sense of brotherly unity (indeed, they call themselves the *Unitas Fratrum*). The Lutheran Reformation brought only further trouble, for the Moravians were caught in the middle of the religious wars that tore Europe until 1648. The one haven they found was the estate of Count Nicholas Ludwig von Zinzendorf in Saxony. Banished for introducing religious novelties, Zinzendorf led his community to the more tolerant religious climate of Pennsylvania in 1740.

Although Zinzendorf remained in America for only two years, he had a lasting influence on the Brethren. He divided the community into ten classes or choirs—one for married persons, one for single men, single women, big boys, little boys, big girls, little girls, etc. Each choir has its own house, elected leader, festivals, and special duties. In this way each member of the community knows his or her place and obligations. Shirking duty—rare in any case among such intense people—instantly brings the frowns of one's peers. It was like witnessing a Christian army in action, for the entire community is mobilized to support a colossal missionary program among the Indians. At times half the adult men are on the road performing the *Diaspora* (or "Scattered Seed"). Given the right of peaceful passage by the Iroquois, who respect their guileless piety, Moravian missionaries range west into the Ohio Valley and north into Canada.

The Brethren are eager to spread the seeds of their faith across the globe, but they are suspicious of strangers who might bring temptations and irreligious notions into their community. Though welcomed courteously enough, I was encouraged to stay at the Crown Inn across the river, even though a new inn had been erected in the town. The ferry across the river was soundly built and pulled by a rope, so the relocation involved little inconvenience. The buildings of Bethlehem are arranged in a rectangle, each part complementing the whole, like the units of an English college. The center is the bell tower, where prayer bands, changing hourly, maintain communion with the Deity from five in the morning until midnight. The tower also contains a balcony for musical concerts, since hymns and chorales are important parts of their religious services. Indeed, Bethlehem possesses the only orchestra I have seen in America, consisting of violins, violas, a cello, a bass, flutes, trumpets, and French horns.

FROM BETHLEHEM THE MAIN HIGHWAY TO PHILADELPHIA is the Delaware River. A shallow-draft barge loaded with barrels of flour carried me to Trenton at the falls of the river. This village thrives on the trade between Philadelphia and New York. Passengers and freight come north from Philadelphia by water to Trenton, and then go by wagon from there to New Brunswick. The constant loading and unloading gives the town an appearance of bustling activity far out of proportion to its size. After a night at the inn and a breakfast of buckwheat pancakes, I boarded a river sloop for the voyage to Philadelphia. The vessel was loaded to the gunwales with oak timbers and barrels of salt pork and made poor headway against a strong south wind. It required nearly a day to beat ten miles downriver to Burlington where we anchored for the night.

Burlington alternates with Perth Amboy as the seat of government in New Jersey, but it avoids any appearance of pretentiousness. Even the governor's house, which overlooks the river, has to be pointed out to strangers, for it is scarcely larger than the other stone houses in town. The first proprietors of New Jersey hoped to make Burlington a major port for the colony, and the town is well-situated for the purpose. The channel flows close to the New Jersey shore at this point, enabling vessels of considerable tonnage to anchor along the bank. Burlington's hopes were never realized, for Philadelphia, twenty miles to the south, dominates the commerce of the Delaware Valley.

I spent the night at an inn recommended to me by a traveler I had met in Trenton. It was operated, he said, by two "amazoons" who "swore and flew about like witches" but who nonetheless were "obliging and good natured." Since I had not encountered female proprietors before, I thought it might be a new experience. The two young women were crude and untutored, but they had an ample supply of opinions. They had come into possession of the tavern as a result of the untimely death of their parents, and because it afforded them a respectable living, neither had any desire to get married. Marriage, they claimed, reduced a woman to total dependence on her husband; he even had control of her property. Even in the best of marriages, they felt, a woman gained only companionship, and in exchange she led a life of dull household routine. In the rare instance where she might obtain a divorce, the law left her husband in possession of all the family property and custody of the children. My hostesses wanted none of this. They were happy in their independence, the companionship of each other, and in the variety of experiences brought by their guests.

The next day a fair wind and outgoing tide swept us quickly down to Philadelphia where I obtained lodging at the Indian King, the inn recommended far and abroad as the best in the city. It has a daily ordinary, well-prepared and priced at only a shilling, and it stops serving liquor at eleven o'clock in the evening, which ensures its overnight guests a peaceful rest.

PHILADELPHIA IS NOW THE LARGEST CITY IN AMERICA and as big as any in Britain, except London. It lies on a two-mile-wide neck of land formed by the Schuykill River, which runs parallel to the Delaware before emptying into it five miles below the city. In 1682, William Penn purchased the tract from three Swedish brothers who had settled on it, and since it was virgin wilderness he had an opportunity to plan the entire city. Penn's scheme called for eight capital streets, running from river to river, and sixteen cross streets intersecting the main streets at right angles. With plenty of space to plot, Penn left ample room for traffic. The largest streets (Broad, Market, and High) are a hundred feet in width; the rest are fifty or sixty. The main streets are paved with brick and along the sides are thin flagstones for pedestrians, who are protected from traffic by rows of posts ten feet apart. At night the streets are lighted with whaleoil lamps.

The Quakers who founded Pennsylvania hoped to create a society in which each person could govern his or her own affairs and worship according to their own conscience. So well did the Quakers succeed that Pennsylvania attracted immigrants from all of northern Europe—Germans, Swiss, Scottish, Irish,

Welsh, and many others—all seeking political rights, economic opportunities, and religious freedom. Although most of these immigrants flowed through the city to the frontier, many stayed on. Germans have occupied the whole northern section of the city along the Delaware; they have their own churches (one Reformed and one Lutheran) and generally preserve their own language and Old World customs. There is a German-language newspaper, and most street signs are printed in both English and German. All this has occasioned a good deal of concern among the English-speaking inhabitants, who regard the Germans as slow-witted and dull.

Even though the Quakers are a minority, even in Philadelphia, they control both the city and the provincial assembly. This they manage to do by a combination of close-knit organization and rabble-rousing attacks on the governing Penn family. Their pacifism and refusal to provide funds for the defense of the frontier during the late war cost them much popular support, however, and the political scene at present is one of much confusion. The Quakers continue to dominate the social and commercial life of the city, however.

Curious about a people who manage to combine such worldly success with private humility, I visited a meeting of the Friends. There was plenty of opportunity, for they attend meeting twice during the week and three times on Sunday. Since each service lasts about two hours, the bone-weary observer is left wondering when they find time to make so much money. I arrived with an acquaintance at ten on Sunday morning. The interior of the church was whitewashed boards, barren of ornaments, except for some tin candleholders. The congregation sat on wooden benches with nothing to lean on for support but a long, horizontal pole on the back. The men and women entered through separate doors and sat apart. On each side was a bench erected a little higher than the others where sat (a pair of men on one side, four women on the other) those who are accustomed to speaking or who anticipated being moved by the spirit on that particular day.

The service was as devoid of frills as the chapel. We sat quietly looking at each other for an hour and fifteen minutes, evidently waiting for someone to be inspired. At last one of the old men on the side arose, removed his hat, looked around the church, and began preaching in an inaudible murmur. Later he grew louder, his voice more singsong, and his cadence slowed so that it seemed like a minute or more between each sentence. He spoke for half an hour, and the gist of it was that the individual could do nothing without God's help. After he sat down the assembly sat silently for a few more minutes before one of the women rose and intoned some prayers in a voice that seemed to be choked with sobs. Shortly after she finished the twelve o'clock bells sounded, and we all departed. I inquired whether I had chanced to visit on a particularly dull day, and my friend responded that occasionally the spirit moves more freely among the congregation, but once in awhile they sit there for two hours without a word being spoken. The fact that women felt free to sermonize, however, was a novelty since most of the churches of the Christian world are dominated by men. My friend told me that women were viewed as the equals of men in the Quaker faith because the light of God was present in every individual. Women had meetings of their own, and some traveled widely around the countryside serving as messengers and ministers to other Quaker meetings. These "public Friends," I was told, were rarely criticized for such "unfeminine" activities.

In need of both food and conversation, we repaired to a nearby tavern for an oyster dinner. The Philadelphia method of preparing oysters is to bake them on hot coals until the shells open. One then picks them up with a napkin (since the shell gets a bit sooty), eats the oyster, follows it with a bite of buttered bread, and washes the whole down with wine. With a blazing fire to add cheer, it is a comfortable way to spend a wintery afternoon.

Having decided to spend the winter in Philadelphia, I had much time to explore the city. The only crooked street in town is Dock Street, which, as the name suggests, runs along the edge of the river. Since the Schuykill is navigable for only a short distance, the city expanded along the Delaware, rather than filling the land between the two rivers as Penn had intended. In a space of about two miles there are some sixty-six wharves, square wooden casements bolted at the corners and filled with stones and gravel. The city corporation operates some, while others are privately owned. Nearly every merchant of any substance possesses his own pier and warehouse and makes a good profit out of docking and storage fees. The city is also an important shipbuilding center, producing about twenty-five vessels a year. All this activity comes to a halt in the winter, however, because the river freezes over.

Philadelphia is not only the largest city in America; it is also the most modern. Many of its civic improvements were inspired by Benjamin Franklin, who is presently representing the colony's interests in London. The most famous of Franklin's projects is the Pennsylvania Hospital, which has now been in operation for four years. When the city's physicians suggested the need for a hospital like those lately erected in England, Franklin backed the idea in his *Pennsylvania Gazette*. There was little enthusiasm for the idea, however. The city corporation felt that the provincial assembly should furnish the money, since the institution would serve the whole colony; and the thrifty farmers in the assembly were reluctant to appropriate funds for anything. At last Franklin hit upon an idea that appealed to the penury of both. He persuaded the assembly to appropriate half the necessary funds, on the condition that the citizens of Philadelphia subscribe the rest. Neither side was willing to lose the opportunity to double its money at the expense of the other, and within a year £4,750 was raised.

The building, designed by Samuel Rhoads, is the most modern facility of its kind. It is designed mostly for the care of the insane, but it will also take sick persons unless they have infectious diseases. Besides a reception room for visitors, the ground floor has apartments for lunatics, equipped with fireplaces and baths. The second floor is a ward for male medical patients and women are on the third. In addition, there is a kitchen, an apothecary shop, and a medical library. So high is the hospital's rate of cure, that it attracts the ill from every colony.

Another landmark of the city, which in part can be credited to Franklin, is the college. Just ten years ago Franklin published some *Proposals Relating to the Education of Youth in Pennsylvania* wherein he suggested an academy that would concentrate on practical subjects such as English and mathematics, instead of theology and "dead" languages. Such an institution, he argued, would save the expense of sending Pennsylvania boys abroad for education, and it would benefit immigrants by offering instruction in English language, laws, and customs. In less than a year £15,000 was raised through public subscription and a grant from the assembly, and the academy opened in 1751. Success of the academy inspired prominent Philadelphians to contemplate the possibility of a college organized on a similar curriculum. Rev. William Smith, whom Franklin induced to come from New York to head the academy, backed the idea, and they obtained a charter for the College of Philadelphia in 1755. The academy was joined to the college as a sort of preparatory school, and William Smith became provost of the whole apparatus. A college which emphasizes practical training seems eminently suited to a society that is concerned with material progress and the conquest of a continent, and it will no doubt serve as a model for educational changes in the other colonies.

Philadelphia does not yet equal Boston's reputation as an intellectual center, but it does possess more libraries. The idea of a circulating library originated with Dr. Franklin's "Junto Club," a circle of artisans and tradesmen who met weekly for conviviality and self-improvement. In 1742 they formed the Library Company of Philadelphia and obtained a charter and a plot of land from the Penn proprietors. Each subscriber paid forty shillings to join and ten shillings annually, the money employed for the salary of a librarian and the purchase of books. The general public could also borrow the books for small fees, paying fines if they returned them late. The library has built up a fine collection of works on mathematics, science, and literature. Because membership in the company is limited and somewhat expensive, other associations have since appeared. One can now find a library to suit almost any taste or interest. Each generously offered me the use of its collection without charge, and the privilege has been an unexpected boon on long winter evenings.

In the daytime, when there is snow on the ground, the main pastime seems to be sleigh-riding. Since these vehicles are less expensive to construct than carriages, all ranks of people have them, and in winter the streets are clogged with sleighs racing hither and yon at prodigious speeds. They are also quite practical in the countryside if the road is well-traveled. On one afternoon we drove to Germantown for dinner, making the eight-mile run in just forty minutes.

CHRISTMAS, A TIME OF CONSIDERABLE MERRIMENT in England, was my one disappointment in Philadelphia. The only holiday recognized by the Quakers is Sunday, and since Christmas fell in the middle of the week this year they went to work as on any other day. The Episcopal church observed the day, but its preparations were no more elaborate than its regular Sunday service. A few Swedish households lit candles, but that seemed to be the extent of the celebration.

Upon resuming the tour in the spring, I decided to see something of the American frontier, following the great wagon road to the valley of Virginia. This route is probably the most heavily traveled in America. In the past thirty years several thousand German and Scots-Irish immigrants have streamed along this highway, settling the backcountry from Pennsylvania to the Carolinas. Separated from the coastal settlements by the Blue Ridge, they send their cattle and grain back along the wagon road to Philadelphia or down the Susquehanna River to Baltimore. The center of all this traffic is Lancaster, Pennsylvania, the largest inland town in America. There Philadelphia merchants have set up branch stores to supply goods for the southern backcountry.

The sixty-mile road to Lancaster was even more crowded with vehicles than I anticipated: I encountered more than a hundred wagons in one day. Nor were they the small carts seen elsewhere in the colonies or in England. The German farmers of the Conestoga Valley have developed a wagon that is almost an inland ship. It has great wheels to negotiate stumps and holes in the road, and the bottom is rounded so the freight will not roll out when going up or downhill. To pull these "Dutch wagons" the Germans have bred huge horses, which also take their name from the river valley. Presiding over this vehicle is usually a professional teamster, whose size and demeanor match his responsibilities. With a load of flour barrels on a narrow gravel road he demands, and invariably receives, the right of way.

Lancaster County is a rolling landscape of well-tended fields interspersed with oak woodlots. The main crops seem to be wheat, corn, and buckwheat, though I saw occasional fields of turnips, which are used to supplement hay as winter feed for animals. As in New York, every farmer has an orchard, though here apple trees are interspersed with peach, cherry, and mulberry. The fields are enclosed with rail fences made from split logs which are notched and wedged into holes in the fenceposts. Three or four rails a foot apart will contain cattle or sheep; pigs carry triangular wooden yokes around their necks to keep them from squeezing between the rails.

I stopped for supper at a small stone farmhouse along the road. Its appearance was unmistakably German, for the exterior was gaily decorated with painted tulips. The farmer spoke only poor English, and his wife none at all. The house was built into the slope of a hill, so it had two stories in front and one in the rear. In the cellar was a spring, which provided both fresh water and cool storage for milk and butter. Supper was apple dumplings, though prepared in a way I had never seen before. The cook made a dough of flour, butter, and water. She then rolled it thin, enclosed a peeled apple in it, wrapped it in a linen cloth, and boiled it. Served with butter and sugar, it is a very tasty dish.

Beyond Lancaster the wagon road turns northwest to Harris's Ferry on the Susquehanna. The river was a raging torrent from the spring thaw in the mountains to the north, and only with great difficulty was the ferryman persuaded to make the crossing. We made it safely enough, though the boat was carried nearly a mile downstream by the swift current. At this point the main wagon road turns south to York, Pennsylvania, before crossing into Maryland. I elected instead to continue west up the Cumberland Valley to Carlisle and Shippensburg. The countryside here is more sparsely settled, and the farms seem poorer. Most are made of logs, one-room affairs with a loft above for sleeping. The population is mostly German and Scots-Irish, with only a sprinkling of other nationalities. Philadelphia friends had warned me of the slovenliness of the Scots-Irish, but their dwellings seemed no worse than any others in this remote country.

The farms are very small, just tiny patches of clearing in the midst of the wilderness. Clearing land is the most tedious process imaginable. A man can clear only five to ten acres a year, depending upon how meticulous he is in removing the tree stumps. The quickest method is to girdle the trees by chopping off the bark near the bottom. This kills the trees and permits the settler to plant a crop in the first year. Later the stumps can be knocked over and burned, with the ashes reduced by boiling to a lye for soap. Stumps and roots prevent plowing for several years, so the first crop is usually wheat, which can be cultivated by scratching the soil with a hoe and sprinkling the seed. Cattle and hogs forage for themselves in the woods since cleared land is too scarce to devote to pasture. Cropland is protected with "worm fences" of split rails which cross at the ends. This type of fence does not require posts, which would be difficult to sink in the thickly rooted forest soil.

Burned-out cabins along the roadside are lingering testimony to the Indian warfare that raged across Pennsylvania in the wake of Braddock's defeat in 1755. The Indians who remain east of the mountains are quite peaceful, however. They have been allowed to keep some lands (usually the poorest), and they grow some corn, beans, and melons. Cows and pigs, however, seem to mystify them, for the only domesticated animal they have is the dog. Pausing for a time in a village of Shawnees, I was treated quite hospitably. After showing some interest in the village school I was allowed to attend an open-air session. Considerable time was spent on the rudiments of survival in the wilderness—hunting and fishing skills—but tribal elders also gave lessons in the history and traditions of the tribe and instruction in oratory. Since they have no written language, rhetorical ability is essential for any young man who aspires to tribal leadership.

We dined on venison and taw ho (a root that is dug in the marshes and baked in the ground under the fire), and after dinner a football game was organized. The game was played on an immense scale—nearly a hundred people were involved and the playing field must have been five or six acres. At each end were goalposts about six feet wide, and the object was to project the ball through the goalposts. Men were allowed only to kick the ball, while women could carry it or throw it. The star of the game was one Amazon who was too strong and agile to be deprived of the ball; she scored every time it came into her possession.

THE CUMBERLAND RIVER VALLEY BENDS GENTLY SOUTH and west from Carlisle to Shippensburg. Mountains rising to about two thousand feet appear on both hands, and almost imperceptibly the south-bound traveler is channeled into the Shenandoah Valley of Virginia. The road crosses the Potomac at Williams' Ferry and meanders through the village of Martinsburg to Winchester. This whole region has been settled only within the last thirty years. Only about a third of the inhabitants are Virginians; the rest are Germans and Scots-Irish who have come south from Pennsylvania. The Shenandoah Valley offers some of the finest farmland on the continent. Deposited on a limestone base, the soil is peculiarly suited for cereal grains that prefer an alkaline environment. In addition, it has an abundance of natural grasses ideally suited for grazing livestock.

However, the land was not free for the taking. Speculators had bought up large parcels of land in the western parts of Maryland and Virginia, and the newly arrived Germans and Scots-Irish had to buy their farms from these grandees. Those without ready cash ended up with life-long mortgages. While passing through Maryland I heard the story of Daniel Dulaney, whose tactics must have been typical of the eastern speculators. In 1744 Dulaney, a prominent Maryland lawyer, purchased a tract of seven thousand acres along the Monacacy River in western Maryland, which lay on the route the Germans were taking into the Shenandoah Valley. He paid only five shillings, eight pence an acre, for the undeveloped land. He found some German squatters living on the land, so he sold five thousand acres to them at a price less than half that he had paid for it. As Dulaney had anticipated, the Germans worked hard to improve their farms, and this enhanced the value of the remaining land. Dulaney was eventually able to sell it for about one pound per acre, thus making his profit. He profited further by founding Frederick Town in one corner of the tract and selling town lots to would-be shopkeepers.

About the same time Virginia speculators were founding Winchester, the county seat for Frederick County. A village of about two hundred houses, it is the largest community in the Shenandoah Valley. Like Martinsburg, it is predominantly German; most of the Scots-Irish seem to have moved farther up the valley. In recent years the inhabitants have done a thriving business selling beef, flour, and butter to the army garrisoning the frontier. In addition it sends considerable produce in wagons through the gaps in the Blue Ridge to Alexandria and Fredericksburg. It boasts a number of taverns, but I evidently chose the wrong one and spent a sleepless night battling numerous insects that infested the bed.

South of Winchester the valley road is considered unsafe this spring for anyone traveling alone. For the past two years the Cherokee have been raiding the settlements of the southwestern mountains. No one here seems to know what inflamed them, but they have long-accumulated grievances against unscrupulous traders and land-grabbing speculators, and no doubt took advantage of the French war to get revenge.

PRUDENCE DEMANDED THAT I ABANDON MY TOUR of frontier settlements and take the wagon road to Alexandria. After a morning-long ride of eighteen miles I reached the Shenandoah River at Sniker's Ferry. This is one of the loveliest streams in America—swift-flowing, crystal clear, and brimming with trout. East of the river the road winds steeply to Williams's Gap in the Blue Ridge. The mountains at this time of year are sprinkled white with blooming dogwood, and the view from the top is magnificent. The Shenandoah shimmers in the sunlight immediately below the mountain, and fifty miles across the forested valley floor rise the lofty Alleghenies. To the east the Virginia Piedmont is a hilly countryside covered with a dense hardwood forest. Here and there the world of oak and hickory is broken by small clearings for tobacco or corn.

Public accommodations are rare in this part of America, but the occasional traveler can almost always count on a warm welcome at any plantation. Virginians seem by nature to be a sociable people, and in their rural isolation they devour visitors the way others read magazines. This is often described as a plantation society, but here on the edge of civilization the farms seem quite small—or at least only a small proportion of the land is cleared. The family with whom I stopped for the night possessed no slaves but had numerous children. I was surprised to learn that they were Baptists, converted by one of the many itinerant preachers who roam these parts. These people practice adult Baptism as a symbol of spiritual rebirth, and in their new regenerate existence they ban all worldly diversions such as gaming and dancing. Supper was a Spartan meal of cold leg of mutton, cornbread, and much talk of salvation. I retired early, thankful that I had not appeared in this rural Zion on a Sabbath.

THE JOURNEY EASTWARD ACROSS FAIRFAX COUNTY represented the unfolding of civilization. The forest yielded to fields and meadows, farm workers—both free white and black slave—were more evident, plantation houses became larger and more elegant. This is corn-planting time, and every field is bustling with plowing and hoeing. The tobacco fields were as yet uncultivated. Since young tobacco plants are susceptible to sunlight and require very rich soil, they are grown in the woods and then transplanted to the fields in late spring. The road to Alexandria skirts the Bull Run Mountains to the north and meets the Potomac River near the Great Falls. Though a barrier to navigation, the falls are a magnificent sight to one more interested in beauty than traffic. The channel is very narrow at this place, pressed between low-lying hills. The Potomac drops for a mile or more through a whitewater rapids and tumbles over a succession of ledges ten to twenty feet high. And then it settles, as if exhausted, into a slow, deep-running pool. As I sat entranced, a fish-hawk, which had been hovering motionless in the air currents, dived into the water and emerged with a small rockfish. Shaking a mist of water from its feathers, it flew off to enjoy its meal. At that juncture a bald eagle swooped down from above causing the hawk to drop the fish, which the eagle dexterously caught in mid-air. A London pickpocket could not have managed a more deft bit of thievery.

Sixteen miles below the falls is the village of Belhaven, or Alexandria. The river at this point widens into a bay, perhaps two miles wide and deep enough to accommodate ocean-going vessels This is one of many tobacco ports in Virginia. None have attained much size because the tobacco trade is almost completely decentralized. Since the colony is blessed with a number of large river-systems, no part of the coastal plain (or Tidewater region) is more than twenty miles from navigable water. As a result, nearly every important planter operates his own wharf, serving his less fortunate neighbors for a fee. Tobacco ships ply the coast from plantation to plantation until they are fully loaded, and then depart for Britain. Tobacco is an "enumerated article" that can be sold only in the mother country. The real center of this trade is Glasgow, which provides both credit facilities and marketing services for the Chesapeake planters.

By chance one of these two-masted tobacco schooners was in port when I arrived. The captain, in conversation, indicated that he planned to stop at several tobacco wharves along the Potomac and then turn north along Chesapeake Bay as far as Annapolis. Since that destination would place me only a day's ride (forty miles and three ferries) from Alexandria, I decided to go along for the cruise.

Below Alexandria the Potomac broadens into an estuary several miles wide, and it is easily navigated, even in adverse winds. Our first stop was at Mount Vernon, home of Colonel George Washington, who commanded the militia regiments on the Virginia frontier in the late war. The colonel had a half dozen hogsheads of tobacco left from the fall harvest, and another half dozen which he was marketing for his neighbors. Because the hogsheads are inordinately heavy (about five hundred pounds), they must be shipped by water. The small, landlocked farmer in the uplands makes his tobacco cask into a wheel by driving an axle into each end, and pulling it to the nearest wharf with horses.

Several stops farther downriver we came to Nomini Hall, home of Robert Carter. This is the eldest son of "King" Carter, who died in 1732 leaving an estate of over 300,000 acres. The elder Carter amassed this princely realm through his post as agent for Lord Fairfax, the proprietor of this whole "Northern Neck" between the Potomac and the Rappahannock. The estate was divided among several sons, and the present Robert Carter (the third) possesses about 60,000 acres and some six hundred slaves. He has a plantation or a farm (the latter being a plantation without a residence house on it) in nearly every county in the colony. He owns his own tobacco ships, but desired us to stop to pick up a few hogsheads acquired in trade during the winter.

The mansion house, where the captain and I spent the night, was located about five miles from the Potomac at the head of Nomini Creek. It is two stories high, made of brick that has been covered with a white lime mortar. It has five stacks of chimneys, so every important room has a fireplace. The great house is at the center of a square formed by four out-buildings—the schoolhouse where the Carter children are tutored, the stable, the carriage house, and the washhouse. In between these buildings are several lesser structures that include the kitchen, bakery, dairy, and a storehouse. Managing such an establishment, with its hundred or more slaves, must be a major task, even with the help of an overseer. In times of agricultural distress these planters are particularly hard hit, because, even when profits are low, buildings have to be maintained and the labor force has to be fed and clothed. Colonel Carter complained bitterly about the low prices that tobacco has commanded for some years past. If prices did not improve dramatically after the war, he thought he might have to shift from tobacco to wheat as a primary crop.

The next morning a fresh west wind blew us the remaining twenty-five miles to the bay. The Potomac at its mouth is about eight miles across, and the bay is perhaps thirty miles wide at this point. These waters present the finest fishing in America; they are teeming with sturgeon, shad, sheepshead, sea bass, drums, and white perch. In the shallows, banks of oysters can be seen, and at low tide every rivulet is crawling with soft-shelled crabs. One wonders how the earliest Virginians managed to starve to death in such a dietary Eden.

Annapolis is a charming town, situated on a peninsula formed by the Severn River as it meanders into Chesapeake Bay. It is built in irregular form, the streets generally running diagonally between river and bay, some terminating at the capitol, others at the still unfinished governor's mansion. None of the streets are paved, possibly because Marylanders, like Virginians, travel mostly by horseback. A few of the houses are brick, but none is built on a pretentious scale. A residence for the governor was started about fifteen years ago, and it is well situated on a small hill that gives it a commanding view of the town and the bay. Owing to a dispute between the governor and the assembly over finances, however, the house was never finished, and it is now an empty shell going to ruin.

Annapolis subsists mostly on its governmental business and court traffic. It is a port of call for numerous tobacco ships, but a few Scottish factors, representing Glasgow mercantile houses, and some local shopkeepers are the entire merchant class. I sought out one of the largest merchant establishments in order to exchange my Pennsylvania currency. The route I had taken from Pennsylvania to Virginia nowhere afforded an opportunity to change money, and I found that Virginians accepted Pennsylvania paper only with dark scowls and heavy discounts. The Annapolis merchant, however, was quite willing to accept Pennsylvania currency since he did a substantial business with Philadelphia importers. He also, by chance, had numerous commercial contacts with Virginia planters in the Northern Neck. Indeed, in addition to supplying me with Virginia money, he wrote a letter of introduction to a Virginian who had married the daughter of a former governor of Maryland—Colonel John Tayloe, of Mount Airy on the Rappahannock.

The ride back to Alexandria was uneventful, though the weather was stormy and the ferries treacherous. The soil in this part of Maryland is quite sandy, and a century of tilling seems to have nearly worn it out. Many tobacco fields have been abandoned to weeds, though much tobacco and corn are still grown. Here and there a progressive farmer has planted clover or timothy to restore the soil. I paused for the night at Marlboro, a pretty little country village on a small tributary of the Patuxent. A warehouse where tobacco was stored and inspected before being shipped abroad seemed to be the main reason for its existence. Yet, incredibly enough, the town offered for entertainment a traveling theater company, which played in a refurnished tobacco shed. Under the direction of one David Douglas, who arrived in America only three years ago, the company put on a very creditable performance.

I ARRIVED IN ALEXANDRIA IN MIDMORNING AND HURRIED on southward through Fairfax County. I crossed the Occoquan River at Colchester, a small tobacco port almost identical to Marlboro. The only distinctive feature of the town was the ferryman, an ancient, grey-haired Negro who seemed barely able to push the boat. In conversation as we crossed, it developed that he had been a slave all his life, and now that he was too old to work in the fields his master had given him a small plot of land and the proceeds of the ferry to support himself. I rode on ruminating about the labor system in America. Was the slaveowner's gift an act of generosity, a reward for a lifetime of service, or an attempt to evade responsibility for the care of an aged and infirmed servant?

Two days' ride brought me to Mount Airy, where my welcome was as warm as my Maryland friend had predicted. The Tayloe plantation consists of six thousand acres on the north bank of the Rappahannock. The mansion house is an elegant seat, constructed of yellow sandstone, rather than the more common brick. Situated on a high hill, it commands a magnificent view of the marshes, the river, and the town of Tappahannock across the way. The outbuildings of this plantation are arranged in a semicircle on the side of the house facing away from the river. On one side was the kitchen, and on the other a guesthouse, each connected to the mansion by a curved portico. The whole arrangement was very similar to the country houses of the English gentry. Behind the guesthouse was the finest garden I have seen in America. It is laid out in a formal manner with intricate paths hedged by boxwoods, and it includes such tropical rarities as orange and lemon trees. Colonel Tayloe has even constructed a glass house for a few rare vegetables, so they can be enjoyed months ahead of the season.

The inside of the house is tastefully furnished with a mixture of imported and American-made pieces. The living room is decorated with portraits of various members of the family, including Mrs. Tayloe's Maryland relatives. In the dining room are pictures of twenty-four famous English racehorses. The colonel is very fond of horse-racing; on the flats below the hill he has even constructed his own track. In the evening the young ladies of the household entertained us on the harpsichord. Supper, served at nine, consisted of soft-shell crab and artichokes, accompanied by persimmon brandy and water.

The next morning, being a Sunday, we all prepared to attend church at Tappahannock across the river. There was some last-minute discussion of canceling the idea, since the sky was threatening, but in the end we elected to go. From beginning to end, the occasion seemed more social in purpose than religious. The men remained outside the church until the service began, discussing tobacco prices and the latest court suits over land titles. I occupied myself reading the advertisements on the church door, which notified the parishioners of beef and pork for sale by the hundredweight. The service itself was a brief series of perfunctory rituals. The sermon was only fifteen minutes long, after which the men stalked out in a body as they had come in. The family then lingered after church for as long as the service had lasted. This was apparently a time of renewing a weekly acquaintance with one's distant neighbors. Numerous dinner invitations were issued. The cooks evidently anticipated company, for by the time we reached home they had prepared a sumptuous feast that occupied much of the afternoon. The courses included boiled rockfish, beef and greens, and roast pig; for dessert there were puddings and cheeses accompanied by Madeira; then the whole was topped by huge bowls of rum toddy for an endless succession of toasts. In the evening a few of the men retired to cards, while the remainder of the company danced. A French horn and two violins accompanied a succession of minuets, jigs, and reels.

Sunday is also a day of rest for the blacks, or, more exactly, it is the one day of the week when they do not have assigned tasks on the plantation. Strolling before breakfast, I saw a circle of black men with fighting cocks in the stable, but much of this day of "rest" the slaves spend cultivating little vegetable plots that the master permits them to establish for themselves in various parts of the plantation. In the evening they gathered in the slave quarters for music and dancing, and the sound of their strings and drums formed a strange counterpoint to the violins in the mansion house. The white people here insist that the slaves are relatively content with their lot, and it is true that the household servants (the only ones with whom one has contact) seem relaxed and cheerful. Yet the constant talk of runaways suggests that the blacks value their freedom as much as any other person. Outside the church, I observed one Negro coachman chained to his seat, evidently because he was inclined to run away, and the male conversation after the service centered on the jailing of three Negroes for conspiracy—an incident that happened more than a month ago.

SEVERAL DAYS OF RAIN DELAYED MY DEPARTURE from the genial surroundings of Mount Airy. The soil in this part of Virginia is a red clay, and rain converts it to a gluey ooze that makes travel nearly impossible. Accordingly, it was the first of May before I resumed my southward journey. Across the Rappahannock I joined the road that connects Fredericksburg with Williamsburg, and reached the provincial capital after a three days' ride. The countryside was much like that of the Northern Neck—a succession of tobacco and corn fields, interrupted by patches of brush where the soil had been exhausted and the land was being reclaimed by the forest. A few miles above the forks, where the Mattaponi and Pamunkey join to form the York River, was a small village of Pamunkey Indians. Though this tribe once roamed much of eastern Virginia, it is now reduced by warfare, disease, and dissipation to a few hundred souls. They possess about two thousand acres of land along the river, which they are restrained from selling or subdividing by act of the assembly. They live in small cabins by the river, dress like Virginians, and subsist by selling fish and game to the neighboring gentry.

The planters living along the York River claim that they produce the best tobacco in the entire Chesapeake region. They use a seed that produces an exceptionally mild leaf, and they have made an art of its cultivation and curing. Colonel Edward Digges, one of the largest landholders in the area, has a reputation for consistent quality that a French winemaker would envy. He marks each tobacco cask with his initials, and even in distant London "E. D." tobacco is said to command a higher price than any other. The pride of Virginians is legendary. One can begin to understand it after seeing their tobacco fields, their armies of slaves, and their greathouses.

Williamsburg is situated on the high land about midway between the James and York rivers. The site was initially chosen because it was above the swamps that plagued Jamestown (which is now abandoned), but its distance from navigable water has retarded its growth. It is a town of about two hundred houses and a thousand people, including slaves. It has an importance far out of proportion to its size, however, for it is the seat of an empire that extends (so the Virginians claim) west and north as far as the Mississippi and the Great Lakes. Hence politics is its source of fame and profit. The annual session of the assembly brings delegates from the most distant reaches of the province; in addition, the governor, council and provincial courts all sit here. As a result, many of the wealthiest planters in the colony maintain residences in Williamsburg to accommodate themselves on their frequent visits.

The main street is exactly a mile long, running nearly east and west from the capitol to the College of William and Mary. The capitol is a solidly built brick structure, more resembling a fortress than a legislative house. The governor's palace, located in the center of town, is modeled on the country seats of the English nobility, and it is one of the handsomest official residences in America. The remaining houses and shops are mostly of wood frame construction and unpretentious design.

The College of William and Mary is second only to Harvard in point of age, but that is almost its only claim to renown. There are no public-supported schools in Virginia, as there are in New England. The children of the wealthy have private tutors (often emigres from Scotland or recent graduates of northern colleges), and the poor remain illiterate. Hence, students come to the college with little formal preparation, and most remain only a year or so. Many Virginians send their sons to northern schools or to Britain for training in medicine or the law.

The chancellor of the college is the Bishop of London, and the president is an Anglican clergyman. Control of the college by the church has been an issue in Virginia politics in recent years, and lay influence has been increasing. The institution possesses a faculty of six professors, each of whom has apartments in the college; they offer instruction in classical languages, moral philosophy, mathematics, and divinity. Associated with the college is a school for Indians, which offers to half a dozen boys some elementary instruction in reading and writing along with a smattering of Christianity.

I lingered for several days in Williamsburg, staying at the sign of the King's Arms, before resuming my southward journey. I crossed the James River at Jamestown, which is now a ghost town consisting of the crumbling remains of houses and the ivy-covered ruins of a church. Below the James the population becomes thinner and the plantations less opulent. White farmers can be seen working the tobacco fields side by side with their slaves. In the woods the ubiquitous oak has given way to long-needled pines. Beneath the trees is a tangle of honeysuckle that makes passage through the forest virtually impossible. The blooms of this vine fill the humid air with a sweet, pungent aroma; passing through it one feels like a ship cleaving water.

The road crosses the Roanoke River at Halifax, a small village which thrives on the tobacco trade and its county court. The North Carolina countryside is much like Virginia, though the farms are generally smaller and slaves fewer. Rare is the planter who owns more than half a dozen Negroes. South of Halifax the land becomes perfectly level, sloping imperceptibly toward the sea. North Carolina is blessed with as many rivers and estuaries as Virginia, but the sandy capes which lie off the coast prevent all but the most shallow-draft vessels from coming in. As a result, most North Carolina tobacco has to be sent to Virginia, either overland or in coasting schooners.

There is no permanent seat of government in North Carolina. The present governor resides at Brunswick, an inconsiderable town at the mouth of the Cape Fear River. Wilmington, about fifteen miles up the river, is the only town of substance in the colony. It is the center of a large trade in naval stores, lumber, and barrel staves, and it serves an immense backcountry that stretches all the way to the mountains. The river valley has been settled within the last few years by Scots immigrants, escaping from their native highlands after the uprising of 1745.

Below Cape Fear the land is very poor, a sandy pine barren, and the few inhabitants subsist in wretched poverty. The rare man who owns a slave usually shares his cabin and table with him. There are no towns, nor any accommodations for travelers. Rather than risk the facilities in some settler's one-room cabin, I purchased some bacon and corn meal from a farmer and camped in the woods along the road. Without recognizing it, one crosses the unmarked boundary into South Carolina.

The first landmark in South Carolina is the village of Georgetown at the head of Winyah Bay. By means of several large river systems which flow into the bay (the Winyah, Peedee, and Waccamaw), this port serves the whole northern part of the colony. The rivers in South Carolina are wide, sluggish, and shallow, capable of navigation a hundred miles inland, but only for small craft. They thus provide access to the sea, but they are not deep enough to permit ocean-going vessels to ride up to the planters's wharves, as in Tidewater Virginia. Thus, inland farmers float their produce downriver in small boats or rafts to Georgetown, Charleston, or Beaufort.

Indigo is the main export crop for the upland farmers. The plant was brought from the West Indies only about twenty years ago, but nearly everyone has started raising it since parliament gave it a bounty of six pence per pound. The plant is a rather undistinguished-looking weed, which is harvested in July, and again at the end of August. The leaves are laid in vats of water for thirty-six hours; then the juice-colored water is drawn off into another vat where lime is added to precipitate out a blue dye. The water is then drained off and the sediment of pure dye is pressed, dried in a special shed, and put into casks for shipment. In contrast to bulky tobacco, indigo has a relatively high value for its weight; hence transportation charges are a relatively small part of a planter's costs. But, like tobacco, its cultivation requires constant attention and some skill, so it can be grown as efficiently by small farmers as by the wealthy.

A few miles south of Georgetown begin the swamps of the Santee delta, and from there to Charleston the road winds its way among cypress swamps and rice plantations. Live oaks dripping with Spanish moss exclude the sun and keep the road in a perpetual twilight, while the air, even in mid-May is hot and heavy. Rice is grown only by the very wealthy because the construction of levees and reservoirs requires a substantial capital investment. Because they are flooded periodically, the rice fields are located on the lowlands next to a river or creek. Reservoirs, erected on higher ground by damming creeks and gullies, maintain a constant source of water. The rice is planted in a dry field in early spring; the field is then flooded and the plants grow in about eight or ten inches of water. During the summer, the water is periodically drained so slaves can hoe out the weeds while standing in the stagnant muck. The grain is harvested in late August or early September, dried in the sun, and threshed by beating. Because of the amount of stagnant water the summer months in the Low Country are considered extremely unhealthy. The slaves suffer from a variety of fevers and agues, and the mortality rate among them is very high. Even so, they survive better than the whites because the climate is not much different from that of their native Africa. During the "sickly season" planters flee to town houses in Charleston or escape to northern resorts like Newport, leaving white overseers and black drivers in charge.

Charleston is the focal point of this rice-planting aristocracy, and the only sizable city in the southern colonies. It has a fine natural harbor formed by the confluence of the Ashley and Cooper rivers, and it is protected from the sea by several islands, which can be fortified in wartime. The Cooper River, which contains the city's docks and wharves, is navigable for about twenty miles inland, and Goose Creek, one of its tributaries, possesses some of the finest rice plantations in the colony. This collection of natural advantages has made Charleston the commercial hub as well as the social and political capital of Carolina society.

Charleston has a population of eight thousand, about a third of it slaves. Blacks, both slave and free, provide nearly the entire laboring force, from dockworkers and shipbuilders to gardeners and domestic servants. The city is laid out, like Philadelphia, on a gridiron plan, but the streets are narrow and poorly maintained. With a recent appropriation of funds by the assembly, the street commissioners are just beginning the task of widening and paving. Churches and public buildings are made of brick; most private dwellings are wood frame. In the last few years—particularly since the great hurricane of 1752—wealthy planters have built elegant town houses so they can reside in the city during the fever-ridden summer and fall months. Many of these houses are three stories high, and each floor has a balustraded porch to catch the sea breeze.

Along the waterfront are a variety of retail stores that dispense everything from hoes, axes, plows, and saddles, to imported satins and muslins. Smaller shops are those of artisans who retail their own hand-made products. These generally seem to be of inferior quality, compared to some of the work I saw in the northern colonies. It is little wonder that the wealthy prefer English-made house furnishings and clothes. Larger stores do a wholesale business, sending consignments of goods to planters and merchants in the interior. The biggest of these deal directly with British suppliers in London; others operate through resident factors who represent British firms. South Carolina is less dependent on Scottish factors than the Chesapeake colonies, having developed a native merchant class, many of them of French Huguenot ancestry.

My final destination in America was Savannah, Georgia, and I elected to travel there by ship. Immense mangrove and cypress swamps prevent a direct overland connection between Charleston and Savannah, and the approaching summer meant the additional discomfort of heat, humidity, and clouds of insects. The ocean passage also afforded me a glimpse of the sea islands, which lie off the coast of South Carolina and Georgia. Hardly recognizable as islands, most of them are separated from the mainland only by grassy salt marshes. The islands are noted for their temperate climate and long growing season. As a result, planters on the islands can grow a peculiar, long-fiber variety of cotton that is very susceptible to frost. Because the fiber is easily separated from the seeds, it can be produced with relatively little labor. There is considerable demand for it in England, so the ship captain informed me, but its culture is confined to the sea islands.

Savannah sits on a bluff about fifteen miles up the river. The land on both sides of the river is a cypress swamp dotted with rice plantations. The proprietors of Georgia initially prohibited slavery, but the import of Negroes has been permitted for the past ten years. The colony is now developing a rice plantation economy similar to South Carolina's. Savannah, however, remains a satellite of Charleston. Its small merchant class operates through Charleston wholesale houses; seldom do vessels arrive here directly from Britain. The port does, however, carry on some trade with the West Indies. It imports some slaves from over-populated islands like Barbados, and it sends to the islands flour, pork, and a variety of timber products. I secured passage on a small vessel bound for Jamaica, where I thought to continue my tour of the empire with an examination of the sugar colonies.

1

England's Atlantic Community

Benjamin Franklin leaned over the side and watched his packet vessel cleave the blue-green waters of the North Atlantic. The year was 1757, and Franklin was journeying to England as colonial agent for Pennsylvania. The Penn family, it appears, had refused to permit their proprietary lands to be taxed to finance the war with France, and Franklin was appointed to represent the grievances of the assembly before the imperial authorities in London. Regular packet service between New York and England had been introduced two years before, and with a favorable wind Franklin could look forward to a voyage of only four weeks.

Never one to be idle for long, Franklin soon turned away from the water and set himself to composing a preface for a new edition of *Poor Richard's Almanac.* Perhaps it was the timeless tedium of shipboard life, for he decided to include the best homilies and maxims, honed at last to perfection, from the almanacs of twenty-five years. "Poor Richard" modestly attributed the collection to an old man he had heard make a speech at a New York auction, and Franklin's Boston printer saw fit to publish the preface separately as *Father Abraham's Speech.* Here Franklin capsulated the middle-class ideology of a land of busy shopkeepers, artisans, and farmers; it amounted virtually to another Testament, a gospel of work. Emphasis upon a new set of virtues—thrift, enterprise, diligence, initiative—expressed in unforgettable aphorisms ("'Tis hard for an empty bag to stand upright," "Lost time is never found again") summarized the ethos of a people who would alter the spelling of "busyness" to "business" and give the word a new meaning. Yet Franklin was more than the philosophical spokesman for a rising middle class in a bright New World. He had already achieved some scientific reputation in Europe for his experiments with electricity, and before long his finesse in imperial diplomacy would be apparent in the councils of London. Philosopher, scientist, inventor, land speculator, and diplomat—Benjamin Franklin symbolized the economic, political, and intellectual interest that bound the imperial community in the eighteenth century.

The Atlantic Economy

The foundation of this community was trade, which grew almost by geometrical progression in the course of the century. The export of British manufactured goods, for instance, increased four-fold—from an estimated value of £250,000 sterling in 1700 to over £1 million by the eve of the Revolution. By the mid-1760s, more than two hundred ships annually departed from London for the colonies. The westbound voyage, running against the prevailing winds, seldom took less than six weeks and often required two months. Few who took the tedious trip ever wanted to do it again, but the risks were not as great as might be supposed. In peacetime, insurance rates on goods shipped from England to America were often as low as 2 percent. Moreover, constant efforts were made to improve communications. In 1755, packet service, carrying passengers and mail, was initiated between New York and Falmouth, and a little later a similar service connected Falmouth and Charleston. In its first decade the service handled over a million letters; by 1770 five packet vessels provided monthly service. The trading community, however, was involved with more than a simple exchange of goods between England and the colonies. It was actually a complex network of commercial relationships among the various mainland colonies, the West Indies and the British Isles.

New England merchants were the pioneers in developing a colonial commerce because they lacked a staple crop (such as tobacco or rice) to finance their purchases of manufactured goods from England. In the last quarter of the seventeenth century, Boston merchants initiated a trade with the West Indians, exchanging grain, lumber, fish, and horses for molasses, a by-product of the West Indian sugar industry. The slave trade, cornerstone of West Indian commerce, was initiated by English merchants, operating under licenses from the Royal African Company; not until after 1700 did the conservative New Englanders enter this risky and unwholesome business. In 1723 a consortium of Newport merchants introduced rum to the African coast, and the classic triangle trade was born. Rum was traded for slaves, gold, elephant tusks, or exotic woods. The slaves were exchanged in the West Indies for molasses or sold in Carolina and Virginia for bills of exchange; the other products were exported to Europe. The trade thus provided New Englanders with currency to pay their debts to English merchants and even afforded a small surplus for investment in manufactures.

The classic triangle, however, was only one pattern in a many-sided trade involving stops in England, various Atlantic islands, Africa, the Caribbean, and the southern colonies. But, whatever the geometrical pattern, the foundation of New England commerce was the West Indian trade. In the year 1748, Rhode Island and Connecticut alone sent more than two hundred vessels to the Caribbean. By mid-century, the mainland colonies were annually exporting to the West Indian goods worth £700,000, while importing only about £400,000; the differential was composed of coin and bills of exchange which helped redress the unfavorable balance of trade with the mother country. An example of the variety of goods shipped to the West Indies can be found in the cargo of a brig owned by Nicholas Brown, prominent merchant of Providence. The cargo manifest listed 72½ bushels of salt, 2,600 feet of pine boards, 9,867 feet of oak boards, 8 barrels of pork, 12 barrels of beef, 400 bricks, 80 barrels of flour, 31 dozen axes, 13 hogsheads of codfish, 27 hogsheads of tobacco, 1 hogshead of sugar, 5,600 barrel staves, 1 horse, 8 sheep, and 200 boxes of spermaceti candles.

The vessels of Brown and other merchants did not always return directly home with West Indian products. Sometimes they carried those products to Europe, a form of commerce called the "carrying trade." The transport of products owned by others was quite lucrative, and the profits from this commerce helped redress the chronic imbalance of trade between the colonies and the mother country.

The far-flung trade of New England gave birth to a number of ancillary manufactures, prime among them being shipbuilding. Geography had forced even the earliest settlers to build watercraft. The Atlantic coast of North America is sliced into segments by gigantic rivers that could be neither forded nor bridged. As a result, commerce until long after the American Revolution moved principally by water. Americans became adept in the building of swift, efficient coastal schooners that plied the coastline from port to port. Blessed with an abundant supply of wood, Americans could built ships more cheaply than others, and the quality of their work put them in world demand. By the time of the Revolution more than half the vessels involved in the Atlantic trade were American-built, and ships themselves ranked fifth in value among American exports (behind fish and ahead of indigo).

Next to ship-building, the most important manufacturing industry of New England was rum. Massachusetts and Rhode Island annually imported two million gallons of molasses, and about half of it was converted into rum. Consumed locally, dispatched to Africa, or sold in the southern colonies, where it was consumed by slaves and poor-whites, rum came close to being the staple crop of New England. Much of it was also sent to Newfoundland where it was exchanged for whale oil, seal skins, and fish, all reexported to Europe in another variation of the triangle trade.

Cod fishing, perhaps the oldest commercial enterprise in New England, suffered a decline in the eighteenth century, ruined by chronic warfare and by competition from the Maritime Provinces. Massachusetts remained the entrepot for the fishing industry, however, for its canny merchants developed a profitable coasting trade with the Maritime Provinces, supplying the Canadian fishing fleets with rum and provisions, in exchange for part of the catch. The sale of cod depended upon the quality of the fish. The "merchantable" fish, after being dried and salted, were shipped to the Catholic countries of southern Europe. Lower-grade fish were consumed locally, forming the principal diet of New England farm families during the winter months. The poorest quality, or "refuse" fish, were exported to the West Indies for consumption by slaves.

The two hundred boxes of spermaceti candles on the cargo manifest of

Nicholas Brown suggest the importance of the whaling industry in the commerce of New England. Although the whaling fleet was concentrated at Nantucket Island, the merchants of Providence and Newport provided the business organization and marketing services. Since whale meat was generally regarded as inedible, only a small portion of the whale was actually used. Whale oil was the most common fuel for lamps in both Europe and America, while whalebone was manufactured into everything from sewing needles to corset stays. Head matter, or spermaceti, a white waxy substance found in the cranial cavities of the sperm whale, was used in making candles. The technique of making candles was introduced into Rhode Island about 1750, probably by European immigrants. Within a decade there were perhaps a dozen candle factories in the American colonies, but Rhode Island remained the center. The Browns of Providence (father and sons) secured an international reputation for making candles of the highest quality. Exporting candles to other colonies, the West Indies, and to England, this single family built its own "triangle trade" in miniature.

New York and Philadelphia, commercial capitals of the middle colonies, traded primarily the products of farm and forest. Like New England, the middle colonies lacked a staple commodity useful to Britain; furs and pig iron were the only major products exported directly to England. Instead the middle colonies developed a thriving trade with the West Indies, chiefly Barbados and Jamaica. In another version of the triangle trade, flour, lumber products, beef, and pork were sent to the sugar islands in exchange for sugar, molasses, and rum. These were transported to England and bartered for textiles, hardware, spices, books, or other manufactured goods. After 1760, a succession of bad harvests in England combined with a growth in population in the colonies provided new markets for the foodstuffs of the middle colonies.

As in New England, the commerce of New York and Philadelphia stimulated the growth of manufactures, primarily iron and flour. The iron industry, of course, was not confined to this region, for there were ironworks in every colony except Georgia. Indeed, by the eve of the Revolution the colonies produced more pig and bar iron than the mother country, and about one-seventh of the total world output. But the industry was most highly developed in southeastern Pennsylvania. There the characteristic unit was the "iron plantation," consisting of several thousand acres of iron-rich soil, forests that could be reduced to charcoal, and fields of grain and vegetables to feed the workers. Though most of the impure and brittle pig iron was exported to England, some was hammered by blacksmiths into bars of wrought iron that could be fashioned into tools or cooking utensils. The iron plantation was thus not only a nearly self-sufficient community but a fairly sophisticated, vertically integrated manufactory.

Pig iron was Philadelphia's primary export to England, but flour was its major commodity elsewhere. Situated in the midst of the vast grain fields of the Delaware and Susquehanna valleys, Philadelphia was a natural milling center. But as markets opened in the West Indies and southern Europe, the mills became increasingly dependent upon the wheat plantations of the Chesapeake. After mid-century, Philadelphia became a vast grain depot which handled more than half of all the flour exported from North America. Flour, in short, was as important in the Pennsylvania economy as tobacco in the Chesapeake or rice in South Carolina.

The southern colonies were often involved in the multiple trading ventures of northern merchants but did not themselves develop any triangular commerce. Instead, the southern colonies generally traded directly with the mother country, importing manufactured goods and exporting staples—tobacco from the Chesapeake, lumber and naval stores from North Carolina, rice and indigo from South Carolina. Of these products tobacco was by far the most important. Production rose steadily in the course of the century, from an annual output of twenty million pounds in 1700 to over one hundred million pounds valued at four million Spanish dollars by 1775. This avalanche of tobacco far exceeded England's capacity for consumption—by the end of the colonial period English merchants were reexporting to the continent nearly 90 percent of the colonial tobacco. The tobacco shipped from Virginia and Maryland accounted for about half the total export value of the thirteen mainland colonies.

From Britain the southern planters purchased woolen and linen goods, coarse cottons for clothing slaves, furniture, Madeira wine, and finished clothing such as stockings, shoes, hats, and silks. In an effort to imitate the fashion of dress, houses, manners, and reading habits of the English gentry, Southern planters frequently exceeded their incomes and went into debt to British merchants. One London businessman observed that Virginians tended to "overvalue their incomes, and live up to their suppositions," a time-honored American weakness. The problem, however, was actually more complex. The great river systems of the Chesapeake region gave nearly every planter direct access to the water. Instead of using American middlemen, the Virginia planters consigned their tobacco to merchants in Britain. These individuals marketed the tobacco and used the proceeds to purchase any consumer goods the planter requested. The remaining profit was returned to the planter in the form of a bill of exchange. The system worked well enough in good times, but after the French and Indian War tobacco prices collapsed and Chesapeake planters found themselves deeply in debt. Because they did not fully understand how European tobacco markets worked, they tended to blame the British merchants for their plight. As relations between the colonies and mother country deteriorated in the 1760s, the Virginians convinced themselves that they were victims of an insidious conspiracy designed to keep them permanently shackled with debt. From that feeling would grow the rhetoric of Revolution.

The planters of South Carolina also relied heavily on the services of British merchants, but they did not fall so deeply in debt because the prices for their staples, rice and indigo, held firm until the Revolution. Carolina planters began growing rice shortly after the colony was founded, taking advantage of the colony's swampy lowlands and numerous rivers. In 1770 rice ranked third among exports from Britain's mainland colonies, behind tobacco and wheat. Indigo production began in the 1740s when Eliza Lucas Pinckney, whose father had been governor of Antigua, imported indigo seeds from the West Indies. Indigo was an ideal complement to rice because it grew on the higher and drier parts of the plantation, and the two crops were planted and harvested at different times of the year. The French wars, which disrupted the trade in West Indian indigo, turned South Carolina into "an Indigo Country," as one planter put it, and parliament further encouraged its growth with a substantial bounty. In the early 1770s indigo culture spread into Georgia and Florida, where a warmer climate produced a crop that was competitive with West Indian indigo. By 1775 indigo ranked fifth in value among the exports of British North America.

The city of Charleston was the commercial hub for the products of the lower South, but it never developed the mercantile facilities or manufacturing enterprises that appeared in the northern cities. It remained a mere "shipping point" for rice and indigo. Like the Virginians, South Carolina planters relied on merchants in Britain for marketing decisions and credit. Why the southern colonies failed to create a merchant class with international connections, such as had appeared in Boston, New York, and Philadelphia, remains one of the minor mysteries of history.

Charleston did, however, rank with Philadelphia as a gateway for the transatlantic migration of peoples. The difference was that Charleston's "immigrants" were the forced arrival of blacks from Africa. The economies of all the southern colonies were built on the foundation of black slavery. Although Virginians had relied principally on white bond servants for labor in the seventeenth century, by 1700 they had concluded that black slaves, bound to life servitude, were more profitable. They soon found also that the reproduction of slaves was an additional source of profit.

This discovery stemmed from one of the incidental features of the slave trade. Most slavers that departed from the coast of Africa headed for the West Indies. Because sugar was the most profitable of all the New World crops, slaves fetched the highest prices in the sugar islands. And, because the mortality rate in the islands was high, there was a constant demand for newcomers. Offered the first choice in a shipload, West Indian planters tended to buy young males, from whom they could expect harder work and a better chance of survivability. The weaker males, as well as women and children, were sent on to the Chesapeake colonies. There was thus a more even balance between the sexes in Virginia and Maryland, and this in turn allowed the slaves to form families. The planters may even have encouraged this because family ties made slaves easier to control, and slave reproduction was the simplest and cheapest source of new labor. Thomas Jefferson, who had about 180 slaves on the eve of the Revolution, expressed a willingness "to indulge connections seriously formed by those people, where it can be done reasonably." On several occasions throughout his life he bought slaves he did not need or sold some that he would have preferred to keep in order to keep husbands and wives together.

Jefferson, like other planters, employed slave women in "feminine" occupations, as cooks, seamstresses, and housekeepers. But he also employed them in light field work, such as hoeing or deworming tobacco and threshing wheat. Jefferson, of course, was a far more lenient master than many, and it must not be forgotten that slavery in any form ultimately rested on the threat, if not the reality, of brutal force. Even so, the success of the Virginia system is measured by the remarkable reproductive performance of Virginia slaves. As early as 1720 the slave population of Virginia and Maryland was self-sustaining, that is, the annual birth rate exceeded the deaths. (Because of the prevalence of malaria and other warm-climate diseases, the white population in the Chesapeake did not become self-sustaining until about 1700.) By contrast the slave population in South Carolina did not become self-sustaining until the 1770s, in Barbados not until 1810, and in Jamaica not until the 1840s.

As these figures suggest, slavery in South Carolina more nearly resembled that in the West Indies. The first settlers in South Carolina came from the West Indies, and they carried with them island precepts about slavery. Unlike the Virginians, the Carolinians never experimented with white servitude; they seem to have assumed from the beginning that only natives of Africa could survive in their miasmic swamps and torrid climate. Once they began cultivating rice, they made the happy discovery that their slave laborers knew more about rice culture than they did. Rice was extensively grown in paddies along riverbanks in western Africa, and it was an important part of the African diet. Not every African slave came from a rice paddy, but enough were familiar with the planting, harvesting, processing, and cooking of rice to shape the rice culture of South Carolina. Nearly all of the tools, for example, used in Carolina rice growing were of African design. And planters were aware of the value of skilled labor. A notice in the Charleston *Evening Gazette* of July 11, 1785, announced the arrival of a Danish slaver with "a choice cargo of windward and gold coast negroes, who have been accustomed to the planting of rice."

Carolina planters may have been correct in their supposition that Africans were more resistant to disease than whites. Both malaria and yellow fever, the two most common of southern ailments, were endemic along much of the coast of West Africa. Blacks probably developed some immunity either through relatively innocuous childhood exposure or through genetic mutation. Sickle-shaped blood cells, for instance, have recently been found to resist attacks of the malaria parasite. The death rate among black slaves was nonetheless very high. Most observers attributed it to overwork. The slaves set each rice plant into the soil by hand and tended it through the growing season with a hoe. When ripe, the rice was harvested and threshed, the last being the most laborious task of all. The grain was separated from its husk by pounding in a large wood mortar. In 1755 Dr. Alexander Garden (the amateur naturalist after whom Carolus Linnaeus named the gardenia) informed the Royal Society that "each Slave is tasked at Seven Mortars for One Day, and each Mortar Contains three pecks of Rice. Some [planters] task their slaves at more, but often pay . . . dear for their Barbarity, by the Loss of many . . . Valuable Negroes, and how can it well be otherwise, the poor Wretches are Obliged to Labour hard to Compleat their Task, and often overheat themselves, then Exposing themselves to the bad Air, or Drinking Cold Water, are immediately . . . Seized with dangerous Pleurisies and peripneumonies . . . which soon rid them of Cruel Masters, or more Cruel Overseers, and End their Wretched Being here."

High mortality lessened the chances for reproduction. In addition, the Carolina planters evinced the same preference for male slaves as the West Indians. A Charleston merchant informed a ship captain in Barbados that the ideal slave cargo for Carolina would be youths of fifteen or sixteen years of age, with a ratio of two-thirds boys to one-third girls. Although the slave birthrate remained low, the number of blacks in South Carolina increased steadily through the eighteenth century due to new arrivals. By 1740 blacks outnumbered whites in the South Carolina low country, causing a new kind of worry for the master class. Indeed, in just the previous year occurred the most serious of pre-revolutionary slave uprisings. Encouraged by rumors that the Spanish were offering freedom, a band of slaves on the Stono River near Charleston started overland for Florida, killing every white they encountered. They were intercepted and executed, but the fear of slave uprising would be a theme of South Carolina history until the Civil War.

The Urban Experience

Although only one person in twenty in colonial America lived in a city, the cities had a disproportionate influence on American development. They were at the cutting edge of social change. It was in the cities that first appeared the elements that we associate with modern capitalism—the use of money and commercial paper in place of barter, open competition in place of social deference and hierarchy, with an attendant rise in social disorder, the appearance of factories using coal or waterpower in place of independent craftsmen working with hand tools, and the organization of work by the clock instead of by the cycles of the sun and moon. "The cities predicted the future," wrote historian Gary B. Nash, "even though they were but overgrown villages compared to the great urban centers of Europe, the Middle East, and China."

Except for Boston, whose population stabilized at about 16,000 in 1760, cities grew by exponential leaps through the eighteenth century. In the fifteen years between the end of the French and Indian War and the outbreak of the Revolution more than 200,000 immigrants arrived on American shores. This meant that a population the size of Boston was arriving every year, and most of it flowed into the port cities south of New England. Philadelphia's population nearly doubled in those years, reaching about 30,000 in 1774. New York grew at almost the same rate, reaching about 25,000 by 1775.

The quality of the hinterland dictated the pace of growth of the cities. Boston's hinterland had always been poor farm country, and by the mid-eighteenth century it was virtually stripped of its timber. The available farmland was occupied; there was little in New England to attract immigrants. New York and Philadelphia, by contrast, served a rich and fertile hinterland laced with navigable watercourses. Scots funneled through New York and into the Hudson and Mohawk river valleys. Irish and Germans landed in Philadelphia and followed the Susquehanna and Juniata rivers into the valleys of Maryland and Virginia. New York and Pennsylvania became the breadbaskets of the New World, sending grain not only to other colonies but to England and southern Europe where crippling droughts in the late 1760s created a whole new market.

Unfortunately, this phenomenal growth did not benefit all alike. Every city, whether it be stagnant Boston or booming Philadelphia, witnessed a widening gap between rich and poor since the beginning of the century. The appearance of poverty in America is most easily seen in expenditures on poor relief. In the years 1710 to 1720, Boston spent on its poor an annual average of £18 per thousand people; in the 1750s its annual spending on the poor was £77. New York's spending rose from £39 per thousand in the 1750s to £123 in the early 1770s. To be sure, these figures may reflect the development of a more humanitarian attitude toward poverty, rather than an increase in poverty, but there were other indicators as well. In 1773 New York officials estimated that there were between six and eight hundred "lower class" persons in the city who "were too poor to survive without public assistance." Not counted, of course, were the thousands who survived from day to day with odd jobs and private charity.

Nevertheless, urban society was not simply composed of an elite of wealthy merchants at the top and a poverty-stricken rabble at the bottom. In between was a broad spectrum of *petite bourgeois:* shopkeepers, craftsmen, day laborers, dockworkers, and sailors. One of the most striking developments of the age was the development of a self-conscious sense of identity among the urban craftsmen and shopkeepers, the men and women who made and sold the items of hand manufacture—from furniture and carriages to bricks and rope. In Boston these artisans characteristically sported a leather apron, a badge of their station and an emblem of their skills. On November 5 of each year—known as Pope's Day in Boston and Guy Fawkes Day in Britain—the leather aprons literally seized control of the town. They held a parade and built floats to reenact the infamous Gunpowder Plot of 1670 when Catholic dissidents tried to blow up the British parliament. It was a way of reinforcing New England's elemental Protestantism, and it presented an opportunity for status reversal that was so common in the holiday festivals of Europe. The lower classes controlled the streets, and young apprentices went from house to house collecting money from the affluent to pay for the drinking and feasting.

Ironically, the world-view that bonded Boston's leather aprons to one another also led them to resist the changes demanded by the dawning entrepreneurial age. Master craftsman and his journeymen employees went through good times and bad together. It never occurred to either that a drop in business might result in layoffs or a cut in wages. In Philadelphia, on the other hand, both masters and journeymen began to understand that the modern concepts of profit and wage-earning were both governed by the law of supply and demand. The construction of the Pennsylvania Hospital in the early part of the 1750s and the war with France in the latter half of the decade created an unusual demand for artisans in the building trades. Carpenters had customarily worked under contracts providing for monthly wages plus subsistance. Finding themselves in great demand in 1755, some asked for a daily wage and agreed to buy their own food. This increased their pay by about a shilling a day, but it also brought insecurity. When demand slackened, they faced periodic unemployment, and many sought to return to the more comfortable moorings of the old system. The development of a competitive labor system would take many years, but there was at least a glimmer of the future in the Philadelphia of 1760.

The succeeding decade witnessed another portent of the future—a postwar commercial depression that caused acute distress in the northern cities as well as among southern planters. Merchants in London began a contraction of credit as early as 1762. The departure of British soldiers and the termination of military contracts meant a drastic reduction in circulating money in the colonies. The silver pocketed by American shopkeepers and tavern owners drained back to England to pay old debts. To make matters worse, the British Sugar Act of 1764 disrupted the West Indian trade, on which all three northern cities depended. In January 1765, a prominent Boston merchant heavily involved in that trade stopped payment on £70,000 in debts that he owed. John Hancock called it "the most prodigious shock ever known in this part of the world." The collapse touched off a wave of bankruptcies among lesser merchants. In New York and Philadelphia merchants dunned the shopkeepers who owed them money, while desperately trying to stall their British creditors. Craftsmen found less demand for their products; dockworkers and sailors went unemployed. The hard times brought home an awareness of class stratification in the cities and fostered a new class consciousness. Addressing his fellow artisans, a Bostonian proclaimed: "From your Labour and Industry arises all that can be called Riches, and by your Hands it must be defended: Gentry, Clergy, Lawyers, and military Officers, do all support their Grandeur by your Sweat, and at your Hazard." Such was the mood of the urban populace in the mid-1760s when the British parliament chose to impose new regulations and new taxes on the colonies. Class rhetoric quickly turned to radical political speech, and the discontented were ready recruits for mobs bent on violence. The ensuing explosion led ultimately to Revolution and Independence.

The Educational Interchange

The Atlantic trading community, of which England was the center, was far more than a commercial operation. The traffic in foodstuffs and merchandise was accompanied by an exchange of books, journals, attitudes, and ideas. The Atlantic commerce brought Americans into intimate contact with Old World cultures, from Scotland to Italy. It introduced American colonists to the intellectual renaissance known as the "Enlightenment," and that in turn excited a burst of intellectual creativity on the American side of the Atlantic.

The foundation of this Atlantic intellectual community was education. By 1776, more than five hundred scions of colonial families had been sent to Britain for schooling. Most of them came from the southern colonies where the gentlemanly ideal of educational travel was reinforced by a lack of local colleges and close commercial connections with Britain. Edinburgh attracted more than any other single university, partly because living costs were cheaper, no religious tests were required for admission, and its medical faculty had an international reputation. Americans, moreover, seemed to have a natural affinity for Scotland. Both were provincial cultures with a sense of inferiority to England, yet their remoteness also enabled them to explore new directions in thought and artistic expression. Scotland, like America, experienced a cultural flowering in the eighteenth century that was most evident in the fields of science, medicine, literature, and painting. The pollinators of this provincial renaissance were middle-class professionals—lawyers, doctors, clergymen, and scientists, who traversed the Atlantic and formed lasting relationships that altered their lives.

American lawyers were forced to rely, for formal training, on the Inns of Court in London. These four centers—Lincoln's Inn, the Inner Temple, the Middle Temple, and Gray's Inn—offered a course of study that led to the rank of barrister, the elite of English attorneys who had a monopoly on all practice before the courts. To qualify as a barrister a student had to attend one of the Inns for twelve sessions, but the attendance requirement could be satisfied by paying fees and eating meals at the Inn. Nor was there any formal curriculum of lectures and moot courts; the Inns were mostly social clubs of men with similar interests. The only generally accepted reading was Sir Edward Coke's *Institutes of the Laws of England,* although only the most conscientious read more than Coke's version of Littleton on property tenures. Otherwise the student read Locke, a little literature, attended Parliament, and occasionally court sessions. A few Americans were admitted to the bar after a stay of three to five years at the Inns, but most returned home without bothering to complete the course. More than two hundred Americans attended the Inns of Court in the colonial period, about two-thirds of them in the years after 1750.

Although dependent upon London for training, American lawyers never developed the rigid social stratification that characterized the profession in England. Northern merchants and southern planters refused to confer a monopoly of court practice upon an elite group of barristers. They preferred instead to handle their own legal affairs on an amateur basis. In the South, the sons of planters read law as a matter of course. It was an indispensable prelude to their social position, and it was essential to their positions as justices of the peace, county sheriffs, and members of the assembly.

The vast majority of professional lawyers received their training by apprenticeship to a practicing attorney. Tapping Reeve offered formal training in the law at his school in Lichfield, Connecticut, but there was no public law school in America until a professorship of law was established at the College of William and Mary in 1779. The apprenticeship system provided on-the-job training, but the quality varied widely. Jefferson thought the system was abused by attorneys who used their students in routine clerical work, although he himself had received intensive training in the Williamsburg office of George Wythe. A few rejected the apprentice program altogether and obtained admission to the bar by independent study. Patrick Henry spent six months preparing for the bar, during which he absorbed some property law from Coke-on-Littleton and coursed through the Virginia *Statutes at Large.* The court's examining committee, however, permitted him to practice only on condition of further reading. Standards for admitting lawyers to practice varied from colony to colony, but usually it only required admission to a court by a judge.

Partly, perhaps, because lawyers never constituted a professional elite and partly because of the wide diffusion of elementary legal knowledge in America, lawyers obtained an influence in colonial society far out of proportion to their numbers. Nearly one-half of the signers of the Declaration of Independence and three-fifths of those who wrote the Constitution had some formal legal training. Moreover, the study of law was intermingled with the general pursuit of knowledge, so that most lawyers were intimately acquainted with the major threads of eighteenth-century opinion. Jefferson, in his many letters to aspiring students of the law, invariably advised them to read widely in the languages, mathematics, and natural philosophy. "This foundation being laid, you may enter regularly on the study of the laws, taking with it such of its kindred sciences as will contribute to eminence in its attainment. The principal of these are physics, ethics, religion, natural law, belles lettres, criticism, rhetoric, and oratory." Such advice, when followed, ensured the practicing attorney a broad acquaintance with the Anglo-American Enlightenment.

Law could not be dissociated from politics, for nearly every lawyer of eminence had read Coke and Locke, who between them had summarized the great revolutionary thought of the previous century. A generation of lawyers, nurtured on Coke, was prepared for the legal rationalism of the Declaration of Independence. Of the great English jurist Jefferson observed: "A sounder Whig never wrote, nor one with profounder learning in the orthodox doctrines of British liberties. Our lawyers were then all Whigs." Although few of them were trained in England, American lawyers actively participated in the Atlantic intellectual community through their reading, their imperial connections, and their absorption of the common law.

American science, to an even greater extent than the law, was the province of amateurs, but it too relied upon the intellectual interchange of the imperial community. In a letter suggesting the formation of an American Philosophical Society, Benjamin Franklin observed in 1743, "The first drudgery of settling new colonies which confines the attention of people to mere necessaries is now pretty well over; and there are many in every province in circumstances that set them at ease, and afford leisure to cultivate the finer arts and improve the common stock of knowledge." The development of American science had been hindered by a lack of libraries, the absence of an aristocracy to provide patronage, and a paucity of universities. But by the mid-eighteenth century there was an international community of scientists who corresponded regularly and formed organizations for the exchange of information.

A notable example was the Swedish botanist Carolus Linnaeus, who established the modern method of plant classification. Linnaeus made frequent visits to England and established a wide circle of friends in both England and America. Among his more important contacts in London was the Quaker merchant Peter Collinson, who in many ways was the focal point of the scientific community. A wealthy woolens draper with a far-flung trade in Europe and America, Collinson made his mercantile firm a clearing house for communications among scientists. Included among his friends were Dr. Joseph Priestley, discoverer of oxygen, and the political radical, Richard Price. Himself an amateur botanist, Collinson made the acquaintance of John Bartram, a Philadelphia Quaker, and enlisted his aid in the collection of American plants. He acquainted Bartram with the Linnaean system of classification and helped the American to secure a royal pension that enabled him to range over the colonies in search of specimens to send to Linnaeus. Another American botanist, Mark

Catesby, received a loan from Collinson that enabled him to publish his *Natural History of Carolina, Florida, and the Bahama Islands.*

Collinson's greatest influence, however, was on the career of Benjamin Franklin. He encouraged Franklin's scientific interests and communicated to him the results of European experiments in electricity. After assiduously collecting Franklin's letters on the subject, he published them in 1751 under the title *Experiments and Observations on Electricity.* The book passed through five English editions and was translated into French, German, and Italian. In the first edition of the *Encyclopaedia Britannica,* the article on electricity was largely dependent upon Franklin's observations. It was an important scientific contribution because it proved the capacity of an American to offer a reasonable hypothesis and marshall experimental evidence to support it. Franklin's concept of electricity as a single fluid flowing from surplus (positive pole) to deficiency (negative pole), though modified considerably by recent discoveries, established the fundamental concepts and terminology still in use. More dramatic, of course, was his demonstration that lightning was a form of electricity. Although this phenomenon had already been discovered in Europe, Franklin was able to put it to practical use by inventing a lightning rod.

The cornerstone of scientific thought in the eighteenth century was the *Principia Mathematica* (1686) in which Sir Isaac Newton developed the mathematics of calculus in his effort to measure the distances among planets in the solar system. Newton's discovery that the planets moved in precisely predictable patterns stimulated the imagination and the curiosity of scientists for the next century. They became concerned with ordering and classifying the observable phenomena of the known world on the assumption that this would reveal the natural laws that governed the universe. One of Newton's earliest disciples in America was George Logan of Philadelphia. After making a fortune in the fur trade, Logan built an elegant mansion near Germantown and began collecting a library that ranked with the collections of Cotton Mather and William Byrd II as the finest in the New World. After reading Newton's *Principia* he constructed a small observatory in 1715 and wrote to London for a telescope and a chronometer (to determine longitude). He then wrestled without success with the problem that had baffled astronomers, the parallax of the earth's orbit around the sun.

The same problem was tackled a generation later with more success by the colonies' foremost scientist, John Winthrop IV. Great-grandson of the first governor of Massachusetts Bay, Winthrop was given the chair of mathematics and natural philosophy at Harvard at the age of twenty-three. He was a creative scientist who wrote on earthquakes, the weather, and mathematics, but his primary interest was astronomy. The transit of the planet Venus across the sun in 1761 seemed to provide a rare opportunity for the measurement of the solar system. Observations of the transit from different points on the earth would enable astronomers to calculate the solar parallax and hence the distance between the earth and the sun. They could then compute the distance between parts of the solar system, which were then known only in terms of the distance from one to another. It would be an immense step toward determining the exact dimensions of the Newtonian universe. Winthrop managed to secure the financial support of the Massachusetts government for an expedition to St. John's, Newfoundland, one of the few places on earth that provided a near-total eclipse. In England the Royal Society with financial support from the crown dispatched two expeditions, one to observe the transit at the island of St. Helena, and one from the Cape of Good Hope. Winthrop traveled to St. John's, established his longitude, and then timed the transit. He sent his observations to an astronomer friend in England. Statistics from the combined observations of the scientific community enabled British astronomers to estimate the distance from the earth to the sun at ninety-four million miles, only slightly longer than the distance now generally accepted.

Eight years later, Venus again moved across the sun, providing scientists with their last opportunity for another 105 years. The transit of 1769 was attended with much publicity in the newspapers and a wide variety of observations, including those of Winthrop at Cambridge. Though the calculations were not much more expert than those made in 1761, the number of observations and calculations received more attention in both America and Europe. Although the American contributions were largely a matter of sending information on the duration of the transit and the longitude, while the calculations were worked out in Europe, the transits of Venus were the most important astronomical events of the century and testified to the existence of an Atlantic scientific community.

Observing the transit of Venus in 1769 from Philadelphia was another prominent American astronomer, David Rittenhouse. A native-born Pennsylvanian, Rittenhouse was a clockmaker with a flair for mathematics and had thoroughly absorbed Newtonian physics. Two years earlier he had begun the construction of an orrery, a mechanical planetarium that would accurately represent the movements of the known planets. Rittenhouse calculated the planetary orbits from limited observations, and his conclusions were confirmed by European astronomers. Yet, like most American scientists, he lacked the instinct for speculation. Confining himself to orbital calculations, he never troubled himself with theories on the origin of the solar system or the composition of comets.

Below Franklin, Winthrop, and Rittenhouse were a variety of lesser lights in the American scientific community. Cadwallader Colden was a Scottish physician trained in Edinburgh and London. He was persuaded to move to New York in 1718 by a fellow Scot, Governor Robert Hunter, who rewarded him with a succession of government posts. During a long political career, he served on the Council and as lieutenant governor, but he also found time to write a *History of the Five Indian Nations* (1727), a pioneering anthropological work on the Iroquois. Less successful was his excursion into the field of physics. His *Principles of Action in Matter* (1746), which presupposed the existence of an interplanetary ether to explain gravity and the laws of attraction, met general derision in Europe. On his retirement from politics in 1750, Colden encountered a copy of Linnaeus's *Genera Plantarum* and developed an interest in botany that lingered for the rest of his life. Through Peter Collinson he came into contact with Linnaeus and sent the Swedish botanist numerous specimens. His

Plantae Coldenghamiae, a list of plants found near his New York farm, was the closest approach to a systematic botanical text by an American colonist.

Thomas Gilpin was another student of nature with catholic interests. On his farm on Maryland's Eastern Shore, Gilpin wrote learned essays on the wheat fly, the seventeen-year locust, a hydraulic windmill, and the migration of herring. His most important contributions, however, were in engineering. He surveyed a route for a proposed canal connecting Delaware and Chesapeake Bays (ultimately completed in 1829), and he drafted plans for a bridge with a three-hundred-foot span over the Susquehanna River.

American contributions to the international scientific community were largely of a practical, rather than speculative, nature. It is hardly necessary to point out that America produced no thinker of Newton's stature. Benjamin Franklin's lightning rod, rocking chair, and enclosed stove, all testimony to American inventiveness, were also symbols of the American concern for practical results. A pragmatic, materialistic people, newly emerged from the frontier condition, were more concerned with the question of "how" than "why." The attitude was best summarized by Charles Thomson when he outlined some of the purposes of the American Philosophical Society:

> Knowledge is of little use when confined to mere Speculation: But when speculative Truths are reduced to Practice, when Theories, grounded upon experiments, are applied to common Purposes of life, and when, by these Agriculture is improved, Trade enlarged, and the Arts of Living made more easy and comfortable,... Knowledge then becomes really useful.

American physicians placed similar emphasis upon empirical methods and concrete results. Medical training in Europe was fettered with dogma; impressed by the simplicity of Newton's mechanical universe, European physicians searched for equally simple explanations for disease. Some attributed illness to a disorder in the body "humors," others to disturbance in the bodily "tension." The celebrated Hermann Boorhaave at Leyden blamed a morbific matter in the blood and treated his patients with medicines designed to alter the qualities of this substance. American physicians, less preoccupied with causes and more concerned with remedies that proved effective, were more inclined to let nature take its course. They occasionally used medicines derived from local herbs and often prescribed such common-sense remedies as rest and fresh air. Eighteenth-century medicine on both sides of the Atlantic floundered in an abyss of ignorance, but the American approach often had the advantage of doing a minimum of harm to the patient.

The reason for the difference in medical practices was the general lack of formal medical training in America. Most physicians gained their knowledge of medicine by serving a brief apprenticeship to a practicing doctor; of the approximately thirty-five hundred persons practicing medicine on the eve of the Revolution only about two hundred had medical degrees. Not until 1734 did the first American go to Europe for medical training, and not until 1766, when the first medical school opened in Philadelphia, did the colonies possess facilities for formal medical education. As a result, the outstanding physicians in America were Scottish immigrants trained at Edinburgh. The Scottish Enlightenment shone most brightly in the field of medicine, and graduates of Edinburgh were men of wide interests and impressive accomplishments in the field of science. The achievements of Dr. Cadwallader Colden have already been noted. Next to Colden, the most prominent American physician was Dr. Alexander Garden, another Scot who landed at Charleston in 1752. After reading the works of Linnaeus, he developed an interest in botany and wrote the Swede offering his services in collecting plants. He traveled widely, collecting specimens of American flora unknown in Europe, and carried on an extensive correspondence with Colden, Bartram, and Franklin. The twelfth edition of Linnaeus's work on plant classification mentioned Garden's name more than that of any other collector, and in gratitude Linnaeus named the gardenia after him, though Garden did not discover it. Garden confined himself to collection and classification, leaving the theoretical work to his European correspondents. His activities nevertheless earned him a membership in the Royal Society, and when the Revolution erupted he moved to England, joining a scientific circle in London.

The American emphasis on practical results led to the first large-scale experiment in innoculation for the dreaded smallpox. The concept of innoculation (injecting a small dose of smallpox into a healthy patient to induce a mild case of the disease and subsequent immunity) was evidently discovered by the Turks. Lady Mary Wortley Montagu, a widely traveled "blue stocking" aristocrat, brought the idea to London, but the news was generally ignored by the medical fraternity. During an unusually severe epidemic in 1721, Lady Montagu persuaded George I to permit the innoculation of his two granddaughters, but the example was followed by only a few members of the Court. The death of two from innoculation occasioned a violent public controversy that ended only with news of American success with mass innoculation.

Smallpox was an endemic disease in Europe. The average person was exposed in childhood, and those who survived were thereafter immune. The disease was unknown to the virgin New World, however, until it was imported from abroad. The result was spectacular epidemics that ravaged the cities and decimated the Indian tribes. Unlike Europe, where only isolated individuals required immunization by innoculation, prevention of the disease in America demanded large-scale experimentation.

The technique of innoculation was introduced to America by Cotton Mather, Boston's foremost theologian at the beginning of the century. Unlike most American ministers, Mather had an intense interest in science and medicine. His essays on plants, birds, snakes, and other phenomena peculiar to America earned him an international circle of correspondents and eventually a coveted membership in the Royal Society. When he read, in the Society's *Transactions for 1714,* a letter from a Turkish doctor describing innoculations, Mather obtained from friends in London information on British experiments. Thus, when an epidemic hit Boston in 1721, Mather quickly appealed to the city's physicians to attempt mass innoculation. Ever jealous of interference in its mysteries (especially by theologians), the medical profession resisted the idea, though Dr. Zabdiel Boylston managed to innoculate some three hundred persons. Only five or six died from the innoculation, while nearly nine hundred succumbed to the epidemic.

Mather promptly collected the statistics and sent them to the Royal Society, noting that the chances of fatality from the disease itself were nine times as great as from innoculation. It was a pioneering endeavor in the use of public health statistics, and it produced a violent pamphlet warfare on both sides of the Atlantic. Gradually medical opposition broke down, however, and the practice became widely accepted when epidemics reappeared in the 1740s. When smallpox hit Charleston in 1743, Dr. James Kilpatrick innoculated some eight hundred persons, sustaining a mortality rate of only 1 percent. When the disease struck England three years later, thousands were innoculated in London, and publication of Dr. Kilpatrick's results helped overcome opposition in the rural areas. Nothing so well illustrated the mutual interchange of knowledge that underlay England's Atlantic community.

The Artistic Community

Another field in which the colonists made an impact on the mother country was painting. When Benjamin Franklin complained that "our geniuses all go to Europe," he probably had in mind American artists. In 1783 he wrote: "In England at present, the best History Painter, West; the best Portrait Painter, Copley; and the best Landscape Painter, Taylor, at Bath, are all Americans." Painters gravitated to Europe in order to acquaint themselves with the style and techniques of the masters. The best often remained because they found patrons among the aristocracy and a ready appreciation for competent work. The wealthy bourgeoisie of America often wanted only likenesses of themselves. While painters were lionized in Europe, in America they were often regarded as mere artisans.

The most successful American painter of the age was Benjamin West. Born in Philadelphia, West demonstrated talent at an early age and was sent to Europe on funds supplied by friends. After spending several years in Italy, he arrived in London in 1763. His Italianate style, which earned him the tag "the American Raphael," became the fashion, and he was an instant success. His talent for portraying historical events, such as the "Death of General Wolfe" (1771) and "Penn's Treaty with the Indians" (1771), started a new vogue in British painting. He became the center of a "historical school" of young painters, and at the death of the great portrait painter Sir Joshua Reynolds, West was made president of the Royal Academy.

Although West never returned to America, he never lost his ties with home. His London studio became the center of an "American school" of young painters. Among his protégés were Charles Willson Peale and Jonathan Trumbull, both of whom returned home to portray the heroes and events of the Revolution.

The best American portrait artist of the colonial period was John Singleton Copley. A native of Boston, Copley earned a modest living delineating the profiles of his wealthy townsmen. One of his paintings, entitled "Boy with a Squirrel," was exhibited in London in 1766 by a ship captain with a discriminating eye, and it won him immediate recognition. West and Reynolds both offered advice on improving his style and urged him to come to Europe. Although Copley bemoaned the cultural desert of America, he delayed a visit to London until 1774. Even then he went less to gain instruction than to escape the violence of the approaching Revolution. He never returned. In his years of residence abroad, the freshness of his early style deteriorated as he increasingly imitated the fashionable modes of British artists.

Copley's disparaging estimate of the cultural level of the American colonies was generally correct. Colonial architecture was completely dominated by English tastes. There were no professional architects in the colonies, merely master carpenters who followed English manuals. The result was a rectangular, symmetrical style, loosely known as Georgian. "Westover" on the James River, designed by the versatile William Byrd II for his own use, illustrates the influence of English baroque in its use of angles and planes, but more typical of colonial Georgian was the box-like Harrison family home "Shirley," a few miles farther up the river. Among musicians the only one worth noting was Francis Hopkinson of Philadelphia. A harpsichordist who played chamber music in the mode of the time, Hopkinson wrote a number of original compositions, distinguished chiefly by being the first produced by an American composer.

A native literature did not exist; in the field of writing Americans showed talent only for history. In the previous century American historical efforts, such as Cotton Mather's *Magnalia Christi Americana* (1702), were theologically inspired, mostly recitations of miracles designed to prove that God had underwritten the Puritan experiment. Robert Beverley's *History and Present State of Virginia* (1705) is the first competent effort at secular history, and though Whiggish and anti-imperial it remains useful today. The ablest chronicler of Massachusetts history was Thomas Hutchinson, lieutenant governor of the colony during the pre-Revolutionary controversy. Though a native of New England, he remained loyal to the empire and fled to Britain when the war began. The first volume of his *History of the Colony of Massachusetts Bay* appeared in 1764. The manuscript for the second volume was partially destroyed when his house was wrecked during the Stamp Act riots, and the third volume was finally completed in England. Unlike the early Puritan apologists, Hutchinson was not concerned with manifestations of God's favor. His well-told, objective account was colonial historical writing at its best.

The disinclination to write books was perhaps characteristic of a society preoccupied with carving a civilization out of the wilderness. Another factor, however, was the cost. There were few artisans skilled at papermaking, typesetting, or bookbinding, and labor costs were high. Since type and ink had to be imported from Europe, both were scarce and expensive. A printer with limited amounts of type on hand was reluctant to commit it to the production of a book. He much preferred to print pamphlets and newspapers, where the type could be set one day and rearranged the next. As a result, Americans found it cheaper to import books, and literary works formed an important segment of imperial trade.

Private collections were usually small and tended to concentrate on practical manuals of law, husbandry, and household medicine. Some collections, however—notably those of Cotton Mather, James Logan, and William Byrd II—numbered in the thousands. Reading was widespread enough to keep more than 150 bookstores in business in the five main colonial cities. The Library Company of Philadelphia, formed in the 1730s, was one of many civic improvements sponsored by Franklin's Junto Club. Though managed by the club, it was open to all who paid a subscription fee. The example was followed elsewhere—Newport had its Redwood Library and the Charleston Library Society boasted of having more than six thousand volumes.

Dependence on the mother country was most evident in the literary tastes of Americans. Private collectors talked some about Greek and Latin writers, occasionally they picked up a copy of Shakespeare or Milton, but their main preference was for the literary giants of the age of Queen Anne—Pope, Addison, and Swift. These satirical writers were widely admired for their urbanity, wit, and elegance of style. Pope's heroic couplet, so easily imitated, was the form for countless American efforts at verse, most of it easily forgettable. Benjamin Franklin sought to improve his writing style by paraphrasing Addison's essays and then comparing his language with the master's. Addison's *Spectator* was also a model for a number of American literary digests. The most interesting of these was the *General Magazine and Historical Chronicle for all the British Plantations in America,* started by Franklin in 1741. It was the first attempt at a periodical for all Anglo-Americans, on the mainland and in the West Indies. Besides reprinting essays and poems from other colonial papers, it edified busy Americans with a column entitled "Accounts of or Extracts from new Books, Pamphlets, etc., published in the Plantations."

Newspapers, however, attracted most of the literary energies of Americans. The prototype of the newspaper appeared in England during the Restoration period, but it was not till the age of Queen Anne that it became an established institution. The idea spread quickly to the colonies—the *Boston News Letter* was born in 1705—and by the time of the Revolution there were thirty-seven newspapers. Philadelphia alone boasted seven papers in the year 1776, more than London itself possessed. Newspaper growth was stimulated by widespread literacy, the vast extent of the continent, and the existence of numerous provincial centers, each with its own news. Useful, relevant, requiring little concentration or leisure, the newspaper filled the needs of a busy people preoccupied with making a living. Devoted primarily to advertisements and shipping notices, it served the needs of merchants and artisans. Where the editor was also the public printer, his sheet was filled with official notices, proclamations, and assembly journals, all of which satisfied the common interest in politics. Extra space was given to poetry, pithy sayings, and practical advice, thus meeting the need for culture without unduly taxing the intellect. Practical, miscellaneous, and inexpensive, the colonial newspaper was the arch-symbol of a civilization in the process of becoming.

Dawn of Enlightenment

The intellectual climate of the eighteenth century was heavily influenced by the scientific revelations of the preceding age. The discoveries of Copernicus and Galileo parted the veil of mystery that had hidden the secrets of the medieval universe. The notion that there were areas of order in the complex universe, patterns that could be comprehended by ordinary men, marked the transition from the medieval to the modern mind. The process was completed by Sir Isaac Newton, whose *Principia Mathematica* (1686) reduced the universe to a uniform system governed by comparatively simple laws of motion. Suddenly the universe was no longer complex and mysterious, subject to unpredictable intervention by the deity; it was consistent, interrelated, and rational. In the aphorism of Alexander Pope: "God said, 'let Newton be', and there was light."

Newton, a physicist and mathematician, failed to comprehend fully the ideological implications of his discoveries. Indeed, he shied away from any temptation toward rational skepticism and sought refuge in religious faith as he advanced in age. But the application of the empirical method to human society was undertaken almost instantaneously by Newton's contemporary and close friend, John Locke. In *An Essay Concerning Human Understanding* (1690), Locke undertook to discover the sources of human knowledge. Disagreeing with earlier philosophers who had assumed the existence of innate ideas, Locke argued that each individual was born with a mind naked of information, a *tabula rasa,* or blank slate on which experience wrote its lessons. The baby was not born with a concept of heat; he acquired it by putting his hand on the stove, just as the physicist formulated laws by observing a certain number of events.

Locke thus elevated the empirical method of science to the status of a philosophy. The social and political implications were enormous. If each person begins life with a blank mind unencumbered by inherited concepts, then each is born equal and differences among people are the result of subsequent experience, or the dictates of society. Totally unintended by Locke, who made a profession of defending the interests of the Whig aristocracy, the democratic implications of his psychology had to await rediscovery by another generation. More important for Locke's purposes was the implication that society itself was a sort of *tabula rasa* on which each generation could write its own concepts of government in accordance with the laws of nature. A system of government could thus be devised by reason, rather than inherited from previous generations. This concept he elaborated in another essay, *Of Civil Government* (1691).

Locke's political theories came from the same well of rationalism as Newton's physics, but they were developed independently. Indeed, as early as 1681 Locke completed a treatise intended to refute the ideas of Robert Filmer, who had argued for authoritarian government and the divine right of kings. Publication of the essay was delayed by the political disgrace of Locke's patron, the Earl of Shaftesbury, founder of the Whig party. After Shaftesbury's death in 1683, Locke sought asylum in Holland where he remained until the Glorious Revolution. Returning to England in 1689, he dusted off his manuscript, added timely allusions to the recent revolution, and issued it under the title, *Of Civil Government, Two Treatises.*

Scientific discoveries were rapidly demonstrating that the universe was governed by immutable laws, written by God but simple enough to be deduced from observation. In the same fashion, Locke sought to deduce from two fundamental premises of natural law a comprehensive political philosophy. His first premise amounted to a labor theory of value. God's bounty, virgin and unused, had no value until a person, by picking fruit or gathering nuts, mixed it with his labor and removed it from nature. In this way an individual created private property, and that person had a divinely sanctioned right to enjoy the fruits of his or her labor. The other premise involved the social contract. The need for government stemmed from the fact that human beings, as the descendants of Eve, are tainted with evil; they covet each other's property, creating disorder and lawlessness. To secure tranquility, the members of society entered into a contract, agreeing to set up a government and appointing one of their number as ruler. But in joining the contractual society, each individual retained the unsurrendered right to his life, liberty, and property which he possessed in the natural condition. If a ruler should infringe upon these God-given rights, the social contract would be broken and revolution warranted.

The intellectual descendants of Newton and Locke in the eighteenth century considered themselves "enlightened," no longer bound by the superstitions and habits that had clouded the human mind. This was the prevailing intellectual climate when Thomas Jefferson, at the impressionable age of seventeen, came down from the hills of the Virginia Piedmont to attend the College of William and Mary. Operated by the Church of England, the college was a provincial backwater in 1760, but Jefferson had the good fortune to be befriended by Dr. William Small, a recent emigre from Scotland who was the college's Professor of Mathematics. Small was, wrote Jefferson, "a man profound in most of the useful branches of science, with a happy talent of communication, correct and gentlemanly in manners, and an enlarged and liberal mind." Small, who taught philosophy, natural history, and rhetoric in addition to mathematics, introduced Jefferson to the Enlightenment. His teaching instilled in Jefferson a love for science and a devotion to reason. Jefferson remained a frequent companion of Small's even after leaving the college and commencing the study of law. His reading of the law induced him to apply the principles of scientific rationalism to the political realm. The complexities of society and government, Jefferson concluded, could be reduced to certain elementary laws as simple and rational as the laws that governed the motions of the planets—"the laws of nature and of nature's God," Jefferson would call them in the Declaration of Independence. Arbitrary governments, relics of an unenlightened age, might be swept aside and replaced by rational systems erected upon such self-evident truths as the principle that governments are derived from the just consent of the governed. A new political edifice, rationally conceived for the benefit of mankind, was certain to produce the greatest human happiness.

Jefferson, like many other disciples of the goddess reason, was prepared also to take the implications of the scientific revolution to their theological conclusion, a body of thought known as deism. Jefferson and other deists came to the realization that, if the universe was subject to rational laws, there was no place for divine intervention. God could not produce a miracle without violating one of His own laws and disrupting the beautifully rational system He had created. God's role in the universe, therefore, was nothing more than that of First Cause. It was He who created the mechanical order out of the chaos, wrote the laws, gave the system a slap to set it working, and, like an indulgent parent, left it alone thereafter. Such religious rationalism was not solely the result of the scientific discoveries of Galileo and Newton. In large part it represented a reaction against the intense religious fervor and conflict that had engulfed England since the Reformation. It was a natural letdown after the Puritan upheavals of the first half of the seventeenth century.

The closest approach to a gospel of deism in the eighteenth century was Matthew Tindal's *Christianity as Old as the Creation* (1730). Arguing for the supremacy of reason over faith, Tindal wished to strip religion of all revelation not supported by scientific facts. He would retain only the basic ethical system found in the teachings of Jesus. Toward the end of the century, Tom Paine, using his talent for expressing the most complex philosophical concepts in phrases comprehensible to all, summarized deist thought in *The Age of Reason* (1794).

Deism was an attitude, not a church, and its adherents came primarily from the upper classes in both England and America. Its importance derives largely from its impact upon the intellectual and political leaders of the century. Cadwallader Colden of New York, Samuel Johnson, President of King's College, and William Smith, first president of the College of Philadelphia, were all deists. Among leaders of the Revolution, Franklin and Jefferson were both committed to religious rationalism, as were Stephen Hopkins of Rhode Island, George Wythe of Virginia, and Ethan Allen of Vermont. Though the outspoken deists were few in number, the prevailing rationalism of the age affected the religious views of many. George Washington, John Adams, and George Mason held liberal religious attitudes, though they shied from the skepticism that accompanied a total commitment to deism.

Deism itself seemed beyond the grasp of the common man, but the prevailing climate of tolerance and rationalism could not help but affect the orthodox churches. In Congregationalist New England, a liberal undercurrent rejected the Calvinist doctrine of salvation for God's chosen few, and offered instead the prospect of universal salvation. Such "heresy" was denounced in the seventeenth century as Arminianism. Jacob Arminius was a Dutch theologian who had pointed out the logical flaw in Calvinism—that God himself was conceivably the author of sin, since He condemned as sinful the vast majority of men whom He had created. The Dutchman's alternative was to offer salvation to all who by their own free will were able to live an upright life. Arminius was burned at the stake for heresy in 1619, but his emphasis upon the individual's choice, rather than the absolute sovereignty of God, troubled Calvinism forever after. In the early nineteenth century, Arminian liberals would give birth to the Unitarian and Universalist churches in America.

Religious Awakenings

Though few could fully grasp the implications of deism, even the most unenlightened were aware of the trend toward religious liberalism. Rationalism induces tolerance, but often it also breeds apathy and indifference. Nor was it very satisfying to the emotional needs of the multitude. Viewing with alarm the decline in church membership and attendance, ministers on both sides of the Atlantic called for a new religious revival that would inject Christianity into the daily lives of their comfortable, prosperous, self-indulgent parishioners. Thus it was that the "age of reason" helped give birth to its own antithesis, a religious revival known as the "Great Awakening" which convulsed the empire through the middle decades of the century.

The revival drew its nourishment from many different segments of the Atlantic community. In England, the brothers John and Charles Wesley were among the first to recognize the gap between the institutionalized formality of Anglican services and the spiritual needs of the laity. At Oxford University in the 1720s, they initiated a religious circle that stressed the importance of elaborate ceremony, earning for themselves the derisive nickname "methodists." In 1735, John Wesley experienced a spiritual rebirth when he made a voyage to the new colony of Georgia. On shipboard he encountered a group of Moravians, members of a pietist sect whose religious beliefs affected the daily conduct of their lives. To such believers, church organization and elaborate ritual were less important than the practice of a Christian existence, dictated by the literal word of the Bible. Impressed by their innocent faith and pious behavior, Wesley saw in their methods a hope at last for the unregenerate poor of England, who had been almost totally ignored by the established church. He returned to England and used his oratorical gifts (and his brother's hymns) to foment a religious revival among the lower classes. The Methodist movement was the English counterpart of the Great Awakening. Pollinated in Georgia, it flowered in England, and then showered its seeds upon every part of the imperial community.

Moravians, Mennonites, and other pietist sects who settled in Pennsylvania influenced the neighboring Presbyterian and Lutheran churches in many of the ways that their brethren affected Wesley. The Scots-Irish who flooded into Pennsylvania after 1715 brought their native Presbyterian church, but under the debilitating influence of a century in hostile Ireland, Presbyterian services had degenerated into an icy formality. Periodic efforts to revive religious enthusiasm were finally coordinated by Reverend William Tennent, who arrived from northern Ireland in 1718. Influenced by the transatlantic sparks of revivalism and by the example of his pietist neighbors, he breathed a new religious spirit into his Presbyterian congregation at Neshaminy, Pennsylvania. He was a "burly, salty, downright man," who preached, said one observer, "like a Boatswain of a Ship, calling the Sailors to come to Prayers and be damned." In 1726 he removed to the Raritan Valley of northeastern New Jersey and established a "log college" for training young evangelists.

The most famous graduate of the school was his son, Gilbert Tennent, who carried the torch of the Awakening from the middle colonies to New England. Concerned with ending apathy, indifference, and secularism, the Tennents focused their sermons on the simple themes of sin, guilt, and redemption. The idea was to convince the assembled multitude of its guilt, of the extent to which it had fallen away from the faith of its forbearers, and then hold out the promise of redemption. Salvation depended less upon the intangible act of grace by a remote deity than upon the actions of the individual, demonstrated by his or her conversion experience, good works, and pure life. The Tennents's appeal was primarily to the poor, those to whom life had dealt a losing hand. Gilbert Tennent heaped scorn on "the Grandees" of America and warned that men tended to "grow in Wickedness in Proportion to the Increase in their Wealth." Unsaid, but certainly understood, was the promise that salvation was the great equalizer; rich and poor stood alike before an implacable God. This was heady stuff for a class of people who were beginning to resent the growing inequality of opportunity in American society.

The Great Awakening in New England, though entirely separate in its origins, was part of the same assault on apathy and outward conformity. There the gradual erosion of religious zeal was an older story, or at least it fretted the Puritan clergy throughout the latter half of the seventeenth century. As it became increasingly evident that a church confined to an inner circle of "visible Saints" had lost meaning to unregenerate outsiders, the clergy fought back with politic compromises and prophecies of doom. The Congregationalists's Half-Way Covenant of 1661 was an effort to extend the influence of the church by permitting nonmembers to participate in the service and authorizing the baptism of their children.

By 1700, many Congregational ministers in Massachusetts and Connecticut concluded that it was impossible to separate true believers from hypocrites who wished to join the church for social or psychological reasons; hence they concluded it was useless to insist upon a demonstration of the conversion experience. This feeling was given wide currency by Reverend Solomon Stoddard of Northampton, Massachusetts, who suggested that communion of the Lord's Supper ought to be offered to any upright adult, even if he had not gone through the emotional experience of regeneration. Stoddardism, spreading across New England, held that the church was no longer confined to an inner circle of Saints; rather it was coterminous with the town. This movement, which proposed to open church membership to all who desired it, evidenced the impact of reason and tolerance upon Calvinist New England. As elsewhere, however, rationalism bred an emotional reaction; critics charged that it ushered into the church the polluting influence of the sinful. Thus a renewed stress upon the sanctifying conversion experience was the theme of the religious revival in New England. It was, ironically, Solomon Stoddard's own grandson, succeeding to the Northampton, Massachusetts, pulpit in 1729, who started the new revival.

Jonathan Edwards brought to his ministry a thorough grounding in the Enlightenment. At the age of thirteen he wrote an essay on the rainbow that demonstrated a familiarity with Newton's *Opticks*. At Yale he received intense instruction in Newtonian physics from the deist Samuel Johnson, and he read

Locke's *Essay*. But, instead of being converted to Newtonian rationalism, he adapted the new science to a Calvinist framework. Locke's epistemology appealed to Edwards as the only way in which the limited human mind could hope to understand the unfathomable mystery of God and His universe. God imparts ideas through sense experience, Edwards concluded; He works on man through the experience of sensation. This seemed to point the way for the restoration of faith. If the only way to impress the understanding was through the senses, the evangelist could abandon rational arguments and appeal instead to men's minds through their feelings.

Blending Lockean psychology with Puritan doctrine, Edwards concluded that only someone who was spiritually enlightened could perceive the truth of an idea. It did not require a storehouse of information, acute intelligence, or professional training. The sense alone could perceive true religion, and a simultaneous act of will translated this into an upright life. By stressing the heart, rather than the mind, will rather than reason, Edwards sought to combat the rationalism, skepticism, and indifference of the age. Although he started from the same point as the deists, he ended with an evangelical theology founded on the emotion-packed conversion experience that signified salvation.

The disparate threads of religious revival were brought together by George Whitefield, who arrived in America in 1739. An Anglican clergyman converted by the Wesleys, Whitefield possessed a gift of oratory second only to that of John Wesley himself. The greatest Shakespearean actor of the century, David Garrick, once observed that Whitefield could throw an audience into paroxysms by pronouncing "Mesopotamia." Other witnesses claimed he could make Hell so vivid they could find it on a map. But Whitefield also had a message. He challenged traditional church authority and called on people to be the instruments of their own salvation. Like Gilbert Tennent, he was offering the dispossessed an escape from the present and a promise for the future.

After a successful tour of the southern colonies, he arrived in Massachusetts in the summer of 1740. He spent four weeks in Boston and then made a triumphal march across Massachusetts. Arriving in Northampton on October 17, he preached for three days from Edwards's pulpit and then departed to fulfill engagements in New Haven and New York. In a triumphant, two-year tour he managed to enchant thousands in every major urban center of the seaboard.

Whitefield's whirlwind tour inspired others, leaving in its wake a string of itinerant evangelists who carried the word to every nook and cranny of the continent. Since most of the itinerants were recent converts who felt the call to exhort others and lacked formal training or ordination, they easily sped away on doctrinal tangents. The result was a chaos of views and an excess of emotionalism that soon disgusted the majority and brought an end to the Awakening. But in the meantime the itinerant preachers brought the new methods to every parish, invited or not, and provided a common emotional experience that cut across colonial boundaries.

The Awakening sliced through the social barriers that divided genders as well. New Light congregations—associations of the regenerate that had split off from the orthodox churches—had a substantial number of women, and the logic of salvation dictated equality among all saints. Rhode Island's Baptists—

spiritually descended from Roger Williams's apostasy a century before—had long allowed women to vote on church affairs, and occasionally they placed female exhorters in the pulpit. New Light churches, though more ambivalent about the role of women than the Quakers, allowed women to serve on church committees and vote on church affairs. One woman, Sarah Osborn of Newport, Rhode Island, even inspired a revival of her own. Until her conversion during the Awakening, Mrs. Osborn was a pious, family-oriented housewife and a member of Newport's First Congregational Church. After her conversion in 1741 she began directing the activities of a female prayer group that met in her home. Religion remained "the chief business" of her life, as she expressed it, even after she was widowed and worked in a shop to support herself. In the spring of 1765 she allowed a number of slaves, who belonged to wealthy townspeople, to attend prayers in her home on Sunday evenings. Before long, she reported to the minister of her church, "Little white Lads and Neighbours daughters also press in" to her meetings. Within a year more than three hundred people, both black and white, were coming to her house each week for religious gatherings. She soon came under criticism, voiced pointedly by the minister of her church, that she was "keeping a Negro house" and breaching the acceptable boundaries of feminine behavior. Her response was that she would continue her spiritual activities "until God in his providence point out a way for it to be better done." And so she did until the revival spirit itself faded in the 1770s.

Most of the southern gentry, on the other hand, remained unaffected by the religious upheaval. Rejecting both the rationalism of the deists and the enthusiasm of the evangelists, they adhered to the Anglican Church because it embraced the middle way. Its emphasis on practical morality unencumbered with theological obscurities suited the temper of men of affairs, just as its modestly decorous services appealed to their sense of propriety. On the other hand, the poor and ill-educated, particularly in Virginia, were more susceptible to the sway of revivalists. In Virginia, as in England, the Anglican Church had degenerated into an easy formality of ritual, providing little ministration and generally ignoring the needs of the poor. The rigid and aristocratic parish system, moreover, prevented the church from accompanying the expansion of the frontier where the emotional needs of the people were often most acute.

The Virginia revival was born in rural Hanover County. Sometime in the 1730s a bricklayer named Samuel Morris decided that he was not getting the true Gospel from his minister, the Reverend Patrick Henry (uncle of the Revolutionary leader). Morris accordingly stayed away from church and collected a close circle of friends who studied the Bible in his home. When Whitefield preached at Bruton Parish, Williamsburg, in December 1739, many from Hanover were converted, and the circle around Morris expanded. For lack of a better name they began calling themselves Presbyterians, adapting it, no doubt, from their Scottish neighbors. In 1743 they received an ordained minister from the New Castle, Delaware, presbytery, who organized them into a congregation and began spreading evangelical doctrines.

Alarmed, Reverend Patrick Henry persuaded the governor to issue a proclamation prohibiting evangelist preachers in the colony, but the Hanover Presbyterians were rescued by the arrival of another evangelist, Samuel Davies, sent by the New York Synod. After charming the governor and council into giving him special permission to preach, Davies spread the religious awakening through the counties of southern and western Virginia. Aided by the influx of Scottish immigrants into the Shenandoah Valley, the Presbyterian Church made great gains in the 1740s, and most of the new congregations were tinged with evangelical concepts. Samuel Davies proved to be the greatest of the itinerant preachers; his oratorical powers were often compared with those of Whitefield himself. Among his avid listeners in Hanover County was young Patrick Henry, who a few years later would prove himself adept at putting the rhetorical techniques of the evangelist to political purposes.

As the tidal wave of revivalism receded it left in its wake irreconcilable divisions in Calvinist churches from New England to Virginia. Those whom the light of Christ had shown the path to salvation called themselves "New Lights," and the moderate orthodox churchgoers received the contemptuous nickname "Old Lights." The core of the dispute continued to be the ancient problem of Arminianism. Wherever unconverted persons were permitted to enter baptism and take communion the New Lights split off and formed their own church. They formed over a hundred new congregations in New England and perhaps an equal number in the middle colonies.

By the 1760s the separatists, or "strict Congregationalists," had embraced the concept of adult baptism. By becoming rebaptized they symbolically shed themselves of former sins, starting life anew. "Believers' Baptism" was also a way of ensuring the purity of the church, for it confined church membership to saints who were assured of salvation. English Baptists had reached a similar conclusion in the early seventeenth century, as had Roger Williams in Rhode Island. The traditional Baptists, however, had made little headway in America until the Great Awakening. With new adherents to the creed of adult baptism following the revival, a union of the two groups became virtually inevitable. The catalyst was Isaac Backus, a Massachusetts farmboy converted by one of the sermons of George Whitefield. After two years of agonizing introspection, this "New Light" Puritan reached the conclusion: "one Lord, one faith, one baptism." After organizing a Baptist church in Middleborough, Massachusetts, in 1756, he took to the road to spread his message, traveling over fifteen thousand miles and preaching over two thousand sermons in the next forty years. He examined his faith in thirty-seven published pamphlets and culminated his work in *A History of New England with Particular Reference to the Denomination of Christians Called Baptists.* On the eve of the Revolution he achieved a union of congregations that marked the formation of the modern Baptist Church, and he took a major step toward making the new church respectable by founding a college (now Brown University) for the training of its clergy.

Others carried the gospel of adult baptism onto the Appalachian frontier. Shubal Stearns was converted by George Whitefield, slipped into the Baptist fold, and then followed an "inner voice" to Virginia. He was joined there in 1754 by his brother-in-law, David Marshall, and the following year the two moved into northwestern North Carolina to organize a church. From this center at Sandy Creek, itinerant preachers spread out across the southern mountains from Virginia to Georgia. In seventeen years the Sandy Creek settlement summoned forth forty-two new churches, 125 itinerant ministers, and countless "revivals." By 1775, the Baptists surpassed the Presbyterians in importance on the frontier, and Baptist itinerants had infused a new religious zeal in the most remote parts of the southern backcountry.

The social impact of the Great Awakening is difficult to assess. In the beginning, at least, it was a movement that met widespread psychological needs, and it cut across social, educational, and geographical lines. Comparatively sober orators such as George Whitefield and Gilbert Tennent appealed to all social classes, and in nearly every town they were offered the use of the local church. Until 1742, at least, the revival was supported by most of the Congregational clergy in New England. But, as the revival evolved into itinerant preaching by lay evangelists, social and intellectual cleavages became evident. Extreme agitators like James Davenport were denied the use of church pulpits. Davenport deliberately antagonized the clergy by insisting that they be examined for regeneracy. Those who declined were invariably denounced, and many who agreed to an interview found to their utter humiliation that they failed to meet Davenport's standards. Excluded from the churches, Davenport exhorted from stumps in the fields and meadows, and his appeal was primarily to the poor and uneducated. Such activities, reinforcing the class appeal of Gilbert Tennent and George Whitefield, conferred a new sense of self-importance among the laboring poor, and it certainly expanded their political consciousness. To be sure, the message of the evangelists did not inspire immediate social revolution, but it did assure ordinary men and women that in certain circumstances they were perfectly justified in taking matters into their own hands. Hard times after the French and Indian War, together with imperial repression would translate that message into political action.

British America in 1763

On the surface, the British Empire in 1763 seemed a marvelously integrated unit. The mutual economic interdependence of mother country and colonies was sustained by the imperial regulations known as the Navigation Acts. Although these laws helped to keep the American colonies in a subservient status, they did give Americans numerous commercial privileges within the empire. Thus, despite its colonial condition, the American economy by the mid-eighteenth century had made considerable progress in agriculture and manufactures, each interwoven with sophisticated patterns of trade. The growth had come in uneven spurts, but it averaged about one-half a percent per year. This seems low by modern standards, but it was about the same as the mother country's growth rate in that preindustrial era. And it was rapid enough for one modern scholar to conclude that the American standard of living in 1774 was "probably the highest achieved for the great bulk of the population in any country up to that time."

Paralleling, and perhaps reflecting, this social and economic progress was the development of fairly sophisticated political institutions. The colonial assemblies created by royal and proprietary charters were originally intended only to ratify executive recommendations on taxes and local ordinances. But in the late seventeenth century they began a quest for power that ultimately limited the authority of both crown and governor. By 1763 they had evolved into miniature parliaments, jealous of their privileges and immunities, proud of their power to initiate and pass legislation. In every colony the assembly obtained, to a greater or lesser degree, the crucial "power of the purse"—the right to levy taxes and appropriate funds. This was the foundation of most of their other powers, for it gave them a leverage against royal officials and, in times of military emergency, against the crown itself.

The authority of the assemblies rested ultimately on the popular will, for in every colony the lower house was chosen by popular ballot. The suffrage was restricted by property qualifications of varying amounts, but in most colonies a substantial number of white males could vote if they wished. Voters, however, usually chose men of the "better sort" to represent them, and hence the assemblies in practice were dominated by the social and economic elite in each colony. The elite, in turn, used the assembly as an instrument to preserve their local autonomy against imperial interference.

It was this undercurrent that belied the superficial unity of the empire in 1763. For several decades while Britain and France struggled spasmodically for imperial hegemony, American political leaders had been left much to their own devices. In the vacuum, they had assumed a considerable amount of local autonomy. Any effort to restore imperial authority or impose stringent regulations was certain to meet resistance, and might even awaken desires for complete independence.

The gentlemanly governance of the colonial assemblies, on the other hand, masked some serious fissures in American society, caused by increasing class consciousness, economic depression, and religious schisms. Amidst such stress, confrontation, even violence, were commonplace. In summary, Americans were combative enough to contemplate Revolution, and they were prosperous enough to make a success of independence.

2

The Imperial Challenge, 1763–1774

At the close of the French and Indian War in 1763, Great Britain stood at the pinnacle of its power. The peace conference at Paris that year was a triumphant recognition of British conquests in seven bloody years of war. The French empire in North America had disappeared; from Canada to the Floridas, the territory east of the Mississippi River was under British dominion. Yet, despite the hardships and the heroism of British arms in North America and India, despite the courage and vigilance of the squadrons that patrolled the West Indies and the Mediterranean, it almost seemed as if the empire had been won too quickly and too easily. Unaccustomed to managing dominions flung in desultory fashion around the world, British politicians were slow to comprehend the meaning of their victory and even slower in developing a comprehensive world-view to match their world-empire. They remained wedded to local politics, encumbered by petty rivalries, stubborn, and unimaginative. As a result, the first British empire began to crumble almost as soon as it was fully formed.

So long as the empire remained a lightly populated collection of seaboard settlements clinging to the mother country for safety and security, it seemed unnecessary to tinker with the administrative machinery. But the "Great War for Empire" and its victorious settlement presented a host of new problems that demanded attention. The very size of the empire set loose centrifugal forces that had to be countered with more efficient administrative ties. Trade regulations had to be strengthened to ensure the continuation of mutual interdependence which underlay imperial unity; above all, if an island were to govern a continent, the staggering burden of costs would have to be shared. Such problems would have confounded a generation of Solons versed in all the governmental experiences of mankind; for the British statesmen of the mid-eighteenth century they were insurmountable. Their groping, tentative efforts to find solutions, coupled with ill-considered threats and hasty retreats, upset the delicate balance between royal authority and local autonomy in America. In a climate of mutual suspicion, each side saw a sinister conspiracy behind every move. The ministry in London became convinced that American leaders were rebels at heart, who would be satisfied with nothing short of independence. In similar fashion Americans concluded that parliament meant to strip away their powers of self-government, perhaps abolish their popular assemblies, and put them under the boot of military rule. It was such fears that drove Americans at last into open rebellion.

The war emergency itself evoked the initial steps toward tightening the imperial administrative machinery. In 1755, General Edward Braddock was appointed commander in chief of all military forces in North America. Creation of this post represented a major step toward unifying military operations which previously had been in the hands of colonial governors and provincial officers. The influx of British regulars after 1755 helped to sustain the colonial defense, but it also threatened the status of provincial military authorities. George Washington, colonel and commmander in chief of Virginia militia, chafed at the necessity of taking orders from mere lieutenants in the regular army and fumed at the overbearing attitude of British officers. Partly for these reasons, he resigned his commission in 1759 and stood for election to the House of Burgesses. Another Virginian, Daniel Morgan, whose exploits in the Revolution are legendary, was given five hundred lashes for striking an arrogant British officer during the French war.

That same year, 1755, the ministry took another step toward administrative unity by creating the office of Indian superintendent, giving him exclusive control of Native American affairs. The following year the office was divided into two departments, supervised by Sir William Johnson in the North and Edmund Aitkin in the South. Relations with the tribes were thus entrusted to officials responsible only to the ministry in London, and colonial authorities were deprived of a power they had exercised since the first settlements were established. Provincial control over the disposition of the West was further diminished in 1761 when the Board of Trade prohibited colonial governors from making grants on lands held by Native Americans. That same year Colonel Henry Bouquet, commander at Fort Pitt, prohibited all settlement west of the Alleghenies in Pennsylvania.

The purpose of these British moves was to prevent border warfare and protect the tribes. The two, of course, were related, for the sharp practices of colonial traders, who subverted the Native Americans with rum, and the encroachments of land-clearing squatters had caused the tribes to strike back with surreptitious violence ever since the two cultures had first confronted each other at Jamestown a century and a half earlier. An urgent need for an imaginative, unified policy was indicated by serious uprisings late in the war. The Cherokee "rebellion" of 1759 in the southern colonies was followed in 1763 by the much more serious "conspiracy" of Pontiac.

Pontiac was an Ottawa leader who organized an alliance of Ohio Valley tribes against further incursions on their lands. His braves struck abruptly in May 1763, and by the end of the summer every British outpost west of Pittsburgh, except for Detroit, fell to the Native Americans. Pennsylvania, whose fur traders and land speculators were largely responsible for the outbreak, bore the brunt of the savage fury, but the Quaker-dominated assembly would do no more than authorize a force of seven hundred militia to guard the eastern towns. After months of vicious fighting, frontiersmen with the help of British regulars rescued beleaguered Pittsburgh and Detroit.

Even before Pontiac's uprising, the ministry in London had been in the process of formulating a new frontier policy. In February 1763, the decision was made to leave an army of ten thousand regulars in the colonies to garrison the frontier (though most of them were eventually stationed instead in Canada and Florida). By summer, royal officials were working on a plan to limit settlement west of the mountains. Pontiac's uprising spurred their efforts, and the proclamation was issued by King George III on October 7, 1763. Seeking to reserve all lands west of the Appalachian ridge for the tribes, the proclamation prohibited any further land grants or sales in the West without royal license and ordered the removal of all white squatters.

The purpose of the proclamation was not to confine American settlements forever to the seaboard; rather, it was intended to centralize tribal relations and land grants in the hands of the ministry, a policy toward which royal officials had been moving since 1755. The ministry intended to negotiate further land cessions from the Native Americans, thus permitting a gradual advance of the frontier; and the proclamation itself permitted land grants to veterans of the French war. Taking advantage of these loopholes, the colonists generally evaded the restrictions, and the proclamation evoked no particular excitement in America.

Writs of Assistance

The Proclamation of 1763, unenforceable as it was, represented only a theoretical centralization of powers. Of more momentous impact was the British effort during the war to enforce the laws of trade and navigation. In wartime the French and Spanish islands in the West Indies, cut off from Europe by the British navy, customarily threw open their ports to American ships. This illicit wartime trade was immensely profitable to New England merchants, but the ministry considered it aid to the enemy. At the suggestion of British officers in Boston, William Pitt ordered a strict enforcement of the trade laws to prevent the smuggling of foreign goods into New England. In their search for illicit goods customs officials armed themselves with writs of assistance issued by the superior court of Massachusetts.

Search warrants required a specific allegation of a crime and were confined to specific objects, but the writs of assistance gave the customs officials general powers of search and seizure. Available in England since Parliament authorized them in the latter part of the seventeenth century, the writs were first used in Massachusetts in 1755, though courts in Connecticut and Rhode Island refused to issue them.

When King George II died in 1760, the writs expired, and the surveyor general requested the Massachusetts superior court to issue new ones. Chafing under the enforcement of trade laws against Massachusetts while Connecticut and Rhode Island smugglers seemed exempt, the Boston merchants decided to contest the writs. The issue immediately became involved in factional politics resulting from the heavy-handed policies of the colony's new governor, Francis Bernard. Initially, Bernard sought to steer a neutral course between the two factions, one led by James Otis, the other by Lieutenant Governor Thomas Hutchinson. Hutchinson's "court party" gave Bernard the most loyal support, however, and Bernard rewarded Hutchinson by appointing him chief justice. Otis and his followers promptly formed an alliance with the Boston merchants, who hired his son, James Otis, Jr., to represent their case against the writs of assistance.

Appearing before the superior court, Otis ignored the arguments of the crown attorney that the writs had English and colonial precedents. He claimed instead that the use of general warrants, which did not list the specific object of the search, so violated the right of privacy that it was "against the fundamental principles of law." Admitting that the writs had been authorized by Parliament, Otis argued nonetheless that a law "against the constitution is void; an act against natural equity is void." Otis lost the case, for Chief Justice Hutchinson found the writs to be legal and reissued them; but in losing he challenged the fundamental powers of Parliament. The rights of citizens, he suggested, were protected by the "constitution" of the empire and by "natural equity," and acts of Parliament contrary to those "fundamental principles" were automatically void. In the next election the Boston populace sent Otis to the House of Representatives, and when the House met, his father was chosen speaker. The alliance of the Otis faction and the Boston merchants provided the nucleus of a "popular party" that led the resistance to British measures after the war. Over the next few years Otis broadened the basis of his popular support by appealing with sulphurous oratory to the feeling of alienation, the hostility to wealthy "aristocrats," among Boston's artisan community.

The next step in the development of a revolutionary opposition in Massachusetts was an alliance between Otis's party and the Boston Caucus. For decades secret caucuses of Boston merchants and artisans had controlled the town meeting. Convening several weeks in advance of the town meeting, wrote one critic who sought to expose the system, caucus leaders "appoint town officers, and settle all affairs that are to be transacted at town meeting." To give a semblance of popular control, they invited all townspeople to speak at the open meeting, and they "prepared a number of warm disputes . . . to entertain the lower sort." By 1763 Samuel Adams, a minor official of the town with numerous contacts among the leather aprons, was an active member of the caucus. Alarmed by its loss of control of the town meeting, the Hutchinson faction in that year sought to discredit the caucus with a public exposé of its methods. The attempt backfired as 1,089 voters turned out for the election that fall, a number not exceeded for a decade, and the candidates backed by the Hutchinson circle took a drubbing. James Otis was elected moderator of the town meeting, and the popular party was in firm control. Boston was prepared to resist, by popular ballot or by violence, any new effort to impose imperial authority on America.

The Parson's Cause

In suggesting that the rights of citizens were founded in natural law and equity, superior even to acts of Parliament, Otis presented a view of the British constitution unfamiliar to most Englishmen. Indeed, its implications shook the very foundations of the empire. Nevertheless, before long Otis was echoed by a voice in the backwoods of Virginia. The occasion was a court trial known as "the parson's cause." The origin of this controversy was the Two Penny Act of 1758, which altered Virginia's tobacco currency. Since the beginning of the century, tobacco certificates had been the common circulating medium in Virginia; nearly all debts, taxes, and salaries were paid in pounds of tobacco. At the beginning of the French war a succession of droughts and bad harvests raised the price of tobacco, making it expensive for planters to pay debts that were expressed in poundage. Responding to petitions for relief, the assembly in 1758 passed a law providing that all debts, contracts, or salaries due in tobacco could be paid with money instead at the rate of two cents per pound of tobacco. Since the market price for tobacco was six pence a pound, the act substantially depreciated the currency. Because the people seemed unanimous in its support, the governor approved the law even though it did not contain the usual clause suspending its operation until approved by the Privy Council in London.

Among the creditors damaged by the law were the Anglican clergy, who were commonly paid by their vestries in fixed rates of tobacco poundage. At the current market price they received only a third of their salary under the new law. The clergy petitioned London, and in 1759 the king in council disallowed the Two Penny Act, though it never made clear whether the act was void from the beginning. In the end, the clergy would have to sue for back pay, and the county courts would have to determine whether the act was ever in effect. In all, five lawsuits were instigated by clergymen, and not one recovered any money because the juries were loaded with unfriendly planters.

The most famous of these "parson's causes" involved the Reverend James Maury, of Fredericksville Parish in Louisa County, Virginia. Since his vestry were also judges of the county court, he removed his suit to neighboring Hanover in April 1762. This choice of venue proved equally unfortunate since this area of the Virginia Piedmont had been a hotbed of Presbyterian dissent since the Great Awakening. In November 1763, the presiding judge, Colonel John Henry, ruled that the act was void from the beginning and the parson was entitled to back pay. Having lost his case, the defense attorney resigned, disdaining further arguments before the jury on the amount of damages to be awarded. In desperation the vestry hired the judge's son, Patrick, a self-taught lawyer who had already failed as a storekeeper and planter. The "parson's cause" was his first case.

Rising in what appeared to be a hopeless position, Patrick Henry's arguments seemed somewhat disjointed at first, and his sympathetic father "sank back in his chair in evident confusion." But then the oratorical powers that were to stir a nation to arms burst forth. The Two Penny Act, he argued, was a beneficial and necessary law; by annulling it the king effectively destroyed the original compact between king and people. Unless a king rules justly, his subjects are not obliged to obey him, Henry continued. ". . . a King, by annulling or disallowing acts of so salutary a nature, from being the father of his people, degenerated into a tyrant, and forfeits all rights to his subjects' obedience." As murmurs of "treason" buzzed through the audience, Henry summarized the accumulated grievances against the clergy, playing on the prejudices of the dissenters on the jury. They would have to award the plaintiff, he reminded the jury, but they did not have to concede him more than a farthing. After brief consideration the jury awarded the parson one penny back pay.

Henry's oratory had elevated a trivial disagreement into a philosophical challenge to the empire. It is highly unlikely that he ever read the works of John Locke or the French *philosophes;* rather, he summarized the concept of "social contract" prevalent in eighteenth-century thought and adapted it to the needs of Americans. Even so, his radical arguments were not heard outside of Virginia. Perhaps the main effect was to enhance Henry's reputation within the colony; two years later he was elected to the House of Burgesses. Like James Otis and Samuel Adams in Massachusetts, Patrick Henry was girded for combat when British ministers sought to reorganize the empire at the end of the French and Indian War.

Parliament Takes a Hand

The end of the French and Indian War brought a change in British ministries. Lord Bute, the king's favorite who mismanaged the last years of the war, resigned in April 1763 and was replaced by the popular and energetic George Grenville. But a few months' investigation was required for Grenville to realize that the ramshackle imperial structure needed an overhaul. The empire had become too overgrown, unwieldy, and expensive to tolerate longer the ad hoc and occasionally contradictory methods of the past. Administrative machinery must be strengthened, trade regulations enforced, and, above all, the colonies would have to contribute more to their own defense in order to relieve the budgetary strain. Actually, there was little new in Grenville's program; indeed, in many ways it was the logical culmination of centralizing measures undertaken during the war. Nor was it a comprehensive program to reform the empire. Grenville and the men around him lacked such vision. Instead, they merely wanted to share the financial burden of the empire, and, above all, they wanted to make the imperial officials in America true to the crown and not subject to the people they governed. Imperial regulations would never be enforced without an independent officialdom with an independent source of income. The colonists, of course, also recognized this, and therein lay the germ of conflict.

The essential difficulty was that British measures after 1763 were based upon a seventeenth-century concept of the empire that no longer squared with reality. The American colonies had thrived on British inefficiency. Ignoring trade laws that were enforced laxly or not at all, Americans had built a complex network of relationships with the West Indies, the Atlantic islands, and southern Europe. The trade was profitable, and Americans particularly depended on it to redress the chronic payments deficit with the mother country.

As the economy had matured since the end of the seventeenth century, so did American politics. The colonial assemblies had become independent-minded legislatures, jealous of their privileges and accustomed to regulating their domestic affairs with a minimum of interference. By 1740 a delicate balance of power had been achieved in most colonies. For the next two decades a relative calm prevailed under a series of tactful governors who knew the limits of their powers, such as William Gooch in Virginia, Gabriel Johnson in North Carolina, William Shirley in Massachusetts, Horatio Sharpe in Maryland, and Benning Wentworth in New Hampshire. But such men were popular precisely because they evaded imperial regulations and were lax in collecting customs duties. George Grenville's aim was to bring these lax officials to heel. His measures and those of his successors, in turn, destroyed the delicate balance of authority in the colonies. Taken to their logical conclusion, Grenville's policies represented a threat to the very existence of the assemblies. Americans responded with a new view of the imperial constitution and a new definition of their inherent rights, and as the threat increased, they slowly evolved a philosophy of revolution.

The first item on Grenville's agenda was the Revenue Act of 1764, commonly called the Sugar Act. The measure increased the duties on a variety of goods imported by the colonies—foreign cloth, sugar, indigo, coffee, wine, and spirits—but the most important feature was a reduction in the duty on foreign molasses from sixpence per gallon to threepence. The Molasses Act of 1732, which imposed a high duty on non-British sugar and molasses, was never properly enforced, and the colonists had persisted in smuggling the much cheaper French molasses. By reducing the duty, Grenville hoped to cut the motivation for smuggling and improve the crown's revenue.

In order to strengthen the enforcement machinery, the Revenue Act established a vice admiralty court for America at Halifax, Nova Scotia. One reason for the lax enforcement of trade laws was that common law juries, often made up of friends and neighbors of the accused smuggler, were notoriously lenient. Vice admiralty courts functioned without juries, and under their rules of procedure the burden of proof was on the accused. Thus merchants whose vessels were seized on the flimsiest evidence found it almost impossible to recover them. The use of such courts actually made Americans second-class citizens, for in England persons accused of violating the trade laws were given the benefit of jury trials. This sort of discrimination was at the root of the colonists's concern for their rights, and the vice admiralty courts (later expanded to four) remained a latent grievance through the rest of the pre-Revolutionary period. In 1765, John Adams called them the "most grievous innovation of all."

Two weeks later Parliament adopted the Currency Act, which prohibited the colonies from making their paper money legal tender in payment of debts or taxes. It provided also that the money then in circulation could not be reissued, thus contemplating the gradual elimination of all paper money once the wartime issues were redeemed. The actual effect of the act is uncertain, since a substantial amount of paper continued to circulate; what is certain is that the act represented a total ignorance of monetary economics in London. The redemption of paper money probably had a general deflationary effect on the economy and aggravated the hard times that followed the war. At least the colonists thought so, and the act thus contributed to the climate of economic discontent that clouded their reception of the Stamp Act the following year.

The Stamp Act

As head of the treasury, George Grenville was largely preoccupied with Britain's staggering war debt and chronic deficit. A major source of the deficit was clearly the cost of imperial defense; military garrisons in America alone cost the mother country £350,000 a year. The revenue anticipated from the duties imposed in 1764 was only £50,000, and the war itself had demonstrated that the colonial governments would not voluntarily contribute to their own defense. A new source of income had to be found, and a duty collected from the sale of stamps to be required on all documents seemed both painless and profitable. Grenville proposed such a tax in 1764, but he agreed to delay it a year to give the colonists an opportunity to consider the matter and suggest alternatives.

The colonial assemblies accordingly prepared petitions against the proposed tax and any other taxation by Parliament. In Virginia, Richard Bland published a pamphlet entitled *The Colonel Dismounted,* a superb defense of American rights. The title was a reference to Parson Maury, but Bland went far beyond the "parson's cause" to expand the American view of the imperial constitution. Having come to the New World voluntarily and conquered the wilderness with no thought of separation, the colonists, Bland explained, retained all the rights of British citizens. Among these rights was the power to regulate their internal concerns and tax themselves through their own elected representatives. This and other protests unfortunately served only to harden the attitude of Parliament.

The Stamp Act, passed with little debate by a nearly empty House of Commons in February 1765, placed duties on every sort of paper in daily use—licenses, legal documents, commissions appointing men to office, ships' papers, private contracts, pamphlets, playing cards, and newspapers. The duties were to be paid in gold or silver only, and the funds were to be set aside for the disposition of Parliament. Violators would be prosecuted in either admiralty or common law courts at the discretion of imperial officials. The specie provision aggravated the colonial money problem, and the enforcement provision meant that all parliamentary enactments, whether for trade regulation or revenue, could be enforced under admiralty law without jury trials. Each colony was assigned a stamp distributor, who would be reimbursed by an 8 percent commission on the sale of stamps. Colonial agents in London, such as Benjamin Franklin, opposed the duties under instructions from the assemblies, but when passage of the law became certain they eagerly sought the lucrative distributorships for themselves or their friends.

A French statesman once observed that the art of taxation consists in plucking the maximum number of feathers from the goose with the minimum amount of squawking. Unfortunately, Parliament in 1765 chose the most tender part of the goose, for the Stamp Act was felt most sensitively by lawyers and printers, the two most vocal groups in America. Word of the measure arrived in April and initial newspaper reaction was hostile; editors generally denied Parliament's power to levy taxes and predicted that it would drain the colonies of specie. The first assembly to take up the issue was the Virginia House of Burgesses, which met on May 1. After transacting routine business most of the members drifted home, but on May 20, 1765, Patrick Henry arrived in Williamsburg, newly elected to fill a vacancy in Louisa County's representation. The colony was already seething with discontent that spring; it was suffering economic distress due to low tobacco prices, debts owed to British merchants, and a scarcity of currency. Lesser lights in the Burgesses chafed under the domination of a small clique of wealthy conservatives; they needed only a leader to catalyze their discontent.

The disgrace of the ruling clique that spring provided Henry with his first opportunity. John Robinson, who had served as both speaker of the house and treasurer of the colony, died that spring, leaving as his funeral pyre an awful scandal. As treasurer, it had been his job to burn the colony's paper money as it was redeemed after the French and Indian War. Instead, he had secretively loaned it to a wide circle of acquaintances, themselves planters deeply in debt to British merchants. Discovery of the scheme on Robinson's death left the debtor-planters exposed to any demands the colony might impose. Three days after his arrival in Williamsburg Patrick Henry was on his feet blasting a "bail out" plan that proposed a public loan office to assist the indebted planters. Thomas Jefferson, breaking from his legal studies to hear the speech, afterwords wrote that he could never forget a particular exclamation of Henry's in the debate:

> It had been urged that, from certain unhappy circumstances of the colony, men of substantial property had contracted debts, which, if exacted suddenly, must ruin them and their families, but with a little indulgence of time, might be paid with ease. "What sir," exclaimed Mr. Henry, in animadverting on this, "is it proposed, then, to reclaim the spendthrift from his dissipation and extravagance, by filling his pockets with money?" . . . He laid open with so much energy the spirit of favoritism, on which the proposition was founded, and the abuses to which it would lead, that it was crushed in its birth.

Henry had pounced on the scheme with all the moral indignation of a New Light preacher. To him indebtedness was itself a sign of extravagance, a badge of lost virtue. To rescue the debtor by public means compounded the sin. A few days later he attacked the Stamp Act with the same sense of indignation. That piece of legislation compromised the colony's virtue in but another way: it represented an external threat to its liberty.

On May 29, only 39 of 116 members of the House were present when Henry presented a series of resolutions on the Stamp Act. His speech was never recorded, but listeners later recalled that he reminded the House that Cæsar had his Brutus and Charles I his Cromwell, and he hoped that "some good American would stand up for his country. . . ." When the Speaker interjected that this was treason, Henry apparently apologized and reaffirmed his loyalty to the king. Such declarations of loyalty were part of the etiquette of the House, but there is no doubt of the emotional impact of the address. Thomas Jefferson, breaking again from his legal studies, was standing at the doorway of the House and remembered every rhetorical image a half-century later.

The next day, five of Henry's resolutions were passed by a handful of discontented burgesses against the startled opposition of the conservative leadership. When Henry left Williamsburg a day later, however, House leaders were able to get the most radical resolution rescinded. The governor then dissolved the assembly. The resolutions actually adopted were no more radical in tone than the views being commonly expressed in the newspapers. They asserted only that the colonists possessed all the rights of British citizens, and that the right of self-taxation was "the distinguishing characteristic of British freedom. . . ." But newspapers to the north picked them up and printed even the fifth resolution, which stated that the assembly was the only body with power to levy taxes on Virginians. Somehow the newspapers obtained several more resolutions that had not even been considered by the Burgesses. These proclaimed that Virginians did not have to obey any law passed by a foreign legislature and declared that anyone who disputed this was "an enemy to this, his Majesty's colony." The conclusion drawn by the casual reader in Baltimore, Philadelphia, and Boston was that the Virginia assembly had actually approved all these revolutionary ideas. Rumor and fiction fanned Patrick Henry's modest flame into a blazing wildfire as it spread northward.

In July, Colonel Isaac Barre's speech opposing the Stamp Act in the House of Commons was reported in the colonies. A follower of Pitt, Barre was only one of three members who spoke against the measure, but in a passionate address he defended the Americans as "sons of liberty" who were fighting for the rights of all Englishmen. The phrase caught on quickly and was adopted by the most militant opponents of the Stamp Act. Little more than amorphous mobs at first, the Sons of Liberty were soon shaped by politicians into well-organized secret clubs.

In Boston, the Sons of Liberty evolved from the old North End and South End gangs, who had an annual battle on Pope's Day, November 5. The battle of sticks and stones in 1764 was particularly violent, and the South End mob, led by Ebenezer Mackintosh, was victorious. Mackintosh, a twenty-eight year old ropemaker, was familiar with poverty. His father, one of the roaming poor of eastern Massachusetts, had been "warned out" of Boston in 1753. Mackintosh himself had served on the expedition that had captured Fort Ticonderoga in 1758.

In its spring meeting the legislature issued only a mild protest against the Stamp Act before being sent home by the governor. But when news of the Virginia resolves reached Boston, "Captain" Mackintosh led his mob on the night of August 14 against the home of the local stamp distributor, Andrew Oliver. The crowd had such widespread popular support that no town officials attempted to stop it. The next day Oliver resigned his post. Emboldened, the mob, on August 26, sacked the house of Thomas Hutchinson, lieutenant governor, chief justice, and leader of the "court party." News of the Boston riots stirred similar violence in Rhode Island and Connecticut, all ending in the resignation of local collectors and virtual nullification of the Stamp Act.

On the eve of Pope's Day in November 1765, several merchants negotiated a union of North and South Enders and then financed a mammoth celebration in a tavern. The result was the creation of a powerful political association, founded on the gangs and their "captains," and managed by a secret committee of merchants and artisans called the Loyal Nine. The leadership included several of Boston's delegates to the assembly, among them Samuel Adams, who was elected to the legislature during the autumn. The new organization, calling itself the Sons of Liberty, embraced the old popular party of James Otis as well as some young radicals, such as the physician Joseph Warren and the lawyer John Adams. By making key decisions in secret caucus, the Sons of Liberty directed much of the business of the town meeting and stood to become a political force in the colony.

No such institution as the town meeting was available to the popular leaders in New York, who relied instead on mass assemblies and mob violence. In the assembly, the DeLancey faction posed as the popular party in opposition to the predominant Livingstons, but both groups were mostly interested in preserving their political privileges and their Hudson River estates. News of the Virginia resolves and the Boston riots stirred mob action against the local stamp distributor. Prominent merchants and lawyers supported the protest at first, but they soon became alarmed at the violence and dropped out. Direction of the mobs thus fell into the hands of a radical group of artisans and shopkeepers—Alexander McDougall, John Lamb, and Isaac Sears. These new artisan leaders kept the city in turmoil throughout the fall of 1765 by dispatching their Sons of Liberty to hunt down supporters of the act. In early 1766 they joined with the Boston "Sons" in forming committees of correspondence that would write radicals in the other colonies and coordinate American resistance. From New Hampshire to Georgia, newly formed popular organizations urged lawyers to open the courts and merchants to dispatch their vessels, all without stamps.

The reception of the Stamp Act in Pennsylvania was also complicated by pre-existing factional rivalries. For decades the Quaker Party had been battling the Penn proprietors and their governors and thus posing as a "popular party." After the Quakers virtually retired from politics during the French and Indian War (due to their pacifism), the party fell under the leadership of Benjamin Franklin and Joseph Galloway. The Penns further antagonized the assembly during the French and Indian War by refusing to allow their vast estates to be taxed, and Governor Thomas Penn's cowardly behavior during the impending attack of the Paxton Boys in 1763 further weakened the influence of the proprietary family.

Seeking to press its advantage, the assembly party undertook to convince the people that the province would be better off under royal control, and Franklin departed for England to request a takeover by the king. The Stamp

Act blasted this initiative to splinters, leaving Franklin, for perhaps the only time in his life, without a political base. In Philadelphia, Galloway tried to rally the artisans that had been traditional supporters of Franklin, but he succeeded only in muting the outcry against the Stamp Act. Bereft of their traditional leadership, the artisans and shopkeepers in Philadelphia took matters into their own hands, formed a Sons of Liberty organization, and sought allies among the Scots-Irish of the frontier, men traditionally at odds with both the crown and the proprietary. Out of this kaleidoscope of shifting loyalties emerged a new political organism, the Presbyterian Party, a dynamic blend of urban radicals, self-reliant frontiersmen, and New Light reformers. The new coalition would eventually include Benjamin Franklin, as he guaged the political wind and shifted to the winning side.

Despite news of street action to the north, South Carolina remained quiet through the summer of 1765, largely because the mercantile leaders of Charleston opposed mob violence. But the arrival of a shipload of stamps in October triggered action. Mobs roamed the city looking for stamps until the governor and the local distributor publicly declared that they would not enforce the law. By the end of the year, Sons of Liberty appeared in Charleston, but they remained primarily the personal following of Christopher Gadsden, hero of a contest with the governor over election privileges two years before.

The final scene in the drama of resistance was in Virginia where it all started. On November 1, stamp distributor George Mercer informed the General Court that he could not provide stamps for legal documents. The court accordingly adjourned until the following spring. Concluded Governor Fauquier with gloomy forboding: "The flame is spread through all the continent, and one colony supports another in their disobedience to superior powers."

An intercolonial congress to draft a protest against the Stamp Act was proposed by the Massachusetts House of Representatives as early as June 1765. Many of the assemblies were able to nominate delegates in regular session; a few had to resort to ad hoc procedures. On October 27, a total of twenty-seven delegates from nine colonies assembled in New York. The members of the Congress were moderate on the whole, although most of them were leaders of the "popular" party in each colony. Not content with objecting to the Stamp Act, the delegates ranged over the whole spectrum of grievances, from trade regulations to admiralty courts. After two weeks of sometimes stormy debate, they approved a "Declaration of Rights and Grievances," which stated the fundamental constitutional position of the colonists that "no taxation should be imposed on them, but with their own consent, given personally, or by their representatives." The Declaration also aimed a jab at the admiralty courts as a threat to the "inherent and valuable" right to jury trial, and it asked for a repeal of the various acts restricting American commerce.

On the other hand, the Congress rejected the idea, suggested by Otis in Massachusetts and Galloway in Pennsylvania, that colonial representation in Parliament might be a solution to the dilemma of taxation without representation. Realizing that colonial delegates in London would be outnumbered and ineffectual, the Congress declared "that the people of these colonies are not, and from their local circumstances, cannot be represented in the House of

Commons of Great Britain." The idea was never again a serious feature of the colonists' argument. The declaration and accompanying petitions were ignored in England, and they even seemed to dampen by their moderation the spirit of resistance in America. Nonetheless, the Stamp Act Congress was the first intercolonial meeting initiated by Americans themselves and attended by official delegates from the assemblies. As such it provided a valuable precedent.

By the time the Stamp Act went into effect on November 1, 1765, distributors in every colony except Georgia had either publicly resigned or promised not to sell stamps. Merchants in New York, Philadelphia, and Boston resolved not to import British goods unless the act was repealed, and during the winter the Sons of Liberty induced customs officials to clear vessels without stamped papers. Newspaper publishers ignored the law altogether and sold unstamped papers without interruption. The law courts suspended business on November 1, but by spring most of them were functioning without stamps. Where lawyers and courts hesitated, caught between their dislike for the statute and their fear of violating it, the Sons of Liberty applied the requisite pressure. Thus by the spring of 1766 the colonial economy was functioning normally without stamps, except in Georgia where the governor enforced the law with militia. The act was effectively nullified by popular action; its repeal could be nothing more than a conciliatory gesture.

Grenville fell from power in the summer of 1765, but his troubles were domestic, rather than imperial, since news of the colonial protest had not yet reached Britain. One factor was Grenville's heavy-handed treatment of a popular hero, John Wilkes, a member of Parliament and editor of a radical newspaper, *The North Briton.* Through the last months of the war, Wilkes's paper carped at the ministry for mishandling the peace negotiations, and then on April 19, 1763, in issue Number 45, Wilkes criticized the king himself, suggesting that "he is responsible to his people for the due execution of the royal functions. . . ." Referring to the struggle with the monarchy in the previous century, he reminded the king that his powers were limited and quoted John Dryden: "Freedom is the English subject's prerogative."

Echoing the views expressed by James Otis and Patrick Henry in America, Wilkes's protest heralded the coming age of republican revolution. Alarmed at such subversive ideas, the Grenville ministry promptly obtained a general warrant; Wilkes was arrested, his quarters searched, and his papers seized. Though he was released from jail as a member of Parliament, the House of Commons expelled him, and he fled to Paris for four years of exile. The incident involved the fundamental rights of Englishmen, including the legitimacy of general warrants, freedom of the press, and the privileges of Parliament. Although in his personal life he was a rascally slanderer, a drunkard, and a whoremonger, Wilkes became a hero to the London populace, and he was widely toasted in the colonies. To Americans his fate was one more piece of evidence indicating a conspiracy against personal liberties the world over.

The Wilkes affair alienated the London populace, and a postwar depression cost Grenville the support of powerful merchants. As a final straw, he made an enemy of the king by omitting the queen-mother from a list of potential regents when George III became ill in the summer of 1765. The king dismissed him on July 10 and turned to Lord Rockingham, leader of the Old Whigs and inveterate foe of Grenville. Despite support from merchants and manufacturers who were alarmed at the din in America, the Rockingham ministry floundered unimaginatively until Pitt came to its rescue with a ringing defense of colonial rights in January 1766. Grasping the fundamental dilemma of parliamentary supremacy versus colonial self-government, Pitt sought to resolve the two: "It is my opinion, that this kingdom has no right to lay a tax upon the colonies. At the same time I assert the authority of this kingdom over the colonies, to be sovereign and supreme, in every circumstance of government and legislation whatsoever. They are the subjects of this kingdom, equally entitled with yourselves to all the natural rights of mankind and the peculiar privileges of Englishmen. Equally bound by its laws, and equally participating of the constitution of this free country. The Americans are the sons, not the bastards, of England." The quandary of preserving these rights amidst the absolute sovereignty of Parliament, Pitt solved by distinguishing between internal and external taxation. Parliament had power to tax for purposes of regulating trade, but internal taxation for revenue was the province of the colonial assemblies. If not a solution entirely satisfactory to radicals in America, it was at least a blueprint for compromise.

The ministry committed itself to repeal of the Stamp Act, and the king had no choice but to agree or let the ministry fall. Benjamin Franklin provided the final push when he informed a parliamentary committee that any attempt to enforce the act would precipitate open rebellion. On February 22 the Commons voted to repeal the act, and two days later it agreed on a measure declaring the power of Parliament to enact laws "to bind the colonies and people of America . . . in all cases whatsoever." This Declaratory Act, passed simultaneously with repeal of the Stamp Act on March 4, 1766, was more than a face-saving device—it was notice to the colonists that if Parliament were tested again, it would react with strong measures. The meaning of the conditional retreat was conveyed by British merchants, who warned their American contacts that further violence would bring new taxes and harsh repression. Americans nevertheless rejoiced openly at their evident victory and erected statues to Pitt.

In the colonies the Stamp Act had been overturned by mob violence, but the social and political implications of that violence divided the colonial leadership. Men who had long identified themselves with popular causes drew back in fright while leaders with a genius for manipulating the mobs came to the fore. Smaller colonies, such as Delaware, New Jersey, Connecticut, and even the Carolinas, remained generally quiet through the uproar, but in Massachusetts, Pennsylvania, New York, and Virginia a new breed of politicians emerged, and they had no intention of surrendering their new-found status.

In Pennsylvania, a Proprietary-Presbyterian coalition tried to ruin Franklin by exposing his failure to oppose the Stamp Act in the initial stages. The Quakers responded by publishing his effective testimony before the committee considering repeal. The result was a victory for the Quakers in the election of 1766 and new fame for Franklin, who became colonial agent for Georgia in 1768, New Jersey in 1769, and Massachusetts in 1770. If the radicals failed for the time being in Pennsylvania, they generated a political revolution in Massachusetts in the spring of 1766. Accusing Thomas Hutchinson and his followers of promoting the Stamp Act, the popular party won control of the House of Representatives. James Otis was elected speaker and Sam Adams became clerk of the House. The House then purged Hutchinson and his friends from the council, replacing them with members of the popular party. It then opened its debates to the public and authorized the construction of a gallery for visitors. Sam Adams naturally saw to it that the gallery was filled daily with his Boston followers. When British troops arrived in Boston in 1768, the Adams party won enough additional support to gain a majority on the council, and it virtually ruled Massachusetts until 1770.

The end result of the Stamp Act crisis, then, was the emergence of radical factions in several important colonies with an arsenal of defenses, ranging from street action to pamphlet warfare, should Parliament once again threaten colonial self-government.

A New Challenge: Townshend Taxes

A new ministerial crisis unfolded in London during the summer of 1766. American rejoicing over the repeal of the Stamp Act and additional complaints about the trade laws weakened Rockingham's position. He was deserted by jealous Whig factions, and he had to face the carping opposition of George Grenville, who insisted that he had been right all along in colonial policy. The most important element, however, was the king, who for six years had been developing a personal following in the Commons, using the methods of bribery and patronage developed by the Whigs over the previous half century. In July 1766, the king dismissed Rockingham and invited Pitt to form a "dignified ministry." For three decades Pitt had publicly criticized royal policies, but he also hungered for political power. The king detested him, but recognized that he was the only man who could handle America.

Unhappily, Pitt immediately threw away any opportunity for success by accepting a peerage, the earldom of Chatham, which removed him from his source of power and prestige, the House of Commons. For the next two years, moreover, he was afflicted with gout and suffered chronic mental depression that kept him out of London much of the time. Direction of the ministry thus fell by default into the hands of the able but truculent chancellor of the exchequer, Charles Townshend. For the next two years the Chatham ministry was a collection of bickering politicians offering a patchwork of ill-considered proposals without direction or policy. Its one accomplishment was a modest reform in the administration of the empire. Colonial affairs had been under the general supervision of the Secretary of State for the Southern Department, who also handled relations with southern Europe. In January 1768, Parliament created the office of Secretary of State for the Colonies, and the post was filled by Lord Hillsborough, president of the Board of Trade and an experienced hand in colonial administration. But any beneficial results that might have come from tightened administration were immediately negated by a new tax policy.

By the end of 1766, a severe depression evoked demands for tax relief from the landed gentry. Searching for a popular issue, Grenville took up the cry in the Commons, coupling it with a demand for taxation of America. In February 1767, Parliament reduced the land tax, which threatened the budget, and forced the ministry to look for new sources of revenue. Without consulting Chatham, "Champagne Charlie" Townshend proposed new taxes on the colonies. Accepting the distinction between internal and external duties formulated by Chatham himself in the previous session, Townshend planned to levy only customs duties on goods imported into America. The idea appealed to Parliament, still smarting from its defeat on the Stamp Act and annoyed by new evidence of colonial intransigence. That spring, for instance, the New York assembly refused to vote provisions for British troops, even after the army had obligingly subdued Hudson Valley tenant farmers who were rioting against the high rents charged by the very landlords who controlled the assembly. In June 1767, Parliament passed the Townshend Acts, imposing new taxes on America, establishing a board of customs commissioners to supervise enforcement, and suspending the New York assembly until it cooperated in the quartering of troops.

The new taxes were levied on British goods brought into the colonies—glass, lead, paint, paper, and tea—and hence were not a regulation of trade at all. Despite the distinction between external and internal taxes, this was clearly a revenue measure, and thus it resurrected the constitutional issue. Moreover, though the rationale was to make up the budget deficit, the revenue was placed in a separate fund earmarked for salaries of royal officials. Establishment of an independent income for colonial governors and other officials would remove them from dependence on the assemblies. This would deprive the assemblies of an essential power of the purse which they had used to great effect, and it would disencumber the executive from any responsibility to the legislature. Thus once again Parliament threatened the very existence of local government in America.

American political leaders suddenly realized that their own distinction between internal and external taxation was a trap. It was evident that their constitutional footing had to be shifted. The task was undertaken by John Dickinson, Philadelphia lawyer trained at the Inns of Court, and a new recruit for the Presbyterian faction in Pennsylvania. In December 1767, Philadelphia newspapers began running a series of "Letters from a Farmer in Pennsylvania." The letters were widely reprinted throughout the colonies, and by March 1768 the whole series was in pamphlet form. Dickinson conceded that Parliament had power to regulate colonial trade and might even use taxation for that purpose, but he denied that Parliament could impose taxes, even customs duties, for revenue purposes. Only the assemblies had power to raise revenue in the colonies.

Dickinson's theoretical defense was soon bolstered by action. In Massachusetts the *Boston Gazette* denounced the ministerial program, and popular leaders demanded a revival of nonimportation. Though in control of the lower house, Massachusetts radicals had to overcome heavy opposition. Merchants were unhappy about the nonimportation scheme because their pocketbooks would have to bear the brunt of the American protest. In addition, they feared a revival of the sort of mob action that had gotten out of control two years before. For a year they managed to prevent any radical action in both the Boston town meeting and the assembly. Then, in the spring of 1768, the popular party pushed through a thin house a circular letter summarizing the constitutional objections to the Townshend program and calling other colonies for a coordinated response.

Upon receipt of the Massachusetts circular letter in April 1768, Secretary Hillsborough sent a virtual ultimatum to Massachusetts Governor Bernard demanding that he "require" the assembly to retract it. Should the assembly refuse, Bernard was to dissolve it and report to Parliament for further action. Hillsborough sent a copy of his instructions to all royal governors, informing them that if their assemblies took the circular letter under consideration they were to be likewise dissolved. By the time Hillsborough's order arrived in June, the Boston radicals had stirred up a new controversy. This involved the customs service and the renewed British efforts to halt smuggling. A major feature of the Townshend program was the establishment of a Board of Customs Commissioners in Boston and the installation of additional vice admiralty courts at Boston, Philadelphia, and Charleston.

The customs commissioners were highly unpopular in Boston, and the adoption of a tentative nonimportation agreement in March occasioned a mob demonstration in front of the commissioners' houses. Alarmed, British officials wrote for help to the naval commander at Halifax, who responded by sending a fifty-gun frigate, the *Romney,* to Boston. The commander of the *Romney* turned out to be a bull in the harbor, impressing sailors, and forcing all ships to obey his instructions. Within weeks the Boston waterfront was seething with discontent, making it easy for popular leaders to assemble a belligerent mob for any occasion. On June 10, the customs officials seized one of John Hancock's vessels, the *Liberty,* for carrying illegal cargo, and towed it out to the *Romney* for protection. That night a mob attacked the dwellings of the commissioners, forcing them to flee for safety to Castle William.

A few days later Governor Bernard submitted Lord Hillsborough's letter to the House of Representatives, together with a threat that if he had to dissolve the assembly, he would not call new elections until ordered to do so by London. This unauthorized threat seemed to remove one more brick from the structure of colonial self-government. By a vote of ninety-two to seventeen the House rejected a motion to rescind the circular letter, and Governor Bernard dissolved the assembly. The House met anyway and petitioned the king for removal of the governor; even the council joined in the petition, indicating the extent to which the governor had alienated the entire province. The "Glorious 92" who had refused to knuckle under were toasted the length of the continent, and nearly every assembly adopted resolutions approving the circular letter and petitioning the king against unconstitutional taxes.

Amidst the turmoil, the radical leaders in Boston decided to revive the nonimportation idea, which languished because of the timidity of the merchants. In July, a "standing committee" headed by John Hancock drafted a new agreement prohibiting the import of all British goods (with minor exceptions) for a year beginning on January 1, 1769, and the scheme was approved by a gigantic meeting in Fanueil Hall. Significantly, most of the signers were artisans who, if anything, benefited from the lack of British competition. Though only a few merchants signed the agreement, most of them cooperated rather than risk the fury of the mob.

A few weeks later New York merchants adopted an even more radical nonimportation agreement. It was open-ended, expiring only when the Townshend taxes were repealed. The signers, mostly artisans and small shopkeepers, agreed to boycott any merchant who imported British goods, thus providing a built-in enforcement mechanism. Despite the rising pressure, Philadelphia merchants held out until March 1769, when they finally agreed to exclude about twenty items normally imported from Britain. Simultaneously encouraged and frightened, merchants in the southern colonies hastened to join the continental front.

In Virginia the question of nonimportation became enmeshed with the old issue of planter debts. When Virginia's governor summoned the assembly for its annual session in May 1769, the House of Burgesses passed a series of resolutions that denied the power of Parliament to tax Americans and called for a petition to the king to intervene and protect his colonial subjects. The governor summoned the Burgesses to attend him in the council chamber, and he dissolved it. Undaunted, most of the burgesses reassembled in the Apollo Room of the Raleigh Tavern, two blocks from the Capitol. The assemblage included in addition to the assembly's leading radicals, Patrick Henry and Richard Henry Lee, two newcomers, George Washington and Thomas Jefferson. Washington had served in the Burgesses in the 1750s, but for Jefferson, aged 26, it was his first political office.

The Virginians followed the northern lead in agreeing not to purchase any of the items taxed under Townshend's Revenue Act. But they went on to pledge a halt in the consumption of a long list of luxury items, such as pewter, clocks, looking glasses, and carriages. Tobacco prices had recovered somewhat since the depression of the mid-1760s, and Virginians had reverted to their old spending habits. The radicals were clearly worried that their fellow planters were selling their souls, along with their constitutional liberties, to British merchants. Nonimportation in Virginia thus had a moral, as well as a political, purpose.

Enforcement of the nonimportation agreements was everywhere sporadic and often ineffectual. Merchants resented the coercion of the Sons of Liberty who visited their shops to inspect the goods on their shelves. Variations in the systems adopted led to mutual distrust among the northern cities. Ironically, it was women who gave the most vocal support to the system. One anonymous poet called on the "Daughters of Liberty" to "nobly arise" and forbear the use of taxable goods. Nonconsummption agreements would reinforce nonimportation, and women, who were responsible for obtaining the family provender, found they had an important role to play. Sometimes they formalized the agreements. In February 1770, the *Boston Evening Post* reported that more than three hundred "Mistresses of Families" had promised to "totally abstain" from the use of tea. This departure from the tradition of feminine noninvolvement in public affairs portended a changing status for women in the approaching Revolution. Nevertheless, despite such efforts the system began to collapse almost as soon as it was initiated, and it would have fallen apart much more quickly but for new British provocations arising from the military occupation of Boston.

"The Bloody Business on King Street"

The presence of British troops had been a latent source of friction ever since the ministry decided in 1763 to maintain a peacetime army in America. Though the ostensible purpose was to police the frontier and the Indian trade, most of the troops were kept in New York City. Despite the comparatively pleasant environment, the army was plagued with problems of morale and desertion, so General Thomas Gage requested changes in the Mutiny Act, the annual act providing for the military, that would permit him to quarter troops in private households. His proposal, which was contrary to accepted practice in England, was toned down, and the Quartering Act adopted in the summer of 1765 represented the final stroke of the Grenville ministry before it fell from power.

The law provided for the quartering of troops in barracks or inns, and, should neither of these be available, it authorized justices of the peace to rent uninhabited houses. These provisions were unexceptionable and caused no opposition in America, but the act also stipulated that the colonial governments must provide food and supplies. When the New York assembly refused to appropriate funds for this purpose, it was dissolved by the governor. The Sons of Liberty tried to take advantage of the situation by provoking incidents with soldiers, but that alienated the city merchants, who swung to the conservative faction in the assembly.

As New York subsided into quiescence, Boston once again seized the initiative. The opportunity came when Secretary Hillsborough ordered a regiment to Boston after learning of the city's rough treatment of the customs commissioners. General Gage and his troops landed on October 1, 1768, and when town officials refused to provide quarters, the British rented vacant buildings with their own funds. The radicals promptly began a campaign of newspaper vituperation against both the army and the governor. They won a temporary victory when Bernard was ordered home to report on conditions in the colony in the summer of 1769, but any rejoicing ended abruptly when their archenemy, Thomas Hutchinson, was named to fill the vacancy.

In September 1769, James Otis became involved in a brawl with British soldiers and was badly injured. He suffered thereafter from periodic fits of insanity and gradually withdrew from politics. Leadership of the revolutionary movement thus fell into the more radical and less erratic hands of Samuel Adams. During the winter, tension mounted as Adams's newspaper propaganda and legal harassment reached a crescendo, while the Sons of Liberty ambushed patrols with sticks and stones. The soldiers responded in kind by assaulting the populace and abusing women on the streets. The climax came on March 5, 1770, when a mob attacked a group of soldiers outside the customs house. Ordered to fire on their tormentors, the soldiers killed three citizens on the spot and wounded a number of others, two of them mortally. A new mob formed to revenge the "massacre," but Governor Hutchinson prevented further violence by ordering the arrest of the soldiers involved and confining the rest to barracks. Not satisfied, Sam Adams appealed in the town meeting for removal of the army, and a few days later the regiments were transferred to Castle William. The populace demanded an immediate trial of the soldiers, but the superior court wisely delayed it until autumn. By that time the British government had retreated once again, and the American protest against the Townshend acts collapsed.

In dealing with colonial ferment Britain's greatest disadvantage was the lack of competent political leadership. The Townshend program was initiated without adequate study or discussion, and when Townshend died in September 1767, the ministry drifted. Chatham, physically ill and morose, resigned in October 1768, and Shelburne, the only friend of America in the government, followed him. The ministry staggered on for two more years under the nominal leadership of the weak and incompetent Duke of Grafton. In the spring of 1768, British politics was further distracted by a spectacular parliamentary election that brought the notorious John Wilkes home from Paris. He campaigned for a seat in the Commons, creating an uproar in London, and he was again the toast of the colonies. Four times Wilkes was elected by his Middlesex constituency over the next few years, and each time the Commons refused to seat him. The agitation gave birth to radical organizations for the defense of civil rights and reform of the House of Commons, and these articulate critics troubled British politics for the next thirty years until they were suppressed during the reaction against French Jacobinism in the 1790s.

It seemed as if government by crown and aristocracy was on the brink of collapse, and opposition Whigs blamed the crisis on the king, who had intervened continually in the affairs of Parliament and ministry. The obvious parallel between the subversion of the electoral process in Britain and the threat to colonial self-government was elucidated by Edmund Burke, young mastermind of the Whig Party, in his *Thoughts on the Cause of the Present Discontents* (1770). Americans fully understood this connection, for when the "Society of the Supporters of the Bill of Rights" in England appealed for funds, the South Carolina Commons House sent it a donation of £1,500. The governor and council, on orders from London, sought to block the appropriation, but the Commons House stood on its rights. The result was an impasse that brought the South Carolina government to a standstill until the outbreak of the Revolution.

The Duke of Grafton finally resigned in January 1770, and Frederick, Lord North, formed a new ministry based almost exclusively on the "king's friends." After a decade of search, which had begun with the appointment of Lord Bute in 1760, King George III at last found a ministry dependent for its existence upon his favor alone. Lord North brought to the government no more perception or program than the quarreling Whig factions he succeeded, but he was a skillful manipulator whose charm, wit, and adroit tactics kept him in office for the next twelve years. He began with a determination to end the domestic turmoil over Wilkes and the friction with the colonies. On March 5 (ironically, the same day as the Boston Massacre), he moved the repeal of the Townshend duties, except for the tax on tea, which was to be retained, like the Declaratory

Act, as a symbol of parliamentary supremacy. The Commons obediently repealed the duties, the action to take effect on December 1, 1770.

When news of repeal reached the colonies, nonimportation collapsed in a matter of weeks. The experiment was of varying success. South Carolina imports were cut approximately in half, but in the tobacco colonies, where each planter did his own importing, trade actually increased. In the cities, where Sons of Liberty enforced the restrictions, the system was fairly effective. Philadelphia imports by 1770 were only a fourth, and New York's only a fifth, of what they had been in 1768. Imports into Boston, despite publication of the names of violators in the *Boston Gazette,* dropped only by half. Suffering in their pocketbooks and mistrustful of one another, merchants became increasingly annoyed at the menacing manners of the Sons of Liberty and alarmed at the assaults on British troops in Boston and New York. Popular leaders in every colony wanted to continue the restrictive system as a protest against the tea duty, but the merchants flatly refused.

The nonimportation experiment left the colonies more divided than ever, plunged into mutual recriminations over alleged infractions. In nearly every colony the radical element was under a cloud by 1770—out of favor with the merchants whom they had so zealously policed and distrusted by the wealthy for their violent methods. After 1770 there seemed to be a general letdown, a relaxation of tension that complemented the desire of the North ministry for peace. This was evidenced by the relatively peaceful trial of the soldiers involved in the Boston Massacre. The commanding officer was judged "not guilty" and returned to England to receive honors and a pension. Only two soldiers were convicted, and both received the light sentences of burning on the hand. Two members of the radical club, John Adams and Josiah Quincy, defended the British soldiers in court, but whether they acted from a sense of justice or a desire to prevent embarrassing cross-examination is impossible to determine.

An Internal Distraction: The Regulators

For the next three years revolutionary fervor seems to have cooled, and the colonies became largely preoccupied with their own domestic problems. Internal divisions, reflecting differences of interest, had complicated the colonial protest from the very beginning, for the colonies were not a monolithic society united in their political aims. The decision to rebel, or even to tolerate a violent protest, was not one to be made lightly, and different social groups reacted in various ways. Yet, despite the lack of rapid and effective communication, a broad consensus was gradually achieved. Social tensions, conflicting economic interests, though never completely harmonized, were at least subordinated to the need for a common front. Only once did the internal divisions reach the point of armed conflict. That occasion was the Regulator movement in the Carolinas.

The social protest called "The Regulation" actually involved two distinct movements in two colonies, fostered by different grievances, and producing different results. The only similarity is that each represented a clash between

East and West, between Tidewater planter and hinterland farmer. The Regulator movement in South Carolina stemmed from deficiencies in the provincial government, which from design and circumstance centered on Charleston. Low-country planters gave little attention to the needs of the upcountry, and the British government actively discouraged movement onto the frontier by prohibiting the creation of new parishes in the West.

For upcountry farmers this meant under-representation in the assembly and inadequate local government. In the West, the only local officials were justices of the peace, who had power of arrest only; civil and criminal court proceedings had to be conducted in Charleston. The usual turbulence of the frontier and dislocations produced by the Cherokee uprising of 1759 made these governmental shortcomings even more apparent. To defend themselves against lawlessness and disorder, upcountry farmers formed vigilante groups (the name "Regulator" came into use in the fall of 1767) to patrol the countryside. Aware of the extra-legal nature of their methods, they usually kept the membership secret and swore oaths to support one another.

Formed in a vacuum of governmental law-enforcement, the Regulators adopted political aims that reflected the needs of the West—demanding county courts in the backcountry, codification of laws and simplification of legal procedures, reduction of lawyers' fees, and more representation in the Commons House of the assembly. The Regulators, for the most part, were farmers of the "middling sort," and their program was hardly revolutionary, but the methods of the Regulators soon led them into conflict with provincial authorities. Taking the law into their own hands, the Regulators meted out "kangaroo justice" and supervised every phase of upcountry life.

Charleston officials, though critical of the violent methods used by the vigilantes, recognized the justice of their demands; and in 1769 the assembly established circuit courts and authorized the appointment of sheriffs for the western districts. Although reapportionment of the Commons House was postponed, these actions softened western discontent. The Regulators did not attempt to ally themselves with the radical Sons of Liberty in Charleston (as the backwoods farmers ultimately did in Pennsylvania), but their leaders, for the most part, joined the Revolutionary cause.

The Regulator movement in North Carolina, on the other hand, was an internal conflict that had little impact on imperial relations. The sectional division of North Carolina was founded upon economic and social differences originating in settlement patterns. The East was English in origin and Anglican in religious tradition. The West was settled by migrants from Virginia and Pennsylvania, a mixture of Scots-Irish, Germans, and Scots. The center of western discontent was the Granville District, embracing the northern third of the colony, where the Carteret family retained a proprietary interest in the land even after surrendering governmental power to the crown. The proprietors charged high prices for land in the region, and their agents exacted excessive fees for issuing patents. There were also political grievances similar to those in South Carolina.

In 1768, the North Carolina assembly levied a poll tax of two shillings and sixpence, to be collected annually for three years to pay for the magnificent palace that Governor William Tryon was erecting at New Bern. Considered by westerners an extravagance "worthy of the residence of a prince of the blood," Tryon's edifice became a symbol of eastern domination. The capitation tax also hit hardest the western farmers who were always short of currency. On April 4, a meeting of backcountry settlers copied the name Regulator from their brethren to the south and drew up a manifesto of grievances. Throughout the summer, rumors, poor communications, and mutual ignorance of the intentions of each side aggravated the tension between governor and frontier. In September, Tryon organized an army of 1,400 militia at Hillsboro and invaded the backcountry, capturing, convicting, and pardoning several ringleaders. In the election of July 1769, the Regulators won a number of seats in the assembly, but before they could introduce reform bills, Tryon cut short the session because of disagreement over the Townshend duties. Significantly, both East and West in North Carolina agreed that parliamentary taxation had to be resisted, and they joined in the colonial protest against the Townshend acts.

Thereafter the Regulator movement centered on the judicial system and legal fees. Their major grievance was that debts, even as little as forty shillings, could be brought by creditors before the superior court, rather than the county courts. The higher court was less friendly to the pleas of debtors, and attendance at its sessions required additional travel. In September 1770, a meeting of the superior court at Hillsboro led to riots and assaults on attorneys. The assembly passed a Riot Act forbidding under penalty of death the assemblage of ten or more persons. Governor Tryon secured indictments of several Regulators for their part in the riots, and in March 1771 he sent an expedition into the west to make the arrests. On May 16, this army of eleven hundred militia encountered a band of two thousand Regulators at the Little Alamance, a tributary of the Haw River. The undisciplined farmers scattered after a couple of hours of skirmishing, and the Regulator leaders were captured. The court at Hillsboro convicted twelve of them and hanged six. The governor pardoned the rest and offered a general amnesty, which was accepted by some six thousand backcountry settlers.

The North Carolina Regulation died out after the Battle of Alamance. Tryon accepted a new post as governor of New York, and many of the Regulators departed for Tennessee and Georgia. Internal tensions subsided as the approaching conflict with the mother country became more certain. Most of the Regulators joined the patriot ranks when the Revolution began, although about two hundred joined the Tory Highland Scots at Moore's Creek Bridge when the British made their first thrust into North Carolina in early 1776. The Highlanders along the upper Cape Fear River sympathized with the aims of the Regulators, but took no part in the uprising. They sided with the governor in 1771 and with the crown five years later.

Controversy Over the Wilderness

During the years of relative quiet on the seaboard that followed the repeal of the Townshend duties, the main source of imperial tension was the frontier. The issue was essentially the same as that involved in parliamentary taxation—

the ministry's desire to make the empire tidier, more efficient, and financially self-supporting. The Proclamation of 1763 was designed to restrict colonial emigration across the mountains, protect the Indian tribes from unscrupulous traders, and prevent expensive Indian wars. Enforcement was entrusted to two Indian agents, William Johnson in the North and John Stuart in the South. Johnson, himself involved in land speculation schemes, made no effort to enforce the prohibition, and after 1763 squatters poured across the mountains of western Pennsylvania. In the South, Stuart took five years to mark the line in the Carolinas, and then Virginia refused to let him proceed further. The Proclamation itself permitted veterans of the French war to take up lands in the West, a loophole that made it virtually unenforceable. Warrants for these soldiers' lands circulated freely and many ended up in the hands of speculators. In 1768, the ministry deprived the Indian Department of further authority over the Indian trade and returned the regulatory power to the colonial governments. For financial reasons, it also ordered the evacuation of all western posts, except for small garrisons at Niagara, Detroit, and Michilimackinac to protect traders. Initiated by Lord Hillsborough when he took over the Colonial Office, this policy of concentrating British troops in New York and Boston meant a virtual abandonment of any effort to enforce the Proclamation line and gave new hope to colonial land speculators. Virginians gleefully began improving the old road from the Potomac headwaters to Pittsburgh, and speculators with claims dating from before the French and Indian War looked forward to a financial return at last. But the plans of Virginians almost immediately ran afoul of the schemes of a group of Pennsylvania speculators, and between them they managed to involve the British government in a new controversy that left disappointment and bitterness on all sides.

In Pennsylvania, a collection of "suffering traders," who had lost their goods during Pontiac's uprising, desired compensation from London in the form of land grants. In 1765 they organized the Indiana Company, and to procure political influence they gave shares of stock to Sir William Johnson, Benjamin Franklin, and his son William, Governor of New Jersey, and to various Philadelphia merchants. In England, Franklin persuaded his friend, Lord Shelburne, to give his blessing to new land cessions by the Indians; and, in the summer of 1768 Sir William Johnson organized a gigantic Indian conference at Fort Stanwix in New York.

The largest Native American assemblage ever held, the meeting was attended by three thousand warriors representing all the major tribes of the North. Concentrating on his Iroquois friends, Johnson convinced them that a cession of claims south of the Ohio River would deflect the migration of settlers away from the Iroquois lands in New York. The Iroquois had only a peripheral interest in western Virginia anyway, so they readily ceded their claims south of the Ohio for £10,000. The position of the Iroquois was actually strengthened because the agreement involved a tacit recognition by the crown of Iroquois suzerainty over the Ohio tribes. The Delaware and Shawnee, who actually used the Kentucky region as a hunting ground, were bitterly opposed to the deal, but they had no choice but to consent.

The Treaty of Fort Stanwix ended any pretense of enforcing the Proclamation line, and a flood of settlers poured across the mountains onto the upper Ohio. A similar movement took place in the South across the low divide that separated the Roanoke River from the headwaters of the Tennessee (the Holston and Clinch valleys). The Cherokee owners protested at first and then followed the example of the Iroquois. Hoping to turn the advancing line of settlers away from their lands in Tennessee, the Cherokees made a series of agreements with Virginia ceding whatever claims they had in Kentucky. The result was that by 1773 population west of the mountains numbered almost thirty thousand, and a stream of settlers was converging on Kentucky from both Virginia and Pennsylvania. The Virginians, with the best title to the West under their charter of 1609, concentrated on obtaining Indian cessions. Pennsylvanians, hoping to outflank the Virginia claim, instead lobbied in England for establishment of a new colony.

To further this scheme the Pennsylvanians sent to London a wealthy Philadelphia merchant, Samuel Wharton, with enough funds to buy his way into ministerial circles. Under the combined pressure of Wharton and Franklin, the Board of Trade in 1773 approved the formation of a new colony in the area of present-day West Virginia and eastern Kentucky. It was to be named Vandalia in honor of the queen, who was allegedly descended from the Germanic Vandals. By early 1774 the details were worked out, but the scheme was interrupted by the Boston Tea Party and parliamentary retaliation. A charter for the colony was never issued, but the speculators never gave up their claims. The rivalry between Pennsylvania and Virginia interests troubled the politics of the American confederation during and after the Revolution.

When Virginia's governor, Lord Botetourt, died in 1771, he was replaced by John Murray, Earl of Dunmore. An impecunious Scotsman, Dunmore came to America to seek his fortune, and he found his opportunity in land speculation. He soon formed an alliance with Virginia speculators and began granting lands in Kentucky. The Shawnee, already unhappy with the cessions made without their consent at Fort Stanwix, were soon on the offensive.

Lord Dunmore's War was an aptly named travesty. London hoped that the war might divert the colonists from petitions and tea parties, Pennsylvania regarded it as Virginia's war, and the assembly in Williamsburg felt it was the governor's. Actually it was the frontier's, for the western settlements from the Potomac to the Holston responded quickly to the governor's call for militia. Under the experienced Indian fighter, General Andrew Lewis, the militia companies marched two hundred miles down the Kanawha River to the Ohio. There at Point Pleasant on October 10, 1774, Lewis was attacked by Chief Cornstalk and his Shawnee braves. In an all-day battle, the Shawnee were decisively defeated and forced to cede their claims to Kentucky. Peace brought a resumption of Virginia's aggressive thrust into the West. In the spring of 1775, Virginia speculators employed Daniel Boone to clear a Wilderness Road from the Cumberland Gap to the Blue Grass region. On April 15, just four days before Lexington and Concord, his party of thirty men began the construction of Boonesboro, the first permanent settlement in Kentucky. But extensive settlement of the region had to await the end of the Revolution.

The speculative interests of Pennsylvania and Virginia made the imperial regime unpopular in both colonies. Reacting against Dunmore's largesse, the Privy Council in 1773 forbade colonial governors from making further land grants in the West. This action threatened the schemes of all colonial speculators. In North Carolina, for instance, Judge Richard Henderson obtained title from the Cherokees to a vast region between the Cumberland and Kentucky rivers and hoped to establish his own colony, Transylvania. British authorities frustrated his plans, but during the Revolution he obtained confirmation of his title from the states of Virginia and North Carolina. Other speculators were frustrated by the Quebec Act of 1774, which turned over lands west of the mountains and north of the Ohio River to Canada. This was a threat to the interests of both Virginia and Pennsylvania, and doubtless alienated leaders in both colonies. The British restrictions on the West were thus a contributing factor in the colonial dissatisfaction, but they were no more than that. The Revolution was triggered instead by the fundamental threat to colonial self-government implicit in Parliament's response to the Boston Tea Party.

Sam Adams: Lonely Rebel

During the calm that followed repeal of the Townshend taxes, the radicals virtually disappeared in every colony. Even Massachusetts settled into an uneasy quiet under its new governor, Thomas Hutchinson, appointed in October 1770. An able politician, Hutchinson set out to wreck the popular party by using the very weapons that the radicals had found so successful in five years of agitation. With the support of loyal newspapers, he launched an attack on Samuel Adams, and he built a personal following by taking advantage of the divisions among merchant groups. The House of Representatives supported the governor, as it had before the Stamp Act, and Adams was left with little except control of the Boston town meeting. Even his opportunistic ally, John Hancock, deserted him for a time. While they awaited a new provocation from Britain, the radicals kept themselves busy organizing a revolutionary substructure. In October 1772, the Boston town meeting at Adams's behest established a committee of correspondence to state the rights of the colonists "as men, as Christians, and as subjects," and other Massachusetts towns created similar organizations.

For a time the principal topic of communication among the committees was the tax on tea. The British government surreptitiously paid the salaries of both Governor Hutchinson and Andrew Oliver, the lieutenant governor, out of the proceeds from the tax on tea. Sam Adams and the Boston radicals suspected this but could not prove it. In 1771 Governor Hutchinson's delay in approving salary appropriations prompted the House of Representatives to inquire if he had some hidden source of income. In June 1772, the government confirmed the truth to the rumors; it also announced that the justices of the superior court were also to be paid from the tax on tea. The House responded by refusing to pay any salary to the governor out of provincial funds. That fall the Boston town meeting voted to begin a correspondence with other towns on the tea tax.

Two other incidents helped spread the correspondence movement to other colonies—the Hutchinson letters and the *Gaspee* affair. In his efforts to damage Governor Hutchinson, Adams found a willing ally in Benjamin Franklin, who had been appointed colonial agent for Massachusetts in 1770. In December 1772, Franklin sent to the Boston radicals a packet of letters written by various officials in Massachusetts, among them Hutchinson. The letters, which Franklin obtained by devious means, contained nothing that Hutchinson had not said publicly concerning the supremacy of Parliament, but, properly edited, they appeared to be part of a conspiracy against colonial self-government. After stirring public curiosity with rumors through the spring of 1773, Adams in June read the letters to the House of Representatives in closed session. A few days later, carefully edited versions began appearing in the radical Boston papers, and soon they were reprinted in other cities. The letters were a public sensation, but the only casualty of the incident was Benjamin Franklin. When his agency in the affair was made public he was summoned before the Privy Council, publicly denounced, and dismissed from his lucrative position as postmaster general of North America. Franklin thereupon resigned his other offices, and in 1775 he returned to Pennsylvania a ready revolutionary.

Coinciding with the Hutchinson letters was a new flare-up over colonial smuggling—this time in Rhode Island. This semi-autonomous republic with a popularly elected governor had long been a notorious center of illicit trade. There was no Board of Customs Commissioners, as in Boston and New York, but Rhode Islanders came into periodic conflict with the Royal Navy, which had chief responsibility for enforcing the trade laws in the colony. In the spring of 1772, the *Gaspee* patrolled the waters of Narragansett Bay, earning the wrath of Rhode Islanders by its heavy-handed enforcement of the trade laws. Its commander, Lieutenant William Dudingston, stopped ships and confiscated cargoes without warrants, sent his crew ashore to commandeer supplies from farmers, and wantonly fired on boats that failed to obey his orders. On June 9, the *Gaspee* ran aground on a sandbar while pursuing a local vessel, and that night a band of 150 residents of Providence boarded the ship, chased its crew ashore, and burned it to the water.

When news of the incident reached England, Secretary Hillsborough ruled that the assault constituted high treason, and the offenders could be tried either in Rhode Island or in England. Before anything could come of this, however, Hillsborough resigned in August 1772 and was replaced at the Colonial Office by Lord Dartmouth. Pressured by mounting indignation in Parliament, Dartmouth appointed a commission to investigate. The commission found nothing, since none of the citizens of Providence would testify, but the colonial newspapers likened the proceedings to the medieval court of Star Chamber.

While the commission met in Providence in the early weeks of 1773, Rhode Island radicals sent out an intercolonial appeal for support. In response, the radical faction in the Virginia House of Burgesses sponsored a resolution creating a legislative committee of correspondence. The Burgesses approved it unanimously, and news of Virginia's action spread rapidly. By the end of 1773 all but three colonial assemblies had set up similar committees. Their primary role was to exchange ideas and enable the radicals in each colony to give each other encouragement. But such artificial efforts to promote radical unity were soon rendered unnecessary by the Boston Tea Party and the British reaction which, by its very harshness, united the colonists as they had never before been united.

Orchestrated Violence: The Tea Parties

Amidst the controversy over the meaning of the constitution, the position of each side gradually hardened in the years after the Stamp Act, but the tragedy is that the British ministry and Parliament never had a coherent program to defend. The root of the dispute was the effort to make the Americans bear part of the cost of maintaining the empire, but the policy never worked or yielded much revenue. Under the various revenue acts between 1764 and 1774 it has been estimated that the British collected about £340,000 in America. Ironically, most of it came from the duty on molasses, the one tax to which Americans never seriously objected. The expense of maintaining the customs service and about forty vessels on the American station to enforce the revenue laws exceeded the amount collected. Moreover, the expense of maintaining the army, which was the original excuse for taxing the colonists, exceeded in any one year the revenue collected over the entire decade. Thus, unable to justify its policy from a financial standpoint, the ministry was forced to stand on a point of principle—the supremacy of Parliament—and the dispute thus became a matter of the integrity of the colonial legislatures.

After 1770, the main symbol of parliamentary supremacy was the duty on tea, yet the duty was widely evaded, not only in America, but in Britain itself. Because of the high duty on tea imported by the British East India Company, tea brought from Asia by the Dutch was smuggled into Britain at the rate of 3,500 tons a year. The effect was to undermine the colonial policy of the ministry, and the East India Company floundered through a sea of financial crises. By the end of 1772, it was on the verge of bankruptcy, unable to sell the huge surplus of tea in its warehouses.

In May 1773, Parliament came to its rescue with a loan and an act permitting the company to dispose of its tea in America through its own agents. By eliminating mercantile middlemen, the British tea could compete with Dutch tea in the colonies, the East India Company could recoup its fortunes, and colonial smuggling would be extinguished in one brilliant stroke. Parliament exacted its due a month later by adopting a Regulating Act that gave the government a measure of control over the company and the administration of India. None of the acts were expected to create any displeasure in America, even though British tea was still boycotted by Americans. Indeed the ministry wished to avoid new provocations. When Dartmouth learned of Governor Hutchinson's defense of parliamentary supremacy before the Massachusetts assembly in early 1773, he ordered the governor to "avoid any further discussion whatsoever upon these questions."

On the other hand, Lord North was unwilling to pamper Americans by retreating on the tea duty. When Burke and the Rockingham Whigs suggested repeal of the tax, the prime minister refused to debate the subject. This disappointed Benjamin Franklin, then terminating his career as colonial agent. Franklin entertained fond hopes that the troubles of the East India Company would force the repeal of the duty on tea, and he regarded the ministerial policy as an effort to "overcome all the patriotism of an American" by offering him cheap tea. Colonial newspapers similarly accused Parliament of a plot to induce Americans to purchase dutied tea and thereby admit the right of Parliament to tax.

As with the Stamp Act, the reaction to the Tea Act in America was conditioned by economics, as well as politics. American merchants had become increasingly fretful of a British practice of selling surplus goods directly through auction or "vendue sales" arrangements with American retailers. This practice bypassed the American wholesale importers and threatened ruin to some of the wealthiest and most powerful of American merchants. When Parliament appeared to sanction this sort of market dumping in approving the Tea Act, American merchants began to wonder if there was some sort of invidious scheme afoot to seize control of the whole American economy. Their suspicions were enhanced by a new downturn in the business cycle in 1772, which caused new failures among American merchants and widespread unemployment. Both Philadelphia and New York were forced to construct new jails to house the numerous persons who, under English common law, were put behind bars for failing to pay their debts. In Virginia the collapse of tobacco prices put new stress on indebted planters. More and more of them were coming to the conclusion that political freedom and economic freedom were two faces of the same coin.

The North ministry knew little of American conditions, and, like its forebearers, it was disposed to ignore American protests. By September 1773, some two thousand casks of tea were ready for shipment to selected agents in Boston, New York, Philadelphia, and Charleston. Neither ministry nor British merchants had any inkling of the storm that lay ahead.

Ironically, Samuel Adams seemed at first unable to recognize the potential for trouble in the Tea Act. When news of the act arrived in September, the Boston press was still aiming its salvos at Governor Hutchinson. New York registered the first criticism, and the Boston papers took up the cry in October. In other colonies the consignees of the East India Company resigned under pressure or promised to return the tea, but the agents in Boston defended themselves in the newspapers with the full support of Governor Hutchinson. Thus the tea became a symbol of the whole contest for power between the governor and the radicals, between the empire and the colony.

When the first tea ship, the *Dartmouth,* landed on November 27, 1773, Adams activated his political organization. The Boston committee of correspondence appealed to the nearby towns for help, and on November 30 about five thousand people assembled in Boston to pass resolutions. The Boston committee placed guards on the teaship to prevent it from paying duties and demanded that the owners secure clearance papers for return to England. Governor Hutchinson refused to issue clearance papers and ordered the warships in the harbor to prevent the vessel's departure without them. Tension mounted as the twenty-day waiting period for discharge of cargo drew to an end. On the morning of December 16, thousands of people poured into Boston from nearby towns to attend another mass meeting. Further negotiations with the governor proved fruitless, and at last Sam Adams closed the meeting with the announcement, "This meeting can do no more to save the country." The statement was evidently a signal, for the meeting instantly broke up amidst shouts of "Boston harbor, a tea-pot tonight!" and "The Mohawks are come!" A crowd of several hundred then adjourned to Griffin's wharf where "a number of brave and resolute men, dressed in the Indian manner," boarded the three teaships. In three hours they broke open 342 chests of tea, leaving the rest of the cargo unmolested, and dumped the contents overboard.

The next day Paul Revere, courier for the committee of correspondence, departed for New York and Philadelphia with a letter from Adams describing the tea party. His arrival in New York four days later gave the Sons of Liberty there the final ammunition they needed to extract a promise from the tea agent not to accept his consignment. In Philadelphia the radical leaders had been agitating against the Tea Act since midsummer but could take no overt action for lack of a target. When a teaship finally arrived in late December, almost simultaneously with Paul Revere's news of the party in Boston, the radicals called a mass meeting and adopted resolutions that the tea should be returned to England. Thoroughly intimidated, the British captain took on necessary stores and sailed off without landing his cargo. The Sons of Liberty in Charleston had also begun agitation against the Tea Act in midsummer, but by the time a teaship arrived in early December, the movement had virtually expended itself. Planters and merchants joined the protest, but they clearly had no stomach for violence. Taking advantage of the radicals' uncertainty, Governor Bull ordered the tea landed and stored in a warehouse. Sam Adams reprimanded the radicals for their lack of decision, and late in 1774 Charleston held a "tea party" as a symbolic gesture of unity.

When news of the Boston Tea Party reached London late in January 1774, the ministry, to its credit, sought means of chastising Boston without the intervention of Parliament. Both Lord North and Dartmouth wished to continue the policy of moderation that had kept the colonies peaceful for three years, and they realized that parliamentary retaliation would bring a critical confrontation. They turned first for advice to the law officers of the crown and to the Privy Council. Did the actions of Boston constitute treason? If so, who could be punished and how?

After an extensive investigation the Privy Council concluded that there was insufficient evidence to bring to trial the popular leaders. North then turned to Parliament where desire for revenge and vindication was reaching the boiling point. On March 7 he introduced a bill to close the port of Boston, supported by 109 documents describing colonial resistance. To him it was no longer a dispute over taxation—Parliament must decide "whether or not we have any authority" in America.

The act, passed by the Commons on March 25 and signed by the king a week later, closed the port of Boston except for the coastal trade in food and firewood. It would not be reopened until the town paid for the tea and compensated customs officials for property destroyed in earlier rioting.

Three days after the Commons approved the Port Bill, Lord North came in with a bill to abolish the Massachusetts charter of government. The purpose, North explained, was to "take the executive power from the democratic part" by substituting a royally appointed council and giving the governor unlimited powers. The governor would appoint all executive and judicial officers, and town meetings, except for annual election meetings, could not be held without his consent. The plan itself was a tacit admission of the extent to which the people and their leaders actually directed the affairs of Massachusetts and the threat to the empire that this created.

The act became law on May 20, and that same day the king signed a third coercive measure, the Administration of Justice Act. Designed for the "suppression of riots and tumults," this measure afforded protection to royal officials who committed a crime while enforcing the trade laws or suppressing a riot. The governor, at his discretion, could remove them to England for trial. The fourth of these "Intolerable Acts," as they were called in the colonies, became law on June 2. It was a new Quartering Act, which made colonial authorities responsible for finding accommodations for the army and authorized the army to seize barns or vacant buildings in towns that failed to provide barracks.

Perhaps the most remarkable feature of the Coercive Acts is the virtual unanimity with which they were passed. Only the Rockingham Whigs raised a critical voice, and their motives were politically suspect. Edmund Burke in an oft-quoted speech gave a lengthy history of British impositions on the colonies going back to the first Navigation Act, but even Burke could not ignore the Declaratory Act and the theory of empire on which it rested. Perhaps the tragedy of Parliament is that it lacked the historical perspective furnished by the American Revolution itself—a perspective that enabled it to accept Lord Durham's recommendations for self-government in Canada three-quarters of a century later. Lacking such foresight (or hindsight), Parliament had no choice but to view the conflict as one involving sovereign power. Political pressures and a concern for its own prestige induced it to challenge the very existence of legislative government in America, for the alternative seemed to be another humiliating retreat. Lord Dartmouth, himself a moderate, admitted that the purpose of the Coercive Acts was to punish the people of Boston for their treasonous behavior. "The question then," he added, "is whether these laws are to be submitted to. If the people of America say no, they say in effect that they will no longer be part of the British empire. . . ." That, of course, was the whole point, and many Americans realized it.

Nineteenth-century historian, Moses Coit Tyler, once observed that the American Revolution was directed "not against tyranny inflicted, but only against tyranny anticipated." The Coercive Acts, after all, were directed primarily at Massachusetts; they were a violent, but probably temporary, effort to punish the vandalism of Boston. Yet they involved an implied threat to all the colonies. Closing the port of Boston and quartering troops on private households were actions without precedent in English or American experience. As for revoking the Massachusetts charter—colonial charters had been annulled by the seventeenth-century Stuart kings, but only through *quo warranto* judicial proceedings. Now Parliament presumed the power, and if Parliament could alter the Massachusetts council, what was to prevent it from abolishing the colonial legislatures altogether? "Had the colonies submitted," wrote one wealthy South Carolinian, "they would soon have been carried on from one degree of slavery to another. . . ." Colonial rights were being lost, not by a direct frontal assault but by gradual attrition, and the need for a united stand was evident.

3

Triumph of Independence

As news of the Coercive Acts filtered across the Atlantic in the spring of 1774 and the dimensions of the British threat to colonial self-government became clear, American political leaders recognized the need for a coordinated defense. When Boston asked other seaports to cut off their trade with Britain as a gesture of sympathy, merchants elsewhere suggested that such a policy ought to be initiated by a continental meeting in order to avoid the distrust that had attended nonimportation five years earlier. That colonial merchants were willing to consider such a scheme at all, in view of their earlier experience with the Sons of Liberty, indicated the extent to which the specter of parliamentary domination united Americans. Conservative lawyers and merchants, however, had learned a lesson over the previous decade. They had to join the ship if they hoped to influence its course. If they held back, radical leaders—such as Adams in Boston, Sears and Lamb in New York, or Charles Thomson in Philadelphia—controlled the ad hoc popular meetings that were becoming an important feature of the political landscape.

The Continental Congress

Popular meetings in New York and Philadelphia suggested a continental assembly to coordinate the colonial response and petition the king, but, as usual, it was the Massachusetts House of Representatives that led the way. Meeting behind locked doors to prevent the governor from dissolving it, the House adopted resolutions offered by Samuel Adams that proposed "a meeting of the Committees from the several colonies" at Philadelphia on September 1, 1774. The Congress thus evolved naturally from the committees of correspondence that had been coordinating colonial policy for more than a year. During the summer every colony except Georgia selected delegates.

In most colonies, the lower house of the assembly, meeting informally, assumed the task. The Virginians had begun to act even before receiving the word from Massachusetts. Its assembly was in session in May 1774, when news of the Boston Port Act reached Williamsburg. Jefferson, Henry, and the Lees, so Jefferson later recalled, "cooked up a resolution . . . for appointing the 1st day of June, on which the port bill was to commence, for a day of fasting, humiliation, and prayer." When the Burgesses approved the resolution, the governor promptly dissolved the assembly. It never met again. The Burgesses reconvened at the Raleigh Tavern and passed resolutions stating that an attack on one colony was an attack on all, and they proposed a meeting of a continental congress. Taking another major step toward independence, the Burgesses also asked the counties to elect delegates to a provincial convention to meet in Williamsburg on August 1. This body adopted an Association to halt all trade with Great Britain and then proceeded to elect delegates for the First Continental Congress. Washington, Patrick Henry, and Richard Henry Lee were natural choices, and Jefferson might have been as well had he not fallen sick on the way to Williamsburg. Before leaving Monticello Jefferson wrote down some instructions for the delegates to the Continental Congress. From his sick bed he forwarded them to Patrick Henry for presentation to the convention. Though hastily penned, Jefferson's instructions opened a new chapter in the emerging ideology of the Revolution. He boldly abandoned the constitutional distinction, worked out by John Dickinson some years before, between *external* and *internal* legislation. Jefferson proclaimed that Parliament had no power at all to legislate for the colonies; it could govern neither their internal affairs nor their foreign trade. This was too much for the conservatives in the convention, who approved a milder set of instructions for their congressional delegates. Jefferson's friends, nevertheless, had his thoughts published in Williamsburg under the title *A Summary View of the Rights of British America.* At once reprinted in Philadelphia and in England, the pamphlet made Jefferson the ideological "point man" of the Revolution.

In New York a "committee of 51," dominated by merchants and landowners, nominated a moderate delegation to the Continental Congress. In Philadelphia the radical leaders organized a succession of mass meetings which eventually forced the assembly to act. Although its hand had been forced, the assembly chose a delegation of seven conservatives, headed by Joseph Galloway, leader of the old Quaker Party. In Charleston a mass meeting chose the South Carolina delegates, but conservative planters and merchants successfully diluted the influence of the Sons of Liberty. Representing the colony were the radical Christopher Gadsden and such moderates as John Rutledge and Henry Middleton. In Massachusetts and Rhode Island the assembly elected delegates, and in Connecticut the task was performed by the committee of correspondence. All three delegations were led by radicals—Samuel and John Adams from Massachusetts, Stephen Hopkins from Rhode Island, and Roger Sherman from Connecticut. Numerically the radicals were a minority in the Congress, but they came prepared with a program, and that gave them the inestimable advantage of having the initiative.

The first decision Congress made when it opened on September 5, 1774, resulted in a defeat for the conservatives. Joseph Galloway, speaker of the

Pennsylvania assembly, offered the State House for a meeting place, but the Congress decided instead upon Carpenter's Hall, which belonged to the most powerful and most radical guild in the city. The decision, observed Silas Deane of Connecticut, was "highly agreeable to the mechanics and citizens in general but mortifying in the last degree to Mr. Galloway and his party." A second defeat came when Congress elected Charles Thomson its secretary, a post he was to hold until the Continental Congress was superseded by the federal government in 1789. Leader of the Philadelphia Sons of Liberty, Thomson was an arch-foe of Galloway, and the fact that he was not even a member of the Pennsylvania delegation made the defeat sting all the more.

Its housekeeping chores completed, Congress turned to procedural problems. The delegates had no precedents to guide them, since this was the first general assembly of colonies, but most realized that their decisions might bind future meetings. The initial difficulty was voting—should it be equal for each colony or proportional? On the second day Patrick Henry suggested that voting be scaled by size, giving more votes to the larger and more populous colonies; and he took the opportunity to give the delegates a sample of the oratory that so entranced Virginians. Charles Thomson described Henry as "dressed in a suit of parson's gray, and from his appearance I took him for a Presbyterian clergyman used to haranguing the people." "Government is dissolved," Henry announced, no doubt pausing dramatically to let the full meaning sink in. "Fleets and armies and the present state of things show that government is dissolved. Where are your landmarks, your boundaries of colonies? We are in a state of nature, Sir. . . . The distinctions between Virginians, Pennsylvanians, New Yorkers and New Englanders are no more. I am not a Virginian, but an American." Despite the seeming nationalism of his address, Henry was championing the interests of Virginia, which was the largest colony and had the most to gain by proportional representation. Unimpressed by his rhetoric, the small colonies insisted upon equality. For the sake of harmony the large colonies gave in, and it was decided to give each colony one vote, to be determined by polling its delegation.

Congress then turned to its two major tasks—drafting a declaration of grievances and organizing a continental system of commercial retaliation. While committees pondered these issues, the radicals once again seized the initiative with the aid of Adams's political machine in Massachusetts. On the morning of September 16, Paul Revere rode into Philadelphia with a set of resolutions drawn by Dr. Joseph Warren and adopted by a Suffolk county convention meeting in the town of Milton. The Suffolk Resolves pledged resistance to the Coercive Acts and promised to support the recommendations of Congress. After presenting the resolves, the radicals pushed through a resolution expressing sympathy for the plight of Massachusetts and requesting other colonies to aid the distressed citizens of Boston. Outflanked once again, Galloway sourly predicted that this action laid "the foundation of military resistance" to the empire.

On September 28, Galloway sought to gain the initiative by introducing a plan for imperial union. In an attempt to compromise the issue of sovereignty by establishing a federal relationship, he proposed a grand council elected every three years by the colonial assemblies and a president-general appointed by the Crown. Together the president and council would form a colonial parliament with broad power over matters of intercolonial concern. Any measure affecting America, even if initiated by the British Parliament, had to have the consent of the colonial parliament, but each colony would retain jurisdiction over its internal affairs. Galloway's plan of union may have envisioned too much colonial self-government to have been acceptable to Parliament, but it met favorable response among moderates in the Continental Congress, who feared that the popular violence was leading to anarchy. John Jay and James Duane of New York and Edward Rutledge of South Carolina, all of whom subsequently voted for the Declaration of Independence, supported it. The radicals did not dare attack it directly; instead they argued that such a gesture of reconciliation amounted to a retreat. Parliament, having put itself in the wrong by assaulting colonial rights, was obliged to take the first step. Even so the plan was defeated only by the narrowest of margins, six colonies to five.

Shortly thereafter Paul Revere again rode into town, this time with a message from the Boston committee of correspondence describing the dissolution of the Massachusetts assembly by General Gage and the construction of fortifications in Boston. Capitalizing on this threat of military tyranny, the radicals persuaded Congress to endorse resolutions urging the people of Massachusetts to create their own civil government and raise troops for defense. Then on October 14 it approved a Declaration of Rights and Grievances, which listed all the accumulated trespasses of Parliament—taxation, admiralty courts, standing armies, destruction of civil government. As a sop to moderates, however, it did concede the power of Parliament to regulate external trade for the advantage of the empire.

A week later Congress completed its labors by adopting a Continental Association. Beginning on December 1, 1774, the colonists would boycott all British goods, even the products of the British West Indies, and six months later (September 10, 1775) they would refuse to export any colonial products to Britain, except for South Carolina rice, which was too perishable to be held in storage. The hope was to impose a uniform, continental system of non-consumption that would paralyze Britain's commerce and, in the words of Richard Henry Lee, "wring immediate concessions from Parliament." Its main work accomplished, Congress adjourned on October 26 amidst a flurry of petitions to the British people, the residents of Canada and the West Indies, and the king. It voted to reassemble in Philadelphia on May 10, 1775, but by then the radicals in Massachusetts had transferred the imperial debate to the battlefield.

Congress wanted the Association to be enforced by elected committees, and during the autumn these organizations (usually styling themselves committees of safety) sprang up in every colony. They inspected the customs houses, fought against price increases, and establshed boycotts against communities that refused to cooperate. Their main weapons were publicity and social ostracism, but occasionally they resorted to the more violent tactics of tarring and feathering. In the process they raised numerous complaints. The New York Loyalist, Samuel Seabury, an Anglican minister, complained, "If I must be enslaved, let it be by a KING at least, and not by a parcel of upstart lawless committee-men. If I must be devoured, let me be devoured by the jaws of a lion, and not gnawed to death by rats and vermin." A Boston Loyalist put the problem more succinctly: "Which is better—to be ruled by one tyrant three thousand miles away, or three thousand tyrants not a mile away?" But, at their best, these extra-legal committees were the instruments of revolution; their efforts to enforce the Continental Association and the subsequent ordinances of Congress represented the first revolutionary assumption of governmental powers. Few of the assemblies were called into session after 1774, and many of the governors abandoned their posts after the battles at Lexington and Concord. The committees of safety moved into this governmental vacuum, providing a measure of administration and justice until the new state governments were created in 1776 and 1777.

The Association brought the Revolution to everyone's door, serving as a kind of loyalty oath; and, like the earlier nonimportation systems, it required the assistance of women. An intercolonial pledge of nonconsumption, the Association could be enforced only with the help of the people who did the household shopping. To win their support orators began appealing to the patriotism of women, assuring them that their boycott of British goods was vital to the future of the country. "Yes Ladies," asserted one Presbyterian clergyman, "You have it in your power more than all your committees and Congresses, to strike the Stroke, and make the Hills and Plains of America clap their hands." If women stopped drinking tea, he went on, it would convince the British "that American patriotism extends even to the Fair Sex, and discourage any future Attempts to enslave us." Women responded enthusiastically and without need for oratory. Even before the embargo went into effect John Adams's landlady refused to serve him tea, even though he requested some that had been "honestly smuggled." Some began referring to themselves as the "Daughters of Liberty," a name that reflected pride in their active political role. In October 1774, fifty-one female North Carolinians met in Edenton to sign an agreement declaring their support for the resolves of the North Carolina provincial congress. They announced it their "duty" to do "every thing as far as lies in our power" to support the "publick good." Implicit in this simple statement was the assumption that women had a responsibility to assume a public role and a "duty" to work for the "publick good." The Revolution was already having a major impact on women's perception of themselves. They were becoming aware that they might be participants in public affairs and not confined to purely private matters of home and family.

The Road to Concord Bridge

New England rippled with tension throughout the autumn of 1774. In addition to the political ferment there was considerable economic dislocation and unemployment resulting from the closing of Boston. Acting upon Congress's recommendation that they arm for defense, a number of towns resurrected their militia units. Through the winter months, town commons all over New England were scenes of troops marching, rehearsing the musket drill, and taking target

practice. To support them, radical leaders stockpiled arms and powder in various towns around Boston. As early as September 1774, a British effort to seize an arms cache near Boston nearly provoked a fight when militia from nearby towns rushed out to resist the effort (soon thereafter they began calling themselves "minutemen"). Through the winter General Gage periodically sent detachments to swoop down on the arms depots of the colonists.

In April 1775, General Gage had an opportunity too good to miss. He learned that his archenemies, Samuel Adams and John Hancock, were in Lexington, and that a sizable arms cache was in nearby Concord. An expedition was quickly organized, but the preparations were observed by vigilant Bostonians. On the evening of April 18, Dr. Joseph Warren sent the Boston committee's courier, Paul Revere, to warn Adams and Hancock. Revere rowed across the Charles River to Charlestown and waited there for signal lights in the tower of the North Church that would apprise him of the timing and direction of the British departure. As a precaution, Dr. Warren sent another rider, William Dawes, by the land route out the Boston neck. Each had a couple of hours start on the British, and both reached Lexington, though Revere was subsequently captured on the way to Concord.

The British force, which departed Boston in the early hours of April 19, numbered seven hundred regulars, light infantry, and marines. As they marched down the Lexington road, churchbells echoed from town to town summoning the militia. Reaching Lexington just after dawn, they encountered about seventy "minutemen" drawn up in two ranks on the village green. It is uncertain who fired the first shot (the British commander reported that snipers in houses and behind a fence fired first); but the issue is academic since both sides were spoiling for a fight. The disciplined British troops fired a volley, and the farmers dispersed, leaving eight dead and ten wounded on the field. Adams and Hancock had escaped, so the British marched off to Concord to discharge the other part of their mission. Entering Concord without resistance, they found that the colonists had carried off most of the munitions. While one group searched the town for stores, another went to secure the North Bridge across the river. About four hundred militia were gathered at the bridge, and in another brief skirmish they drove the British back into town.

By noon militia from all over eastern Massachusetts were responding to the ringing bells. The British force started for Boston, pressed by snipers from behind every tree, rock, and fence along the road. Only the timely arrival of a thousand reinforcements halfway back saved it from complete disaster. By the end of the day some four thousand "minutemen" were engaged in the fray, solid evidence of American zeal; British casualties of 273 (from an estimated ten thousand rounds expended by Americans) is evidence of their marksmanship. With the British ensconced in Boston, the militia settled in Cambridge to conduct a "siege" that would last for eleven months.

Siege of Boston

On April 22 the Massachusetts Provincial Congress met in Cambridge. It had been elected in the autumn under the new charter, but was never officially convened by General Gage. Now it undertook direction of the war effort, issuing a call for 13,000 men and appointing aged Artemas Ward, who had seen service in the French war, to command the army in Cambridge. News of the battles stirred radicals in every colony into feverish activity. By the end of April the siege force was augmented by troops from neighboring colonies, units that had been put together and were commanded by John Stark of New Hampshire, Nathanael Greene of Rhode Island, and Israel Putnam of Connecticut.

Among the more imaginative of these arrivals was Benedict Arnold, New Haven shopkeeper and captain of a company of Connecticut militia, who appeared in Cambridge on April 29 with a plan for capturing the forts on Lake Champlain. The committee of safety accepted the scheme, made him a colonel, and authorized him to recruit an expedition. Hastening northward Arnold encountered another adventurer with the same idea—Ethan Allen, leader of the Green Mountain Boys, an irregular force originally formed to resist New York's claims over Vermont. Allen claimed authority from the Connecticut Assembly for an attack on Fort Ticonderoga, and Arnold, rather than risk a quarrel, agreed to a joint command. On the night of May 10 the combined force, numbering about 250, caught the slumbering garrison by surprise and captured the fort. This sudden move secured for a time the back door of New England, and it provided the Americans with some badly needed cannon, which were hauled on sleds from Ticonderoga to Boston the next winter.

On that same day, May 10, 1775, the second Continental Congress met in Philadelphia. The radical ranks were strengthened by the appearance of John Hancock, Benjamin Franklin, and Thomas Jefferson, while the retirement of Galloway left leadership of the conservatives to John Dickinson. Information from London indicated that Parliament had rejected the petitions of the first Congress, but it had approved a conciliatory measure of Lord North's, promising no more taxation if the colonies would contribute to their own defense. Propitiating as it seemed, North's plan did not go to the heart of the issue, for Parliament did not abandon its theoretical power of taxation, and it actually increased the standing army in America. During the spring, reinforcements totaling nearly five thousand men were sent to Boston, along with three new major generals, William Howe, Henry Clinton, and John Burgoyne.

Impressed more by the menacing posture of the British army than by the conciliatory gestures of Lord North, Congress prepared for war. It called upon New York to muster three thousand militia and construct fortifications at the Highlands of the Hudson. As a nucleus for a continental army, it authorized twelve companies of riflemen to be recruited from Pennsylvania, Maryland, and Virginia; and, on June 15 it decided to appoint a general to command "all the continental forces, raised or to be raised, for the defense of American liberty." The unanimous choice was George Washington, once again a delegate from Virginia. Washington had considerable military experience in the French war—perhaps he was not so subtly reminding delegates of this when he appeared in the uniform of a colonel of Virginia militia. Yet there were other possible candidates who could boast more. The main reason for the choice was political. As a Virginian he represented the largest, most heavily populated colony; as a southerner he gave a truly continental flavor to the American resistance. He was also a gentleman with a considerable fortune and moderate views; his leadership would give the lie to those who charged that the colonial cause was led by an incendiary rabble. A day after Washington accepted the post, events in Boston made evident the need for a disciplined army under unified command.

In early June, General Gage, whose reinforced army numbered approximately ten thousand, decided to seize the low hills of Dorchester that overlooked Boston to the south. When the committee of safety picked up this intelligence, it decided to counter the move by occupying Bunker Hill on the Charlestown peninsula north of Boston. On the night of June 16, Israel Putnam led a force out to Bunker Hill, and then, on sudden inspiration, threw up breastworks on Breed's Hill, which was closer to Boston and commanded the shipping in the harbor. It was an error, for it exposed him to the cannon of warships in the harbor. Luckily for the Americans, Gage compensated with an error of his own. He decided to drive the Americans from the hill with a morale-breaking bayonet charge that would crush the incipient rebellion then and there.

Command of the assault was given to William Howe, but an adverse tide prevented the British from crossing the Charles River until early afternoon. By two o'clock, the British force of 2,500 was drawn up in magnificent red lines before Breed's Hill. The first two attacks were beaten back with heavy losses, but then the Americans ran low on ammunition and a bayonet charge sent them scurrying in confusion across the neck to Cambridge. In the flight, Dr. Warren was shot, and his body was left where it fell. The colonists lost 100 killed and 271 wounded, mostly in the retreat, while the British suffered 1,054 casualties, or about 42 percent of the attacking force. Another such victory, said London wags, and there would be no one left to bring the good news home. For the defeated Americans the battle brought a tremendous boost in morale, if only because it proved that untrained farmers could stand up to British regulars (or at least they would if protected by breastworks). But the battle also taught them the need for trained soldiers, a centralized command, and a coordinated strategy.

Washington took command on June 20, and spent the next nine months trying to shape a motley collection of farmers and shopkeepers into an effective fighting force. His problems mounted as the conflict settled into a lackluster siege. Unaccustomed to the routine of camp life, the "minutemen" drifted home in boredom. Housed in crude barracks and chilled by approaching winter, the thirty- and sixty-day militia refused to renew their terms of service. In December the Connecticut troops marched off home en masse, their enlistments having expired. Washington was left with fewer than two thousand effectives; but the British remained huddled in their winter quarters in Boston. If nothing else, the desertions alleviated his logistical problems; and, the troops were relatively well-fed and clothed that first winter.

Through all of this Washington actually improved his standing, both within the army and in his relations with the provincial governments. As his army melted away he complained privately about "the dearth of public spirit and want of virtue" among the soldiers from New England, but he made no effort to threaten or coerce them into staying. New Englanders had always enlisted for stated periods of time, and in all past wars they had gone home when the contracts expired. In the end, Washington's patience paid off. When he asked New England's political leaders to draft auxilliaries to meet the emergency, they responded with a prompt mobilization of militia. Washington's experience with legislative bodies in both Williamsburg and Philadelphia was another asset that winter. He sensed that he was cast in the role of a diplomat in a coalition war. During the nine months that he was encamped at Cambridge, he wrote fifty-one letters to the president of Congress, thirty-four to the Massachusetts legislature, forty to the governor of Connecticut, and thirty to the governor of Rhode Island. If the political leaders failed to give him all the support he desired, it was for lack of resources; there was certainly no communications gap.

At the end of January 1776, General Henry Knox appeared with forty-three cannon from Ticonderoga. As spring approached, reinforcements flowed into Cambridge, and Washington decided to take the offensive. On the night of March 4, he occupied Dorchester Heights and placed cannon in a position to command the city and the harbor. Howe, who had replaced Gage during the winter, had to risk another Breed's Hill or evacuate the city. Actually he had already decided to remove his army to New York, where a bigger harbor and a sizable concentration of Loyalists promised a better base of operations. He sailed on March 17. The evacuation of Boston was carried out with mutual forbearance—the British did not burn the city and Washington refrained from bombarding the troopships.

"Common Sense"

In the course of the long siege of Boston, the fundamental absurdity of the American position gradually became evident. Americans were battling the military forces of the empire in order to maintain their rights within the empire. Was the position merely inconsistent, or was it really self-defeating? Yet the only alternative, in lieu of an unexpected surrender by Parliament, seemed to be a declaration of total independence. And that course, considering the disparity in military power between Britain and the colonies, was fraught with danger. Moreover, it involved a break with a familiar culture and old ties of business and friendship; it was a step not to be taken lightly. In February 1776, Henry Laurens of South Carolina predicted, "One more year will enable us to be independent. Ah! That word cuts me deep—has caused tears to trickle down my cheeks." A period of mutual adjustment was necessary, and the revolution was a year old before much serious consideration was given to the idea. In the meantime a variety of extra-legal committees and congresses filled the governmental hiatus.

The battles at Lexington and Concord sent about half the royal governors scurrying to the nearest royal warship for safety. Virginia's Lord Dunmore confiscated the powder stored in Williamsburg and transferred it to ships in the James River. This enraged the radicals, who had been remarkably quiescent throughout the spring; and, Patrick Henry led a militia band to Williamsburg where they forced the governor to reimburse the colony. When Henry departed the governor branded him a rebel, but his proclamation was drowned out by the din of marching militia. In June, Dunmore took refuge on a British man-o-war and issued a call for slaves to rally to the crown. This hint of slave insurrection ended any vestige of royal authority in Virginia. In August the radical Burgesses, who had been meeting unofficially as a convention for a year, elected a committee of public safety. Until a constitution was drawn up a year later, this executive junta of eleven prominent planters established an army, issued paper money, and levied taxes in Virginia.

In the quasi-republics of Connecticut and Rhode Island, where the governors were elected annually by the assemblies, there was no royal government to overthrow. So smooth was their transition to independence that Connecticut did not bother to write a state constitution until 1818, and Rhode Island not until 1846. In the middle colonies, the royal and proprietary governors held their ground with the support of Tories and moderate Whigs. In Maryland the popular Robert Eden remained in control until the Declaration of Independence. As the siege of Boston continued, Congress encouraged the transformation from colonies to states. When New Hampshire reported that it was in a "convulsed state" and asked for advice, Congress recommended that the provincial convention "call a full and free representation of the people, and that the representatives, if they think it necessary, establish such a form of government as in their judgment will best produce the happiness of the people. . . ." Significantly, Congress refrained from any reference to New Hampshire as an independent state, though John Adams tried unsuccessfully to include one. Sentiment for independence did not gain momentum until the early months of 1776. The catalyst was the pamphlet *Common Sense* by Thomas Paine.

Tom Paine was the son of a poor Quaker corset-maker, self-educated, and a failure in every business he had tried in England. Persuaded by Franklin to move to America in 1774, he absorbed the main currents of popular feeling in Philadelphia and spent the autumn of 1775 preparing a pamphlet advocating complete independence. *Common Sense,* an aptly titled attempt to get at the heart of the matter, was published in January 1776. The decade of controversy had produced many great polemicists, but none had the appeal of Paine because they were directed toward the educated elite. Paine wrote in the language of the common man. He shunned all esoteric appeals to the "social contract" and "natural law," all the subtle distinctions regarding the powers of Parliament; his was a candid appeal for independence.

But it was more than that. It was also a plea for a republican form of government in America, and Paine sought eagerly to divest Americans of their emotional attachment to monarchy. He pointed out how the selection of rulers by heredity was logically ridiculous since birth was no assurance of talent. "One of the strongest natural proofs of the folly of hereditary right in Kings is that nature disproves it, otherwise she would not so frequently turn it into ridicule, by giving mankind an Ass for a Lion." Another bulwark of monarchy, the claim of divine right, he undermined by recalling the first of the modern English kings, William the Conqueror: "A French bastard with an armed Banditti and establishing himself King of England against the consent of the natives, is in plain terms a very paltry rascally original. It certainly hath no divinity in it." Then with mockery and contempt he traced the institution of monarchy through history, coming to the conclusion that "Of more worth is one honest man to society, and in the sight of God, than all the crowned ruffians that ever lived."

Paine concluded his tract with a strong plea for independence and the establishment of a constitutional republic with a one-house legislature, similar to the Continental Congress. His parting words echoed through the colonies:

> O ye that love mankind! Ye that dare oppose not only the tyranny, but also the tyrant, stand forth! Every spot of the old world is overrun with oppression. Freedom hath been hunted round the Globe. Asia and Africa have long expelled her. Europe regards her like a stranger, and England hath given her warning to depart. O! receive the fugitive and prepare in time an asylum for mankind.

Here in unforgettable prose was the sense of mission, the promise of destiny, so necessary to every successful revolution. In a population that numbered a little more than two million Anglos, Paine sold 120,000 copies of *Common Sense* in the first three months. His flaming rhetoric reached every corner of the continent and crystallized the movement for independence.

Through the spring of 1776, state after state began instructing its delegates in Congress to support independence. After a battle between Whigs and Tories at Moore's Creek Bridge, the provincial congress of North Carolina voted for independence in April. New England and Virginia followed suit in May; only the middle colonies lagged. In Pennsylvania, John Dickinson had made himself the leader of those who still hoped for reconciliation with the empire. In the fall of 1775, the Pennsylvania assembly had instructed its delegates in Congress to vote against independence whenever the issue was raised, and the other middle colonies took the same stance. In New York the DeLanceys leaned to the Tory side, and the Livingstons floundered in fearful uncertainty. After months of hesitation, Robert R. Livingston finally advised his followers to join the movement for independence on the grounds that "they should yield to the torrent if they hoped to direct its course."

On June 7, 1776, Richard Henry Lee sought to focus the debate in Congress by offering a resolution "That these United Colonies are, and of right ought to be, free and independent states. . . ." The provinces should sever all connections with Great Britain, form a confederated union among themselves, and seek foreign allies to aid them in the contest. The motion was seconded by John Adams and a fierce debate began. The conservatives, led by Dickinson and his young disciple James Wilson, argued for delay: the time was not ripe, and England might yet yield to colonial demands. Moreover, they feared that a precipitate break with the mother country would lead to anarchy and social disorder; at the very least a confederation should be formed before the imperial tie was severed. On June 10, Edward Rutledge moved that a vote be postponed until early July, and the radicals agreed. Delay would give public sentiment in the middle colonies time to jell, and elsewhere uninstructed delegates could check with their assemblies. To appease the radicals, an amendment was added appointing a committee to draft a declaration of independence in the interim, and the postponement package was adopted by a vote of seven states to five.

The most important member of the drafting committee was Thomas Jefferson, who had proved his facility with a quill by his pamphlet *A Summary View* two years before. The other members of the committee—Benjamin Franklin, John Adams, Robert R. Livingston, and Roger Sherman—agreed to let Jefferson undertake the initial draft. Later in life Jefferson stated that his intent in the declaration was "not to find new principles, or new arguments, never thought of . . . ; but to place before mankind the common sense of the subject, in terms so plain and firm as to command their assent. . . ." Jefferson's primary objective was to convince the world that the colonies were in the right in separating themselves from Great Britain. But Jefferson went beyond this, seizing the occasion to set forth an ideological foundation for the new nation. His draft began with a statement of Lockean doctrine that already had become a familiar feature of the American argument. All men, Jefferson proclaimed, are created equal, and each is endowed with certain inalienable rights, among them the right to life, liberty, and the pursuit of happiness. It is to protect these rights that governments are instituted among men, and when government infringes upon these rights, men have the right to rebel. Jefferson then carried the Lockean defense of revolution one step further by suggesting that governments themselves derived their powers from the just consent of the governed. The democratic implications of the right of revolution were thereby transformed into a philosophy of government by majority vote. Posterity in moments of disillusionment has occasionally considered the Declaration "a salad of illusions," a potpourri of unfulfilled promises, but it nevertheless reflected the fundamental idealism of a revolution based ultimately on popular consent. Having laid his philosophical foundation, Jefferson "with a decent respect for the opinions of mankind" proceeded to list all the transgressions of the king that had induced his subjects to rebel.

While the committee labored over Jefferson's draft, making minor changes in wording, the political situation solidified in the middle colonies. In June the Pennsylvania radicals, a coalition of Presbyterians and Sons of Liberty with some leadership from the old factions, finally seized the initiative and summoned an ad hoc convention. This body proceeded to rule alongside the more conservative assembly, calling for independence and a state constitutional convention. In New Jersey the committee of safety finally arrested Governor William Franklin, and the provincial congress voted in favor of independence. Maryland, too, fell in line by the end of the month. When Lee's resolution was taken up for debate on July 1, every colony except New York had instructed its delegation by one means or another. July 2 dawned hot and humid—Jefferson's newly purchased thermometer registered eighty-one degrees at nine o'clock. Horseflies streamed in through the open windows, and debate grew increasingly irritable. The vote on Lee's resolution revealed substantial opposition. Pennsylvania, Delaware, and South Carolina were badly divided, and the uninstructed New York delegates abstained. Even so, the resolution passed and the next day Congress took up the committee's draft. A few of Jefferson's more extreme statements were deleted, among them the indictment of the king for forcing slavery on the colonies. More forceful instructions arrived from the Pennsylvania convention, and new pressure was applied to the South Carolina laggards. On July 4 the declaration was approved; five days later new instructions for the New Yorkers made it unanimous. Engrossing and printing required several more weeks, but the signing was completed by early August.

The Revolution as Civil War

Adoption of the Declaration of Independence marked the founding of a nation, and that fact alone gave new definition to the words "loyalty" and "patriotism." Hitherto, Americans had been divided bitterly over the proper course to pursue in maintaining their rights within the empire; now suddenly the course of the radicals was the course of a nation. Those who wished to stay within the empire were a threat to the republic; imperial loyalty was potential treason. During the great constitutional debate, Americans divided into "Whigs" and "Tories," though the appellations had no connection with British parties except in name. When the Whigs endorsed the independence movement they identified themselves with the cause of the new nation and thus became "Patriots," while the opposition thereby became "Loyalists" or, in common parlance, "damned rascals." As potential traitors, the Loyalists were hounded by Patriot committees and deprived of their property. Many avoided trouble by swearing loyalty oaths and some joined the British army, but a large number (possibly half) chose instead voluntary exile in Canada, Britain, or the West Indies.

The Loyalists were conservatives in the most elemental sense—they wished to preserve the status quo against revolutionary change. But they were also conservative in a secondary sense, for many of them were men of wealth and property who feared social disruption more than parliamentary rule. Suddenly launching a new ship of state without even the rudder of centralized government, they predicted, would bring drift and confusion, mob rule, and eventually tyranny. In this, of course, they were no different from the conservative Whigs, who also feared that the eddies of revolution would bring the "lower orders" of society to the surface. But at least the conservative Whigs—men like John Dickinson in Pennsylvania and James Duane in New York—were willing to commit their ideas to the tribunal of public opinion, and in the end they elected to join the revolution in the hope of steering it in a moderate, stable direction.

Tories, lacking a faith in public opinion, failed to develop any apparatus of popular appeal; no Samuel Adams appeared among them to coordinate, encourage, and propagate their ideology. It is significant that no important Tory pamphlet appeared in print until the very eve of the war. Even then they were unable to offer a viable alternative to the revolutionary movement, except a status quo defense of the imperial relationship. The one comprehensive program conceived by a Tory—Galloway's plan of union—was offered only in the secrecy of the Continental Congress and never submitted to public debate. This lack of faith in the populace weakened the Loyalists and bound them even closer to the mother country; the more dependent upon England they became, the less effective they were as political advocates.

Conservatives are, by their very nature, on the defensive, for those who demand change necessarily have the initiative. Tories accentuated this disadvantage during the rush of events that preceded the revolution by abdicating their political responsibilities. They ignored the extra-legal conventions and committees, refused even to participate in elections, and thus deprived themselves of political influence. New York, for instance, had a higher proportion of Tories than any other colony, but they refused to participate in the crucial elections of 1774 and 1775. In some of the Tory counties of the lower Hudson Valley a mere handful of radicals was permitted to select delegates to the provincial congress without opposition. In contrast, the conservative Whigs in New York controlled the revolution by cooperating with it, and they eventually succeeded in writing the conservative state constitution of 1777.

Referring to the Tories as conservatives does not mean that they were all men of wealth, or that the revolution was a class struggle between rich and poor. There were many wealthy men who sided with the revolutionary cause, George Washington being perhaps the best example. And the Tories themselves covered the entire spectrum of wealth and interest. The one unifying factor among the various Tory groups seems to have been that each of them had a project, interest, or status that required British support. This was certainly true of officeholders, from governors to customs collectors, who were appointed by and responsible to the imperial regime. This group included both British-born officials, who considered themselves temporary exiles from their homeland, and "native sons," such as Governor Thomas Hutchinson of Massachusetts and Justice William Allen of Pennsylvania.

The Anglican clergy were also dependent upon the mother country for status and support, though in the southern colonies they were so enmeshed with the planter gentry who controlled the vestries that most of them became Whigs. But in the north, Anglicans were a minority in most colonies, and in Congregationalist New England their very existence seemed to depend upon imperial support. For a decade, Anglicans in the northern colonies had demanded the establishment of an American episcopacy to relieve the difficulties of ordaining clergy and strengthen the organization of the church. In New England particularly, the demand had hardened political attitudes, for Congregationalists generally assumed that an American bishop was only the first step toward establishment. As John Adams observed, "If Parliament could tax us, they could establish the church of England." In the heterogeneous middle colonies, the Anglican clergy also tended to be Tories, though only in New York did they provide an articulate opposition. The Reverend Samuel Seabury, a New Englander who had studied at both Yale and Edinburgh before being sent to New York by the Society for the Propagation of the Gospel in Foreign Parts, was perhaps the best of the Tory propagandists. His *Letters of a Westchester Farmer,* published in the winter of 1774–75, appealed to the anti-Yankee and anti-urban prejudices of New York farmers while piously denouncing extralegal conventions and revolutionary violence.

In terms of economic interest and geography, the highest incidence of Loyalism seems to have been among the fur traders of the frontier and the merchants of the seaboard cities. Many frontiersmen were too remote from the revolutionary struggle to choose sides, and a substantial proportion of trappers and traders became Loyalists. Remote from the political issues and isolated from the developing sense of American identity, these men labored for an imperial market and ignored colonial boundaries and jurisdictions. The most famous were Matthew Elliott and Simon Girty, who escaped from Pittsburgh to live among the pro-British tribes of the Northwest. After the war they became Indian Agents in the British outposts at Detroit and Malden; from there they provided diplomatic and occasionally logistical support to the Northwestern tribes until the War of 1812. At the other end of the economic spectrum a substantial number of seaboard merchants became Loyalists. Most of these were men of substance who feared social upheaval, or they were international traders with a cosmopolitan outlook. In the southern colonies, most Scottish factors representing British firms returned to their homeland at the outbreak of the revolution.

Besides those who were dependent upon England for substance or status, the other major source of Loyalism was found in cultural minorities. The Dutch of New York and the Germans of Pennsylvania tended to be Tory in those enclaves where they retained their own religion and language. In other localities where they had been assimilated by the prevailing Anglo-American culture, the same ethnic groups were neutral or Whiggish. Similarly, the Highland Scots, whether they lived in the Hudson Valley of New York or the upper Cape Fear Valley of North Carolina, were overwhelmingly Loyalists. Most of them were recent immigrants with little sense of identity with their new land. They had little love for the Hanoverian dynasty, having rebelled against it in 1745, but British reprisals after "the '45" together with British generosity in granting crown lands in America made them unwilling to risk their fortunes on another insurrection. As Presbyterians, they were also a religious minority in the predominantly Anglican Carolinas. Other religious minorities in the southern colonies, such as the Quakers and German Pietists, tended to be neutral or passive Loyalists.

The one thing that all these social groups had in common was a fear of being overwhelmed by the majority, not merely in political terms at the ballot-box, but in the set of assumptions that characterized American culture. The Revolution was a bourgeois upheaval by a middle-class society; philosophically it rested on the liberal doctrines of English and French commonwealthmen and *philosophes*. In economic terms the tenets of this society could be found in Benjamin Franklin's injunctions to hard work in the *Almanac* and *Father Abraham's Speech*. They received more profound analysis in *The Wealth of Nations* by the Scotsman Adam Smith, published in 1776 and widely read in America thereafter. Politically, they found their best expression in the Declaration of Independence and in the numerous state constitutions. So pervasive was this intellectual climate that it quickly absorbed those Loyalists who returned after the war. The first of the liberal revolutions, the contest for independence was a major step in forming the essentials of the distinctively American creed—faith in the social contract, written constitutions, individual rights, and free enterprise.

An Island Versus a Continent

It was one thing to assert independence, it was quite another matter to win it. The American states challenged an empire that stretched from the plains of India to the jungles of Honduras. They faced a navy that had dominated the seas for a century. At three million, their population was less than a third that of Great Britain. They lacked both the manufacturing industries and the financial organization to sustain a total war. And they were painfully slow learning the art of war.

Military tactics in the eighteenth century were dictated by the weaponry, and the standard infantry firearm was the musket, a smooth-bore, muzzle-loading gun with an effective range of less than a hundred yards. Because of the range and the time required for reloading, the bayonet was an essential feature of the weapon. Armies commonly fought in lines of battle two to three men deep, the assailing force marching to the tap of drums, relentlessly forward toward an opponent strung out along a defensible ridge or stream. Each force hoped to draw fire while the range was still great, advance quickly, loose a coordinated volley, and charge with the bayonet, catching the enemy with broken ranks and empty weapons. In the course of the century, warfare developed into a fine art, one resembling a chess game. Armies of professional soldiers, finely trained to undergo the physical and psychological rigor of such battles, were too expensive to risk losing. The business of war, therefore, became a matter of efforts to checkmate the enemy by cutting his lines of supply or threatening his capital city.

Americans, however, knew little of the formal rules that had developed, and, unused to regimen, they did not adapt readily to the line of battle. The weapon with which they were most familiar, the rifle, was too long to carry a bayonet and was useful only in skirmishing. Their army, moreover, was maddeningly decentralized—in fact, it was not one army but fourteen. Each state maintained its own force of militia. The militia were part-time soldiers whose enlistments varied from three to six months; they were ill-trained, undisciplined, and generally unreliable. But, despite these deficiencies, they were the hope of the American cause. Under a Daniel Morgan or a Nathanael Greene, generals who understood their potential as well as their limitations, the militia could be made to fight; and, in times of crisis they often appeared in numbers sufficient to tip the balance of military power. Congress maintained a separate force, the Continental Army. Signed for longer terms, varying from three years to the duration of the war, the continental troops were usually more effective; but they learned the art of war only in the hard school of military defeat.

The conflict, nevertheless, was not so unequal as it appeared. In suppressing the rebellion, Britain faced a number of difficulties which ultimately proved decisive. To begin with, Britain entered the war in diplomatic isolation. The extent of its victory in 1763 aroused jealousies on the continent, and its perfidious treatment of allies during the struggle with France left her without a friend in the world. In particular, Britain's ancient rivals, France and Spain, kept close watch on New World developments and rubbed their hands with ill-disguised glee when Britain's empire began to crumble.

Britain had long preferred to fight its wars by subsidizing allies, and had never found it necessary to maintain a large standing army. When the Revolution began Britain could put no more than 15,000 redcoats in the field and was soon forced to solicit the services of hired mercenaries from the continent. The strength of the Royal Navy rested more on reputation than reality. Neglected since 1763, the famed wooden walls were old and rotten, the ships ill-equipped and poorly manned. France, meanwhile, had completely reconstructed her navy and presented a serious challenge to Britain's naval superiority.

Incompetent administration further hampered the British war effort. George III, in his crusade to restore royal authority, had systematized corruption and demoralized the government. Cabinet positions of key importance were occupied by men whose only recommendation was a willingness to dance to the king's tune. Lord North lacked both the ability and spirit to conduct a lengthy war; the Earl of Sandwich, in charge of the navy, and Lord George Germain, colonial secretary, were political hacks dependent upon the favor of the king. George's attempts at personal rule provoked considerable domestic opposition, and Britain seethed with discontent throughout the war.

The conditions under which the war was fought also worked to Britain's disadvantage. After the evacuation of Boston, they were faced with invading a hostile continent three thousand miles away. The voyage across the Atlantic required three to four weeks, and in adverse weather might take six or eight. The vast distance thus created a colossal communications problem and made the supply of an army enormously expensive. The geography of America, together with the Americans' ignorance of the proper conduct of a war, also hindered the British. In Europe the capture of a capital city such as Paris or Vienna was sufficient to end a war, but America possessed no strategic urban centers whose conquest was a mortal blow, either actually or psychologically. The vast expanse of wilderness permitted American generals to retreat indefinitely without demoralizing their cause, while British generals, as Burgoyne was to discover in upper New York and Cornwallis in the Carolinas, might conduct long, wearisome marches only to find that they controlled nothing more than the soil under their feet, a hostile countryside having closed in behind them.

The endless woods, rugged hills, and dense swamps of the American terrain hindered military operations in the European style, but were well suited to the type of guerilla warfare at which Americans were skilled. With a population experienced in the use of firearms, America could produce at a moment's notice a host of armed farmers who seemed to rise up out of the native soil as if dragons' teeth had been sowed. And the British were under the psychological disadvantage of invading and conquering a foreign land, while Americans fought for their freedom on their home soil. As Tom Paine observed, "It is not a few acres of ground, but a cause that we are defending."

Many Englishmen, aware of the difficulties of suppressing the revolution, urged a policy of compromise. John Wilkes contended in the Commons that a military victory, even if achieved, would mean nothing; the colonists would have to be kept in permanent subjection by the military. Even Lord North doubted the wisdom of force, but George III considered compromise weakness and resolved to meet insurrection with overwhelming power. Indeed, the king and ministry decided to declare war even before the Americans declared independence. In November 1775, Parliament instituted a naval blockade of the American coast and authorized the seizure of all American vessels on the high seas. By December, the government was scouring the continent for mercenaries to fill out ranks of the British army, entering into contracts with German principalities for about 30,000 men. The landgrave of Hesse-Kassel alone supplied 17,000 men—hence the use of "Hessian" to describe German soldiers serving in America.

From Long Island to Trenton

The spring of 1776 saw reinforcements flowing across the Atlantic. Ten thousand were sent to Sir Guy Carlton, governor of Canada, who was instructed to invade the New York frontier. In Halifax, Sir William Howe with a force that reached 30,000 by midsummer, planned to seize New York City and make it his headquarters for suppressing the rebellion. On July 2, 1776, the very day on which Congress severed the ties between Britain and America, Howe sailed into New York harbor with a battle fleet and troop transports for one of the largest amphibious landings to that time. Although Howe brought peace overtures (which to Americans seemed to offer only an amnesty if they would lay down their arms), the time for compromise had passed. It was to be a mortal struggle, and the stakes were high: the preservation of an empire or the birth of a nation.

General Washington anticipated the British move into New York; indeed, two days after they left Boston, he sent the first American contingents southward. New York was a complex of islands—Manhattan, Long Island, and Staten Island—and it was impossible to defend in the face of superior naval power; yet, Congress ordered it held and even sent a committee to supervise the operation. Washington, who arrived in April 1776, agreed that the loss of New York without a fight might wreck the morale of his army and deal a fatal blow

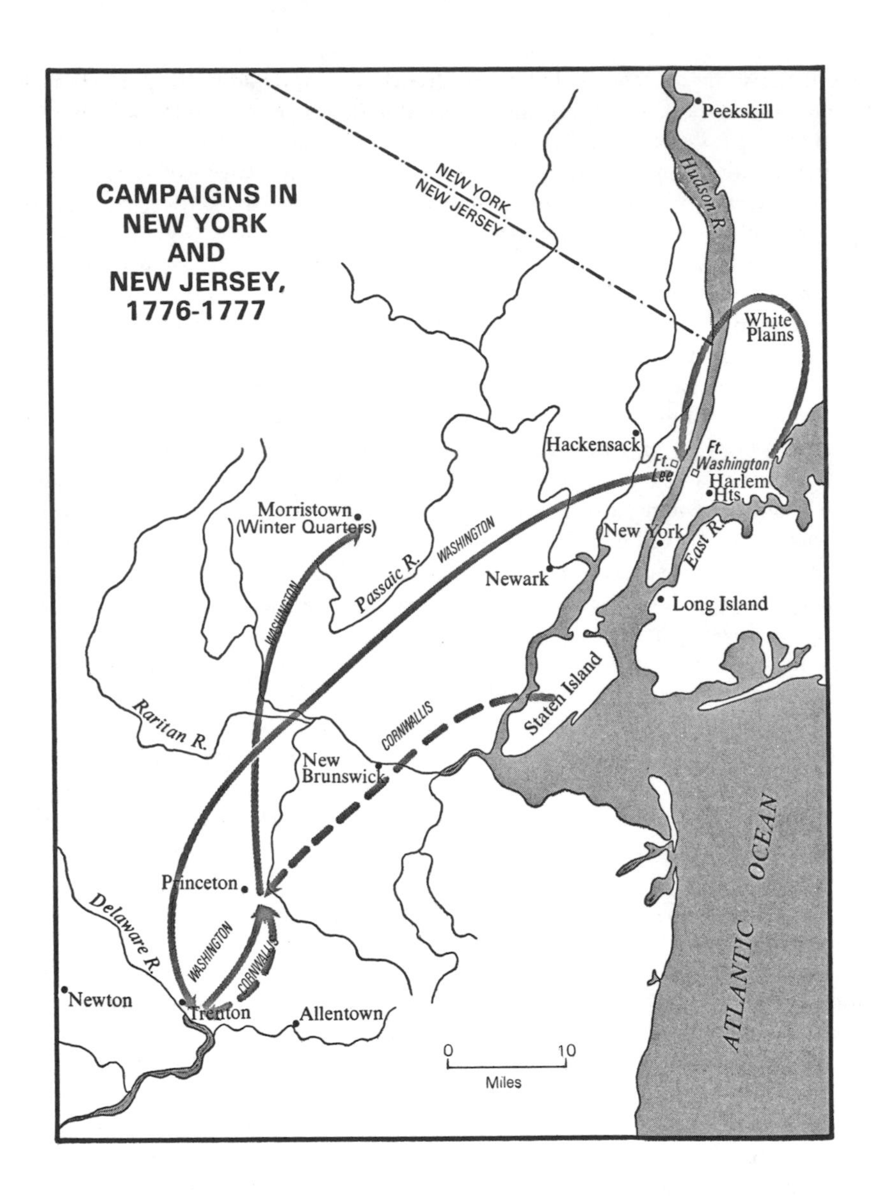

to the patriot cause. After surveying the defenses, he decided to occupy Brooklyn Heights on Long Island. The decision involved grave risks, for the British might sail up the Hudson River, land on Manhattan, and cut him off from the mainland. Yet, for the same purposes of internal morale that motivated Washington, Howe would have to meet the American army head-on. Washington could choose the site, and Brooklyn Heights afforded the most promise. Through the summer he labored to make its ridges another Breed's Hill.

After consuming a month in futile peace negotiations, Howe put his army in motion on August 22, landing on the southwestern tip of Long Island at Gravesend Bay. Surveillance had revealed the strength of the American position, and Howe, profiting by his experience at Breed's Hill, decided on a flank attack. Dividing his army, he personally led a demonstration against the American front while sending Lord Charles Cornwallis to fall on the American left. Guided by local Tories, Cornwallis on August 26 marched along the Jamaica Road through the unguarded Jamaica Pass and descended on the American flank. Taken by surprise, the inexperienced Americans fled in confusion, abandoning their fortifications. Despite a strong defense by continental regiments from Maryland and Delaware, the Battle of Long Island was an overwhelming British victory. Two American generals and one thousand men were captured; British casualties numbered about three hundred. At the conclusion, Washington's army was in a desperate plight. At its front was a triumphant British army; to the rear the British navy lay at anchor in the East River. Luckily, Howe chose to conduct the war in the leisurely fashion characteristic of the eighteenth century, and delayed the final blow that might have pushed Washington into the river. Rain and fog on the night of August 29 enabled the Americans to row across the river under the bows of the British ships and make good their escape.

Manhattan was subject to the same tactical disadvantages—an amphibious landing in Westchester might cut off the entire American army. General Nathanael Greene urged that the city be evacuated and burned to deprive the British of a base of operations. While Washington paused indecisively, the British on September 15 landed at Kip's Bay half way up the island on the East River. The green militia assigned to defend the bay broke and ran despite frantic efforts to make them fight, and the American army retired northward toward the Harlem River. After a few skirmishes in Harlem Heights, Washington retreated across the river to the hills around White Plains. There a brief and indecisive battle at last halted the British advance. From White Plains, American troops kept watch on the British in New York for the rest of the war.

Washington, numbed by this succession of disasters, seemed unable to make up his mind what to do next. In November he watched helplessly while the British captured a fort on the Manhattan side of the Hudson River, taking about three thousand Americans prisoner. He moved half his army across the Hudson in a half-hearted gesture to protect another fort on the New Jersey shore, but that too fell to Howe's energetic lieutenant, Lord Cornwallis. Then Cornwallis turned in pursuit of Washington, and suddenly there was no longer time to dally. The American army fled for the Delaware River, hoping to find safety in the wilds of Pennsylvania. Washington reached the river on December 1, gathered all the boats he could find, and crossed. Cornwallis arrived two days later, found no boats available, and decided to call it quits for the winter. With Howe's approval, he set up an advance base at Trenton, from which the British might descend on Philadelphia the following year, created small supply bases at Princeton and New Brunswick, and returned to enjoy the winter social season in New York.

Disheartened by the string of defeats and the approach of winter, Washington's army melted away. Enlistment terms for most of these who remained were due to expire at the end of the year. It was at this critical juncture that the magical pen of Thomas Paine produced the first number of *The American*

Crisis. Like the Declaration of Independence, it was read to the troops, and the effect of its opening words was electric: "These are the times that try men's souls. The summer soldier and the sunshine patriot will, in this crisis, shrink from the service of their country; but he that stands it now, deserves the love and thanks of man and woman. Tyranny, like hell, is not easily conquered. . . ." As a contemporary wrote, "Hope succeeded to despair, cheerfulness to gloom, and firmness to resolution."

Washington too hoped to rebuild morale. The dispositions made by Cornwallis had a serious weakness, for his isolated garrisons strung out across New Jersey invited attack. The British did not notice the danger. Their chain of unbroken successes had made them overconfident; and, they were certain the Americans had had their fill of battle. No doubt they also assumed that Washington would behave like a gentleman and retire to winter quarters when the campaigning season was ended. But Washington, his plea for reinforcements having brought several thousand Pennsylvania militia to his camp in mid-December, saw the opportunity. He could win a victory and restore morale by concentrating his small force in a surprise attack on a British outpost. Choosing the Hessian garrison at Trenton as his victim, he planned to envelop the town by dividing his army and crossing the Delaware both above and below the town.

It was a daring plan, nimbly executed. Even though the detachment that was to cross below Trenton was intimidated by floating ice and failed to get across, Washington led his wing of 2,400 over the river above Trenton on Christmas night. Early the next morning the Continentals descended on Trenton by two parallel roads, surprised the force of 1,500 Hessians, and captured the entire lot. Washington prudently returned to the west bank of the Delaware with his prisoners; then, encouraged by success, his generals persuaded him to undertake further adventures. On December 30, he again crossed the river and reoccupied Trenton. The enlistments of many of his men were due to expire the following day, but Washington appeared before each regiment with a plea that they stay on for another six weeks as a special favor to him. He won over two-thirds of the soldiers scheduled for departure. It was a day they never forgot. Many vividly remembered that moment years later when they described their service in applying for Revolutionary pensions.

In the meantime, word of the capture of Trenton reached Cornwallis, and he started south in haste, collecting troops from the garrisons at New Brunswick and Princeton, and entered Trenton on January 2. Washington's army, camped south of town, seemed in danger of being trapped against the icy river, but that night it left campfires burning to deceive the British and marched east to Princeton. The next morning Cornwallis heard firing from the direction of Princeton and started in hot pursuit, but the Americans, having surprised the garrison and captured the supplies, headed north just as Cornwallis entered the town.

Deciding at last that it was time for winter quarters, Washington chose Morristown in the hilly section of northwestern New Jersey. There he was relatively secure from British attack, yet still presented a threat to the chain of British bases. Howe accordingly ordered the evacuation of Trenton and Princeton, and the British retired to New Brunswick and the Hudson. In a fortnight

Washington had freed western New Jersey, temporarily removed the threat to Philadelphia, and restored American morale.

Contest for the Fourteenth Colony

The Hudson and Delaware were the main theaters of the war in 1776; Washington, Howe, and Cornwallis, the principal actors. But all the while a minor drama was being enacted to the north, a portent of what would be the most important campaign of the Revolution. The acquisition of Canada as a fourteenth state was a cherished dream of the Continental Congress. The Canadians, it was thought, might be eager to share the blessings of republican liberty, and even if they proved loyal to the empire, the conquest of Canada would forestall invasion from the north. Soon after Ethan Allen and Benedict Arnold opened the gateway to the north by capturing Ticonderoga in May 1775, Congress created a separate army department and placed it under the command of New York's General Philip Schuyler. Though solid and capable, Schuyler was slow to make decisions, and as a New York aristocrat he was disliked by the democratic Yankees who made up most of his army. He was fortunate, however, in his chief lieutenant, Brigadier General Richard Montgomery, youthful, decisive, and energetic, a soldier who provided the qualities Schuyler lacked. After consulting Washington, Schuyler proposed to descend on Montreal by way of the Lake Champlain-Richelieu River waterway, the classic route used by Lord Jeffrey Amherst in 1759–60. The expedition would be entrusted to Montgomery, while from his headquarters in Albany, Schuyler would handle problems of supply and reinforcements.

Washington accepted Schuyler's proposal, at the same time approving a plan submitted by Benedict Arnold for a surprise attack on Quebec by way of the Kennebec River in Maine. The two expeditions, he felt, would complement each other, for the British would not be able to defend both Montreal and Quebec simultaneously, and at least one would fall. Thus evolved, from the planning of Congress, Schuyler, and Washington, a coordinated two-pronged assault on Canada in 1775 that came very near to success.

The key elements in the plan were speed and surprise—a quick thrust at Canada might crystalize a hoped-for revolutionary spirit among the Canadian people and catch the British unprepared. But the slow-moving Schuyler, overwhelmed by the problems of creating and supplying an army in the wilderness of upper New York, frittered away the summer. Not until early September did Montgomery's army move up Lake Champlain to invest Fort St. Johns on the Richelieu River. Defended by a force of five hundred British regulars, the fort was too strong to be carried by assault; and the Americans lacked the cannon to reduce its stout wooden walls. Montgomery was compelled to undertake a prolonged siege, and not until November 2 did the British abandon the struggle and retire to Montreal. The delay of fifty-five days probably saved Canada for Britain.

Montreal proved easier prey. The capital had no important fortifications, and the predominantly French citizenry was unwilling to fight. Governor Guy

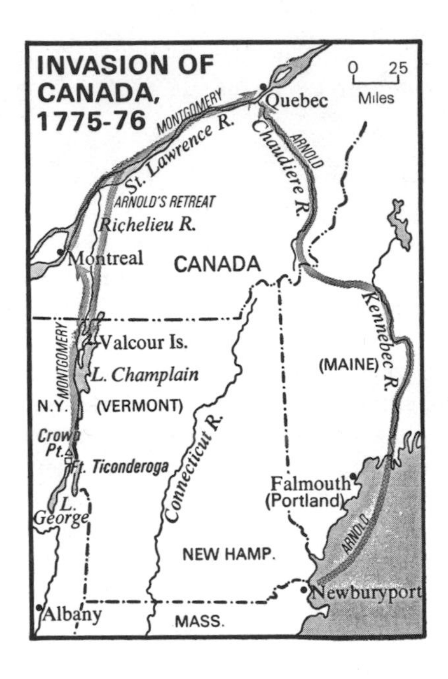

Carlton abandoned the city and retired with his little army toward Quebec; the citizenry opened the gates to Montgomery on November 13. He delayed for two weeks in Montreal, resting his army and procuring supplies from the south. Then, at the end of November, he hurried forward to join Benedict Arnold before Quebec.

The organization of Arnold's expedition, too, had suffered from frustrating delays. General Washington himself organized the force of 1,100 men, giving Arnold ten companies of New England militia and three companies of Pennsylvania and Virginia riflemen from his army in Cambridge. But it was not until September 25 that Arnold began his push up the Kennebec; had he been able to start a month earlier, perhaps even a week earlier, Canada might have been his. The march to Quebec is one of the great sagas in American military annals, a punishing tramp through dense woods, accompanied by starvation and dysentery. From the Kennebec the small force, its ranks thinned by desertion, alternately waded and crawled over the divide to the headwaters of the Chaudiere River, which flows northwest into the St. Lawrence. On November 10, Arnold arrived at Point Levis opposite Quebec with five hundred half-starved, ragged men. Quebec was at his mercy; its citadel was undefended, its population restless and inclined to surrender. But a storm and a lack of boats delayed his crossing for three days, during which Carlton's army of regulars straggled up from Montreal. With characteristic energy Carlton restored civilian morale and repaired the fortress. After the agonizing march, Arnold was denied his prize.

On December 2, Montgomery joined Arnold, bringing the total American force on the Plains of Abraham to a thousand men. Profiting by the disastrous experience of Montcalm sixteen years before, Carlton refused to sally forth to give battle. The American commanders contemplated besieging the city, but such an operation was doomed from the start. Montgomery lacked the cannon to breach the stone walls, winter was at hand, and enlistments were due to expire. In desperation Montgomery and Arnold determined upon a night assault, carried out on December 30 under cover of a blinding snowstorm. Forewarned by deserters, the British repelled the assault, killed Montgomery, wounded Arnold, and captured Colonel Daniel Morgan, commander of the Virginia riflemen.

With what remained of his army Arnold encamped on the Plains of Abraham and spent the winter conducting a futile siege from forts of snow. The spring thaw brought a British fleet up the St. Lawrence with reinforcements, and Arnold at last retired southward. He arrived at Ticonderoga in July 1776, his army broken in spirit, starving, and rotten with smallpox—and with Carlton in hot pursuit.

One of the most daring feats of the war, the assault on Canada was ill-starred from its inception. Its success was jeopardized by delays in getting started, and the expedition was doomed by the unforeseen energy of Carlton and the unwillingness of the Canadians to respond to the call of liberty. In fact, it almost ended in disaster, for the New York frontier was wide open to invasion in the summer of 1776, while Washington was busy defending the lower Hudson. Only the initiative and determination of Arnold prevented Carlton from pushing down the Hudson to join Howe in New York, thus severing the republic at its birth.

Realizing that a successful defense required control of Lake Champlain, Arnold sent for New England shipwrights and constructed an odd fleet of two schooners, two sloops, four galleys, and eight gondolas (a type of heavy flat-bottomed barge). This forced Carlton to pause at the head of the lake in order to build his own fleet, and not until October was he ready to fight. Arnold drew up his ships in line of battle under the shelter of Valcour Island near the northern end of the lake, and there the British found him on October 20. Better armed and better manned, the British fleet had the better of the fight, but the Americans held on for seven hours until darkness ended the battle. During the night Arnold slipped away under cover of fog, ran his ships aground, burned them, and returned to Ticonderoga. Carlton, though now in control of the lake, decided that it was too late in the season to undertake a siege of the stone fortress and returned to Montreal. Arnold thus prevented an invasion of upper New York in 1776, and without Ticonderoga the British were deprived of a base of operations for an attack the following year.

The Hinge of Fate

The operations in the North in 1776 nevertheless predetermined, to a large extent, the British strategy for the following year. During the winter Carlton's chief lieutenant, Major General John Burgoyne, returned to London with a plan for an assault on the New York frontier which held the promise of ending the war with one quick stroke. Briefly, Burgoyne proposed a combined attack on Albany and the strategic Hudson Valley. He would lead one expedition down Lake Champlain and the Hudson River, while another force marched on Albany from the west by way of Lake Ontario and the Mohawk River. Simultaneously, Howe would move up from New York City effecting a junction with Burgoyne near Albany that would split off New England and break the back of the Revolution.

The king and Colonial Secretary Germain accepted Burgoyne's plan, but with surprising agreeability they also approved a plan submitted by Howe for an attack on Philadelphia, an inconsistency in strategic planning that contained the seeds of disaster. In approving Howe's move southward, Germain may have been guilty of overconfidence in British arms, but his reasoning seemed sound enough. By permitting Howe to divert Washington's attention toward Philadelphia, Germain hoped to remove the only military force of importance in the Hudson Valley, thereby permitting Burgoyne to cruise without resistance down the river into the welcoming arms of New York Loyalists.

Of the diverse British expeditions, Howe's was the first to get underway. Wary of a long march across New Jersey, whose farmers were skilled at knocking down bridges and felling trees across the road, Howe decided to move on Philadelphia by sea. Proceeding with his usual deliberation, he loaded his army on transports at the end of June and then sat in the harbor until July 23 before sailing. At Morristown, Washington was completely mystified. Burgoyne was already at Ticonderoga, and Washington could not believe that Howe intended to desert his fellow countryman. Days of anxious uncertainty were ended when the British fleet was sighted off Delaware Bay, and Washington began moving his ragged troops south through Philadelphia. Forts and sunken ships prevented Howe from entering the Delaware, and he again disappeared into the blue only to reappear in Chesapeake Bay. The British at last disembarked at the head of the bay on August 25, 1777.

Washington made his stand for the defense of Philadelphia at Brandywine Creek in southern Pennsylvania, almost on the Delaware line. He arrayed his army along the creek bank at the ford where the road from Baltimore to Philadelphia crossed, hoping to force the British into a frontal attack across the water. Howe declined battle on Washington's terms, however, and used a repeat performance of the tactics used at Long Island. Leaving most of his army at the ford, he led a strong force of five thousand men upriver where he could cross a series of small branches and descend on the American flank. An expedition of five thousand men is difficult to conceal, however, and Maryland farmers brought word of the British movement into the American camp. Unfortunately, Washington dismissed their stories as the exaggerated estimates of simple rustics and believed the British force was only a foraging party.

The British attack came on September 11. While Hessian troops demonstrated against the center, Howe and Cornwallis pounced on the right. Taken by surprise, the right wing dispersed in panic, but a courageous rearguard action by Nathanael Greene's corps enabled the American army to retire from the field in good order. Washington had been outgeneraled again, but worse was to come. After resting his troops several days, Howe, moving with unac-

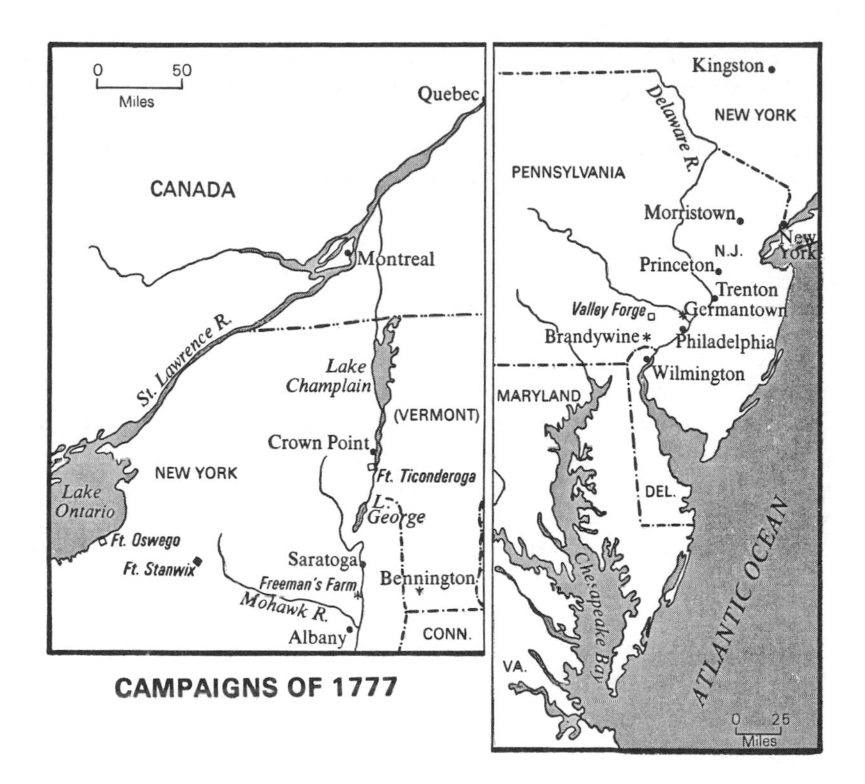

CAMPAIGNS OF 1777

customed speed, faked to the west, broke to the east, and ended up in Philadelphia on September 25.

Washington withdrew up the Schuylkill River to await an opportunity for battle while Congress set up shop in York, Pennsylvania. The loss of a capital would have crushed any other nation, but Americans were too provincial to look upon any one city as their center. In Paris, when Benjamin Franklin was informed that Howe had taken Philadelphia, he replied, "I beg your pardon, Sir, Philadelphia has taken Howe."

And so it seemed. Having performed his part of the British strategy, Howe ensconced himself in Philadelphia to enjoy the fruits of his victory, leaving Washington's army to face a cold and hungry winter in the woods. Yet despite his victorious campaign, he had failed to capture the Continental Congress, and he had not recovered any significant amount of imperial territory. In fact, he controlled only the city about him. Washington's army was still intact and presented a constant and embarrassing threat. To guard against surprise Howe placed a large garrison of nine thousand at Germantown, five miles northwest of Philadelphia, while other detachments were sent to open the Delaware River. That his placement was subject to the same disadvantages as the attempt to garrison New Jersey the previous winter seems not to have occurred to Howe. But Washington caught it and made plans for an attack on the Hessian outpost at Germantown.

His strategy was similar to that used in Trenton. To achieve surprise he proposed to descend on the town from four different directions, timed to meet simultaneously at the city. The complicated plan required perfect timing, and, unhappily for the strategist, it fell victim to a dense fog and green troops. Americans accidentally fired upon one another, panicked in the murky confusion, and retreated in disorder. After penetrating the Hessian defenses, the Americans, in the bitter phrase of General Anthony Wayne, "ran from victory." Washington then led his exhausted troops twenty-five miles westward up the Schuykill and went into winter quarters at Valley Forge.

Just as Sir William Howe snuggled into Philadelphia in the early autumn of 1777, the other feature of British campaign strategy was nearing a thunderous climax in the north. The Saratoga drama was played before the backdrop of the beautiful lake and mountain country of upper New York and Vermont, where the hardwood forests changed from a lush green to a variety of yellows and reds as the plot thickened. The leading protagonist was dashing "Gentleman Johnny" Burgoyne, engaging courtier and brilliant tactician, accompanied by his mistress, assorted troops and Indian irregulars, and a baggage train bearing his choice wines and extensive wardrobe. Arrayed against him was an untrained, ill-equipped "rabble in arms" (as Burgoyne contemptuously called them)—New England farmers who sprang suddenly from the murky forest to oppose the British advance.

Returning to Canada in May 1777, accompanied by three brigades of British regulars and three of German mercenaries, Burgoyne was able to muster an army of 9,500 men. This was augmented by several hundred Canadian and Loyalist militia and perhaps four hundred Indians. His impedimenta included 138 cannon for the reduction of Ticonderoga, scores of camp followers, and 1,500 horses to move the unending baggage train. The army departed from Fort St. Johns in late June, sailed up Lake Champlain to Crown Point, and then proceeded overland toward Ticonderoga, manned by a force of three thousand Americans under General Arthur St. Clair. Ticonderoga was a formidable bastion in the wilderness, a stone fortress protected by entrenchments designed by the Polish engineer Thaddeus Kosciusko. The trenches extended up Mt. Independence on the Vermont side of the lake, which was connected to the fort by a footbridge. The only weakness in the defense was Mount Defiance to the west of the fort, which St. Clair had left undefended partly for lack of manpower and partly because he felt its slopes were too precipitous for British cannon.

When the siege opened on July 2, the British disappointed American hopes for a frontal assault. Instead, Burgoyne's men scaled the undefended mountain and trained their cannon on the fort. Totally outmaneuvered, the American forces retreated overland to the Hudson. The most they could do was to slow Burgoyne's march by felling trees, but in the narrow gorges of the Adirondacks this proved impediment enough. Not till the end of July did Burgoyne reach the Hudson, and by then the hinge of fate was swinging to the American side.

General Philip Schuyler, the genial aristocrat whom New Englanders denounced as "that damned Dutchman," was saddled with the loss of Ticonderoga. In early August, Congress replaced him with Major General Horatio Gates, a professional soldier who had settled in Virginia a few years before the war and whose democratic manners appealed to New Englanders. Gates took command at a fortuitous moment, for by the time he arrived in Albany the whole military situation had changed. The northern army had increased to nearly nine thousand men, in part reinforcements sent by General Washington, including the newly repatriated Colonel Morgan and his regiment of Virginia riflemen, but in larger part by New England militiamen. Aroused by the invasion threat and rumors of atrocities by Burgoyne's Indians, thousands of Yankee farmers picked up their muskets and started off "agin Burgine."

Burgoyne, meantime, found himself in an ever more difficult situation. As he marched southward the forbidding wilderness closed in around him, and his tenuous supply route to Canada was at the mercy of the "Green Mountain Boys." When he sent a detachment of five hundred Germans to raid an American supply depot at Bennington, Vermont, they were surprised and captured by New Hampshire militia. Thereafter British foraging parties hovered close to camp.

The final blow to Burgoyne's fortunes was the defeat of the British force in the Mohawk Valley. Burgoyne's original plan had envisioned that his own advance would be complemented by a flanking attack on the Mohawk. This second expedition was commanded by Lieutenant Colonel Barry St. Leger, who landed on the New York side of Lake Ontario with a force of eight hundred regulars and Canadian militia. Joining him were a thousand Iroquois led by the Mohawk chief Joseph Brant, a cosmopolitan Indian educated at Dartmouth and who had been presented to the court of George III. The only place at which St. Leger could be stopped was Fort Stanwix at the head of the Mohawk River, manned by 450 Continentals. St. Leger appeared before the fort on August 2 and settled down to a siege. Recognizing the danger, Schuyler sent Benedict Arnold with a thousand men to relieve the fort. Arnold, aware that his army was too small to engage St. Leger, seized and dispatched a half-witted Tory named Hon Yost to the British camp with news that Arnold was at hand with an overwhelming force. The Native Americans, who had a mystical regard for the feeble-minded, believed the story and began drifting off into the woods. Abandoned by his Indian allies, St. Leger was forced to lift the siege and return to Canada. Burgoyne was on his own.

Though shaken by the news of St. Leger's failure, Burgoyne felt that he had no choice but to push on. He crossed to the west bank of the Hudson on September 13, cutting off any chance of easy retreat and committing his army to victory or surrender. On the advice of Arnold and Kosciusko, Gates chose for the defense of Albany a hilly ridge along the river called Bemis Heights, in front of which lay the broad expanse of Freeman's Farm. To the west of the farm was a low hill and a dense wood that protected the American left.

Burgoyne opened the battle on September 19, sending a flanking force to occupy the hill and woods. Urged by Benedict Arnold to take action, Gates sent Morgan and the Virginia riflemen into the woods to meet the British attack. Arnold sent in additional reinforcements, but Gates was unwilling to commit his entire army. Dusk finally forced an American retirement and the Battle of Freeman's Farm came to an end. Burgoyne held the field of battle, but the

Americans proved quite effective in the woods. Burgoyne's losses were almost double theirs, and the British thrust had been halted.

For the next two weeks, the opposing forces menaced each other across the yellowing fields. Neither felt very comfortable or sure of victory. Burgoyne's once-fine army was now tattered, exhausted, and critically low on supplies. The general continued to nurse hope of relief from Sir Henry Clinton, commanding in New York City, but after Howe took the main British force to Philadelphia, Clinton could do little. The Americans, meanwhile, nervously argued among themselves. Gates, aware of the unreliability of militia in the open field, wished to play a waiting game that forced Burgoyne to attack his well-entrenched hill. Arnold, on the other hand, felt that idleness would break American morale and send the farmers home to their crops. So vehemently did he insist on action that Gates relieved him of command.

On October 7, Burgoyne made a final effort to push past the Americans with a "reconnaissance in force." If the flanking probe succeeded he would order a general assault the next day. A detachment of 1,500 entered the woods on the American left, and Gates sent Morgan's riflemen to counteract it. After a short struggle, the British retired toward their entrenchment, but the riflemen, without orders to pursue, hesitated. At that moment Arnold galloped onto the field on a great brown horse. "Now come on, boys. . . . We'll have them all in hell before night," he shouted and led an attack on the nearest British redoubt. Beaten back, he reorganized the troops from various regiments around him, threw a motley force against a second redoubt, and carried it, sustaining a leg wound himself. Though dusk prevented further action, Burgoyne's position was now untenable, and he ordered a withdrawal that night.

The British retired a few miles up the Hudson to previously prepared redoubts on high ground near Saratoga. Gates followed slowly, while his militia infiltrated through the woods, surrounded the British, and cut off further retreat to Ticonderoga. When Burgoyne offered to parley, Gates demanded unconditional surrender. Burgoyne instead suggested a convention by which his army would return to England on condition that it would not again serve in America. Uncertain of the whereabouts of Clinton (then withdrawing to New York after an attack on the Hudson highlands), Gates agreed. On October 17, 1777, Burgoyne's once splendid army, deserted by its Indian allies and reduced to five thousand ragged men, laid down its arms.

The convention negotiated at Saratoga was never carried out. General Washington felt Gates had been overly lenient because nothing prevented Burgoyne's army from relieving other troops in England, who might be sent to America. He thus took advantage of minor British violations of the agreement to order them detained in Boston. Eventually they were transferred to Virginia where they remained prisoners for the duration.

A World War

Saratoga initiated a chain of events that converted the American Revolution from a domestic spat between Britain and her colonies into a world war that involved much of western Europe. France had kept a watchful eye on American events from the beginning, plotting revenge for the humiliating defeat of 1763 and hoping to gain advantage from the breakup of Britain's overextended empire. The outbreak of hostilities in 1775, however, posed a dilemma for French Foreign Minister Charles Gravier, Comte de Vergennes. The king was suspicious of the republican doctrines being espoused across the Atlantic; and Finance Minister Turgot predicted that substantial aid to the rebellious colonies would bankrupt the government. Vergennes thus compromised on limited aid privately administered. As agent in the business he chose a man with all the credentials—Pierre Beaumarchais, amateur playwright (author of "The Barber of Seville" and "The Marriage of Figaro"), dashing courtier who charmed even the experienced Madame Pompadour, and professional espionage agent.

In 1775, Beaumarchais organized the fictitious mercantile firm of Roderigue Hortalez and Company, and the governments of France and Spain each supplied him with gifts of one million livres. Beaumarchais then got in touch with Arthur Lee, colonial agent of Virginia who had lingered in London, and soon French munitions were flowing to America by way of the West Indies. Thus the Bourbon powers, acting in their own interests, extended the first "foreign aid" before a single American agent reached French soil.

In the spring of 1776, the Committee of Secret Correspondence, Congress's agency for foreign relations, sent Silas Deane, a Connecticut merchant, on a mission to France. After the Declaration of Independence, Benjamin Franklin was added to the delegation in Paris, and the American commissioners were instructed to obtain military support and a trade agreement. Contacted by Beaumarchais on his arrival, Deane recognized him as an agent of the French government and quickly entered into a contract for the purchase of munitions. The Frenchman neglected to mention his earlier arrangement with Arthur Lee, and Deane knew nothing of it, since Lee had not seen fit to confide in the Continental Congress. By the time Franklin arrived in December 1776, the two had amassed enough arms and clothing to supply an army of 30,000. Extra space on the vessels was filled with French silks and wines consigned to Deane's business partner in Philadelphia, Robert Morris.

At that juncture Arthur Lee crossed the channel from London, already piqued at being superseded by Franklin and Deane. A suspicious, tactless, overbearing man, he soon alienated foreign minister Vergennes, who hinted to Franklin that negotiations would be easier if Lee were off seeking alliances in eastern Europe. Lee also objected to the contract that Deane had negotiated, claiming that by his earlier understanding with Beaumarchais the supplies were to be a gift. His protest ignored, Lee quickly concluded that Beaumarchais and Deane, perhaps Franklin as well, planned to pocket the money paid by the United States, and he returned home to convey his suspicions to the Continental Congress.

The Deane-Lee embroglio polarized factions in Congress. Richard Henry Lee rallied to his "brother's defense" and brought in train his old radical friends from Massachusetts, the Adamses. Delegates from the middle states, led by Robert Morris, generally sided with Deane. Although most of the delegates remained aloof from the factional struggle, the temptation to regard the arms as a gift was great. As a result, Beaumarchais was never reimbursed, though in 1835 the United States finally paid his heirs 800,000 francs. In 1778, Congress recalled Silas Deane, partly because of Lee's accusations, but mostly because of Deane's propensity to issue American military commissions to every European adventurer who desired one.

In the meantime, Franklin and Deane worked smoothly and efficiently after Lee's departure. Deane administered the flow of military supplies, blandly mingling public and private business (at times even mixing the two accounts), while Franklin handled the diplomacy. The French were willing to furnish secret aid to the new republic, but they balked at an open military alliance. Except for the raid on Trenton, Washington was defeated every time he took the field; and, Vergennes demanded assurances that the Americans could hold up their end of the war. In addition, the French navy was unprepared for war. Vergennes was advised that it would be the spring of 1778 before a squadron could be fitted out for service in America.

While he waited for good news from America, Franklin kept himself busy watching balloon ascensions (the rage in Paris that year), inventing bifocal glasses, converting his mouth organ into a harmonica, and working out a plan for daylight saving time. His renown as a scientist and inventor, his friendship with several of the *philosophes,* made Franklin a great favorite in Paris. With his straggling gray hair, fur cap, spectacles, and plain Quaker-like clothes, he was viewed no doubt as something of a curiosity, an impression which Franklin did nothing to dispel. At last in December 1777, news of Burgoyne's surrender reached Paris, and Franklin promptly suggested that it might be a propitious moment to open peace talks with Britain. Vergennes was not fooled, but he conveyed the threat to the king, who had been dragging his feet on the question of war. With the king's apprehensions overcome, Vergennes presented Franklin with the draft of a treaty modeled on proposals made by Franklin a year earlier.

The treaty of alliance was signed in February 1778. France recognized American independence and offered formal military aid. If France entered the war—a near certainty—neither would conclude a peace with Britain without the consent of the other. In addition, the United States would help to defend the French islands in the West Indies against British attack. A separate commercial agreement provided for mutual trade on a most-favored-nation basis. France declared war on England in May 1778, and then turned to the task of bringing Spain into the alliance. Though willing to supply small amounts of financial aid to Americans, Spain was cool to the idea of entering the war. It had no love for this New World society of upstart merchants bubbling with subversive notions of republicanism, and its West Indies empire was terribly vulnerable to British attack. Yet the possibility of revenge for past defeats was alluring, and France did promise aid in recovering Gibraltar and Florida. In the spring of 1779, Spain signed an alliance with France and entered the war, but it neither recognized nor ever became a formal ally of the American republic.

Spain's military contributions were nevertheless of considerable importance in achieving American independence. The Spanish governor of Louisiana, Bernardo de Galvez (after whom Galveston, Texas, is named), proved to be one of the most successful generals of the war. He cleared the Gulf coast of British troops and captured the strategic naval base of Pensacola. The French and Spanish fleets combined outnumbered the British, and their threat to such British colonies as Jamaica forced the British to divert resources to the West Indies. This diversion made possible the final American victory at Yorktown.

Winter at Valley Forge

While Franklin worked to enlarge the war, Washington and the American army suffered through a vicious winter at Valley Forge. The camp lay in an area swept clean of food and fodder during the autumn campaign around Philadelphia. What meat and flour remained, the thrifty German farmers preferred to sell to the British for hard money. Worst of all, the ever-inefficient commissariat broke down under the strain, leaving the army to starve and shiver, without food, clothing, or blankets in their hastily built huts.

As if the winter were not punishment enough, Washington was further discomfited by congressional interference and political intrigue. He had long been the object of some suspicion in Congress. Aware of the usual fate of republics, Congress was leery of military heroes and reluctant to permit the army independence of action. Moreover, some were growing skeptical of Washington's abilities. Would it not be better, they wondered, to entrust America's fortunes to a general who could at least boast a victory in the field? These two notions conjoined in November 1777, when Congress created a Board of War to supervise army operations. Horatio Gates, hero of Saratoga, was appointed to head the board, a position that made him technically superior to Washington.

The move did not threaten Washington's position, but it did expose him to intrigue. Among those to see an opportunity was Thomas Conway, one of the more unfortunate protégés of Silas Deane. In a search for military talent, Congress had authorized Silas Deane to grant commissions to European professionals willing to serve in the American army. Deane issued far too many commissions, and Washington was driven to distraction by foreign generals petulantly demanding regiments to command. Some of these foreign officers—notably the Marquis de Lafayette, Thaddeus Kosciusko, the Baron de Kalb, and Count Casimir Pulaski—were invaluable additions to the army, but others were worthless adventurers. Among the worst was Conway, an Irish-born colonel in the French army, who appeared in Philadelphia with a promise from Deane that he might be a general. In December, 1777, Congress made him inspector general of the army over the objections of Washington, who feared the appointment would cause mass resignations. Conway thereupon became an enemy of Washington's and wrote an incautious letter to Gates, hinting that he hoped Gates would supersede Washington. Washington learned of the letter and, without discovering the details, dashed off a stinging rebuke to Gates. The incident brought the intrigues against Washington into the open, rallied his supporters in Congress, and Conway was removed.

The only bright spot of that awful season was the appearance of Frederick William Augustus, Baron von Steuben. A professional soldier, Steuben arrived in February 1778, armed with letters of introduction from Franklin and Deane, letters which called him "a Lieutenant General in the King of Prussia's service," an aide-de-camp of the great Frederick himself. The rank, title, and position were all false; actually he had been only a captain, and that fourteen years earlier. He was, however, an able soldier with some experience and a martial bearing. Pleased with his attitude and address, Washington made him inspector general and charged him with training the army.

The task was not easy. The baron prepared a rudimentary drill, which was translated, printed page by page on the army's solitary press, and distributed to brigade commanders. He formed a model company of 100 men which he himself trained and drilled, and which in turn he used as a cadre for other companies. Steuben's ignorance of English and his semicomprehensible French necessitated an interpreter, and the troopers' ignorance of the facts of military life led him frequently to strong language. Once in utter exasperation he sputtered to his translator, "Viens, Walker, mon ami, mon bon ami! Sacre! Goddam de gaucheries of dese badauts. Je ne puis plus. I can curse dem no more!" But his popularity among all ranks was high, and he taught the army how to march in column instead of straggling along single file, and how to deploy from column to line of battle. He taught it the use of the bayonet, which had previously been used mostly for cooking meat, and the all-important drill for reloading a musket. In short, he converted the American army into a disciplined force able to match the British army on its own terms. Never again would Washington be defeated in the open field.

Stalemate in the North

As the meadows and farms around Philadelphia turned green with the approach of spring, the new British commander, Sir Henry Clinton, who had replaced Howe during the autumn, made plans for the coming campaign. Cabinet orders to abandon Philadelphia met his approval, for he had disliked the operation from the first. It had accomplished none of Howe's original aims, and the British army was a virtual hostage to an inimical countryside. To return to New York by sea was the safest route; but, it meant abandoning the Philadelphia Loyalists and leaving New York exposed while the army was aboard ship. Clinton finally decided to pack the Loyalists and their belongings on the ships while the army went overland.

Evacuating Philadelphia on June 18, 1778, Clinton began the long march across New Jersey to Sandy Hook. Washington moved his own force into New Jersey and followed on a parallel road, waiting for an opportunity to strike. Not all the American commanders favored an attack, however. Most vocal in opposition was General Charles Lee, who felt that instead of hindering the British they ought to build a "bridge of gold" across New Jersey. Washington nevertheless ordered his advance guard under Lafayette to harass the British and attack if opportunity arose. As the advance unit gradually built up to five thousand men, Lee, outranking Lafayette, demanded the right to command it and Washington consented.

On the evening of June 27, the British were camped at Monmouth Court

House. Washington ordered Lee to attack as they resumed their march the next morning. Opposed to the whole idea, Lee did not bother to reconnoiter or form a battle plan. Perhaps he anticipated defeat, perhaps he felt he could handle each problem as the battle progressed. The morning of June 28 dawned extremely hot, the temperature reached one hundred degrees by noon, and the American attack was uncoordinated and sluggish. The British regulars wheeled into line and quickly stopped the advance units, whereupon Lee ordered a withdrawal. Washington, rushing to the scene with the rest of the army, found Lee's troops in disorderly retreat, the British in pursuit. Angered to the quick, he dashed up to Lee, cursed his stupidity, and removed him from command. He then rallied the Americans behind a ravine, stopped the British assault, and attempted a counterattack. At dusk both armies collapsed in exhaustion. During the night the British moved off toward New York leaving their wounded behind.

Washington could claim a technical victory, having been left with the field, but otherwise the battle was indecisive, with about three hundred casualties on each side. Charles Lee demanded a court martial, which was quickly granted. He was found guilty of disobedience of orders and misbehavior before the enemy; he was suspended for a year, and Congress later dismissed him from the service.

As the British settled into New York, Washington encamped once again at White Plains, noting with satisfaction that after two years of fighting the British were back where they started. Except now they were on the defensive. Even so, the lengthy and dull siege of New York presented its own problems of boredom and discipline for the American commander. The only important action of 1779 was the capture of Stony Point by "Mad Anthony" Wayne and his Pennsylvania light brigade. The rest of the army grew stale from lack of action, and its numbers dwindled.

Morale deteriorated further in the severe winters of 1779–80 and 1780–81 at Morristown, where the army faced greater agonies than at Valley Forge. In January 1781, a dangerous mutiny broke out in the Pennsylvania line. The threat was ended by timely promises of supplies and pay from the Pennsylvania Assembly, but when the New Jersey troops mutinied a few days later, Washington restored discipline by shooting the ringleaders.

The women who accompanied the army were also a source of concern to Washington during the routine of the siege. Perhaps not surprisingly, given the attitudes of the day, Washington never viewed them as a source of morale or a potential work force. Although most of the women who accompanied the army were probably wives of soldiers, Washington and other officers regarded them as a nuisance. Washington repeatedly issued orders that women were not to ride in military wagons if they were able to walk. When provisions were scarce, as they were in the formidable winter of 1779–80, only married women were allowed to draw rations, and unmarried women were "sent off." Washington also regarded female camp followers as an embarrassment. When he marched through Philadelphia on his way to the Brandywine he gave strict orders that the baggage wagons were "to avoid the City entirely. . . . Not a woman belonging to the army is to be seen with the troops on their march." However, even

Washington ultimately had to concede that, in a sense, women did "belong" with the army. As the army settled into more or less permanent quarters during the siege, women were employed as cooks and clothes washers. An orderly book for a New York regiment allowed women "two shillings a dozen for all articles which they wash reckoning both large and small provided they find their own soape." Washington himself recognized the value of women as nurses, since this was obviously related to their domestic skills. However, because most of the skilled tasks of nursing were performed by male surgeon's mates, the work of the females was mostly custodial and therefore ill-paid. Washington's rationale for recruiting women for this labor was that the men employed in such tasks would be "entirely lost in the proper line of their duty."

The only notable event of 1780, was the treason of Benedict Arnold, itself evidence of deteriorating American morale. Though probably the army's most effective combat officer, Arnold repeatedly had been forced to stand aside while less capable men were promoted, often for political reasons, ahead of him. In February 1777, Congress denied him a promotion to major general primarily because his home state of Connecticut already had two generals of that rank. After losing his leg at Saratoga, Arnold was given command of Philadelphia when the British left. A military hero, he was swept up in the social life of the city; but the round of activities proved too much for his meager army pay, and he was soon in financial difficulties. Facing a possible court martial for misusing army materiel, he persuaded Washington to transfer him to the command of West Point on the Hudson. Even before this, however—indeed, shortly after his marriage to Peggy Shippen, daughter of a Tory physician in Philadelphia—he had begun a secret correspondence with General Clinton that continued for sixteen months. Ultimately, it led to a bargain by which he agreed to turn over West Point to the British for £10,000.

The plot was discovered when Clinton's agent, Major John André, was captured while crossing American lines, and Arnold escaped to New York City. His motives for treason remain a mystery. He later claimed that he considered the Revolution a failure; by helping to end it he was doing a service to his country. Yet he bargained long and hard over the financial and military rewards for his services. His marriage, disappointment at seeing incompetents promoted over his head, and a desire for money were doubtless all factors.

Despite difficulty holding his army together, Washington managed to send detachments west for the defense of the frontier. In 1779, an expedition under General John Sullivan broke the power of the Iroquois in central New York. In the same year Washington's fellow Virginians challenged British control of the Northwest. Claiming title to the territory south of the Great Lakes under their charter of 1609, the Virginians had extensive speculative interests in the region. In 1778, Governor Patrick Henry gave the task of conquering the Northwest to George Rogers Clark, bolstering it with a commission as colonel of Virginia militia. After recruiting a band of 175 frontiersmen in Pittsburgh, Clark started down the Ohio to the Illinois country. There he found the French population disposed to cooperate and quickly captured Kaskaskia on the Mississippi and Vincennes on the Wabash.

Learning of Clark's adventure in December 1778, the British marched out from Detroit and recaptured Vincennes. Clark, wintering at Kaskaskia, hiked his men across ice-covered prairie and flooded rivers, reappeared outside Vincennes in February, and compelled the British to surrender. He wanted then to push on to Detroit, but his shivering and exhausted men were unable to move. The campaign thus ended in a stalemate, but Clark's heroics did give the United States a substantial claim to the Northwest at the peace table.

Campaign in the South

After the British retired to New York, the main theater of war shifted to the southern states. In some respects, the British move was a tacit concession that the northern states were hopelessly lost. The staple-exporting colonies had always fitted better into the imperial economy, and evidence of substantial Loyalist sentiment in Georgia and the Carolinas bared the possibility that at least part of the empire might be salvaged. Primitive roads and broad, unbridged rivers, moreover, made it difficult for the Americans to send reinforcements southwards, while the British had easy access from the sea.

Thus far, the southern states had escaped the brunt of the war. Their turn came in December 1778, when a British army landed near Savannah, brushed aside the Georgia militia, and took possession of the state. Congress hastily created a Southern Department, placing Benjamin Lincoln in charge of an army of a thousand Continentals and five thousand militia. Making Charleston his headquarters, Lincoln undertook to recover Georgia. Two forays into the state were stopped by the British, and the year 1779 was consumed in futile maneuvers across and through the swamps and rivers of South Carolina.

Clinton himself appeared in the South with an army of 14,000 in the spring of 1780, laid Charleston under siege, and forced Lincoln to surrender his entire army. Clinton then returned to New York, leaving Lord Cornwallis in charge of mop-up operations. Tories flocked to the British standard, and by midsummer South Carolina was ostensibly under British control. To hold the state Cornwallis set up a string of garrisons from Augusta on the Savannah River to Fort Ninety-Six on the Saluda, Camden on the Wateree, and Cheraw on the Peedee. The disposition was reminiscent of his effort to garrison New Jersey in 1776—and consequently subject to the same pitfalls. Each was exposed to surprise attack, and British supply lines were constantly menaced by the guerilla forces of Andrew Pickens, Thomas Sumter, and the "Swamp Fox" Francis Marion.

In June 1780, Congress placed Horatio Gates in command of the Southern Department without consulting Washington. With a corps of Maryland and Delaware Continentals under Baron de Kalb, Gates started south, picking up militia as he went. He hoped to surprise the British garrison at Camden, but word of his advance reached Cornwallis, who hastened to the rescue. The two armies stumbled into each other near Camden on August 16. Gates arrayed his army along a road, militia on one side, Continentals on the other. Cornwallis accordingly sent his regulars smashing into the militia, who broke and ran, carrying General Gates with them. Fighting gallantly as a rear guard, the Con-

tinentals turned back two British assaults, until at last, with Baron de Kalb dead, they too retired under the assaults of Banastre Tarlton's Loyalist cavalry.

Three days later Gates was in Hillsboro, North Carolina, 160 miles away. To say the least, he had managed one of the fastest disengagement actions in history. Gates's explanation was that he wished to get far enough from the British to raise a new army; but Congress, disillusioned with him at last, asked Washington to name a new commander. He chose his ablest lieutenant, Nathanael Greene. By the time Greene arrived in the late autumn the military situation had improved substantially.

Exploiting his victory, Cornwallis started north in September 1780, advancing on two fronts. In the east he moved the main army of regulars; scouting the mountains on the west was a detachment of Tory militia under Major Patrick Ferguson. When Ferguson suddenly found himself opposed by a large gathering of riflemen from the mountains of Virginia and North Carolina, he retired to King's Mountain, some thirty miles west of Charlotte on the border between North and South Carolina. On October 7, 1780, some nine hundred riflemen swarmed up the hill firing in frontier fashion, from tree to tree, and forced the Tories to surrender. The battle of King's Mountain, notable because it was an exclusively American fight, left Cornwallis's flank exposed and made him retrace his steps to Camden.

When he assumed command of the American army, General Greene felt too weak to take decisive action. Dividing his army, he sent Colonel Daniel Morgan to threaten Fort Ninety-Six while he encamped at Cheraw Hill on the falls of the Peedee to watch Cornwallis. Anxious to protect his flank, Cornwallis sent Banastre Tarlton against Morgan, and after much maneuvering the two met on January 17, 1781, at the Cowpens a few miles from King's Mountain.

Morgan's tactics in the battle were quite unorthodox. He chose open ground with the Broad River at his back, which prevented any retreat. "Had I crossed the river," he explained after the battle, "one half the militia would immediately have abandoned me." Then he arranged his army in a way that would counter the familiar British tactics of disciplined volley and terrorizing bayonet charges—and at the same time accommodate the tendency of American militia to flee. Sharp shooters hidden in front harassed the British advance, aiming at "the men with the epaulets." Then stood a line of militia required only to shoot twice before retiring to the rear of the Continentals. The plan worked to perfection. The British line, ragged and staggering by the time it reached Morgan' Continentals, broke and fled after a half hour of fighting, leaving 900 casualties and prisoners behind (of a total force of 1,100).

Cornwallis rushed west hoping to trap Morgan's battle weary army, but Morgan retreated into North Carolina where he joined Greene. Adapting to this kind of hit-and-run warfare, Cornwallis destroyed his baggage wagons, took only such supplies as his troops could carry, and started after the Americans. Greene fled northward across the Dan River into the security of Virginia, beating Cornwallis by a day. Reinforced by a large body of Virginia militia, aroused by the sudden threat to their homes, Greene took the offensive and met Cornwallis on March 15 at Guilford Court House. He arrayed his army in the Morgan manner, for Cowpens had taught both generals how to use militia. An extra touch, however, was a hidden cavalry regiment under "Light Horse Harry" Lee, which slammed into the British just as their attack faltered in front of the Continental line.

After repelling two British charges, Greene retired from the field rather than risk a defeat. The British, who suffered some five hundred casualties, could not afford many more such victories. Moreover, Cornwallis concluded that the Carolinas would never be secure so long as the Americans had an untouched sanctuary in Virginia. After resting his army for a month at Wilmington, Cornwallis started north in April 1781, hoping to distract Virginia enough to give the British a secure hold on the rest of the South. The scheme backfired, for Greene instead of pursuing Cornwallis, sidestepped him and headed west to the mountains. There he was joined by the partisan forces of Pickens and Marion; and as Cornwallis moved into Virginia, Greene captured the British bases in South Carolina, one by one. By the autumn of 1781, the British possessed only Charleston. The long campaign in the Carolinas had come to naught.

The Road to Yorktown

The British invasion of Virginia, which ended in disaster at Yorktown, was plagued from the start by differences over strategy. Despite the hopes of the king and his ministers, the cautious Clinton had never envisioned a complete conquest of the South. Instead he planned to hold strategic parts of the coastline and any additional territory that Loyalists could command. He thus had serious misgivings about the invasion of Virginia, but Cornwallis had the support of Lord George Germain. During the preceding winter Clinton had sent the now-British officer Benedict Arnold to preoccupy Virginia with amphibious raids. Arnold landed on the James River in early January, marched thirty miles to undefended Richmond, and wrote a cheeky letter to Governor Jefferson demanding a ransom for the capital. Jefferson instead called out the state's militia to resist the invasion. Arnold retired to Portsmouth on the lower James, where the British had established a permanent base the previous year. During his two-day "invasion" Arnold destroyed substantial amounts of arms and powder that Jefferson had been stockpiling for General Greene.

Greene's move into South Carolina left Virginia defenseless. Untested militia, organized as a home defense corps, proved helpless against Arnold, and in May 1781, Cornwallis joined his 5,000 regulars to the 2,000 already at Portsmouth. In response to Governor Jefferson's frantic pleas for help, Washington sent Lafayette with 1,200 Continental troops. Although augmented by several thousand Virginia militia, Lafayette's force was too small to challenge Cornwallis, and the British devastated central Virginia with ease. One raiding party headed by Tarleton struck Charlottesville and sent Jefferson and the Virginia assembly scampering ignominiously over the Blue Ridge. Cornwallis himself set up headquarters at Jefferson's Elk Hill plantation. In later years Jefferson recalled bitterly the destruction that the British commander loosed on his property. The British burned barns and fences, destroyed large quantities of corn and tobacco, and either ate or carried away his farm animals. Cornwallis also took twenty-seven of Jefferson's slaves with him when he departed. "Had this been to give them freedom he would have done right," Jefferson later wrote, "but it was to consign them to inevitable death from the small pox and putrid fever then raging in his camp." This was indeed the fate of most of the slaves; Jefferson recovered only five of them.

In midsummer Cornwallis retired to the Williamsburg peninsula to rest his army. Clinton ordered him to establish a supply base at Old Point Comfort, but after visiting the point Cornwallis decided it was unsuitable and moved his army to Yorktown, a few miles up the York River from Chesapeake Bay. Lafayette, shadowing him, settled in Williamsburg. From there the young Frenchman wrote Washington suggesting that with adequate reinforcements and temporary naval control of the Chesapeake he might trap Cornwallis and force his surrender.

Washington had big plans for a campaign that summer. For the first time in years he could count on French naval support. The French had tried and failed to recapture Savannah in 1779, and they had occupied Newport, Rhode

Island, in 1780. But the French navy seemed more interested in looting British islands in the West Indies. When Washington learned that a squadron under Admiral de Grasse was assigned to North American waters in 1781, he met with General de Rochambeau in Wethersfield, Connecticut, and the two planned a concerted attack on New York City. Then came word from de Grasse that he was sailing, not for New York, but to the Chesapeake. Arriving almost simultaneously was the letter from Lafayette suggesting that Cornwallis had trapped himself. A quick decision was made. Washington transported his army across the Hudson, made a feint toward Staten Island, and quickly marched south. Ferried down the bay by the French fleet, the allied army reached Yorktown by September 28—7,800 French troops and 12,000 Americans against Cornwallis's army of 7,000 effectives.

The siege of Yorktown was conducted in the fashion dictated by the military textbooks of the day. With plenty of time to prepare, Cornwallis fortified the town with redoubts, circular earthworks guarded by pointed stakes and armed with cannon. The allies resorted to the spade, digging approach trenches which zigzagged ever closer to the British lines. The aim was to advance far enough in trenches so the redoubt could be taken by a sudden rush of infantry. On the night of October 14, allied forces stormed redoubts nine and ten on the British left along the river. Alexander Hamilton, Washington's aide-de-camp, successfully led the American charge on one, while the French carried the other. From these key points the allies could shell the town with artillery.

Clinton received word in New York that unless he sent immediate help he could expect "the worst." One supply expedition had been turned back by the French hovering off the Virginia capes. He hastily put together another and sailed on October 19—ironically, the very day that Cornwallis surrendered. The victory at Yorktown ended the serious fighting and virtually assured American independence. Further maneuvering was confined to the peace negotiators. The war faded into a seemingly endless siege of New York and Charleston (evacuated in July 1782), punctuated only by Washington's fears that Americans would relax their efforts now that victory was in sight.

The Peacemakers

The peace negotiations began well before Yorktown. Galvanized by the French alliance into pondering American war aims, Congress in 1779 sent John Adams to Britain to explore the possibility of peace. He was instructed to insist on independence, possession of Canada, and a boundary that extended to the Mississippi River on the west and the thirty-first parallel (the northern boundary of Florida) on the south. The military situation did not justify such claims, and Congress retreated under French diplomatic pressure. In June 1781, a new peace commission of Franklin, Adams, and John Jay was instructed to insist only on independence; on all other matters it was to be governed by the position of France.

Unpretentious as they were, the new instructions reflected the deteriorating American position. In addition to nearly uniform British success in the

South, Congress was in deep financial trouble. The war was financed in the time-honored American way, by issuing paper money. Floated at first in conservative amounts, the money was generally accepted and circulated nationally. Eventually, the lack of tax revenue and the requirements of the army forced Congress to frequent use of the printing press. The states financed the war in the same way; and, by 1779 the nation was deluged with public paper. As it became increasingly clear that such vast amounts of money could never be redeemed, people became reluctant to accept it, and the value depreciated. By the end of 1779 a Spanish milled gold dollar was worth a hundred Continental paper dollars. In the spring of 1780, Congress took the drastic step of devaluating the currency by calling in the old issues and exchanging them for new bills at the ratio of forty to one. Even this expedient was no permanent solution, for the new bills would depreciate unless Congress mobilized the financial resources of the nation.

The irony was that the nation remained generally prosperous during the war. The needs of the armies for food and supplies presented splendid opportunities for profit to farmers and merchants alike. Both British and French paid their bills in hard cash, bringing more specie into circulation than the colonists had ever seen. Manufactures bloomed behind the protective wall of the British blockade. Foreign trade declined, but commercial interests compensated by investing in privateers. This form of legalized piracy brought fabulous profits to the lucky. In the year 1780 alone, when Washington struggled along with a mere 7,000 men, New England sent 165 ships and 6,000 men to prey on British commerce. So successful were these speedy marauders that they cost England about 2,000 ships, £18 million, and 12,000 captured sailors.

The economy, moreover, was not seriously damaged by the runaway inflation. Merchants, farmers, and craftsmen merely raised their prices to compensate for the depreciation of the currency. There was no important salaried or wage-earning class to be hurt by inflation. The army suffered, to be sure, but the part-time militia supplemented their incomes by farming. The problem, in short, was not poverty but the inability of government to tap the reservoir of wealth.

In the summer of 1781, amidst general recognition of the need for administrative reform, Congress created the office of Superintendent of Finance and filled it with Robert Morris, a wealthy Philadelphia merchant. Morris took office with a comprehensive plan for placing the nation's finances on a businesslike footing. To meet the immediate emergency he issued "Morris notes," bills of credit backed by his own fortune, which temporarily solved the currency problem. As a more long-range solution, he proposed a national bank that could loan the government the funds it needed. In December 1781, Congress chartered the Bank of North America, a partnership of business and government modeled on the Bank of England. These measures eased the financial crisis, and after the autumn of 1781, the American situation improved.

Had the peace treaty been signed immediately after Yorktown, the United States might have gained more in the settlement than it finally did. For just as the American scene brightened, British prospects became increasingly dark. In utter isolation by 1780, Britain sullenly watched the northern powers—Russia,

Sweden, Denmark, and Holland—form a League of Armed Neutrality to defend themselves against British seizures on the high seas. In moody revenge, Britain declared war on Holland in 1780, and swept down on the Dutch island of St. Eustatius in the West Indies. Not only did the move add to its enemies, but the British West Indian squadron, preoccupied with getting its booty safely back to England, neglected de Grasse and permitted the French to gain control of the Chesapeake. In 1781, France took the initiative in India, while Spain seized Minorca in the Mediterranean and began a siege of Gibraltar.

At home the British government faced a major domestic crisis. The cutoff of colonial markets depressed British industry, and unemployed laborers roamed the northern cities. In June 1781, anti-Catholic riots in London rocked the government to its foundations. The Yorkshire Association, formed that spring, won wide support among the gentry by demanding reform of the House of Commons. Seizing the opportunity, the Whigs focused the attention of reformers on the royal household and demanded a professional civil service. The ministry of Lord North teetered throughout the year and finally collapsed in March 1782.

It may well be, as some historians have suggested, that Britain weathered its own "French Revolution" in the year 1781. Public reaction against violence following the London riots took the steam out of the reform movement and perhaps forestalled any further threat to the monarchy, while the resignation of North silenced the critics of the government and paved the way for the formation of a conciliatory Whig ministry under the Marquis of Rockingham. With domestic tranquility restored, the British peace negotiators were able to sit down at the diplomatic poker table with strong hands.

Nevertheless, the situation both internally and throughout the world was such as to require an accommodation with the former colonies. The Earl of Shelburne, the new colonial secretary, was an old friend of Benjamin Franklin's, and in the spring of 1782, he sent a special emissary, Richard Oswald to Paris. Franklin and Oswald were in the midst of hard bargaining when Foreign Secretary Charles James Fox muddied the waters by sending his own agent to Paris. The death of Lord Rockingham in July 1782, relieved the tangle. The king asked Shelburne to be first minister, Fox promptly resigned, and Shelburne emerged at the head of a united government disposed to compromise.

As the negotiations proceeded in earnest in the fall of 1782, the Americans found themselves hampered by the instructions to rely on the advice of France. It was clear that France was in the war to further her own interests, and if the commissioners depended on French diplomacy they would secure little more than American independence. While maintaining the front of allied unity, they decided to conclude a separate agreement with England and then present Vergennes with *a fait accompli.*

The boundaries of the new republic were traced on John Mitchell's map of 1755, the inaccuracies of which occasioned many a future border dispute. The northern boundary followed the St. Croix River in Maine, the forty-fifth parallel to the St. Lawrence, and the Great Lakes. The western boundary ran from the Lake of the Woods (erroneously marked on the map as the source of

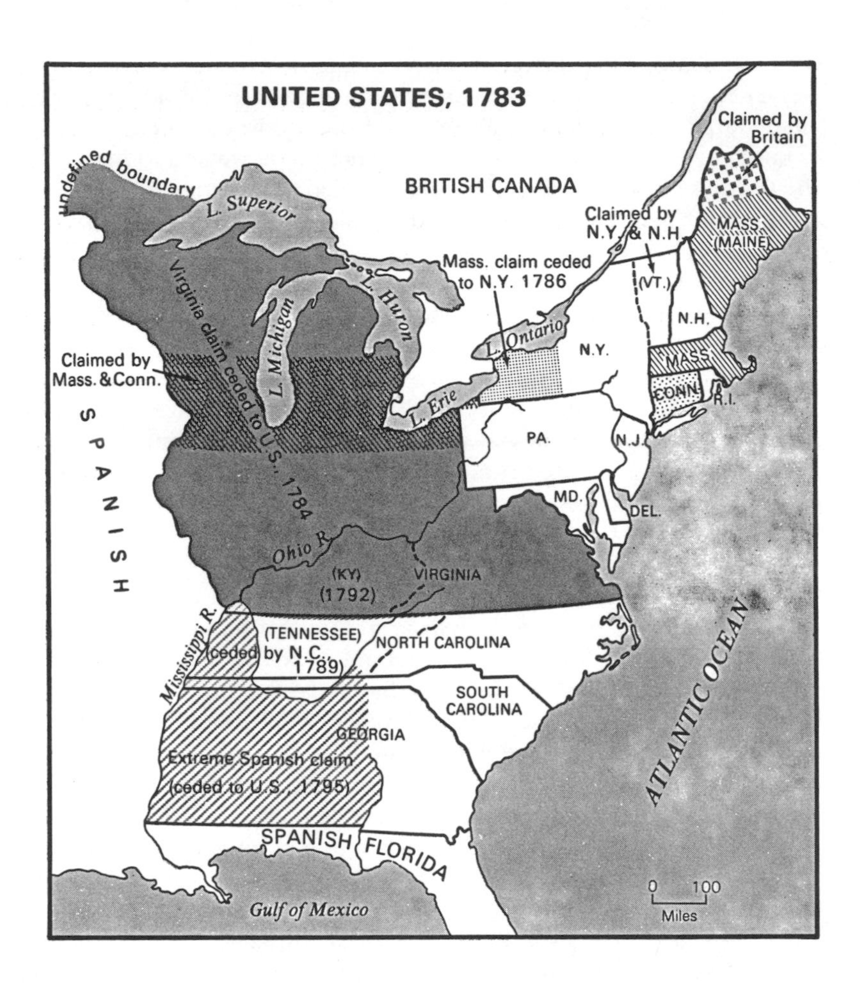

the Mississippi) down the Mississippi River to Spanish Louisiana. The southern boundary followed the thirty-first parallel, the northern border of Florida.

Minor problems seemed to give the most trouble. At the insistence of John Adams, the British permitted Americans who fished off the Grand Banks to dry their catch on the shores of Newfoundland. When the British demanded that confiscated Loyalist property be restored, the Americans countered with a bill for British depredations in the South. After standing firm for the Loyalists through weeks of bickering, the British finally agreed to an article under which Congress would recommend that the states compensate the Loyalists for their losses. Compensation for property destruction and freed slaves was silently omitted. The Americans also agreed to remove any impediments to payment of prewar debts owed to British merchants.

Preliminary articles embodying these agreements were signed on November 30, 1782. Franklin was then given the delicate task of showing the articles to Vergennes. The French minister was predictably dismayed, but hardly surprised, since his spies had kept him abreast of the Anglo-American negotiations. Franklin apologized for the American "breach of etiquette," and then with astonishing nerve he suggested that an additional loan of six million livres for the empty American treasury would demonstrate to the British that the alliance could not be broken. Vergennes agreed. The money and the peace agreement sailed on the same packet.

Fighting in America ended. A peace treaty embodying the Anglo-American articles was signed in Paris in September 1783, and the British evacuated New York in November 1783. The world settlement providing for a mutual restoration of conquests, except that England, in recognition of its defeat, was forced to surrender Florida to Spain.

The United States was now an independent republic, ready to assume its role in world affairs. Yet the war and the peace settlement left a legacy of foreign and domestic problems. The French alliance, so valuable in wartime, contained some embarrassing commitments, notably the promise to help defend the French West Indies. Spain, never a firm ally, viewed the sprawling young republic with a mixture of disdain and suspicion. Ignoring the Anglo-American agreement that the thirty-first parallel would be the southern boundary of the United States, Spain claimed everything south of the Tennessee Valley, and in 1784 it closed the mouth of the Mississippi River to American commerce. The twin actions were a source of Spanish-American friction until 1795.

The war also left a full share of domestic problems. In the aftermath of the last British campaign, the South lay in ruins. Production of the southern staples, rice and tobacco, would not reach prewar levels until after 1790. The frontier suffered from sporadic Indian raids encouraged by the British, who held on to Detroit and other western posts in violation of the treaty. Returning Loyalists, seeking to regain their positions and property, caused social disruption, riots, and some bloodshed. Yet the problems themselves helped to forge a new American unity. Born in the crucible of war, the new republic was quickly assuming its own identity, commanding a new loyalty and respect. This emerging feeling of pride in the American experiment would culminate, only a few years after the war ended, in a stronger, more effective instrument of republican government.

4

From Many, One

THE AMERICAN REVOLUTION WAS FAR MORE THAN a colonial struggle for independence; it was also a republican rebellion against monarchy. In this sense it was the first of a long series of Liberal revolutions aiming at government by and for the governed. What Jefferson once called "the unquestionable republicanism of the American mind" precluded any serious thought of establishing an American monarchy, and only a very few even contemplated the possible value of a New World aristocracy. Except in Congregationalist New England, religious establishments were abolished everywhere during or shortly after the Revolution. The ocean barrier and the availability of free land prevented the transplanting of European feudalism to America during the colonial period, and the Revolution wiped out such feudal relics as the monarchy and the established church.

A middle-class society demanded a republican form of government managed by elected representatives, but that did not mean direct popular participation in the government, nor did it necessarily involve a surrender to the "lower orders" of society. "Democracy" was still an epithet in the eighteenth century, commonly used disparagingly, because it evoked much the same emotional response that "Bolshevism" did in the twentieth. To gentlemen educated in the Greek and Roman classics, democracy was inevitably associated with mob rule and demagoguery. Plato's *Republic,* it will be recalled, classified democracy as the second-worst form of government, for it invariably degenerated into tyranny, which was absolutely the worst.

In the formation of republican institutions, American political leaders could find few models or precedents. They had to rely primarily on their own colonial experience and on various theoretical treatises written by British and French radicals over the previous two centuries. James Harrington's *Oceana* (1656), produced during the English Civil War, outlined a model republic with an elected executive chosen by property owners. Republished twice in the eighteenth century, it was eagerly absorbed by Americans and profoundly influenced both Jefferson and John Adams. Of equal importance were the writings of the *Philosophes,* French rationalists who sought to inject order, reason, and progress into the art of government, and laid the theoretical basis for world-wide republican revolution. Montesquieu's *L'Esprit des Lois* (1748) ranged over laws, customs, economics, and religion from Roman times to contemporary France, but Americans were chiefly interested in his description of executive, legislative, and judicial powers under the British system. Montesquieu, of course, had only the vaguest conception of the British constitution and he failed to perceive the evolution of the cabinet, but his misinformed concept of "separation of powers" appealed to Americans who had battled royal governors and judges for more than a century. In his commonplace book, Thomas Jefferson took more notes on Montesquieu than any other author.

From Montesquieu, as well as from British polemicists of the eighteenth century, Americans also derived the principle of "balanced government." This concept, which can be traced back to Aristotle, envisioned a balance of interests among the one, the few, and the many. In the British government the principle took form in the relationship between the king, the Lords (both spiritual and temporal), and the Commons. John Adams became the leading American advocate of the principle, arguing that the upper houses of American legislatures were the natural home (and defense mechanism) for persons of wealth and status.

Ironically, perhaps, the most fruitful source of governmental concepts was the British colonial legacy. Americans discarded monarchical forms for which they had no use, but they eclectically absorbed the traditions of common law jurisprudence and the enormous body of civil liberties obtained by Englishmen in the previous century. The Virginia Declaration of Rights, drawn up by George Mason in 1776, embodied all the fundamental English liberties—right to jury trial, protection against cruel and unusual punishments, restrictions on search warrants, freedom of speech and press, and subordination of the military to civil power. The Declaration was widely imitated in other states and was re-expressed in the first ten amendments of the federal Constitution (the Bill of Rights, ratified in 1791).

The most prominent influence of the colonial past, though most Americans may have been unaware of it, was the legacy of written charters of government. The British constitution itself was an "unwritten" collection of legislative and judicial precedents; but the colonial charters, instructions to governors, and regulations of the Board of Trade all conditioned Americans to written expressions that both outlined the structure of government and defined its powers. Indeed, the concept of a social contract itself, on which the Revolution was founded, might easily suggest to the legal mind (and there were many lawyers in the revolutionary leadership) that a written contract was the most durable and easily comprehended. As a result, the exodus of royal governors and the Declaration of Independence caused a flurry of constitution-writing among the states.

Thirteen Republics

Although utterly inexperienced in the art of constitution-making, Americans were in fair agreement as to what it required. Everywhere it was assumed that a constitution was a form of higher law, superior to ordinary legislative acts. It was further assumed that the authority to establish a constitution flowed directly from the people themselves. Thus, most of the states summoned conventions that were specially elected for the purpose. And all the states, including those in which the legislature drafted the constitution, submitted the documents to popular vote for approval. In Massachusetts the voters rejected a draft submitted by the legislature, and the chastened assembly asked the people to elect a convention, which was done.

Every constitutional convention found itself obliged to balance continuity with change. The Revolution (or, rather, the events leading up to it) had brought new elements into the political arena. These "popular leaders" hoped to consolidate their position by expanding the suffrage and loosening access to public office. The elites, on the other hand, wished to preserve as much of the past as possible; they would eliminate the empire but otherwise preserve the system. The amount of change varied from state to state.

The constitution of Pennsylvania was by far the most democratic, partly because it utilized the democratic features of the colonial charter, including a unicameral assembly and a relatively broad electorate. The Proprietary-Presbyterian coalition in the assembly provided moderate leadership through the early stages of the Revolution; but, in June 1776, radicals took the initiative and called for a constitutional convention. The radical group represented a new alliance between the popular leaders of Philadelphia and the Scots-Irish of the frontier. The convention, which met on July 15 in a room across the hall from the Continental Congress, was chosen in a general election without property qualifications on the suffrage.

Radicals dominated the proceedings and drafted a remarkably progressive frame of government. It set up a one-house legislature elected by all white adult male taxpayers (only non-Christians and Tories were excluded from the suffrage); the executive, instead of a single governor, consisted of a council with delegates elected from each county. So confident were the radicals in their handiwork that they did not bother to provide for ratification, and the constitution went into effect by common consent. But the consent was not universal, and the democratic features of the document combined with its obvious defects, such as the plural executive, engendered a conservative opposition. After the war the constitution became the center of a party conflict in the state, and in 1790 the Anti-Constitutionalists framed a new instrument with a single executive and two-house legislature modeled on the federal Constitution. Significantly, however, the revision did not alter the virtually universal white manhood suffrage established in 1776.

Georgia, also a state with a sizable frontier population, underwent a similar experience. Relatively happy and prosperous under the royal regime, Georgia was dragged into the Revolution by the actions of other colonies. Its governor retained the allegiance of the militia, and its conservative rice planters ignored the directions of the Continental Congress. Then in July 1775, a small group of radicals set up a council of safety and took effective control of the government. A year later the council issued a call for a constitutional convention and permitted all white male taxpayers to vote for delegates. Radicals consequently dominated the convention, and the constitution which emerged in February

1777, was a democratic document, providing for a unicameral assembly elected on nearly universal white manhood suffrage (anyone with property worth ten pounds and all "mechanics" with or without property could vote). As in Pennsylvania, the conservatives eventually regained the upper hand, and in 1789 the constitution was revised. The Georgia revision was also patterned on the new federal Constitution. It established a two-house legislature and strengthened the executive branch. The suffrage was extended to all white male taxpayers, but high property qualifications for officeholding and disproportionate representation for coastal counties ensured control by the seaboard planters.

Besides Pennsylvania and Georgia, the most liberal constitutions were written in Delaware and New Hampshire, both of which required only payment of taxes as a requisite for voting. Virginia and North Carolina wrote constitutions in 1776 that can best be described as middle-of-the-road. Both possessed all-powerful legislatures and weak executives; North Carolina even deprived the governor of any veto or power of appointment. Both set up small freehold qualifications for voting (fifty acres of land) that could be met by nearly all white adult males, but the system of representation by counties, rather than population, ensured a disproportionate influence for the Tidewater region at the expense of the Piedmont and the West. The Whiggish squirearchy, which controlled the colonial assemblies and managed the Revolution, dominated the politics of Virginia and North Carolina for half a century thereafter.

In 1780, Massachusetts, after several drafts and two referenda, gave birth to a moderately conservative constitution that was based on the colonial charter. Drafted by John Adams, it was a new departure among revolutionary constitutions, for it provided for an independent judiciary and a popularly elected governor with veto and appointive powers. Other state constitutions tended toward legislative supremacy, but Adams was more concerned with a separation of legislative, executive, and judicial functions, balancing powers among the three branches. His draft foretold effective government, but it made few concessions to democracy.

Suffrage and representation provisions were carried over virtually intact from the colonial charter. On the surface, this seemed unimportant since about nine-tenths of the white adult males could meet the suffrage qualifications in colonial Massachusetts, and representation by towns appeared to favor the numerous villages of the hinterland. However, no salaries were provided for members, and few rural communities could afford to send delegates. Indifference, insolvency, and provincialism effectively prevented many interior communities from exercising any effective voice in the state government. Popular influence was further hedged by high property qualifications for officeholding. Membership in the senate was restricted to men with £300 freeholds, and the governor had to possess a freehold worth £1,000. As a result, a mercantile elite effectively dominated the politics of the state in the postwar period, managing debts and taxes to suit its own interests. When the farmers of the interior awoke to their plight in the 1786 depression, they exercised their power, not at the ballot box, but through rebellion.

The most conservative constitutions of all were written by New York, Maryland, and South Carolina. All three had high property qualifications for voting and holding office, ensuring governments dominated by wealthy landowners. In Maryland, for instance, an individual had to possess property worth £1,000 just to be sheriff. Moreover, all three gave coordinate legislative power to the upper house (or Senate), and then imposed rigid property qualifications for a seat. Maryland even provided for indirect election of senators through an electoral "college," thus removing it further from popular influence. South Carolina required property valued at £2,000 if a senator resided in his district and £7,000 if he did not. The governor of South Carolina was required to possess an estate of £10,000, roughly the financial equivalent of a modern-day millionaire.

Despite the obvious differences, there were a number of similarities among the first state constitutions. The principle of separation of powers was universally accepted, though in most states the legislative branch was supreme. Except in Massachusetts and New York, governors were granted extremely limited powers and were usually subject to election and removal by the assembly. As a result of the bitter colonial experience with royal and proprietary governors, executives were given no direct control over elections and possessed no power to summon, prorogue, or dissolve a legislature. In most states they could not even exercise the veto. Separate provision was made for the judiciary, which was given tenure during good behavior in eight states and confined to specified terms in five. But it, too, was subjugated to the legislature which had the power of appointing and removing judges in most states. Except in the most conservative constitutions, the lower houses were more powerful than the upper, which merely confirmed the trend of the late colonial period.

The political changes accompanying independence do not seem very revolutionary, the most obvious being the reduction in the power of the executive. Even this did not last long, for the constitutional revisions that took place in the next few decades redressed the balance of power among the three branches of government. Yet more subtle changes, largely unnoticed by contemporaries, were taking place. Comparing the composition of the revolutionary legislatures with the colonial assemblies reveals substantial change. The appointed colonial councils were dominated by lawyers, merchants, and large landowners, those with enough social and economic prestige to earn recognition by the governor. After 1776, the upper houses were elected, albeit by a restricted suffrage, and there was a substantial increase in the proportion of farmers and planters. To a lesser extent, the same was true of the lower houses, where the number of lawyers and merchants serving in the 1780s was half what it had been a decade before. These figures suggest a substantial dilution of the governing elite, a growing identity between the voting populace and its leadership, and an increased participation by the "lower orders" in government.

Representative government implies a certain amount of democracy, in the sense that representatives are subject to the voters, however restricted in numbers, at election time. There was thus a certain amount of democracy inherent in the colonial regimes. Despite the efforts of a number of conservative leaders, the Revolution itself brought substantial advances in democratic theory and practice. A genuine revolution (as opposed, say, to a *coup d'etat*) is a democratic process inviting popular participation, and the American Revolution to establish government on "the just consent of the governed" increased the theoretical importance of the commonality, just as the mass appeals of patriot propaganda heightened their political awareness. Several state constitutions broadened the electorate by reducing or eliminating property qualifications, though continued apathy and provincialism prevented any sudden increase in voter turnout. The foundation was nonetheless laid for the strides of another generation, which would remove the legislative restrictions on voters (in most states after 1815) and develop the political machinery, symbolism, and rhetoric that would bring them to the polls.

Articles of Confederation

Constitution-writing in the states was accompanied by a search for some form of central government that would unite the thirteen sovereign republics. Even without a written instrument of authority, Congress exercised a number of governmental powers—by the end of 1776 it had declared the nation's independence, encouraged the states to draft constitutions, established a committee to negotiate treaties with foreign nations, created a continental army and appointed its commanding officers, established a navy and marine corps, and printed paper money. The need to prosecute a war impelled Congress to act, but it also pointed out the need for a written instrument of government.

Richard Henry Lee's resolution recommending independence suggested also that "a plan of confederation be prepared," and on June 12, 1776, Congress appointed a committee to draft some articles of confederation. A majority of the committee of thirteen were conservatives, such as John Dickinson, Edward Rutledge, and Robert R. Livingston, who desired a federal union before independence was declared in order to prevent a governmental hiatus that would bring social chaos. Dickinson undertook the drafting assignment, and in August he submitted his handiwork to Congress. The government Dickinson envisioned was actually the existing Congress with vastly expanded powers. Congress would have competence over foreign affairs, the war, appropriations, the Native American tribes, and western lands. Although authority was not specifically delegated, there was no limitation on the creation of executive and judicial agencies.

Distracted by the press of military affairs, Congress did not resume consideration of Dickinson's draft until the spring of 1777. In the meantime, states' rights sentiment increased, mostly among the southern states where the planter gentry, free for the moment from the threat of British attack or internal tension, felt little need for centralized authority. When the Articles of Confederation were finally approved in October 1777, Dickinson's plan was considerably watered down. On the motion of a North Carolina delegate, the article granting broad powers to Congress was replaced by a clause reserving to the states "every power, jurisdiction, and right which is not . . . expressly delegated. . . ." Congress lacked the power to tax, subsisting instead on funds provided by the states under assigned quotas, and each state would continue to have one vote, regardless of the size of its population. Instead of a strong central government, the Articles represented a "league of friendship" among thirteen sovereign states. Congress had a strong claim to sovereignty in its own right, since it had come into existence before the states did and even authorized the colonies to convert themselves into independent states. But it surrendered that claim in the second article of the Confederation, which declared that "each state retains its sovereignty, freedom, and independence." The question of "states rights," or "state sovereignty" would haunt American politics until the Civil War.

Despite the war emergency, ratification of the Articles proved nearly impossible. The main opposition came from the small states, Delaware, New Jersey, and Maryland, who feared domination by their larger neighbors, even though they possessed an equal vote in Congress. The crux of the issue was the possession of western lands. The "landless states" had either well-established western boundaries, or, in the case of New England, only the most fragile claims in the West. Virginia and North Carolina, who possessed the best and most extensive titles in the West, prevented all efforts to give Congress control of the West under the Articles. North Carolina had an uncontested title to Tennessee and Virginia to Kentucky. North of the Ohio River, Virginia's claims were based on its charter of 1609 and the expedition of George Rogers Clark in 1778–79.

Speculators in Philadelphia and Baltimore reinforced the stand of the "landless" states. Before the Revolution they organized the Illinois, Wabash, and Indiana land companies, and to circumvent Virginia's title they purchased lands in the Northwest directly from the Native Americans. This, of course, was contrary to British policy; but, the outbreak of revolution raised the possibility that the speculators might have their title validated by Congress. Thus, the most prominent stockholders in the land companies—Robert Morris, Benjamin Franklin, James Wilson, and Charles Carroll of Carrollton—sought to include a provision in the Articles for congressional control of the West. When this failed, they used ratification as a lever to pry the West from Virginia's grip. In December 1778, Maryland, whose own speculators were heavily involved, declared that it would not approve the Articles until the other states ceded their western claims to Congress. By then, every other state had approved the Articles, but Maryland's action delayed ratification for another two years.

In the interim, the authority of Congress declined steadily. At the beginning of the war it was very popular, and people would no doubt have acquiesced in any powers that it wanted to assume. But as the war went on its popularity filtered away. The loss of status was best seen in the decline of state subsidies, which weakened Congress even further. Chronically insolvent, Congress resorted to issuing bills of exchange on its foreign emissaries, hoping that they could borrow funds abroad to redeem them. Its other recourse was more paper money, and after 1779 the continental press flooded the nation with depreciating paper. In 1780, the states took over the obligation of paying the army, thereby assuming part of the national debt and further weakening the influence of Congress. The fall of Charleston in May 1780, and the British conquest of South Carolina was a heavy blow, but at least it reawakened southern nationalism. In the fall of 1780, the Virginia Assembly reversed itself and ceded its claims north of the Ohio to Congress on the condition that previous purchases by speculators be invalidated. Maryland accordingly ratified the Articles in February 1781, though opposition to Virginia's proviso delayed congressional acceptance of the cession until 1784.

Ratification of the Articles by no means ended the problems of Congress. The situation in the South deteriorated further as Cornwallis moved into North Carolina. The new currency depreciated (since Congress lacked a tax power), and the unpaid army seethed with discontent. In February 1781, the nationalists in Congress took the initiative and gained the support of southern delegates whose homes were suddenly threatened by Cornwallis. Congress requested the states to approve an amendment to the Articles that would permit it to levy a 5 percent tax on imports. Two weeks later, Congress reorganized its administrative machinery, creating an Office of Foreign Affairs with Robert R. Livingston as secretary, and a Department of War headed by General Benjamin Lincoln.

Nationalist efforts to create a nascent executive branch of government climaxed in July with the appointment of Robert Morris as superintendent of finance. The tax power was the key to his system. With an independent income, Congress could pay interest on its debt, thus preventing further depreciation in its paper money, and it could borrow in the future. To ease the credit situation Morris proposed creation of a bank that would hold the national debt and charge the government a uniform rate of interest. This plan for a "funded debt" would thus restore the credit of Congress and mobilize the financial resources of the nation for the war effort. On the last day of 1781, Congress chartered the Bank of North America, capitalized at $400,000. Most of the stock was purchased by Morris and his friends, although the secretary eventually had to use treasury funds to set the bank going. On the basis of its capital, the bank issued notes which circulated at par and solved for the time being the government's problems with paper money. On the whole, the banking experiment was a success, and when investors clamored to buy stock Morris sold them the government's shares.

In addition to loaning money to the government, Morris hoped the bank would serve "to unite the several States more closely together in one general money connexion, and indissolubly to attach many powerful individuals to the cause of our country by the strong principle of self-love and the immediate sense of private interest." The bank was thus part of a comprehensive scheme of political nationalism, designed to unite the country and stabilize the government. Despite its political overtones, Morris's plan passed Congress with relatively little opposition. The fiscal crisis, unrest in the army, and the British invasion of Virginia all silenced those who feared centralized government.

Unfortunately, however, the entire edifice rested on the impost amendment. Without the power to levy taxes, Congress could not pay its debts or borrow further from the bank. In the emergency, most states acted with unusual speed, and by the end of 1782, all but Georgia and Rhode Island gave their assent. Since Georgia was in British hands, it could be ignored, but Rhode Island was another matter. The state was dependent on foreign trade, and its merchants traditionally opposed any tax burdens on their commerce. Besides, the state felt it had its own debts to pay. Since unanimous approval was required, Rhode Island's refusal killed the impost amendment and scuttled the nationalists' program. When the war ended, anti-nationalists resurfaced in Congress, and the bank charter was allowed to expire in 1784.

From their inception, then, the Articles of Confederation engendered a contest between supporters and critics. Most nationalists considered the Articles too weak; they desired amendments giving Congress the power to levy taxes, regulate interstate and foreign commerce, and create a national judiciary. Anti-nationalists, approving of the Articles, favored a federal system of union that would leave essential powers in the hands of the states. The two groups were hardly political parties in the modern sense, for they lacked organization and popular support. But they did develop the electoral techniques, the interstate alliances, and the ideology on which a party system could be built.

The nationalist faction included a number of merchants, particularly those with interstate connections, as well as former army officers and others who served the continental government. Farmers along arterial river systems, such as the Connecticut, the Delaware, and the Potomac also generally favored a strong government that could regulate commerce and negotiate trade treaties. The anti-nationalists, on the other hand, included a variety of groups whose interests were primarily local. Small farmers, whether in North Carolina or New England, tended to be local-minded and provincial, and mistrustful of governmental authority. Similarly, politicians with strong local organizations, such as John Hancock in Massachusetts, Patrick Henry in Virginia, or George Clinton in New York, took a dim view of surrendering any of their authority to a central government.

The debate over the extent of federal power involved a variety of interests and motives, but it would be a mistake to label either group as "progressive" or "conservative." The nationalist faction, to be sure, included a number of social conservatives, such as Morris in Pennsylvania, Jay in New York, or the Rutledges in South Carolina, who desired a government strong enough to preserve law and order and maintain social stability. But the group also included a number of reformers. Nationalist James Madison guided the Virginia Statute for Religious Freedom through the state assembly; and another nationalist, Edmund Pendleton, helped reform the state's penal code. In New York, John Jay, Alexander Hamilton, and Rufus King were all active in one of the nation's first antislavery societies.

A number of anti-nationalists, on the other hand, successfully promoted political democracy at the state level and feared that a strong central government might somehow undermine their efforts. The Presbyterian Party in Pennsylvania, which wrote a democratic state constitution, abolished slavery, and instituted educational and legal reforms, was generally anti-nationalist in complexion. But elsewhere the anti-nationalists seemed to be more particularist than democratic. George Clinton consistently championed the interests of Hudson Valley land barons, while in Massachusetts Samuel Adams defended the established Congregational Church and the conservative state constitution. In Virginia, the arch-particularists, Patrick Henry and Richard Henry Lee, led the fight against separation of church and state.

Organizing the West

Despite the inherent weakness of the confederation, it could boast a number of achievements. The Articles, after all, did afford Americans experience in governing a continental domain under a written constitution. They were an essential ingredient in the shift in popular attitudes that overcame local jealousies and promoted a sense of national identity. It is entirely possible, indeed probable, that without this initial experience in interstate cooperation, a stronger government would never have been approved in 1788.

In more specific terms, the confederation government also established a rudimentary bureaucracy that formed the basis for the executive departments set up in 1789. The War Department under Henry Knox, who became secretary in 1784, was carried over intact into the Washington administration. The Department for Foreign Affairs, which was handed to John Jay in the mid-1780s, was the prototype for the modern State Department. Operating out of New York City's Fraunces Tavern, Jay sent ministers to France, Britain, and Spain, and he maintained consuls in nineteen foreign ports to oversee American commercial interests. A post office department had been established by Congress as early as 1775 with Benjamin Franklin as postmaster general. He was succeeded first by his son-in-law Richard Bache and then by Ebenezer Hazard who ran the system on a paying basis from 1782 to 1789, by which date the country had seventy-five post offices and 2,400 miles of post roads. That office, too, was carried intact into the Washington administration, though it did not then have cabinet rank.

By far the greatest achievement of the confederation government, however, was the formation of a national land policy and a territorial administration for the West. State cessions dumped into the lap of Congress a vast national domain west of the Appalachians. Acceptance of Virginia's cession in 1784 clarified the situation north of the Ohio River. That same year Massachusetts relinquished whatever claims it had in the region, and Connecticut surrendered its claims in 1786, retaining only a "Western Reserve" of four million acres on the south shore of Lake Erie for war veterans.

Congress thus obtained clear title to the area between the Ohio River and the Great Lakes, but cession of the Southwest was slower. Both North Carolina and Georgia hoped to pay off their state debts through the proceeds from land sales. In 1783, North Carolina opened its Tennessee lands for sale, at five dollars per hundred acres, and then a year later ceded the region to Congress. The cession alarmed the settlers of Tennessee, who feared that federal possession might jeopardize their titles. A meeting of residents of the Holston Valley, dominated by one of the largest of the speculators, John Sevier, decided to set up a separate state of Franklin and petition Congress for admission to the Union. North Carolina promptly withdrew its cession, but the residents of Franklin drew up a state constitution and launched an independent government. The new "state" was plagued with factional rivalries between North Carolina and Tennessee interests; and when Sevier's followers were defeated in a brief skirmish in 1788, the statehood movement was dead. In 1789, North Carolina again ceded Tennessee to the federal government, and a year later Congress erected it into the Territory Southwest of the River Ohio. Georgia similarly tried to profit from its claims over Alabama and Mississippi, making two gigantic sales in the region to land companies before ceding it to the federal government in 1802.

The state cessions of the 1780s provided Congress with a national domain at its own disposal. The acquisition of this territory had profound political implications, for the Confederation Congress now possessed one of the fundamental attributes of sovereignty. No longer could it be considered a mere "league of nations," handling matters of war and diplomacy as an agent of the states. A giant step had been taken toward the establishment of a sovereign national government; and Congress moved quickly to exercise its new responsibilities. The cession of the Northwest brought a host of problems—the domain had to be organized for sale to pioneers and some sort of government had to be provided. The second problem proved to be stickier, for it had all sorts of political ramifications. Was ultimate statehood the destiny of the region? If so, under what conditions and how many states? The answers to these questions involved fundamental issues of democracy and home rule, as well as a conflict of interests: hinterland versus seaboard, resident pioneers versus eastern speculators.

In 1784, Congress appointed a committee headed by Thomas Jefferson to draw up a plan for administering the territory between the Ohio, the Great Lakes, and the Mississippi. Jefferson's blueprint proposed to carve fourteen territories from the region, each two parallels of latitude in width and burdened with such neoclassical names as Sylvania, Michigania, Metropotamia, and Illinoia. Jefferson pretty much left government to the settlers themselves, fearing that they might object to a "colonial" regime imposed by Congress. Accordingly, his proposal envisioned only a temporary government in each territory set up upon the request of the free white adult males and a formal territorial government when the population reached twenty thousand. The only requirements were that the territory must erect a republican form of government, remain part of the Confederation, and abolish slavery after 1800. When the population equalled the number of inhabitants in the least populous original state, Congress could admit the territory to the Union as a full-fledged state.

Jefferson's plan thus contemplated quick, easy, and painless access to statehood for the West. It was also eminently democratic, for it provided local autonomy with a minimum of control by Congress, and it permitted all free white adult males to participate in western politics. These virtues unfortunately proved its undoing. Land speculators feared the establishment of strong local governments in the West that might threaten their interests; and conservatives predicted that an excess of frontier democracy would lead to chaos. The ultimate creation of fourteen states in the area, moreover, would give the West control of Congress and smother the influence of the old thirteen. As a result, Jefferson's report was badly gutted before Congress incorporated it into the Ordinance of 1784. The specific provision for fourteen territories was deleted, along with the ponderous names suggested by Jefferson, and the ban on slavery was removed. It was this last alteration that bothered Jefferson the most. He regarded slavery as an evil; and, though he could see no way of eliminating it in places like Virginia and South Carolina where it was well entrenched, he wanted to see it barred from the virgin lands of the frontier.

Jefferson did not concern himself with the sale of the land in the West. Indeed, he was prepared to give it away on a theory that the government would best profit by the development of the West and the resulting tax receipts. Squatters—persons who settled and farmed the land without paying for it—were precisely what concerned Congress. By 1784 several hundred of them had moved into the wilderness north of the Ohio River and were carving out farms in widely scattered settlements. If the Ohio country grew as fast as Kentucky had (Kentucky had seventy thousand people by the census of 1790), the spread of illegal settlement would prevent Congress from ever profiting from the sale of its lands. And by 1785 land sales were the best potential source of income for Congress, and the only feasible way of paying off the Revolutionary War debt. Congress felt it had to attract industrious, market-oriented settlers to the West. To do so, it had to survey the West and set up conditions for the sale of its lands.

The Land Ordinance of 1785 followed the New England system of imposing a grid of rectangular towns on the landscape. The Ordinance divided the public lands in the Northwest by base lines (east-west) and range lines (north-south) into townships six miles square, each containing thirty-six sections of 640 acres (one square mile). The initial base line would run west from the point where the Ohio River emerges from Pennsylvania, and the range lines would run south from that line to the river. The land would be sold at auction, with a minimum price of one dollar an acre and a minimum sale of 640 acres. In effect, Congress elected to trade immediate sales for an orderly future. The provisions for prior survey eliminated any conflict over titles, but it would be months or years before any significant portion could be surveyed and sales begin. Nevertheless such stately regularity had advantages of its own. The settlement of Kentucky and Tennessee had bred a host of stories about the wild frontier. Congress did not want to replicate that experience in Ohio. Compact settlements that developed slowly were part of a socializing process, turning new settlers into law-abiding farmers. Washington, who had had his own troubles with lawless squatters on his land in western Virginia, favored "progressive seating" in the West. Congress also recognized that an artificially limited supply would keep land prices up.

Congress also acted on the premise that it would be best if the Northwest were populated, not from adjacent settlements in the West, but by migrants from the East. George Washington even expected (and probably hoped) that it would by settled by immigrants from abroad. To further this policy the Ordinance provided that federal land offices would be located in the East so that everyone would have an equal chance to buy. To ensure that easterners had access to information about the western lands the Ordinance stipulated that each state was to nominate a surveyor to join the official United States geographer in the field.

Despite the vision of orderly development that would attract orderly and industrious settlers, profit from land sales remained Congress's principal objective. And sales were disappointingly slow. When the lands from the first surveys were brought to auction in 1787, only 72,934 acres were sold, and the proceeds amounted to a meager $117,108. Congress realized that it had to devise other means to attract customers. As a result, it was prepared to lend a friendly ear to the Reverend Manasseh Cutler, a Congregationalist minister from Massachusetts who arrived in New York with a proposal to buy a huge tract of land beyond the surveys. Cutler represented a new land company, the Ohio Company, that was formed in March 1786. The Ohio Company was the brainchild of General Rufus Putnam of Connecticut, and most of its chief subscribers were New England speculators. In July 1787, the deal was made. The Ohio Company agreed to pay $1 million in depreciated continental paper money for 1.5 million acres of land in the valley of the Muskingum River. Half was offered as a down payment; the remainder was due when the company completed its surveys. Congress received considerably less in the bargain than the dollar an acre prescribed by the Land Ordinance, but it expected to achieve its other goals for the West. The Ohio Company was expected to fill the West with New Englanders, "a description of Men," as one Virginia delegate joyfully reported, "who will fix the character and politics throughout the whole territory, and which will probably endure to the latest period of time."

In the meantime, a congressional committee had again taken up the question of a government for the Northwest. The Ordinance of 1784 provided for too much local control of government to suit either Cutler or the "robust and industrious" settlers he promised to send to the West. Working closely with Cutler, the committee drafted a new ordinance, which was adopted on July 13, 1787, a scant ten days before the Ohio Company sale was completed.

The Northwest Ordinance of 1787 authorized the division of the region between the Ohio River and the Great Lakes into three to five states and then set up the procedure under which a wilderness evolved into statehood. In the initial stage the government would consist of a governor, three judges, and a secretary, all appointed by Congress. The laws for the "colony" would be enacted by Congress, adapting "such laws of the original States, criminal and civil, as may be necessary and best suited to the circumstances of the district." When the adult male population reached five thousand, the territory was permitted an elected legislature, which in turn could appoint a nonvoting delegate to Congress, but the governor would still be appointed by Congress. Then, when the total population reached sixty thousand (which was at that time the number of inhabitants in Delaware, the least populous state), the territory could summon a constitutional convention, draw up a state constitution, and apply for admission to the union. When the application was approved by Congress, the state was admitted "on an equal footing with the original states." Finally, the Ordinance incorporated a bill of rights for the territories, guaranteeing freedom of religion; the right to jury trial, habeas corpus, and due process of law; and prohibiting "cruel and unusual punishments." The Ordinance also prohibited slavery from the territory .

In its general features, the Ordinance represented a conservative retreat from Jefferson's Ordinance of 1784, which it repealed. The limitation to five states reduced the amount of western representation in Congress, and the stringent requirements for statehood meant indefinite control of the region by Congress. (Ohio, the first state created in the area, was admitted in 1803, and Wisconsin, the last, in 1848.) The Ordinance also represented a setback for popular participation in politics—where Jefferson's plan of 1784 permitted all adult males to vote, the Ordinance of 1787 restricted the franchise to owners of fifty-acre freeholds and required officeholders to possess two hundred acres of land.

Although the Ordinance was written by and for land speculators, it nonetheless represented a substantial contribution to the American experiment in republican government on a continental scale. The highly centralized government which it imposed on the West may have kept democratic influences at a minimum, but it did provide a stable regime for the turbulent frontier that effectively countered any potential secessionist movements. Moreover, the Ordinance, to its credit, did contemplate ultimate statehood for the area at a time when many eastern politicians were demanding that it be kept in a permanent colonial status, and the pattern for governmental progression which it created provided a blueprint for the expansion of the United States down to the admission of Alaska and Hawaii in the mid-twentieth century. The guarantees for the rights of citizens, moreover, included a number of provisions that would shortly be incorporated in the first eight amendments of the federal Constitution, and the prohibition on slavery reflected the fundamental idealism of the Revolution. Taken as a whole, then, the system of land organization and government instituted by the Ordinances of 1785 and 1787 were a signal achievement for the Confederation Congress.

Demobilization and Depression

Despite this record of achievement, the Confederation government faced a number of problems, which in the end proved its undoing. Most of them were not the result of weak government nor the fault of Congress. Nevertheless, Congress's inability to handle satisfactorily the vicissitudes it encountered undermined its authority and fostered demands for stronger government. The first problem it faced, as the war dragged to an end, was demobilization, always productive of social tension and economic dislocation. The army was chronically discontented because it was paid irregularly, and when it was paid the money evaporated with inflation. After mutinies were quelled in 1781, the demands of the troops centered on a pension of half pay for life.

After the British evacuated New York in December 1782, the army had little to do but contemplate its meager rewards for service. Within a few weeks it was enmeshed in politics, for the likelihood of pensions was tied to the fate of the impost amendment and Robert Morris's plans for a funded debt. In January 1783, a delegation of army officers rode to Philadelphia to petition Congress for a grant of postwar pensions. They warned that if Congress did not act, it could expect "at least a mutiny" in some parts of the army. Congress responded by naming a committee to look into its financial resources. Robert

Morris picked that moment to tender his resignation as superintendent of finance. He added to the pressure by informing Congress that he could not advance a shilling to the army unless the impost were improved. Morris and a few other nationalists, including Alexander Hamilton, apparently hoped to use the threat of military takeover to frighten the country into granting Congress more power.

In early March anonymous "addresses" circulated among officers stationed at Washington's headquarters in Newburgh, New York. The author was a young officer named John Armstrong, an ally of General Horatio Gates in army politics (ironically, Armstrong would later become a very able secretary of war under President Madison during the War of 1812). The first address denounced Washington for his supposed moderation and urged a tougher stand with Congress. A subsequent address called for a meeting of officers to discuss a possible refusal to disband until Congress conceded their demands. Such a meeting without the consent of the commander in chief verged on mutiny, and the implicit threat of military force verged on treason. Alarmed that the discontented officers might turn to Gates for leadership, Alexander Hamilton wrote to Washington to warn him what was transpiring. Hamilton no doubt also hoped to enlist Washington in the movement to strengthen Congress's power. Washington acted swiftly. He denounced the call for a meeting as "disorderly" and "irregular" and summoned a meeting of his own. Shifting ground, the malcontents issued a new address endorsing this meeting and implying that Washington had become one of their own. Presiding over the meeting on March 15, 1783, Washington cooled the tempers of the assembled officers by expressing his faith in the justice of Congress and offering to present their demands himself. Then he pulled from his pocket a letter from a friend in Congress, pausing dramatically to put on his glasses, which few realized that he required—"Gentlemen, you will permit me to put on my spectacles. I have grown gray in the service of my country and now feel myself growing blind." The audience sat stunned. Some officers openly wept. In that one dramatic gesture Washington had won over his army. There would be no mutiny, nor a march on Congress. The letter was an expression of congressional sympathy for the demands of the army; and Washington concluded by suggesting that the army do nothing to detract from the honor and glory it had won during the war. When the general withdrew, the assembled officers voted to leave their problems in his hands and specifically rejected "the infamous propositions" previously circulated.

After a long debate in the spring of 1783, Congress rejected Morris's program for funding the debt, but on Washington's intercession it did make a gesture of conciliation to the army. Commissioned officers were voted pensions of full pay for five years after discharge, and enlisted men received half-pay for four months. In the meantime, the army, anxious to get home, was disbanding itself. A number of states rewarded their returning veterans with their only available commodity, land; but, since few soldiers were willing to remove to the frontier to carve farms from the forest, most of the land certificates fell into the hands of speculators at a heavy discount. From the demobilization crisis,

Congress emerged with its reputation badly tarnished, and its soldiers looking to the states rather than the central government for relief.

One incidental result of the Newburgh movement was the founding, in May 1783, of the Society of the Cincinnati. This was the brain-child of Henry Knox who did not relish the unglamorous descent from artillery commander to bookstore proprietor. He conceived of the Cincinnati as a social fraternity of former officers who sought to keep up wartime friendships. It soon developed political overtones, however, for most of its members had experienced the ineptitude of Congress during the war and favored a revision of the Articles of Confederation. Though denounced in New England and the South as a step toward an hereditary aristocracy, the Cincinnati retained public respect in the middle states where it was a potent force of nationalism.

No sooner had the Continental Congress resolved the demobilization problem than it encountered an economic depression that dominated the rest of its history. The depression was not the product of weak government, but it did create social and economic tensions that further emphasized the destitute condition of Congress. No regime is popular in a time of depression—to which former President Herbert Hoover would be the first to testify. The confederation government had the misfortune to coincide with a downturn in the business cycle which ended, again coincidentally, with the adoption of the Constitution. It was a typical postwar depression, presaged by an orgy of consumption that began when the serious fighting ended at Yorktown. Americans, who had been deprived of manufactured goods by the war and the British blockade, eagerly made purchases through the newly opened channels of trade with the Continent. Specie flowed back to Europe in exchange, severely aggravating the domestic fiscal crisis. Adding to the money shortage were state efforts to retire the paper they had issued to finance the war. Paper money had always been regarded as a temporary expedient, justified only by military emergency. Consequently, when the war ended the states collected the paper in taxes and destroyed it as fast as they could. Nevertheless, the boom continued into 1784, financed largely on credit advanced by British merchants who were anxious to recover their American markets. Since the nation lacked a sophisticated network of financial institutions, there was no spectacular "panic," but the situation gradually got worse; and, by the spring of 1784 the nation was in a severe commercial depression. Unsaleable goods glutted the market, prices fell, and specie was almost nonexistent.

Throughout the colonial period Americans had paid for their import of manufactured goods by selling their agricultural surpluses, primarily the staple crops of the South. Unfortunately, the South had been hard-hit by the Revolution, and its depressed condition aggravated the specie drain. Indigo was a casualty of independence; it could not be grown profitably without the bounty paid under the British navigation acts. Rice culture was similarly devastated. The great rice plantations of the Carolina Tidewater were wrecked by British and Tory depredations; and in 1782, the evacuating British carried off an estimated 25,000 slaves. Not until 1790 did South Carolina rice production return to pre-war levels. Chesapeake tobacco production was little affected by the war, however, and the end of the fighting brought renewed British demand, new markets in France, and consequent high prices. In the year 1784, Virginians received nearly twice as much for their exported tobacco as in the prewar years, but toward the end of that year the price began to drop. By late 1785, the price of tobacco was cut in half; and Virginia was returned to its chronic condition of depression, characterized by a lack of coin and increasing debts to British merchants.

New England suffered most from the depression. The region was relatively free of marching armies after the British evacuated Boston in 1776, and it prospered during the war from privateering and the sale of farm products to the French army occupying Newport. Farm prices remained high throughout the war, nourished by French gold and domestic paper money, but they fell drastically in 1785. Aggravating the situation were the tax policies of the New England states which levied taxes on land by the acre regardless of value and demanded that they be paid in unobtainable specie. Britain's order-in-council of July 1783, which excluded American ships from the imperial trade, presented additional problems. The view of Parliament was that Americans could not have their cake and eat it too; having left the empire, they did not deserve to benefit by the imperial trade relationships. The effect was to sever New England merchants from their traditional markets in the British West Indies and remove one leg from the profitable "triangle trade." Since this trade was New England's primary source of specie, the region's economy teetered on the brink of collapse.

Critics of the Confederation blamed the economic distress on weak government. Artisans demanded a government with power to install customs duties that would relieve them from competition with cheap British manufactured goods. Merchants and exporting farmers demanded a government with stature enough to negotiate trade treaties that would open new markets in the closed empires of the world. Nationalists seized every opportunity to emphasize the woes of the times, but in general the depression was not as severe as they portrayed. Chronic low prices and lack of specie were real enough, but the impact of the depression was somewhat mitigated by an expansion of American trade into new regions of the world. Although Americans were excluded from the British West Indies, they opened a brisk trade with the French islands, stimulated by a commercial agreement with France negotiated by Jefferson in 1786. Relieved of the British navigation system, Americans for the first time traded directly with northern Europe; France and Holland both became important customers, especially for American tobacco.

Peace and independence also brought the first American contact with Asia. In 1784, Robert Morris dispatched the first American ship to China with a cargo of manufactured goods and ginseng (a root-herb which the Chinese believed would restore vitality to the aged). His ship, *The Empress of China,* returned a year later with a load of tea and silk, turning a substantial profit for the investors. Within a few years American ships were second only to the British in the Canton trade, but there was a limit to the Chinese consumption of ginseng (and, presumably, to Chinese gullibility), and the trade found a better economic base in Pacific furs. In 1788, the first American ships visited Nootka Sound (Vancouver Island) where they bought sea otter furs from the Indians and swapped them in Canton for tea and silk. In the meantime, in 1786, a Baltimore merchant sent a vessel to India, which won a concession from the East India Company that in ports under its control Americans would be treated as most favored foreigners. Prior to the development of the sea otter trade with China, American tonnage in Indian ports may have exceeded that at Canton. Trade with Asia, of course, remained a small fraction of the nation's foreign commerce, but it symbolized the new horizons opened by the Revolution.

Economically, however, Americans certainly paid a price for independence. It has been estimated that the level of performance of the economy of the United States as a whole fell by almost half between 1775 and 1790, which is approximately the amount of decline in production that occurred during the depression of 1929 to 1933. But the depression of the 1780s was at least short-lived, and by 1790 the United States had embarked on a period of general prosperity that lasted until the panic of 1819. In the meantime, however, the depression stirred up a number of important political issues that Congress seemed unable to resolve, and that furthered the demand for a more viable central government.

The Fight Over Paper Money

Prime among these was the problem of paper money, easily the hottest political issue of the decade. By 1786, seven states had resorted to the issue of paper money in one form or another, and it was a source of fierce debate in the rest, contributing to political tensions and hardening factional lines. The states had redeemed much of the wartime paper, and, unfortunately, the new nation had not developed other sources of money and credit. The success of the Bank of North America (which continued for a time as a Pennsylvania corporation after Congress refused to renew its charter) inspired the establishment of two other banks—the Bank of New York and the Bank of Massachusetts. Neither had enough capital to meet the national need for credit, however; both made only short-term thirty-day loans to local merchants.

As a result, a demand arose for new issues of paper by the states, and this instantly created a political firestorm. Paper money had always been suspect by fiscal conservatives; it had been tolerated in military emergencies and retired at war's end. A number of colonies regularly issued paper money on loan to farmers during periods of economic depression. This "pump priming" helped combat the extreme deflation caused, in part, by the lack of a circulating medium of exchange. But the runaway inflation of continental and state paper currency during the Revolution made creditors wary of paper money in the postwar years. They viewed the demand for such currency as a form of debtor relief; that is, the money was expected to depreciate in value and thereby allow debtors to escape their burdens. In truth, the primary demand for paper issues came from rural areas that lacked the currency to pay debts and taxes. In five states, for instance, paper money was loaned to farmers on the security of land (an ingenious experiment in government farm mortgages that was not tried again until the New Deal), but it was far more than a debtor-relief mechanism.

In most states paper money was also used to pay interest on the state debt, and thus attracted the support of security-holders. In general, paper emissions in the 1780s functioned about the way they did for the colonies. When merchants recognized its value in relieving the capital shortage and accepted paper in payment for goods, it worked. When they deliberately depreciated it by raising prices, it failed.

Pennsylvania, in 1785, was the first state to issue paper money after the war. The state printed £150,000 in bills of credit, two-thirds to be used to pay interest on the state debt, the remainder to be available for loans on farm mortgages. The primary support for the act came from farmers and holders of state securities; its main opponents were Robert Morris and the Bank of North America. Philadelphia merchants generally accepted the notes, however, and they circulated at close to par; by 1789 most of them were redeemed. New York and South Carolina, both of which issued paper money in 1786, had a similarly successful experience. South Carolina's was exclusively debtor-relief legislation, but in that state the leading debtors were also the leading planters—Rutledges, Pinckneys, Izards, and others who dominated the politics of the state. Their creditors were British merchants with resident factors in Charleston, many of whom were repatriated Tories. In 1786, the assembly authorized the issue of £100,000 in paper currency, to be lent on real estate mortgages; simultaneously it passed the Pine Barren Act which permitted debtors to tender worthless lands in payment of their debts. The action eased South Carolina planters through the worst of the depression; and, an improved rice crop brought the state its first favorable balance of trade since the war. In 1787, the assembly embarked on a program for complete recovery, prohibiting the further importation of slaves and the collection of debts for three years. The system involved considerable government intervention and juggling the state's credit system, but by 1790 South Carolina had completely recovered its prewar prosperity. Virginia did not issue paper money, but it did adopt other expedients to relieve its currency-shy farmers. In addition to tobacco, which had long been used as a substitute for money, it allowed people to pay taxes in commodities such as deerskins (thus equating the dollar with a buckskin or "buck").

In a few states, paper money operated with less success, partly because they suffered more complicated economic problems. New Jersey was the weakest of the middle states, its politics torn by the ancient sectional division between East and West, its economy debilitated by commercial dependence upon New York and Philadelphia. It was partly to relieve this dependence that New Jersey engaged New York in one of the more notorious quarrels of the period. When New York, along with several other states, imposed tariff duties on British goods in retaliation for the order-in-council of 1783, New Jersey refused to cooperate. Hoping to build up one of its own ports, such as Perth Amboy, into a trade center, it refused to discriminate against British goods. New York accordingly levied a tax on foreign goods entering through New Jersey, and New Jersey retaliated by taxing the lighthouse maintained by New York on Sandy Hook at the rate of £30 a month.

The whole affair, of course, was an exercise in trivia; but, it was used by the nationalists to illustrate the balkanization of America and the need for a central authority with power to settle such disputes. Although no state ever levied customs duties on the goods of another state, the New Jersey affair reminded merchants that such tariffs were possible and led them to support a federal power over interstate commerce that would ensure uniform regulation. The same thing, in general, happened to New Jersey's paper money. New Jersey's issue of public paper was designed to pay the interest on both the state's debt and on its share of the continental debt. Each year the paper was redeemed by taxes and then reissued to pay interest. It was an ingenious scheme, but unhappily much of it ended up in the hands of New York and Philadelphia merchants who discounted it heavily. Eventually the state found itself under an unmanageable burden of debt, its debtors received no relief, and alarmed merchants outside the state demanded that New Jersey stop flooding the country with paper.

Even so, the most notorious example of paper money abuse was provided by Rhode Island. The motive for the Rhode Island issues was much the same as New Jersey's—to pay interest on the state debt and incidentally provide some relief for rural interests. Rhode Island emerged from the war in a prosperous condition, having profited immensely from privateering and the presence of the free-spending French army; but it also had a staggering burden of state debt and a huge unpaid subsidy owed to the Continental Congress. A group of shrewd politicians concocted a scheme to issue a sum of paper money equal to the state debt and loan it to anyone who could furnish the requisite security. The interest on the loans would thus approximately equal the interest on the state debt. Because more currency was in circulation, the populace would tolerate a high level of taxes, and the revenue could be used to pay off the debt and retire the paper money.

The plan seemed foolproof, and it was enthusiastically approved in a popular referendum held early in 1786. Unfortunately, however, it overlooked two interests—merchant-creditors of Providence and Newport, who would have to accept the paper in trade, and holders of continental securities who were left out in the cold (since Rhode Island did not contemplate either paying its subsidy or assuming part of the continental debt, as other states were doing). In Providence and Newport the two interests were commonly united, the most prominent merchants being holders of continental securities. As a result, they deliberately undermined the plan, charging excessive prices for goods or refusing to accept Rhode Island paper at all. The value of the state's paper skidded to eight cents on the dollar. In retaliation the assembly made the money legal tender and levied a fine of £100 on anyone who refused to accept the bills at face value. When merchants closed up shop and retired to Boston to avoid payment in depreciated paper, the assembly permitted debtors to discharge their debts by depositing the sum in paper with the courts.

With mercantile support the scheme might have worked, for the state's debt was gradually retired and its commerce prospered. But the ludicrous image of debtors chasing creditors to pay off in worthless paper, grossly exaggerated by merchant-refugees, blackened the state's reputation and undermined public paper everywhere. The successful experiments in paper issues by several states were ignored in the uproar over Rhode Island. All along the seaboard, merchants denounced the practice and demanded a central government with sole authority over the money supply. After the federal Constitution was submitted to the states for approval in the fall of 1787, James Madison wrote to his friend Jefferson in Paris that "the evils issuing from [paper money] contributed more to the uneasiness which produced the [federal] Convention . . . than those which accrued to our national character and interest from the inadequacy of the Confederation."

"A Little Rebellion . . ."

Amidst the furor, it was generally forgotten that the issue of paper money had been approved by a substantial majority of the citizens of Rhode Island. Instead, the explanation of merchants that fanatical rural-debtor interests were responsible was widely accepted. To many eastern conservatives this was the sort of social upheaval they had long feared would result from the Revolution. Their mounting concern reached the dimensions of panic at the news of an agrarian upheaval in Massachusetts, led by a number of economically-pressed farmers, but associated in the minds of easterners with the name of Daniel Shays.

Shays's Rebellion was the product of both the depression and the paper money dispute. The Massachusetts economy was disrupted both by independence and the depression. The war destroyed the state's fishing fleet, and the industry did not recover until Congress granted a bounty on cod in 1790. Many of the state's most enterprising merchants were Loyalists who departed with the British army, and with them went skills and experience that were hard to replace. This in turn accelerated the decline of Boston, whose economy had been sputtering for some years before the Revolution. The British order-in-council of 1783, which disrupted the triangle trade and dented the flow of specie, was only the final blow.

Rural Massachusetts suffered commensurately. Farm prices plummeted, money was scarce, and debts mounted. In addition, the state's tax system, devised by eastern merchants, fell particularly hard on farmers, for the main revenue-producing device was a tax on real estate levied by the acre without regard to value. Western farmers complained that they were overtaxed and underrepresented. But they seldom paid taxes, for lack of specie, and they did not send delegates to the assembly (which they could have controlled) because they could not afford the transportation expenses. During the early 1780s the lax and genial administration of Governor John Hancock was widely popular, and the West settled into a narrow provincialism that permitted eastern merchants to manage the state.

When Hancock retired in 1785 (possibly foreseeing trouble), James Bowdoin, candidate of the Boston merchants, began to reorganize the state's tangled finances. To undertake payments on the public debt, much of which was held by Boston merchants, Bowdoin induced the assembly to impose a new excise, to increase the poll tax, and, in a monumental blunder, to adopt a stamp tax. New collectors were sent into the hinterland, and the flow of additional revenue eased the fiscal crisis, but new levies increased the hardship in the penniless West. Rural interests, hoping to imitate Rhode Island by using paper money to pay interest on the debt, were bitterly disappointed when the assembly rejected a paper money bill in the spring of 1786.

Western farmers soon directed their wrath at the courts, which were the main instrument for the collection of debts. Lawyers had long been suspect in Puritan Massachusetts, and fees charged by judges and attorneys were an ancient grievance among farmers. Courts, moreover, were the only governmental agency with statewide influence. The assembly in Boston was remote, devious, and controlled by the East, but the county courts were something the farmers could get their hands on.

Throughout the month of August 1786, the West simmered with discontent. On the twenty-sixth, a meeting of delegates from thirty-seven towns in Worcester County drafted a petition of grievances denouncing the costs of justice, the tax system, and the shortage of money. Three days later a mob of 1,500 angry farmers interrupted a meeting of the Hampshire County court in Northampton. The discord was not confined to the Connecticut Valley and the Berkshire Hills, however; during September, county courts were disrupted in Great Barrington, Taunton, and Concord, at the very gates of Boston. In November, court proceedings in Hampshire and Middlesex counties in the middle of the state were halted by a band of several hundred armed men led by Daniel Shays, a bankrupt farmer who had been a captain in the Revolution. The authority of the state government west of Boston gradually dissolved.

The "rebellion" sent a shiver of fear along the eastern seaboard. "Our affairs seem to lead to some crisis," wrote John Jay from the relative security of New York, "some revolution—something I cannot foresee or conjecture. I am uneasy and apprehensive; more so than during the war." The Massachusetts Assembly reacted with a mixture of panic and conciliation. During the autumn, it reduced taxes by 75 percent, reformed the court system, and suspended judgments against debtors for eight months. But it also called for help from Congress, and Congress responded by authorizing Secretary at War Knox to raise 1,340 men for the defense of Massachusetts against Native Americans, though no belligerent tribes had been seen in the state since the French war. The farmers knew well who the "Indians" were, and they made plans to seize the federal arsenal at Springfield. When Governor Bowdoin learned of this threat, he recruited a state army of four thousand volunteers under General Benjamin Lincoln and sent it to the defense of Springfield. In late January 1787, Lincoln defeated Shays in a brief battle and scattered his band of 1,200 rebels. Within a few weeks the other rebel groups surrendered or dispersed, and the rebellion was over.

Rebellion is hardly the word for it; "mob action" would be more appropriate. Shays and his followers never seriously threatened the existence of the state government; in the end they were suppressed by volunteer forces financed largely by Boston merchants without the help of the Continental Congress. But the reaction of eastern conservatives verged on hysteria. This was just the sort of radicalism that they had long feared. David Humphreys, Connecticut merchant, poet, and later secretary to President Washington, detected in the fall of 1786 "a licentious spirit prevailing among many of the people; a levelling principle; a desire of Change." Even in distant Virginia, Washington, informed by his Massachusetts friend Henry Knox that the rebels were "levelers" who aimed to redistribute property, shivered in apprehension.

On the other hand, Thomas Jefferson, benefiting from the perspective afforded by three thousand miles of ocean, viewed the incident with equanimity. To the son-in-law of John Adams he observed:

> We have had 13 states independent for 11 years. There has been one rebellion. That comes to one rebellion in a century and a half for each state. What country before ever existed a century and a half without a rebellion? And what country can preserve its liberties, if its rulers are not warned from time to time that their people preserve the spirit of resistance? Let them take arms. . . . What signify a few lives lost in a century or two? The tree of liberty must be refreshed from time to time, with the blood of patriots and tyrants. It is its natural manure.

But Jefferson's faith in republican government was not shared by many. Closer to the scene of violence, merchants, lawyers, and landowners in New England, many of whom had doubted the value of central authority, now looked for a government that might have power to protect property and put down domestic violence. Shays's Rebellion thus gave added momentum to the movement already under way for strengthening the Articles of Confederation. One Philadelphia merchant, foreseeing a crisis in the summer of 1786, suggested that "a Convulsion of some kind seems to be desirable," for it affords "the only chance we have of restoration to political health."

Toward a Stronger Union

The movement to strengthen the Articles of Confederation was underway from the moment they were ratified. Indeed, many of those who generally approved the Articles saw room for improvement. When the war ended, attention focused on two vital powers—commerce and taxation. Most merchants desired federal regulation of interstate and foreign commerce to insure uniformity at home and leverage abroad in bargaining for trade concessions. To retaliate against the British order-in-council of 1783, Congress asked for power to pass a navigation act of its own. But the amendment was never approved because southern states feared it would give northern merchants a monopoly of their trade.

The power to tax was even more important, for as long as Congress was dependent upon the voluntary contributions of states it could have neither authority nor influence. After the war, a few of the states began assuming part of the continental debt held by their citizens, instead of sending subsidies to Congress, and the authority of Congress slipped another notch. After its first request was killed by Rhode Island, Congress in 1783 tried again, asking for power to levy customs duties for twenty-five years. Rhode Island and eleven other states approved this amendment, but this time New York balked. Under anti-nationalist Governor George Clinton, New York in 1786 agreed to the amendment with the stipulation that collections be made by state officials and the state's paper money be acceptable in payment of duties. The conditions were contrary to some of the expressed stipulations of other states, and Congress could not accept them. The impost amendment was dead.

That same year Congress made one last effort to save itself from total atrophy. It appointed an investigating committee, headed by James Monroe of Virginia (a "trimmer" who consistently worked to improve the Articles but later voted against the Constitution). The committee recommended extensive changes that would give Congress power to regulate commerce, power to levy an impost when only eleven states agreed, and authority to force the states to pay their annual subsidies. It also suggested a national judiciary with power to enforce the regulations of Congress. The proposals did not alter the essential character of the Confederation; they were designed, rather, to make it work. Congress debated the report for several weeks in the spring of 1786, but it never came to a vote, largely because most nationalists by then had lost interest. They had come to the conclusion that only a total overhaul of the government would do. The problem of government, they had come to see, had more than one dimension. In drafting their revolutionary governments they had focused on preventing oppression, but by creating weak governments they now risked anarchy. The Philadelphia physician and political radical Benjamin Rush expressed it thus: "In our opposition to monarchy, we forgot that the temple of tyranny has two doors. We bolted one of them by proper restraints; but we left the other open, by neglecting to guard against the effects of our own ignorance and licentiousness."

By 1786, in corresponding with one another, the group who favored constitutional reform had begun to refer to themselves as "Federalists." This gave new meaning to a term that had previously been loosely applied to any association of sovereign states. Federation—as opposed to confederation—meant a balance of power between a central government and the states, a system that endowed the central government with adequate powers in the realm of taxation, trade, and foreign relations, while leaving the daily chores of government to the states. The most diligent disciple of this new, and as yet very nebulous, creed was James Madison of Virginia. Son of a respectable Piedmont planter and educated at Princeton, Madison was elected to the Virginia Assembly before he reached the age of twenty. He served on the council of state while Jefferson was governor, and the two men formed a working relationship that would last the rest of their lives. The assembly sent Madison to Congress in 1781 where he became acquainted with Alexander Hamilton and other nationalists. Madison plunged at once into the work at hand, and he played an important role in managing the fiscal crisis and responding to the army's threats of mutiny. Each new crisis, however, strengthened his conviction that the government must be reformed. After finishing his three-year term, he returned to the Virginia House of Delegates where he did battle with Patrick Henry over paper money, repayment of British debts, and disestablishment of the Anglican Church. His most signal achievement of these years was steering through a reluctant assembly the Statute for Religious Freedom drafted by Jefferson nearly ten years before. He maintained contact with Jefferson in Paris and Monroe in Congress, writing lengthy descriptions of Virginia politics and the progress of the movement for constitutional reform.

Madison also assiduously courted Washington, striking up a correspondence even though the two had never met. Washington's support was essential to the success of any movement for constitutional reform, and Washington was a natural ally. His war experience had made him fully aware of the shortcomings of Congress, and he fretted continually about the nation's drift into anarchy. He also had substantial landholdings in the West that had come to him as a reward for his military service. These would be greatly improved in value with the installation of a government strong enough and solvent enough to suppress Native Americans, build roads, and improve rivers. In January 1785, Washington agreed to serve as president of the Potomac Company, a newly created stock company that planned to open the Potomac to navigation as far as the Blue Ridge and the Shenandoah River.

It was navigation of the Potomac that, almost by coincidence, presented the Federalists with a means by which to reform the government. Down to 1786, they seem to have concentrated on securing amendments to the Articles of Confederation, working within the Continental Congress, rather than trying to bypass it. As early as 1780, Alexander Hamilton had boldly proposed a constitutional convention to revise the government, but the idea had not caught on. Many years later Madison would claim credit for orchestrating the series of meetings that culminated with the Federal Convention of 1787, but the contemporary evidence—including his own private correspondence—indicates that the idea of bypassing Congress, scrapping the Articles, and starting afresh was slow in developing. Indeed, the initial meeting was almost accidental. It all started with the Potomac River.

By its colonial charter the boundary of Maryland extended to the south shore of the Potomac, rather than the middle of the river, and the state of Maryland asserted the same claim upon independence. In 1784, Madison visited Alexandria and was shocked to discover that foreign vessels unloaded goods on the Virginia shore without paying taxes to either state. He decided that it was time that Maryland and Virginia formulate some joint rules on the navigation of the Potomac. The two legislatures agreed and nominated delegates for a meeting in Alexandria in March 1785. Someone blundered on the Virginia side, however, and the Virginia nominees were not notified of their appointment or of the time and place of the meeting. When the Maryland commissioners arrived in Alexandria, they went to the home of Thomas Henderson, one of the Virginia commissioners. Henderson quickly recovered from his surprise and promptly notified George Mason, another of the Virginia delegates. That gout-ridden gentleman, obviously embarrassed, decided that the meeting should proceed without delay, even though Madison and Edmund Randolph, the remaining Virginia delegates, were still at home. Washington learned of the meeting and, as president of the Potomac Company, took an immediate interest. He invited the delegates to Mount Vernon where he offered the hospitality of his estate.

At Mount Vernon the commissioners agreed on regulations for Chesapeake Bay and the Potomac River, and they recommended another convention to establish uniform tariff duties for the area. The following winter the legislatures of both states ratified the agreements reached at Mount Vernon. In the Virginia Assembly Madison proposed that the agreement be submitted to Congress for its approval, but the anti-nationalists were unwilling to involve that body. Instead the assembly adopted a resolution submitted by John Tyler, a political fence-straddler who more often than not sided with Patrick Henry in assembly balloting. Tyler's resolution proposed a meeting of delegates from all the states at Annapolis, Maryland, to discuss "such commercial regulations [as] may be necessary to their common interest and their permanent harmony." What prompted Tyler's move remains a mystery. In any case, the Henryites did not oppose it, perhaps because they saw nothing wrong with agreements among the sovereign states. Madison went along with the idea, but he was skeptical that much would come of it. To Jefferson he complained about the size of the Virginia delegation, fearing that it was so large that it would be unable to agree on anything. By the summer of 1786, however, as other states responded favorably and named delegates to Annapolis, Madison was becoming cautiously optimistic. After a late-summer visit to Philadelphia he told Jefferson that some people wanted to make the Annapolis meeting a steppingstone to a "Plenipotentiary Convention for amending the Confederation."

The Annapolis Convention met in September 1786, while New England was in an uproar over Shays's Rebellion. Only twelve delegates appeared, but most were ardent nationalists, representing New York, New Jersey, Delaware, Pennsylvania, and Virginia. Maryland, though host, ignored the proceedings for fear that they might undermine the authority of Congress. The Clinton faction in New York took little interest in the convention, so Alexander Hamilton nominated himself. The rest of the delegates were sent by their assemblies. The twelve had no difficulty deciding upon a plan of operations. Instead of discussing a commercial agreement, they issued a statement drawn up by Hamilton citing the weaknesses in the Confederation and calling for a new convention to meet in Philadelphia on the second Monday in May 1787, to consider commerce and "such other purposes" as public affairs might require.

The report of the Annapolis meeting was suitably vague, designed to frighten no one, yet leave the way open for the Philadelphia convention to write a new constitution. The summons placed the opponents of change in a dilemma. Many of them recognized the defects in the Articles and backed the amendments suggested by the Monroe committee in Congress. So long as the Philadelphia meeting was authorized only to recommend reforms within the existing framework, they could not oppose it. But they saw no need for radical innovations. The proposal, however, gave the advocates of change the initiative, and they never lost it. Madison returned to the Virginia Assembly and obtained its endorsement for another convention. Madison then got himself elected to Congress and secured that body's approval. As state after state nominated delegates during the winter of 1786–87, all seemed to be going according to plan. At that juncture foreign affairs intruded, causing a sectional-economic conflict that threatened the entire movement for a new constitution.

Spain had joined the war in 1779 as an ally of France, but it neither recognized nor approved of the United States. In a move to exclude rough frontiersmen from Spanish territory and prevent the spread of subversive ideas, Spain in 1784 closed the Mississippi River to American traffic. A year later Spain sent a special emissary, Don Diego de Gardoqui, to negotiate a treaty of amity and commerce with the United States. Congress accordingly instructed its secretary for foreign affairs, John Jay, not to give up the right to navigate the river and deposit American goods at the port of New Orleans. The privilege was essential to the people living west of the mountains. Since it was not feasible to transport farm products across the mountains to the eastern seaboard, their only access to the markets of the world was downriver, by way of the Ohio or the Tennessee, and the Mississippi. In the course of the Jay-Gardoqui negotiations it became evident that Spain would not open any part of its empire; but, it would make concessions on American exports to Spain, especially fish, if the United States would recognize Spain's exclusive control of the mouth of the Mississippi. In August 1786, Jay so reported to Congress and requested permission to be relieved of his instructions concerning the river in order to reach some sort of commercial agreement.

The issue had sectional implications that threatened to destroy the movement for constitutional revision. New England enthusiastically approved the idea of opening new markets in Spain, even at the risk of abandoning the West. Virginia, whose sons were rapidly populating Kentucky and Tennessee, reacted with alarm. In November, the House of Delegates unanimously passed resolutions declaring the American right to use the Mississippi, while Patrick Henry hinted darkly that George Rogers Clark might be unleashed on New Orleans. Jay's request, Henry informed Virginians, was just the sort of thing they might expect under a federal government dominated by northern merchants. Recognizing the threat to his plans for the Philadelphia meeting, Madison spent the spring sniping at Jay from the floor of Congress. He never secured a public disavowal of the intended concessions which he could hand to Patrick Henry, but the negotiations were quietly dropped in April 1787. The young Virginian then set off for Philadelphia to prepare for the coming convention.

The Federal Convention

Observing American events from Paris, Thomas Jefferson was impressed enough with the stature of the men convening at Philadelphia to call it an "assembly of demi-Gods." In that instance, distance lent romance rather than perspective, but, then, Jefferson was often inclined to hyperbole when he took quill in hand to address a friend. He might have noted, for instance, that many of the great republicans who had spearheaded the movement for independence were conspicuously absent. His colleague on the committee that drafted the Declaration, John Adams, was representing the nation in London. Samuel Adams and John Hancock were not chosen as delegates, while Patrick Henry and Richard Henry Lee were elected but declined to serve. All four generally approved the Articles and were suspicious of the intentions of the Philadelphia meeting. Henry summed up their attitude when he explained, "I smelt a rat."

Despite these absences, Jefferson was correct in his judgment that the Philadelphia convention was the most distinguished body of men yet assembled on the North American continent. The Virginia delegation, even without Jefferson, was spangled with notables—Washington, Madison, Edmund Randolph, George Mason, John Blair, George Wythe, and Dr. James McClurg. Randolph was governor of the state, and his selection emphasized the importance Virginia attached to the meeting. George Wythe was a signer of the Declaration of Independence, a justice of the Court of Chancery, and a professor of law at William and Mary who trained a generation of Virginia jurists (including Jefferson and John Marshall). George Mason generally shunned public office, but his role in drafting the Virginia Declaration of Rights and the state constitution of 1776 made him one of the outstanding representatives of Virginia republicanism.

The Pennsylvania delegation was almost equally impressive. It was led by Robert Morris and his protegés, Gouverneur Morris and James Wilson. Gouverneur Morris was a colorful, talkative New York aristocrat, a rhetorical genius with voice or pen. He had served his governmental apprenticeship under Robert Morris in the Department of Finance. James Wilson was a Scottish emigre in his mid-forties who had become one of the most prominent lawyer-politicians in the state. Featured in the Pennsylvania delegation was Benjamin Franklin, who, like Washington, added more in the way of prestige than ideas to the proceedings. John Dickinson, leading advocate of centralized government since the contest over the Articles a decade before, was missing from the Pennsylvania group, but he came into the convention wearing the livery of Delaware where he had served as president.

South Carolina dispatched its usual collection of Rutledges and Pinckneys. John Rutledge had been a member of the First and Second Continental Congresses and presided as governor of the state during the war. Charles Cotesworth Pinckney, English-educated and a general in the Continental Army, was a strong nationalist who subsequently filled a number of posts in the federal government. From New York came Alexander Hamilton, Robert Yates, and John Lansing, Jr. Only thirty years old, Hamilton was born on the West Indian island of Nevis, educated at King's College (Columbia), worked as aide to General Washington during the war, and served a two year term in Congress—a career that shaped him into the most ardent nationalist in the Convention. But Hamilton's influence was diluted by Yates and Lansing, both followers of Clinton who battled the nationalistic drift of the Convention until they finally went home in disgust.

Other states contributed individuals of distinction. William Paterson of New Jersey was a brilliant lawyer, attorney general of the state, and subsequently a member of the Supreme Court. Roger Sherman of Connecticut, a cobbler turned professional politician, possessed the distinction of being the only man to sign the Continental Association of 1774, the Declaration of Independence, the Articles of Confederation, and the Constitution. Rufus King, the only spark in a rather drab Massachusetts delegation, was a young lawyer unknown outside his home state, but he surprised the Convention with his deft tactics, oratory, and imagination, all of which gave promise of a productive political career that would last into the 1820s.

The Convention was scheduled to open on May 14, but on that date only the Virginia and Pennsylvania delegations possessed quorums. The assembled delegates marked time for two weeks until a majority of states were represented. To many it was reminiscent of the most vapid days of the Continental Congress. The Rhode Island legislature on three occasions voted not to send a delegation to the convention, and the New Hampshire delegation did not arrive until late July. Georgia was represented by only one man through most of the summer. A few states were too embarrassed financially to sustain their delegates; and, poor roads, mired by the wettest spring in memory, accounted for the tardiness of the rest.

Madison, who arrived eagerly on May 3, spent the interim devising a plan of government and lining up supporters. At last, on Friday the twenty-fifth, seven states were present, the Convention was called to order, Washington was elected president, and a committee on procedure was appointed. On the following Monday the committee made several proposals whose adoption would determine to a large extent the course of the convention. The first decision was to conduct the proceedings in secret. The idea was certainly novel, but it was also reasonable. No one, including Madison, had any clear-cut ideas on a form of government, and all wanted the freedom to change their minds in debate without being accused of inconsistency. The result was a genuine forum for the exchange of ideas; and, the enemies of change outside the hall were deprived of ammunition until it was all over. The other important procedural decision involved voting, a matter that had contributed to the debilitation of Congress. The Convention sat through the usual arguments for proportional representation, but in the end it decided to avoid dissension by giving each state one vote. The Convention agreed that a majority of seven states constituted a quorum, that a majority vote of the state delegations in attendance was needed to adopt any measure, that at least two delegates had to be present for a state to be conidered represented, and any issue once decided could be reconsidered.

Finally ready for business, the Convention on May 29 faced the crucial question of what to do. Should it offer suggestions for revision of the Confederation (as many delegates were instructed to do), or should it attempt to frame an entirely new form of government? While waiting for a quorum the delegates had ample opportunity to explore one another's views; and, not surprisingly, they discovered among themselves a general willingness to undertake a new departure. The question was how far to go. At one extreme was the possibility of creating a purely national government with a virtual monopoly on power. This was the view of one delegate, George Read, who suggested abolishing the states altogether. Hamilton probably agreed with that idea but regarded it as impractical. Most of the delegates wanted to preserve the states, while drawing a line between national and state authority, and they desired some provision, to ensure that the supreme authority would reside in the national government. The problem was how to establish the proper relationship between the national government and the states. Addressing the convention on June 6, John Dickinson came up with a solution that was both theoretically sound and practical. He suggested a mixed system, partly national and partly federal, in which one branch of the government would "be drawn immediately from the people," while the other branch would represent the states as states and be chosen by the state legislatures. The Constitution thus would achieve the classic balance of the one, the few, and the many, with the states serving the function of the English House of Lords. Dickinson thus provided the theoretical foundation for the new Constitution; however, there was many a battle to be fought in achieving the reality.

On taking the chair Washington, in a rare moment of eloquence, warned the delegates:

> It is too probable that no plan we propose will be adopted. Perhaps another dreadful conflict is to be sustained. If to please the people, we offer what we ourselves disapprove, how can we afterwards defend our work? Let us raise a standard to which the wise and honest can repair. The event is in the hand of God.

Governor Randolph then "opened the main business" with a speech detailing the defects in the Articles of Confederation and submitted a series of fifteen resolutions that constituted the "Virginia Plan." Conceived by Madison and modified in minor ways by his colleagues, the plan reflected Madison's concern for separation of powers, rather than a "balanced government" that protected the interests of the upper class. Unlike such nationalists as Hamilton and Dickinson, Madison was deeply concerned that the government contain internal checks, lest it become an engine of tyranny. Early next year in essay Number 51 of *The Federalist,* Madison described the fundamental problem that the Convention faced: "But what is government itself but the greatest of all reflections on human nature? If men were angels, no government would be necessary. If angels were to govern men, neither external nor internal controls on government would be necessary. In framing a government which is to be administered by men over men, the great difficulty lies in this: You must first enable the government to control the governed; and in the next place, oblige it to control itself."

Accordingly, the Virginia Plan proposed three independent branches of government—executive, legislative, and judicial—each with specifically delegated powers. The legislature would contain two houses, apportioned among the states by population or wealth, which reflected Virginia's long-held view that the larger states ought to have representation in proportion to their size. The powers granted to both the executive and legislature were stated in general terms (Madison obviously contemplated some bargaining), but by virtue of being general they also seemed unlimited. The scheme even included a power to legislate in cases where the individual states proved incompetent.

Randolph's proposals were discussed for the next two weeks, and in the course of debate it became obvious that the Convention was divided between large states, who favored proportional representation and centralized power, and small states, who demanded equal representation and limited power. The division was predicated less on current population than on access to western land and the promise of future growth. Hence, sparsely populated Georgia voted with the large states. The division was further affected, of course, by the personal predilections of the delegates, some of whom voted politics rather than interest. New York's stance with the small states, for instance, was determined by Yates and Lansing, both anti-nationalist Clintonians; when they went home in July, Hamilton consistently represented the nationalist position, but being the only delegate from the state, he could not vote on any issue. During these days of adjustment and exploration there was no consistent alignment, but Massachusetts, Pennsylvania, Virginia, the Carolinas, and Georgia generally supported the Virginia Plan, while New England, New York, New Jersey, Delaware, and Maryland opposed it. The division was thus sectional, as well.

On June 15, William Paterson of New Jersey offered an alternative set of proposals on behalf of the small states. The New Jersey Plan started with the existing Confederation and sought to make it workable. The unicameral Congress and the system of representation by states were both retained, though the plan envisioned an independent executive and judiciary. Paterson also wanted to grant Congress enough powers to make it a sovereign government; its laws would be supreme and binding upon the states as well as individuals. The small states' program thus looked to the formation of a strong central government, but these states wanted to make sure that the federal government was not dominated by their larger neighbors. The plan proved unacceptable to the Convention, however, and it received only the votes of New York, New Jersey, and Delaware (with Maryland divided). The meeting then returned to considering the Virginia Plan, but the issue of representation remained paramount. The debate raged through two more weeks, while tempers rose along with the thermometer, but neither side would budge.

The division in the Convention was more than a simple disagreement between large and small states; it was also a split between North and South. Central to the issue of representation was the question of whether one counted slaves as "persons," even though they had no rights. Southerners naturally wanted them counted, arguing that slaves, whether considered people or property represented wealth. "Money was power," a South Carolinian bluntly told the Convention, "and the States ought to have weight in the Government in proportion to their wealth." Southern delegates pointed out that South Carolina and Connecticut had approximately the same number of inhabitants, but that in South Carolina more than 100,000 of the inhabitants were slaves. If slaves were not counted, wealthy South Carolina would have less influence in federal councils than Connecticut.

At the outset of this discussion southerners offered to compromise on a ratio of three-fifths, that is, only three-fifths of the slaves would be counted for purposes of representation. This ratio was familiar to all delegates because in 1783 the Continental Congress had proposed, and eleven of the states had accepted, that this ratio be used in calculating the sum each state was to contribute for the support of the Confederation government. Elbridge Gerry of Massachusetts objected to any sort of compromise, insisting that slaves were property of the sort that cattle and horses were in the North. He did not see why one species of property should be counted as population any more than the other. Nevertheless nine states approved the three-fifths compromise. Application, however, depended on resolution of the larger issue of representation by population versus equal representation by state.

To end the impasse, Roger Sherman of Connecticut on July 2 suggested the appointment of a select committee, consisting of one delegate from each state, to work out a compromise. No one much liked the idea, but the only alternative was to confess failure and return home. In three days the committee, headed by Franklin, formulated a compromise based on the theoretical foundation offered by Dickinson at the beginning of the Convention. Franklin proposed that the large states concede equality of voting in the second house, and the small states in turn should allow the first house to be apportioned according to population and to be given exclusive power to initiate money bills. The large states were not completely happy with this niggling concession, but North Carolina's switch enabled the compromise to pass, five states to four with one divided (New York and New Hampshire not represented).

Adoption of the "Connecticut Compromise" assured the small states an equal voice in one house and preserved their integrity against both a consolidated central government and their larger neighbors. Their interests protected, the delegates from the small states demonstrated their latent nationalism, quickly agreeing to the remainder of the Virginia Plan. They agreed to grant adequate powers to Congress, create a single executive with extensive authority, and an independent judiciary.

Having agreed on a general framework, the Convention on July 26 gave its resolutions to a five-man Committee of Detail and adjourned for ten days. Utilizing the sense of the meeting as expressed in resolutions, speeches, and private agreements, the committee drafted a constitution consisting of a preamble and twenty-three articles. The result was a practical merger of the Virginia and New Jersey plans, creating a strong national government with extensive but specifically enumerated powers. The committee also conferred names on the various branches of government—President, Supreme Court, Congress, House of Representatives (for the "first house"), and Senate (for the "second house").

The Convention reassembled on August 6 to view the result and spent the next month on minor changes that pacified special interests. Property interests were protected by clauses prohibiting the states from emitting paper money or interfering with contracts. The South obtained a prohibition on export taxes that might interfere with its staple trade and managed to prevent any federal restrictions on the slave trade until 1808. Southern states also desired a two-thirds vote in Congress for the approval of any navigation acts, but this was blocked by the commercial interest of New England. The landless states wanted power over western lands to be lodged in the Senate, where they had equal representation, but the large states prevented this and even secured a provision that protected a state from being subdivided without its consent.

The one major change that resulted from the August discussions was the selection of the president by an electoral college, instead of by Congress. The alteration made the president independent of Congress, and since the president nominated federal judges it made them too less susceptible to legislative influence. The presidential veto, moreover, and the senatorial power of advice and consent over appointments enabled each branch to check the other two. The concept of checks and balances—probably the Convention's most important contribution to the theory of government—was implicit in both the Virginia and New Jersey plans, but it required considerable negotiation and adjustment to achieve its final form. Ironically, although it achieved Madison's aim of checking tyranny, it did so only by abandoning his initial concept of a rigid separation of powers. The Constitution was thus a unique blend of the political philosophies current in the eighteenth century; and it was a foundation for a new political order.

On September 8, the Convention referred the document to the Committee of Style to give it final form. The most important member was Gouverneur Morris, whose literary flair was widely recognized, and it is largely to his talent that the Constitution owes its clear, concise style. Morris took a few liberties with the text, but the only notable one was a change in the Preamble. The original language listed each of the states as ordaining and establishing the Constitution; Morris substituted "We, the People of the United States. . . ." Few delegates noted any significance in the change, and, indeed, it was dictated by necessity since it was quite possible that one or more states might refuse to ratify. Yet the change in wording represented a subtle change in philosophy that did not escape later generations. In contrast to the Articles of Confederation, which nowhere referred to the people but always to the "States in Congress assembled," the Constitution placed its foundation on the will of the people in language reminiscent of the Declaration of Independence. If nothing else, the change symbolized the reunion of the American people under a new central regime, more powerful, but also more popular, than the British empire.

On September 12, the Committee of Style submitted its report together with printed copies of the Constitution. Then a hitch developed when George Mason of Virginia demanded a bill of rights that would protect the essential liberties of citizens. Mason, along with his colleague, Edmund Randolph, and Elbridge Gerry, of Massachusetts, had become increasingly concerned with the total impact of the powers granted the federal government and the lack of any protection for private rights. His proposal was rejected by weary delegates who felt that such a list was unnecessary since the Constitution did not give Congress power to abridge the rights of individuals. On September 17, thirty-nine men signed the Constitution. Most of those who objected to the trend of the Convention had already gone home; only three still in attendance refused to sign—Mason, Gerry, and Randolph. Their criticism was ominous, however, because the demand for a bill of rights soon became the loudest argument against ratification.

The Great Debate

The Constitution itself outlined the ratification procedure. The Convention deliberately bypassed the state legislatures where the Constitution might become entangled in other issues or mired in local jealousies. Since most state legislatures consisted of two houses, legislative ratification would double the number of contests necessary to adopt the Constitution. It, therefore, was decided to submit the Constitution to specially elected ratifying conventions; the approval of only nine states was required to put the instrument into effect among the adopting states.

On September 28, Congress referred the Constitution to the states without recommendation one way or the other. Congress's approval was certain, but Federalists worried about the appearance of division because of the objectives voiced by delegates such as Richard Henry Lee and William Grayson of Virginia; Nathan Dane of Massachusetts, and Melancton Smith of New York. Both sides compromised: Federalists gave up the idea of a congressional endoresment of the Constitution, and Antifederalists agreed not to place their objectives or proposed amendments on Congress's journals. The fact that Congress transmitted the Constitution to the states by a unanimous vote suggested approval to most newspaper readers, and for the moment that was enough.

Once the Constitution was submitted to the states for ratification the secrecy was over, and sides quickly formed. Supporters of the Constitution publicly assumed the name Federalists, a term their opponents had previously used to describe themselves because it seemed to emphasize the importance of state powers. Nationalists had quietly been appropriating the name for some years, however; and the Constitution itself gave new meaning to the term, suggesting that it was possible to have a stronger central government while still retaining essential rights in the hands of the states. The Federalists thus considered the name an honest description of their political beliefs, but it was also a shrewd strategem because it forced the critics of the Constitution to assume the name Antifederalists, a title that was neither catchy nor positive.

Indeed, the vacuity of the name itself suggests the fundamental dilemma of the Antifederalists. Lacking a program, they could do little more than endorse the status quo. Even this was not common to all of them, for they had been divided on the question of amending the Articles, divided on the necessity for a convention, and divided on its result. Some Antifederalists dismissed the Constitution as a "national" government that would leave the states with a mere shadow of their powers, while others felt they could live with it provided changes were made, such as limitations on the tax power. In addition, most of the Antifederalists were men accustomed to local politics who knew nothing of one another and cared little about affairs outside their own states. Under such conditions a concerted effort to prevent approval of the Constitution was virtually impossible, even if they could command (as they probably could) a popular majority. Those who defend existing conditions are necessarily at a disadvantage, for the proponents of change inevitably have a positive program and an interested group to support it. The only question, usually, is whether they can command enough public support to put it over.

The Federalists seized the initiative when they promoted the convention idea, and they never relinquished it. A seemingly innocuous convention, assembled to discuss mutual problems, produced in utmost secrecy an entirely new frame of government, which was suddenly submitted to the people for approval. Federalists moreover, hinted broadly that alterations by any one state, however minor, would cause the entire scheme to flounder in a morass of petty bickering. Hence the only choices were "aye" or "nay," and a negative might well mean chaos. These arguments were effective, but most individuals made up their minds in the light of their own social, philosophical, or economic advantage.

For many it was a vote against the past—they had become disgusted with the seemingly chaotic political conditions and hoped for something better. This was certainly true of many former members of Congress and military officers, all of whom had struggled with governmental ineptitude during the war. The war affected in similar fashion those who suffered devastation from military campaigns or prolonged British occupation. On the other hand, there were others who failed to make progress in the postwar years and desired change. The states of Connecticut, New Jersey, and Delaware were commercially stagnant, dependent upon their larger neighbors, and unable to go it alone, while Georgia felt itself threatened by the Spanish on its flank and the Indians at its back. In all four the voters were overwhelmingly Federalist, regardless of their individual status or vocation.

Besides the hope born of change there were many who saw special advantages in the Constitution. Men of wealth and property generally, whether landowners or merchants, seized upon the promise of stability and maintenance of law and order in a stronger federal regime. Creditors generally benefitted from the prohibitions on state paper money and debtor-relief laws, and those who held securities of the national debt were certain to be reimbursed at substantial profit from the new federal tax power. Yet support for the Constitution was by no means confined to the wealthy. Artisans in the cities, who fashioned primitive manufactured goods in their own shops, hoped to gain tariff duties that would protect them from foreign competition. Even farmers stood to benefit from the shift in taxation from landed property (at the state level) to customs duties (at the national level).

Unfortunately, most farmers were too far removed from the political dialogue to be aware of such sophisticated and problematical benefits. Those who lived near channels of communication, such as in the great river valleys or in proximity to important cities, were often Federalists; but, those scattered across the vast American hinterland were hostile or indifferent to the Constitution. Since 90 percent of the population lived in rural areas, it is probable that a majority of Americans were opposed to ratification; but these were also the most provincial who cared least about the outcome. In the election of delegates to the state ratifying conventions in the winter of 1787–88, about two-thirds of the white adult males in the nation did not participate. A few of these were excluded by property qualifications for voting, others were kept from the polls by bad weather and worse roads, but most were claimed by apathy and indifference.

The advantage of Federalist momentum was almost immediately evident in Pennsylvania, a crucial state because of its size and central location. Pennsylvania, moreover, possessed a fairly well-developed party system. For more than a decade two political factions, divided between critics and supporters of the democratic state constitution of 1776, had struggled for control of the state

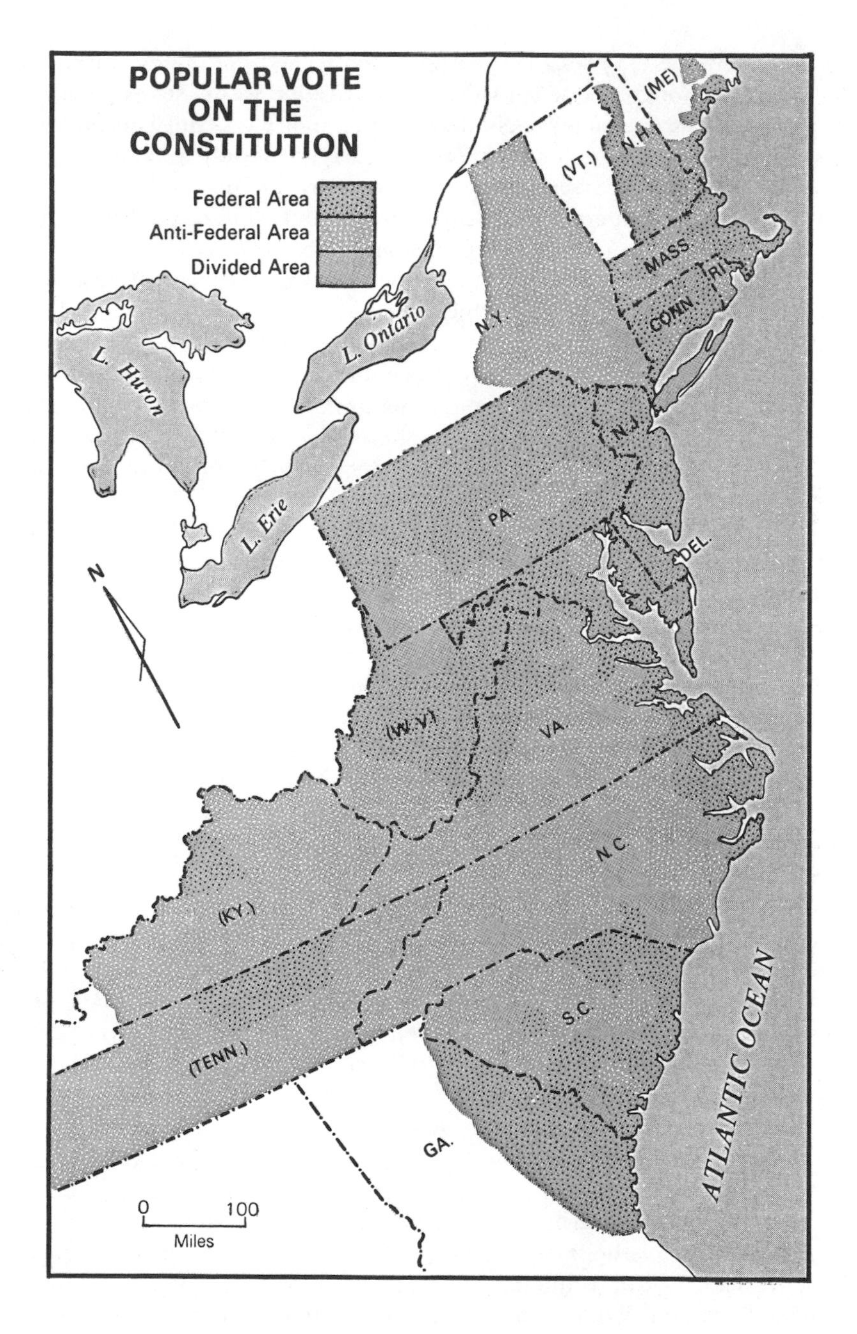

with neither gaining a decisive advantage. The Republicans, who drew most of their popular support from the city of Philadelphia and the more settled counties of the Delaware and Susquehanna valleys, were led by Robert Morris and generally favored strong government on the national level. Having won the 1786 election, this faction had a slight edge in the Pennsylvania Assembly, but unfortunately the 1787 session was scheduled to end on September 29, only one day after Congress transmitted the Constitution to the states. Speed was essential, for a new assembly might delay summoning a ratifying convention for months. The opposition Constitutionalist Party, generally anti-nationalist in federal affairs, drew its strength from the Scots-Irish settlements on the northern and western frontiers. Delay would thus permit them to publish the Constitution in the backcountry and organize an opposition.

The instant Congress adopted the resolution transmitting the Constitution, a courier sped from New York to Philadelphia, arriving only a few hours before the assembly was to adjourn. To block assembly approval nineteen members of the opposition walked out in order to prevent the necessary two-thirds quorum. The Federalists accordingly sent gangs to scour the city for the absent members; two were found and dragged back to the house for the necessary quorum. The assembly then scheduled an election for delegates to a convention that would open on November 20. The Federalists launched an intensive election campaign in the city and county of Philadelphia, the crucial area that had swung back and forth politically for a decade. The campaign was spectacularly successful. Federalists swept the city 1,198 votes to 160, won all five delegates in the county, and even carried two previously anti-nationalist counties in the West. When the convention opened on November 20, the Federalists had a two-thirds majority, and they rammed through the Constitution in three weeks.

By the time the Pennsylvania convention met, six other states had arranged for elections, and by the first day of February 1788, five states had ratified. All except Pennsylvania were small, insecure states—Delaware (actually the first to ratify, on December 7), New Jersey, Georgia, and Connecticut (the first three by unanimous votes). By the end of January, every state except Rhode Island, which ignored the proceedings entirely, had made provisions for a convention, but then the Federalist steamroller seemed to falter. During the fall, the Antifederalists began to communicate with one another, arranging strategy, and pouring out a torrent of criticism. In November, Luther Martin of Maryland, who had departed the Philadelphia Convention in August, published *The Genuine Information* in an effort to lift the veil of secrecy from the transactions of the Convention and expose the extent to which the delegates had violated their original instructions.

A month later an anonymous essayist produced the most persuasive of the Antifederalist tracts, *Letters from a Federal Farmer.* The Federal Farmer argued that the Constitution had gone too far in altering the substance, as well as the form, of the central government. To call it a "federal" system, he argued, was sheer hypocrisy, for the states were deprived of any direct role in the government. Instead, the Constitution created a truly national government whose laws were binding upon all the people. More than anything else, the Federal Farmer and his Antifederalist cohorts feared power, and in every phrase of the Constitution they saw a grant of power—to Congress, to the president, to the judiciary—unfettered and unrestrained. Nowhere could they detect any genuine guarantee of popular liberties or any listing of fundamental rights; and, the national character of the government seemed to destroy the bulwark of liberty that was most important of all, the sovereign states. Yet the general tone of Federal Farmer's arguments was moderate. He conceded the necessity for some alteration in the Articles of Confederation, and he even indicated that the Constitution could be made acceptable by the addition of a few amendments that would safeguard the rights of individuals.

The Federal Farmer pamphlet had a profound influence on opinion in Virginia and New York, where it was widely disseminated; but it also revealed the developing strategy of the Antifederalists. Avoiding a purely negative position, which might prove self-defeating, Federal Farmer and his allies decided to seek a second general convention to make necessary alterations. If nothing else, such a meeting would disrupt the nationalist movement and delay ratification for months, possibly years, and it would surely rearrange the Constitution. The strategy was shrewd, but it failed for lack of timing. A month after the Virginia Assembly approved the election of delegates to a ratifying convention, it adopted a resolution proposed by Patrick Henry instructing the governor to send a circular letter to the other states advocating a second convention. Even though the only governor likely to respond to such a proposal was George Clinton of New York, a Virginia-New York alliance might have nevertheless proved fatal to the ratification movement. But for some unaccountable reason, it took three months to reach New York. By the time Clinton received his copy of the circular on March 7, the New York Assembly had already agreed to summon a ratifying convention in June.

In the meantime the Virginia Federalists went to work on Governor Randolph whom his cousin, John Randolph of Roanoke, once called "a chameleon on an aspen: always quaking, always changing." Randolph's refusal to sign the Constitution was dictated by republican ideology, which required a bill of rights, and by his estimate of the political temper of Virginia, which was hostile. Both motives were subject to persuasion. His misgivings about the Constitution were relieved by the reasoned arguments of Washington, Madison, and John Marshall, while his political ambitions were satisfied by hints of a station in the new government. In 1789, President Washington appointed him the nation's first attorney general. Since Virginia was likely to elect an Antifederalist majority to its convention in June, the governor's conversion to the Federalist cause was nothing less than a political coup. "Loaves and fishes," Gouverneur Morris suggested when the ratification debate began, "must bribe the Demagogues. They must be made to expect higher offices under the general than the State Govts."

The same strategy worked in Massachusetts where the ratification convention, meeting in January 1788, was evenly divided. The merchants and lawyers of the seaboard were solidly in favor of the Constitution, while the Shaysite farmers of the interior were just as solidly against it. But it was an extremely large convention, containing more than three hundred delegates, and nearly half were uncommitted—farmers, artisans, village merchants, men of substance in their local communities who were open to persuasion and looked for leadership to the aging heroes, Samuel Adams and John Hancock. Both politicians had been suspicious of the nationalist movement; both were critical of the Constitution.

Samuel Adams was growing conservative in his advancing age. He openly approved of the state constitution of 1780, defended the established Congregational Church with a zeal the bordered on fanaticism, and shuddered at the anarchy of Shays's Rebellion. But the Federalists cleverly staged a mass meeting in Boston managed by Paul Revere and other old Sons of Liberty, and they adopted strong resolutions in favor of ratification. Adams then announced his conversion on the floor of the convention. Adams could control perhaps twenty delegates, but twice that many were in the pocket of John Hancock, who had dominated the politics of the state since 1780. Vain and ambitious, Hancock was brought into the fold by vague promises of the future vice presidency (which would obviously go to a New Englander if Washington were elected president). It was even possible that Virginia would reject the Constitution, thus making Washington ineligible, and who but Governor Hancock would be the logical choice for the highest office of all? On February 8, Massachusetts ratified the Constitution by a vote of 187 to 168.

Massachusetts's approval was critical, for it was the first state to ratify over a substantial opposition. As the price of ratification, Federalists agreed that the convention would instruct the state's future members of Congress to work for the proposal of amendments to the Constitution in the manner provided for in Article V of the new frame of government. Six of the remaining seven states ratified the Consitution in this manner. Massachusetts's ratification had a profound influence on opinion in New Hampshire and New York, both states in which a majority of the people opposed the Constitution. A shift of ten votes in Massachusetts would have stopped the ratification movement cold, but with that important hurdle cleared, Federalist momentum picked up once again. During the spring, two southern states, Maryland and South Carolina, ratified with comparative ease. Conditions in the two were similar. Each had an important commercial center, Baltimore and Charleston, and each was governed by a wealthy planter-gentry that favored order and stability. In late April, Maryland approved the Constitution by sixty-three to eleven; South Carolina followed suit a month later, supporting the new government by a margin of two to one. When New Hampshire followed the lead of Massachusetts and ratified on June 21, the requisite nine states was achieved.

Even so, the Federalists were worried, for the ratification drive seemed to stumble badly on the threshold of success. During the spring, the North Carolina electorate returned delegates that were solidly opposed to ratification, and Rhode Island held a referendum that rejected the Constitution by ten to one. Moreover, neither New York nor Virginia had given its consent, and without them the Union would have two gaping holes. If they disapproved, other states might be encouraged to withdraw, and the whole edifice would crumble. By all estimates a majority of the people in both states were hostile to the Constitution. The election in Virginia followed a familiar sectional pattern. The counties along the Potomac and lower James rivers had for several years looked to Madison for leadership and they elected a phalanx of Federalist delegates, while the tobacco-growing counties of the Piedmont followed Patrick Henry and elected Antifederalists. The only surprise was a shift in the stance of the counties in the Shenandoah Valley and the Alleghenies. It was here that the fate of the Constitution was decided, for these counties, previously wedded to Patrick Henry, voted solidly in favor of the new government. Evidently they hoped that the new regime would give them protection from the marauding Ohio tribes and remove the British from the forts along the Great Lakes.

In a sense, the Virginia election foretold the impact of the Constitution on American politics. In the representative system that had existed hitherto, men were elected because of their standing in the community. Once in the assembly they were expected to vote for the commonweal, making up their minds after the issues were discussed in intelligent debate. In the ratification election delegates became nothing more than proxies for an idea, or a platform if you will; they were chosen precisely because they were either Federalists or Antifederalists. And any who changed his mind after the election risked popular displeasure in the next contest. Electoral commitments to a program were a major step toward the evolution of modern political parties. Madison's circle, at least, was aware of the importance of such commitments. After the election was over, and some three months before the convention was to meet, a friend of Madison's predicted that the Constitution would be ratified in Virginia by a vote of 89 to 79. He hit it right on the nose.

The tradition of high-powered oratory, swaying listeners on the spot, was nevertheless far from dead. And each side entered the convention with a "murderers' row" of orators. The Federalist lineup combined the oratory of Edmund Randolph, the unchallenged republicanism of Edmund Pendleton and George Wythe, and the carefully reasoned arguments of Madison and John Marshall. Although Washington was not a delegate, convention Federalists used his prestige to good effect. The Antifederalists were also a distinguished lot—George Mason, James Monroe, Theodorick Bland—but all they really needed was Patrick Henry, a host in himself. For twenty-three days Henry held the delegates in his grasp, enthralled by his magic voice. Speaking two, three, and four hours at a time, he appealed to principles, to passion, and to prejudice. From the outset his tactics were clear—conditional ratification that would make enough changes in the Constitution to force another federal convention, or, at the very minimum, require the other states to summon new conventions to consider the alterations. He predicted that the tax power would raise the price of goods Virginians imported, the commerce power would mean domination by northern merchants, and the treaty-making power would force Virginians to pay their British creditors. But, most of all, he hammered at the lack of any guarantees for the rights of citizens.

Doctrinaire republicanism was a characteristic of Virginia planters, and Henry's arguments had broad appeal, which worried the Federalists. Madison had originally dismissed the idea of a bill of rights as unnecessary and potentially dangerous. It was humanly impossible to conceive or list all the potential rights of man, he had argued some months before, and a partial list might imply that there were no others. Rather than restrict freedom by trying to define it for all time, it would be far better to depend on the fact that the government was delegated only specific powers and the rest were retained by the people. But to undermine Patrick Henry, Madison shifted his ground and promised on the floor of the convention that he would personally work to secure amendments once the Constitution was ratified. The promise was welcome but probably unnecessary. There is no evidence that the lengthy debate changed a single mind. On June 25, Virginia ratified, 89 to 79. The Federalists immediately sped the good news to their beleaguered colleagues in New York.

It had been anticipated from the beginning that New York would be the most difficult because the state was under the thumb of an antinationalist, Governor George Clinton. A few days after the Philadelphia Convention adjourned, Madison traveled to New York to help Federalists get the Continental Congress to forward the Constitution to the states. About a month later, Madison agreed to collaborate with Hamilton and Jay on a series of essays designed to influence opinion in the state. Between October 27, 1787 and August 16, 1788, a total of eighty-five essays appeared in the New York press under the pseudonym "Publius," fifty-one turned out by Hamilton, twenty-six by Madison, and five by Jay (the remaining three a joint effort by Hamilton and Madison). Collectively published in the spring of 1788 as *The Federalist,* the essays remain today the most perceptive analysis of the American scheme of constitutional government. Yet they had only a small influence on the ratification movement, and even less on opinion in New York where the electorate in the spring of 1788 voted two to one against the Constitution. The Federalists carried only the city of New York and adjacent Long Island, along with two counties in the Hudson Valley; the rest of the upstate area clung to Clinton.

When the New York convention assembled in Poughkeepsie on June 17, the Antifederalists possessed a majority estimated at forty-six to nineteen. For a week they tore the Constitution apart clause by clause, pursuing their strategy of conditional ratification that would force a new federal convention. Hamilton and his following conducted a holding action until word arrived that New Hampshire and Virginia had ratified unconditionally. The Federalists then spread the rumor that the city of New York and the southern counties might secede from the state if the convention refused to join the Union. In hasty caucus the Clintonians decided to approve the Constitution "in full confidence" that amendments would subsequently be made, and on July 26 New York ratified by 30 to 27. The fact that North Carolina had voted a few days earlier not to ratify the Constitution no longer mattered, and in November 1789, that state belatedly joined the union. Intransigent little Rhode Island, faced with the threat of being subjected to tariff duties as a "foreign" country, finally approved the Constitution in the spring of 1790, but then only by the slimmest of margins, 34 to 32.

Formation of the federal government brought the American provinces full circle to the unity under a central regime that they had known as colonies. Yet there were important differences, for the new government would be responsible, however indirectly, to the average citizen. The Constitution was too hedged against popular rule to be an instrument of democracy, but it was nonetheless a radical innovation. It was an experiment in representative government on a scale that had never been attempted before. Few, even of its critics, demanded that it be democratic. Most Antifederalists were more concerned with popular rights than with popular rule. In that regard it lived up to the fondest hopes of its founders by ensuring new respect for the nation in the world abroad and providing relative stability at home. Yet it did nothing to hinder political reform and social progress. The promise of the Declaration of Independence that "all men are created equal" could still be pursued within the new framework of representative institutions. In January 1787, Benjamin Rush offered hope for the future of the great experiment: "The American war is over; but this is far from being the case with the American Revolution."

5

The Search for National Identity

The new Federal Constitution incorporated several progressive innovations, among them a national census every ten years. The national charter apportioned both direct taxes and membership in the House of Representatives by population and for this purpose it was clearly necessary to take a periodic head-count. In a rapidly expanding society with a mobile population, periodic reapportionment was an essential ingredient of popular government. It meant that the national legislature would never be burdened with the "rotten boroughs" that corrupted and debilitated the British House of Commons. In England alterations in the constituency of the Commons led to bitter partisan conflict throughout the nineteenth century; in America provision for change was incorporated into the original frame of government. The United States in 1790 was thus the first government to institute this reform (Britain conducted its first census in 1800).

By the census of 1790 the American population numbered nearly four million persons, a figure that would double by 1815 and double again every twenty-five years through the next century. The population was overwhelmingly rural—more than 95 percent of the people lived on farms or in small villages. It was also very youthful; nearly half the population was under sixteen years old because of early marriages and large families. Life expectancy was short (under forty years), but this was due to a high rate of infant mortality. Those who survived childhood could normally expect to live a half century or more. Thomas Jefferson lived to the age of eighty-three, and his longevity was not considered remarkable.

Ethnic composition of the white population was determined by the colonial immigration. Eighty percent were of British descent—English, Scottish, and Scots-Irish. Another 10 percent were Germans, and the remainder included a sprinkling of Welsh, French, Swiss, Dutch, and Scandinavians. The Revolution virtually halted immigration (except for Hessians who elected to stay after the war), and the new nation was eager to encourage a revival of the transatlantic flow of humanity. In 1790, Congress enacted a law that enabled aliens to become naturalized citizens in just two years, while private land speculators combed Europe for likely settlers. Immigration nonetheless was retarded by the European wars which lasted, with only brief intermissions, from 1793 to 1815. The British government also stemmed the flow of manpower by prohibiting emigration of skilled artisans and outlawing indenture contracts for transportation. As a result, immigration from 1790 to 1815 averaged only about eight thousand a year, a tiny fraction of the increase from the natural birthrate.

A Bourgeois Republic

The two most important geographical factors in American history were the Atlantic Ocean and the wilderness. The first virtually predetermined a middle-class society in America; the second hindered the subsequent development of class stratification by offering opportunity and encouraging mobility.

The Atlantic filter was a highly selective one—the voyage was tedious, dangerous, and expensive. The abject poor of Europe could not afford the trip. To be sure, many came as servants, working under contract for four or five years to reimburse their benefactors for the price of the crossing. But even these were usually people of imagination and initiative, often possessed of some property even though they lacked the cash for an ocean voyage. Most were British or German farmers displaced by the agricultural revolution of the eighteenth century. Conversely, the oppressed peasants of eastern Europe and the ragged denizens of the slums of London and Liverpool stayed home, at least until the late nineteenth century when communications were better.

The Atlantic barrier also discouraged the very wealthy. Anyone with position and status in the old country had little desire to pull up roots and start anew in the American woods. Soldiers and courtiers came to America to repair their fortunes, but few remained. Only one titled aristocrat, Virginia's Lord Fairfax, lived and died in America, and he retired to the frontier where he could indulge his love for hunting and fishing. Thus, from the beginning America was a middle-class society. There were substantial economic differences, of course, and Old World wealth was often translated into landed estates in the New World. Moreover, in some regions, such as the Connecticut River valley, the Hudson Valley, and low-country South Carolina, oligarchies of wealthy farmers and merchants were politically and socially dominant. But there was neither peasantry nor nobility—if one ignores for a moment the slave population—and that alone was something new for mankind.

The availability of free land preserved and even encouraged the middle-class character of American society. In its simplest form, the presence of free land was a constantly available alternative to the discontented and the unemployed. Efforts to establish a manorial system in Maryland in the seventeenth century, for instance, failed largely because no one was willing to serve. Why put up with a manorial court and the imperious edicts of its "lord" when a cheap farm and public justice were only a few miles away? It did not always work this way of course. Human beings are not perfectly mobile; they cannot and often will not pull up stakes and start afresh when things go wrong. In the 1760s the oppressed tenant farmers of New York's Hudson River valley fought their landlords with pitchforks and guns, instead of looking for new opportunities on the frontier. Similarly, every colonial city had its riotous element of discontented journeymen, abused apprentices, unemployed dockworkers, and bored sailors. For these people a frontier farm was not a viable alternative, if only because they did not know how to grow corn or tobacco. Even so, the wilderness offered many the opportunity for self-improvement.

America was an "underdeveloped" nation. It had land and natural resources aplenty and an industrious people who felt it almost a moral duty to exploit both. So long as the supply of investment capital was adequate, labor was certain to be in short supply. As a result, the daily wage for an American worker, whether urban or rural, was often 25 to 50 percent higher than in England. At the same time, very few Americans were actually getting rich. Capital, though often adequate, was never plentiful. In a colonial economy, the nation faced chronic trade deficits, and specie flowed to Europe to pay debts. Moreover, in a preindustrial economy the opportunities for advancement were limited. Merchants and land speculators occasionally turned handsome profits, but both ventures were risky. Robert Morris, the opulent financier of the Revolution, ended his career in a debtor's prison. Most Americans were farmers, and nobody has ever got rich with a horse and a hoe. Although there was a great deal of mobility in American society, much of it was sideways. Yet the movement itself represented a never ending search for opportunity; the promise was always there. The result was a social structure in which the differentials were primarily economic and occupational. At the bottom were the servants, both black and white. African American slavery will be discussed in another connection; white servitude was dying out. In the late colonial years most of the indentured servants who came to America were German "redemptioners," but that flow had slowed considerably by 1775. The Revolution stopped it completely, along with most other immigration. By 1790, most states prohibited indentured servitude, and the institution disappeared completely by 1815.

Within every region, no matter how well developed agriculturally, there were substantial social and economic differences among individuals. The differences, of course, were rather less on the frontier where society was newer and conditions more primitive. But Buckingham County, Virginia, in the heart of the tobacco country on the upper James River, is probably typical of the social structure of rural America. In the year 1790 about one-fifth of the country's taxpayers possessed property (land and buildings) worth less than twenty-five pounds in Virginia currency. The value of land varied with fertility, but it averaged about a pound an acre in that county. A substantial number of these rural poor were women (probably widows) and free blacks. Sixty percent of the taxpayers owned between twenty-five and one hundred fifty pounds in property. The very wealthy (eight hundred pounds and more) made up 5 percent of the country's taxpayers. Half of the people in the county owned no slaves, and a third owned fewer than five. Only four planters had more than twenty-five slaves; none had as many as fifty. This cross section thus reveals a fundamentally middle-class society, but one in which there was still a considerable gap between the very rich and the very poor.

The Revolution did initiate some changes in the colonial social structure. The alterations were relatively minor and bloodless—especially when compared with the bloody purges that accompanied the French and Russian revolutions—but they did herald the coming of democracy. The removal of imperial authority alone opened new political and economic opportunities. The departure of crown officials enabled men of inferior rank, such as Samuel Adams and Patrick Henry, to rise to positions of power. The flight of Loyalists, especially in northern states, skimmed off some of the cream of society and allowed new men to rise in their places. The confiscation of Loyalist estates, as well as the appropriation of the vast tracts of land held by the crown and its proprietors, paved the way for a substantial redistribution of property. Most of it in the short run went into the hands of speculators, but these resold it in small parcels, often on credit. The long-run effect was expanded opportunities.

African Americans, Slave and Free

African Americans benefited from the Revolution perhaps more than any other element of American society. Free blacks were among the "minutemen" who flocked to Boston after the battles of Lexington and Concord, and they were initially welcomed in the army. When Washington took command of the army, he ordered a halt in black enlistments, but at the end of 1775 the need for manpower forced him to change his mind. New England led the way in enlisting African American soldiers, encouraging slaves to join by promising them freedom when the war was over. The southern states followed suit when the war came to them, except for South Carolina and Georgia. About five thousand blacks served in the Continental Army, nearly all in integrated units. There were a few all-black units, but each numbered only a couple hundred men. Another two thousand served in the navy, constituting about one-tenth of the nation's sailors.

One factor in General Washington's change of heart toward the use of African American troops was the British effort to enlist them. In November 1775, Virginia's royal governor Lord Dunmore proclaimed all slaves "free, that are able and willing to bear arms, they joining his Majesty's Troops as soon as may be. . . ." The invitation alarmed white Virginians and eliminated any lingering vestige of royal authority in the colony, but it also attracted a large number of blacks. In the course of the Revolution about 25,000 slaves fled their masters to gain freedom with the British. Some served in the British army, and some were employed as laborers. However, there were also a substantial number of women and children among the runaways. British embarcation records indicate that almost half of the refugees were female, and about 40 percent of the women had children with them. Entire families, it would seem, had fled from slavery when opportunity beckoned.

When the British evacuated the southern colonies at the end of the war, they took the African Americans with them to Halifax. The Nova Scotia climate proved too severe, however, and those that were sent on to the West Indies subverted the slaves laboring on the sugar plantations. In 1787 Britain moved to solve its free black problem by establishing the colony of Sierra Leone on the west coast of Africa, the first important effort to resettle American blacks in Africa.

On the American side, the Revolution stimulated the first important criticism of slavery. Previously, antislavery sentiment was almost exclusively religious in origin. Mennonites in Germantown, Pennsylvania, voiced opposition to slavery as early as 1688, and in the mid-eighteenth century the Quakers actively discouraged their members from owning slaves. A Quaker, John Woolman, published the first antislavery pamphlet in 1762, and one of his disciples, Anthony Benezet founded the country's first antislavery society in 1775. In the Declaration of Independence, Jefferson included the slave trade in his list of accusations against King George III. The charge was hardly fair since American merchants were as much involved in the iniquitous trade as the British. It did reflect, however, the growing opposition to the further import of blacks from Africa. The northern states led the way in prohibiting the slave trade, and by 1794 every state outlawed it. Rapidly expanding South Carolina was the most reluctant, and the last to do so. The Federal Convention sought to give Congress broad powers over commerce, which would have included the authority to ban the foreign slave trade, but the opposition of the South Carolina and Georgia delegates forced a compromise that delayed the prohibition until 1808.

Revolutionary idealism was also evident in Jefferson's declaration that "all men are created equal." Though Jefferson himself did not pursue immediately the implications of his statement, there were others who did so. "To contend for liberty," observed John Jay of New York, "and to deny that blessing to others involves an inconsistency not to be excused." Jay, along with Alexander Hamilton and Rufus King, was instrumental in founding the New York Society for Promoting Manumission in 1785, and within a few years every state from Massachusetts to Virginia possessed a similar organization. The growing sentiment against slavery yielded some results. Vermont, which considered itself an autonomous republic, prohibited slavery by its constitution of 1777. Massachusetts' slaves were freed by judicial decision in 1783 when the state supreme court, acting on Quork Walker's suit for freedom, declared slavery to be incompatible with the state's constitution. Other northern states passed laws providing for gradual emancipation, though some were so loosely drawn that they required later revision. By 1790, however, there were still 40,000 slaves in the North, more than the region's population of free blacks. And in New York and New Jersey, both of which had adopted plans of gradual emancipation, slaves could still be seen in the 1820s. Even so, a start had been made. Emancipation of slaves was certainly the most important social change accompanying the War for Independence.

Southerners were not untouched by the enlightened idealism of the age, but they remained caught in the dilemma of race. Laws easing the restrictions on private manumission were widely adopted, but invariably they contained the proviso that freed blacks be removed from the state. Jefferson himself symbolized the southern quandary. He frequently voiced his opposition to the institution and was largely responsible for the prohibition of slavery in the Northwest Ordinance. But in his *Notes on Virginia,* published in 1785 while he was minister to France, he expressed the view that both African Americans and Native Americans were culturally inferior. Whether this was due to any innate inferiority Jefferson was unsure.

A living example that it was not was Benjamin Banneker, a free African American born in Maryland and educated by Quakers. He was a brilliant mathematician and astronomer, and in 1791 he began publishing an annual almanac, modeled on Benjamin Franklin's. That same year President Washington appointed him to serve with Pierre Charles L'Enfant on the commission to lay out the federal capital. The appointment was made on the recommendation of Secretary of State Jefferson, but Banneker was still chafing from the secretary's published disparagement. In August 1791, he wrote Jefferson a militant letter pointing out the inconsistency between Jefferson's attitude toward African Americans and the sentiments of the Declaration of Independence. He enclosed one of his almanacs as proof of what blacks could do if given a chance. Jefferson replied reassuringly that "Nobody wishes more than I do to see such proofs as you exhibit that nature has given to our black brethren talents equal to those of the other colours of men, and that the appearance of a want of them is owing merely to the degraded condition of their existence, both in Africa and America."

Private acts of manumission increased with the Revolution, but most southerners, like Washington, freed their slaves only by last will and testament. Jefferson doubtless would have done so if his estate had not been so encumbered with debt by the time he died. But even acts of this sort hardly demonstrated idealistic commitment. One who genuinely abhorred the institution would have freed his slaves during his lifetime, perhaps even prepared them for freedom with education and land, as the Quakers did. Southerners, in short, never came to grips with the basic racial dilemma, even in the heyday of revolutionary idealism. But even if they had, their efforts would have been hampered by the racial attitudes of northerners. When John Randolph, for instance, freed his three hundred slaves on his death in 1833 and provided them with lands in Ohio, the munificent act was largely negated when Ohio refused to admit the freedmen.

In 1790, the South contained more free blacks (32,000) than the North (27,000), and neither region treated them with justice. Southern slave codes placed severe restrictions on them. They were not allowed to possess firearms or dogs, and they had to carry identity papers wherever they went. Southern cities all possessed strict vagrancy laws, designed mostly to keep free blacks busy and away from slaves. There were fewer restraints on them in the North, but they were still the objects of prejudice. As the French visitor Brissot de Warville perceived, "There still exists too great an interval between them and the Whites, especially in the public opinion. This humiliating difference prevents those efforts which they might make to raise themselves. . . . Though free, they are always accustomed to consider themselves as beneath the Whites." New York and New Jersey both permitted free blacks to vote, but when the revolutionary idealism faded the privilege was revoked. The Revolution thus brought a few hesitant steps toward a recognition of African American rights, but there was still a long way to go.

Liberty's Daughters Become the Republic's Mothers

The experiences of white women during the war depended in large measure on their husbands' political activism. Wives of men who joined the army or rode off to Congress were left alone for long periods of time. Some women accompanied their husbands on military service, but this was not an attractive alternative for most. Instead they found themselves thrust on their own resources to manage a shop or maintain a farm. Abigail Adams wrote lengthy letters to her husband John, describing her adjustment to farm chores, which varied from digging potatoes to making hay.

The responsibilities thrust upon women, however, greatly improved their sense of self-esteem. Women who, prior to 1770, offered profuse apologies whenever they dared to discuss politics, proudly shouldered the burden of enforcing the tea boycott in 1774, and by the 1780s they were reading political literature and engaging in public debates. Abigail Adams, for one, recognized that the change in governments presented a rare opportunity to legislate rights for women. In 1776 she wrote to her husband John in Philadelphia:

> . . . in the new code of laws which I suppose it will be necessary for you to make, I desire you would remember the ladies, and be more generous to them than your ancestors. Do not put such unlimited power in the hands of husbands. Remember, all men would be tyrants if they could. If particular care and attention are not paid to the ladies, we are determined to foment a rebellion, and will not hold ourselves bound to obey the laws in which we have no voice or representation.

Unfortunately, the Revolution brought no substantial change in this regard, in part because the state constitutions and laws were written by men. John Adams, who was comparatively liberal for his time, refused even to take the matter seriously. "A fine story indeed," he replied to his wife's plea. "I begin to think the [British] ministry as deep as they are wicked. After stirring up Tories, . . . bigots, Canadians, Indians, . . . at last they have stimulated the [women] to demand new privileges and threaten to rebel!"

Although almost nothing was done in a formal way to improve the position of women in American society, the Revolution did have a profound impact on their status. As already noted, women's sense of self-esteem increased immeasurably. Several years after the war Eliza Wilkinson, a resident of South Carolina, recalled the impact of the British invasion of her state in 1780s. During that emergency, she recalled, "none were greater politicians than the several knots of ladies, who met together. All trifling discourse of fashions, and such low chat was thrown by, and we commenced perfect statesmen."

When Charleston fell to the British in May 1780, Philadelphia merchants began soliciting funds for enlistment bounties to raise a new army in the South. According to the *Pennsylvania Gazette,* the merchants' wives and daughters also responded to the crisis with "public spirited measures." Among these was a plan to found the nation's first women's organization. A month later *The Sentiments of an American Woman* appeared on the streets of Philadelphia, a broadside composed by Esther DeBerdt Read. Esther Read was an Englishwoman who had lived in Philadelphia only since her 1770 marriage to Joseph Read. She was nevertheless a staunch patriot who thought that women ought to do more than offer "barren wishes" for the success of the army. Women, she argued, wanted to be "really useful," like "those heroines of antiquity, who have rendered their sex illustrious." She thought Joan of Arc an especially appropriate role model because she had driven from France "the ancesters of these same British, whose odious yoke we have just shaken off, and whom it is necessary that we drive from this Continent." Reminding her readers of the contributions that women made during the nonimportation movements, she proposed that they renounce luxuries and send the money saved to the army as *"the offering of the Ladies."* Three days later thirty-six Philadelphia women met to organize themselves and agreed that their donations would be sent to Martha Washington for the benefit of the troops. They divided the city into districts for the solicitation of funds and recruited some of the most prominent women in town to make solicitations, including Sarah Franklin Bache and Julia Stockton Rush, wife of Dr. Benjamin Rush.

The success of the Philadelphia association encouraged the formation of similar organizations in Trenton and Annapolis. Women in the latter city raised some $16,000 in currency during the summer of 1780. In Virginia, Martha Wayles Jefferson, wife of the governor, received a copy of the Philadelphians' plan directly from Martha Washington. Being in poor health, she endorsed it but decided not to take an active role in it. Interestingly, her response to Martha Washington on this occasion is the only surviving letter we have from Jefferson's wife.

Martha Washington had returned to Virginia by the time the collections were completed that summer, so the Philadelphia association voted to leave the disposition of the funds to the general. Unfortunately, Washington suggested that they purchase shirts with it. Esther Read's response, much revised in order to be as tactful as possible, pointed out that the soldiers would not particularly appreciate an item that the government was expected to furnish anyway. She suggested giving each soldier two dollars to spend as he wished. Washington stiffly replied that the soldiers would spend it on drink. That ended the interchange. The ladies bought the linen and made the shirts themselves, embroidering each with the name of the woman who had made it. The whole incident demonstrated a proud sense of involvement in public affairs that would not disappear with the end of the fighting.

Lucy Flucker Knox, wife of Washington's general of artillery, spent much of the war managing the family's finances on her own. In March 1777, the general wrote her to ask that she have his brother Billy sell some horses for him. Lucy did as she was told, but she later told her husband that she could have done a better job. The horses had gone for only £75, she wrote Henry, "owing to your not trusting me with the sale of them." She suggested that he employ her as "your future agent," describing herself proudly as "quite a woman of business." Two months later, speculating about her husband's return to civilian life, she predicted that the change in their relationship would be permanent. "I hope you will not consider yourself as commander in chief in your own house," she declared pointedly "but be convinced . . . that there is such a thing as equal command."

The Revolution thus dealt a blow to male dominance of the family. In 1790, when Jefferson's daughter Patsy was marrying Thomas Mann Randolph (a future governor of Virginia and, so Jefferson claimed, his "own first choice" for her), Jefferson explained to a French friend that, "according to the usage of my country, I scrupulously suppressed my wishes, that my daughter might indulge her own sentiments freely." Arranged marriages were also a casualty of the Revolution and the new respect accorded women. "In a matter of such importance," a New Englander declared in 1784, a young woman "ought to be left entirely to herself."

There are two other indices of women's improved status within marriage after the Revolution—a decline in fertility and a rise in divorce. Two independent studies, one of New England and the other examining Quaker families in Pennsylvania, have found that women who married after 1780 had fewer children than women who married prior to 1765. The fertility rate dropped again among women married after 1800. Given the debilitation suffered by women as a result of repeated pregnancies, it is likely that colonial women would have preferred to have fewer children; and, they were well aware of at least one contraceptive method, prolonged nursing of a previous child. But given their total subjection to the dominant husband, their wishes were probably given little weight. The dramatic drop in family size after the war strongly suggests a more egalitarian approach to marriage.

Changes in state laws and the disestablishment of the Church of England made divorce easier after the Revolution, and there is considerable evidence that women took advantage of the opportunity. Massachusetts records for the last quarter of the century indicate that an increasing number of people, including notably larger proportions of women, sought legal separation from their spouses. A reasonable conclusion is that women were experiencing rising expections from marriage, and they were increasingly willing to assert themselves when they were dissatisfied. A related and equally telling statistic is an increase in the number of women who chose to postpone marriage or not to marry at all. "I keep my name still," wrote a New England woman in 1782. "I think it a good one and am determined not to change it without a prospect of some great Advantage." She did eventually marry, but only very late in life.

The republican ideology that developed during and after the Revolution reinforced the new status of women. Central to this ideology was the assumption that the republic would not long survive unless its citizens were virtuous in both public and private lives. Virtue in the eighteenth century meant more than moral behavior; it meant public spirit, a willingness to work for the common good. As one Harvard student asserted in 1785, "to be destitute of virtue, is to cease to be a citizen." The secondary assumption was that the teaching and practice of virtue began in the household. The republic itself was in danger, wrote David Ramsey of South Carolina, if too many families failed to practice "industry, frugality, temperance, moderation, and that whole lovely train of republican virtues."

This line of thinking had significant implications for American women. If the household was the most important repository of virtue, the wife and mother, who directed most of its activities, had new responsibilities. Women had long been linked to morality in European thought; it was commonplace in western thinking that the morals of women determined the morals of men. In the context of republican ideology this notion took on new significance. It meant that women had a crucial role to play in instilling patriotism and civic responsibility in their children. Their influence on their sons was particularly important because these were the future citizens of the republic. The concept of republican motherhood not only added to the status of women within the family, but for the first time it accorded them an importance in the public sphere.

In the vanguard of this thinking were the numerous, and unfortunately short-lived, literary magazines that were founded in the early years of the republic. The publishers of these journals explicitly addressed them to women as well as men. The preface to the *Lady and Gentleman's Pocket Magazine of Literature and Polite Amusement* in 1796 explained that a number of its articles would be specifically addressed to the education and amusement of the "Fair Sex." The publisher went on to explain that "to distinguish works offered in part to the Fair, by making them trifling and insignificant, however sanctioned by custom, would, in our opinion, at this period, be inexcusable." Such magazines, in turn, became an outlet for the essays and poems of women, including, most significantly, some strongly argued pleas for greater equality.

The ideology of republican motherhood neverthless had its limitations. Its basic assumption was that woman's destiny was to marry and have children, and that girls should be trained solely for this goal. The dawning recognition of women's intellectual equality, of women's social and political importance to the republic, remained in the context of household and family. Significantly, the publication of *A Vindication of the Rights of a Woman* (1792) by the English radical Mary Wollstonecraft, an appeal for legal and political equality for women, met almost universal condemnation in the United States. Some women secretly admired the work, but they publicly condemned it. Among its critics also were some of the foremost exponents of republican idealogy. Republican womanhood would thus evolve into Victorian womanhood, a cult of domesticity that bound women to home and family. Even so, the egalitarian rhetoric of the Revolution would provide a basic vocabulary for women's rights when that movement appeared a half century later.

Reform with Caution

The impact of the Revolution on women perhaps can best be described as ambiguous. Ambiguity also shadowed other efforts at social change. Republican ideology, with its accent on virtue, dictated that society be purified if the republic were to survive. Thus independence, in addition to giving rise to constitution-making, inspired a number of movements for social reform. Reformers generally were of two varieties—those who sought a moral solution to the problem of the republic's survival (i.e., to make better people), and those who sought a socio-economic solution (i.e., to make better laws and social arrangements).

Samuel Adams is perhaps the best example of the moralist at work. In the Massachusetts constitutional convention of 1779–80, he personally drafted the religious article, which retained the Congregational establishment and required all citizens to pay taxes for the support of religion. Adams was convinced that religious faith was the foundation of all morality, that church and republic leaned upon one another. During the 1780s, Adams expended a prodigious amount of energy battling a nightclub in Boston. "Sam the Publican" had no ojections to masculine taverns, but the *Sans Souci* proposed to admit female customers. Adams predicted that it would lead to Roman-style orgies and reintroduce Old World decadence. Although Adams never realized it, a campaign such as this merely trivialized the broader concern for republican virtue.

In Pennsylvania Benjamin Rush took a more practical approach to reform, although it was in part religiously inspired. Brought up in a Presbyterian household, Rush had been deeply affected by the Great Awakening, which imbued him with a strong revulsion against the corruption and decadence that had infiltrated America from the mother country. At the same time, Rush was touched by the Enlightenment. In the 1760s, he journeyed to Edinburgh for medical training, and the tour exposed him to the thinking of the Scottish rationalists. Unlike Jefferson, Rush never saw an inconsistency between the message of the evangelists and the climate of reason. What he did see was that the Revolution was an opportunity to purge American society of the corruption that had crept in under the imperial regime.

The most obvious of these evils was of course slavery. Rush wrote a pamphlet denouncing slavery in 1773, and when Quakers founded America's first antislavery society two years later, Rush became its secretary. During the war Rush joined the revolutionary army as a physician, but he soon became embroiled in a controversy with the Philadelphia doctors in charge of the military hospitals, charging them with corruption and the theft of medicines. In 1785, he was instrumental in the founding of Dickinson College in Carlisle, Pennsylvania. He had become disenchanted with Franklin's College of Philadelphia (which had become the University of Pennsylvania) because he thought the college students too susceptible to the corruptions and distractions of the big city. In remote Carlisle, surrounded by the moral climate of the virgin wilderness, Rush thought they would better tend to their studies. He hoped also that the college would have some influence on the Scots-Irish farmers in its neighborhood, a people notorious for their lack of manners, patriotism, and civility.

In 1787, Rush delivered an address to the Philadelphia Young Ladies Academy (which he had helped found) entitled "Thoughts Upon Female Education." Rush not only endorsed the concept of higher education of women; he proposed a curriculum to prepare them for republican motherhood. American women, he declared, should be trained in math and bookkeeping so they could assist their husbands in business and eventually administer their estates. He also thought women should be acquainted with history, geography, natural philosophy, and religion so they could bring up their children more effectively. Rush thought such courses ought to replace frivolous subjects, which women had previously undertaken, such as drawing, French, and instrumental music. Although Rush's thought failed to escape the confines of republican motherhood, his emphasis on utilitarian courses initiated a change in American attitudes toward female education.

That same year Rush read another essay, this time at the home of Benjamin Franklin. Having steeped himself in the work of the Italian reformer, Cesare Beccaria, Rush argued that public punishment, such as a whipping or placing persons in stocks, neither reformed nor isolated the most dangerous criminals. He proposed instead that they be confined in a specially constructed building (the word penetentiary had not yet come into common use) located in the distant countryside and put to work in complete silence. Rush also advocated that the sexes be separated in Philadelphia's jails and that debtors be separated from criminals. His reforms were enacted in 1789 and 1790, though the state penetentiary that he advocated was not built until some years later. His campaign against capital punishment also led to legislation that limited the death penalty to murder in the first degree.

Almost single-handedly Benjamin Rush put Pennsylvania in the forefront of social reform. Only Virginia among the states accomplished as much. The instrument in that state was Thomas Jefferson.

Jefferson was a secular reformer; his inspiration was not morality but reason. He was inclined to accept people as they were; he wanted only to improve their environment. Unlike some European rationalists, Jefferson had no rage against the past, nor did he have a blueprint for the future. He was attached to the Virginia of his birth; he wished only to eliminate its abuses—the relics of feudalism, the privileges accorded the few, its massive popular ignorance, its religious establishment, and its dependence on human servitude.

Jefferson was serving in the Continental Congress in the spring of 1776 when the Virginia assembly formed itself into a convention for the purpose of drafting a state constitution. Jefferson drafted a model constitution and gave it to George Wythe for presentation to the delegates in Williamsburg. To his utter dismay, the delegates ignored his draft and drew up a far more conservative document of their own. Jefferson thus began a lifelong quarrel with Virginia's constitution, but he never met with success. The document drafted in 1776 was not revised until 1829, three years after his death. Jefferson's model, though never used, is nevertheless instructive, for it represented the essence of his political thought at the outset of the revolution.

Jefferson argued, first of all, that the Virginia constitution was illegitimate because it was not drafted by a body specially elected for the purpose. Nor did the convention provide for popular approval of the document. Jefferson's plan not only included a provision for popular ratification, but it also included a provision for periodic amendment and revision.

Jefferson's model also differed substantially from the document drafted at Williamsburg on the issues of suffrage and representation. Although he was unable to break entirely with the notion of a freehold suffrage qualification, he reduced the amount of property by half to fifty acres. He also included a unique provision for a governmental gift of land to any adult who possessed less than fifty acres. This, of course, would have brought about virtually universal male suffrage. On the matter of representation, Jefferson proposed that the Senate and House of Delegates be based on electoral districts of equal size. The county-unit system of representation, inherited from the colonial charter, gave a disproportionate power to the Tidewater where the counties were smaller and hence more numerous than in the West. Because wealth and privilege were concentrated in the Tidewater, the county-unit system also gave control of the government to the wealthy few. Jefferson regarded equal representation as "capital and fundamental."

Jefferson's draft also contained a number of liberal reforms—on religion, slavery, inheritance, and punishment of crimes—none of which were incorporated in the constitution. Although he was unable to modify the constitution, he saw that these reforms, at least, could be enacted by the all-powerful assembly created by the constitution. He accordingly retired from Congress on September 2, 1776, and after a month at Monticello he took a seat in the House of Delegates in Williamsburg.

On October 12, the House gave him leave to draft a bill for the general revision of the laws. The bill passed two weeks later, and the House named a committee of five, chaired by Jefferson, to carry out the work. The result was eminently Jeffersonian. The committee did not discard the body of colonial law; instead it streamlined it by deleting what was obsolete and useless. It also acted on the principle that the law should be reasonable and comprehensible, as well as humane. The revision of the law code took the committee almost three years; it finally issued its *Report* in June 1779. In later years Jefferson bracketed legal reform with two other measures that he drafted during his legislative service, freedom of religion and educational reform, and viewed the whole "as forming a system by which every fiber would be eradicated of ancient or feudal aristocracy; and a foundation laid for government truly republican."

Unfortunately, the revision of the laws had occupied nearly all of Jefferson's years in the assembly. Not long after his *Report* was published he moved on to the governorship, to the Congress, and then to diplomatic service abroad. The many bills he had drafted in those three and a half years would be guided through the assembly by his young friend, James Madison. The *Report* itself was never acted on as a unit; instead it became, as Madison expressed it, "a mine of legislative wealth" that occupied much of the assembly's time for more than a decade.

Jefferson's first bill, abolishing entail (feudal limitations on land inheritance), passed the assembly in November 1776. A related measure, abolishing primogeniture (inheritance by the eldest son when a person died intestate or without a will), was finally adopted on Madison's motion in 1785. Together with the abolition of quit rents, these measures eliminated the relics of feudalism from the Virginia land system and ensured that freeholds would be the prevailing land tenure thereafter in Virginia. Jefferson thought he was striking a blow against aristocracy; in a sense he was, but he was also laying the foundation for free enterprise capitalism.

Like Benjamin Rush in Pennsylvania, Jefferson sought to reduce the number of crimes punishable by death to two—treason and murder. Unlike Rush, however, Jefferson had no concept of a penetentiary to confine criminals, an idea just gaining a foothold in Europe. Instead he proposed to employ criminals on public works, in mines, roads, and shipyards, shaving their heads and dressing them in uniforms to discourage efforts to escape. Madison brought the bill enacting these reforms before the House in 1786, but it went down to defeat. Madison thought a "rage against horse stealing" responsible. That was an especially nefarious crime among Virginians and had been a capital offense since the middle of the century. However, a decade later most of the features of Jefferson's bill were enacted into law.

Freedom of religion was the next item on Jefferson's agenda. George Mason's Declaration of Rights committed the new state to the idea that "all men are equally entitled to the free exercise of religion." However, this promise of toleration did not affect the fact that public taxes were used for the support of the Anglican establishment. Jefferson's conviction that church and state must be kept separate was founded on reason. The question of what is truth, he felt, must be submitted to the free marketplace of ideas; it could not be determined by the state and imposed by coercion. "It is error alone which needs the support of government," he declared. "Truth can stand by itself."

Jefferson's reasoning ran counter to the idea, endorsed by both Patrick Henry and Richard Henry Lee, that religious faith was essential to morality, and public support for religion was necessary for the survival of the republic. Fortunately for Jefferson, however, disestablishment appealed to Baptists and Presbyterians who objected to paying taxes for the support of the Episcopal Church. The Lee-Henry forces tried to counter this by introducing a bill for a general assessment on behalf of religion, to be distributed to the various churches at the designation of the taxpayer.

Jefferson drafted his own Statute for Religious Freedom in 1779. The Anglican Church was effectively disestablished in that year, but the assembly was not yet ready for Jefferson's concept of the total freedom to believe, or, equally controversial, the freedom to disbelieve. The statute, which Jefferson later regarded as one of the three supreme achievements of his life, was finally steered through the assembly by Madison in 1786.

Jefferson's proposals on education and slavery met with less success. Educational reform was tied to republican virtue, a concern for which Jefferson shared with Benjamin Rush and the Adamses. Even more so than the Adamses, Jefferson believed that government rested on the will of the people, and it would not long survive republican and free unless the people were adequately informed and instructed. Education, accordingly, was too important to be left to chance, or to wealth, which was much the same thing. It was one of the primary functions of republican government.

In 1778, he brought before the assembly a Bill for the More General Diffusion of Knowledge. He projected three distinct levels of education: elementary, middle, and higher. At the elementary level each county would be subdivided into wards, each of a size suitable for a school. All free children, male and female (and presumably including free blacks), would be educated at governmental expense for three years; they could stay in school longer at the expense of their parents. At that level, in addition to reading, writing, and arithmetic, they would receive instruction in the rights and duties of citizens. The moral lessons in this regard, however, were to be drawn from history, not the Bible.

At the secondary level the training was also at governmental expense, except for students "in easy circumstances," who would be charged tuition and board. Democratic though his inclinations were, Jefferson could not temperamentally escape Virginia's hierarchical social system. Under his plan one-third of the students in the secondary schools would be eliminated after the first year, and the remainder after the second year, except for the best scholar in each of the district schools. By this method, Jefferson wrote, "twenty of the best geniuses will be raked from the rubbish annually, and be instructed, at the public expense, so far as grammar schools go." Ten of these twenty would be allowed to attend the College of William and Mary, which stood at the apex of Jefferson's educational pyramid. He drafted a companion bill to convert the College from an Anglican-controlled institution into a state university offering instruction in all branches of knowledge.

Nothing came of Jefferson's plan; it was far too radical for the assembly. Indeed, the idea of tax-supported public education did not become current in the North until the 1830s, and southern states did not embrace the idea until after the Civil War. As governor, however, he was able to make some changes in the College. He replaced professorships in divinity, oriental languages, Greek, and Latin with professorships in law and government, anatomy and medicine, and modern languages. These changes foretold the revolutionary changes in university curriculum that he would institute in founding the University of Virginia thirty-seven years later.

The fate of Jefferson's efforts to modify the institution of slavery revealed the limits of revolutionary social reform, as well as the limits of Jefferson's own idealism. His model draft for the Virginia constitution prohibited the holding in slavery of any person who henceforth entered the state, which presumably applied to imports from other states as well as from Africa. The legislature was unwilling to go this far, but in 1778 it did slam the door on further imports from Africa. Jefferson later claimed authorship of this measure, and that seems likely. In its original form the bill sought to encourage private manumission of slaves, but that provision was deleted by the assembly before passage. In his *Notes on Virginia,* published in 1785, Jefferson outlined a plan for gradual emancipation, but neither he nor any other Virginian was willing to risk political influence and social standing to fight for it. The prohibition on slavery in the Northwest Ordinances was his only other achievement. Thereafter, to the end of his life, his attitude toward slavery was at best ambiguous.

Toward a National Economy

Despite the declaration of political independence from England, the United States in 1790 still labored under a colonial economy. The center of population was only a few miles from the seacoast; its main exports were still the products of farm and forest. New England, with the exception of Maine and Vermont, was the only area that could be described as well populated. There the average farm was about 150 acres, though most of it was in woods and pasture. Except in the Connecticut River valley, the soil of the region was too thin and rocky to permit much more than a small garden crop on each farm.

New York was still largely uninhabited west of the Hudson River. The Iroquois, who held the military balance of power between the English and French through much of the colonial period, controlled vast tracts of land in the center of the state, and their possessions were guaranteed by countless treaties. During the 1790s, the line of settlement pushed steadily up the Mohawk Valley turning the wilderness into a land of small farms similar to that of New England. In contrast to the freeholders of New England, however, New Yorkers remained tenants of land speculators who had engrossed huge estates through political influence and the bribery of American Indian tribes. The largest of these, the Holland Land Company, possessed 2,500,000 acres covering the whole western end of the state south of Lake Erie.

The Pennsylvania frontier in 1790 ran roughly along a line from Philadelphia to Harrisburg and Pittsburgh, cities that were connected by the crude wilderness trail carved by General John Forbes during the French and Indian War. South of Forbes' Road, German and Scots-Irish farmers tilled the fertile valleys of the Susquehanna, Cumberland, and Juniata rivers and grew a variety of cereal grains. During the decade, settlement moved steadily northward, virtually covering the state by 1800. In New Jersey and Delaware, prosperous middle-sized farms raised a wide variety of crops for the New York and Philadelphia markets.

The land northwest of the Ohio River was still virtually untouched by whites in 1790; Marietta, the first settlement north of the Ohio, had been founded only two years earlier. Pioneers traveled south around the Allegheny plateau of Virginia (present-day West Virginia) following the Wilderness Trail that Daniel Boone blazed from the Cumberland Gap into Kentucky in 1775. The Kentucky settlements, clustered in the Blue Grass region some thirty-five miles wide and eighty miles long, centered on Lexington. In this extremely fertile, lightly wooded region, emigrants from Virginia produced fine horses and excellent bourbon, as well as good crops of hemp, wheat, and tobacco. From this isolated center, population spread into the rest of Kentucky and north into Ohio.

Tennessee, in contrast, developed from two nuclei, which created a sectional division in the state that profoundly affected its politics for a century and a half after the Revolution. East Tennessee originated from isolated settlements on the Holston and Broad rivers, which join to form the Tennessee River at Knoxville (founded in 1791). Rugged terrain and hostile Native Americans combined to limit the development of this region, and it remained for many decades a land of primitive, subsistence farms. Economically and politically, east Tennessee was soon overshadowed by the northcentral region around Nashville, founded in 1779 on the Cumberland River. More level in terrain and fertile in soil, middle Tennessee developed a slave plantation system, exporting tobacco, hemp, and, by the end of the decade, cotton.

The agricultural economy of the South Atlantic states was in a severe depression in 1790. The price of tobacco in Virginia and Maryland had been declining for a century because of overproduction, and planters in Tidewater Virginia and Maryland were rapidly shifting to cereal grains. In both states almost two centuries of wasteful practices led to soil exhaustion, and farmers were only beginning to experiment with fertilizers and crop rotation. South Carolina and Georgia were even worse off. Both states were hard hit by the guerilla campaigns of the Revolution and the depredations of the British army. Rice, the primary staple of the South Carolina low country, still commanded a good market, but many dams and levees had been damaged by the fighting. Not until the mid-1790s did rice production recover its pre-revolutionary prosperity. Long-staple cotton could be grown on the sea islands along the coast, and it had a ready market in the textile cities of Britain. But it was too sensitive to frost to be produced in the uplands. Short-fiberd cotton, on the other hand, could be grown as far north as Virginia, and it too was in demand abroad because of the revolution in textile technology. However, its seed was deeply imbedded in the fiber and could be extracted only with time-consuming labor. Eli Whitney's invention of the cotton gin in 1793, by providing a mechanical means of separating the short-staple seed from fiber, offered a new crop for the Carolina upcountry and laid the basis for expansion of the slave-plantation economy throughout the lower South.

Overland transportation was still extremely primitive in 1790. Roads were few and short, usually extending from inland communities to the nearest river town or seaport, and they were little more than trails through the woods, full of stumps and rocks, dusty in summer and impassable in winter. Nearly all interstate commerce was carried by coasting schooners which plied the bays and harbors of the seaboard. Yet, in 1790 the nation was on the threshhold of the "Turnpike Era." Unable to finance road construction, the states turned for help to private companies, organized by merchants and land speculators who had a personal interest in improved communications with the interior. The pioneer in this move was Pennsylvania, which chartered a company in 1792 to construct a turnpike from Philadelphia to Lancaster. The legislature gave the company authority to erect tollgates along the road, though it carefully regulated the rates. (The states had unquestioned authority to regulate private businesses in this period.)

The company built a gravel road within two years, and the success of the Lancaster Pike encouraged imitation. Northern states generally relied on private companies to build their toll roads, but Virginia constructed a network at public expense. Such was the road-building fever that by 1810 New York alone had some 1,500 miles of toll roads extending from the Atlantic to Lake Erie.

The most common freight carrier was the Conestoga wagon, a land vessel developed in the mid-eighteenth century by German immigrants in the area around Lancaster, Pennsylvania. It featured large, broad wheels able to negotiate all but the deepest ruts and holes, and its round bottom prevented the freight from shifting on a hill. Covered with canvas and drawn by four to six horses, the Conestoga wagon rivaled the log cabin as the primary symbol of the frontier. Passengers traveled in a variety of stagecoaches, the most common of which had four benches, each holding three persons. It was only a platform on wheels, with no springs; slender poles held up the top, and leather curtains kept out dust and rain. The Concord coach, popularized in modern Hollywood westerns and associated with the far-western frontier, was not developed until 1828.

Nearly all river transportation went one way—downstream. The simplest, and perhaps most common, vessel was the raft, which could carry a farmer's annual crop and then be broken up and sold for lumber at its destination. Only slightly less primitive was the flatboat, a shallow box with freight on the deck and a crude shelter for persons and livestock. It floated with the current, guided by poles, and it too was usually broken up for lumber at the end of the journey. The most sophisticated form of river transportation, prior to the steamboat, was the keelboat, a canoe-shaped vessel with oars, sails, and a walking plank for poling upstream. Varying in length from forty to eighty feet, the keelboat could carry up to thirty tons of freight; in the West it was the primary form of freight transportation until the steamboat arrived on the Ohio River in 1811.

Foreign trade expanded steadily after the Revolution, which freed Americans from the restrictions of the British navigation acts. Even before the war ended, new markets for American tobacco were found in Sweden, Russia, and the Netherlands, while New England fisheries discovered almost unlimited consumers in southern Europe. In 1790, the United States still imported more than 90 percent of its needed manufactured goods from England, but the biggest customer for American exports was France. A commercial treaty negotiated by Jefferson in 1786 opened the French West Indies; and by 1790, these islands consumed 25 percent of all American exports, mostly flour, beef, rum, and fish.

Business organization remained essentially the same as in colonial times. Most common was the individual proprietor—whether storekeeper, artisan, or slave-owning planter—who owned or rented his premises, sold his own goods, and was responsible for his own debts. The partnership involved two or more persons, who pooled their capital and shared risks, profits, and debts. This system was most widely used by merchants and shipowners, who often bought shares in cargoes or ships rather than risk a fortune in one journey. The most sophisticated type of business organization was the corporation, still in the process of evolution from the colonial joint stock company. The corporation permitted the pooling of large amounts of capital under centralized management, and it offered investors an independent existence (partnerships were usually dissolved upon the death of a partner) and limited liability for debts. It derived its existence from a charter issued by a legislature which defined its structure, purposes, capital, and often conferred a monopoly. Seven such business organizations were in existence before 1775, most of them city water companies or private wharves. The first corporation chartered after independence was Robert Morris's Bank of North America; and by 1790, state legislatures were actively chartering banks, waterworks, and insurance companies, as well as canal and turnpike corporations.

In 1790, the most important industries were those of a colonial economy—agriculture, lumbering, and fishing. Even the manufacturing enterprises that had developed were those associated with a colonial economy, producing half-finished goods that were exported abroad for further refinement.

Shipbuilding, the most important colonial manufacture, had been in the doldrums since the Revolution, retarded by the postwar depression, a lack of trained carpenters, and the need to import sailcloth and rigging. Technological difficulties were overcome by 1790 through development of domestic manufactures, and the outbreak of war in Europe in 1792 created new demands on American shipping. Shipbuilders in Boston, Philadelphia, and Baltimore also proved adept at constructing speedy ships with large capacity. By combining speed with carrying capacity, American shipowners could carry freight at rates that were less than half those of the British, and the success of Yankee captains in capturing a major share of the world's carrying trade after 1800 would cause conflict with Britain and contribute ultimately to war.

The iron industry had ranked with rum and shipbuilding among colonial manufactures, but it was still in a primitive condition in 1790. Centered in Pennsylvania, Maryland, and Virginia, American furnaces produced a highly carbonized pig iron by melting ore with charcoal (even in Pennsylvania coal was not used extensively for another generation). Hammering (for tools) or remelting (for cast-iron utensils) removed impurities. American iron furnaces, however, produced far more pig iron than its reworking furnaces needed, and until well after 1815 this remained an important export to Britain.

Flour milling was another derivative of the staple-export economy, although it had not been an important export prior to the Revolution. American mills began producing a surplus for export in the 1790s as a result of the inventive genius of Oliver Evans, one of several originators of automation. In his mill near Philadelphia, Evans invented a series of machines that weighed, cleaned, and ground the wheat, and packed the flour in barrels. Mills of the Delaware and Chesapeake quickly adopted his invention, and after 1800 he hooked up a steam engine to the apparatus so that the mill would not be tied to water power. Largely because of Evans's innovations, American flour mills led the world in efficiency and productivity by 1800. Realizing that steam engines could be employed in other industries, Evans in 1803 set up a shop to fabricate engines. This marked the beginning of the manufacture of machinery as a separate branch of industry.

The industrial revolution, which was to transform the western world, began in Britain in the last quarter of the eighteenth century. It was triggered by dramatic progress in textile technology. The spinning jenny (1764), which enabled one person to operate as many as thirty spindles, came into use in America during the Revolution, and by 1790, there were a half dozen jenny mills in New England. Richard Arkwright's water frame (1769) improved on the jenny and attached it to water power, thereby vastly accelerating the spinning process. Awkright's machine was too large for use in a household; it required a "house" of its own, or a factory. Factories attracted workers from the countryside, and the needs of the workers for housing, food, and clothing stirred urban development. Industrialization and urbanization went hand in hand.

In 1790, an English immigrant, Samuel Slater, constructed from memory an Arkwright machine, and with the financial backing of Moses Brown of Providence he constructed a water-powered spinning mill at Pawtucket, Rhode Island. The technology expanded rapidly, particularly under the impetus of Jefferson's Embargo and the War of 1812, which temporarily cut off British competition; and by 1815, there were 213 spinning mills, most of them concentrated in southern New England. Prior to 1813, the weaving of cloth was a separate operation often done in the home of a weaver. In that year the Boston Manufacturing Company established at Waltham, Massachusetts, a textile mill that combined all operations for converting cotton into cloth by powered machinery. The "Waltham System" produced a standardized course cloth and required little skill of workers. The Boston associates employed young New England farm women to operate the machinery, the first instance of female labor in a factory setting. To protect the young women and avoid public criticism the associates housed them in dormitories.

By that date substantial advances had been made in both textiles and iron manufacturing, but the United States was still far from industrialized. For long after 1815, most manufacturing was still done by hand—weaving, sewing of clothing and shoes, and home furnishings. Rural families in particular were almost completely self-sufficient, producing all but a few necessities in the household. It has been estimated that the average productivity, income, and standard of living for Americans was about the same in 1820 as in 1790. Early advances laid the foundation for future industrial development, but not until 1840 did the nation begin a self-sustaining economic growth.

Religion: Institutionalizing Faith

American religious thought in the late eighteenth century had evolved in three distinct strains. First, the legacy of the Enlightenment produced a rationalist view of the scriptures, reduced the agency of God to that of "first cause" in creating the world, and viewed salvation as a matter for the individual to choose by leading an upright life. This view affected a wide variety of men, from low-church Episcopalians like Washington to outright deists such as Franklin and Jefferson, for whom religion was less a theology commanding faith than a philosophy governed by reason. A second element of religious attitude included the remnants of seventeenth-century Puritanism, which left a legacy of orthodox Calvinism, austere, disciplined, and pious. Centered among the Congregational churches of New England and institutionalized at Yale College, this strain of religious orthodoxy remained a bulwark of social and political conservatism into the first quarter of the nineteenth century. A third legacy stemmed from evangelical movements in the mid-eighteenth century—the Methodist movement in England and the Great Awakening in the colonies—and produced an intensely emotional Protestantism that stressed the individual's conversion experience as manifested in piety and rectitude.

To most orthodox church people in 1790, deism still seemed the major threat to organized religion. Deists viewed the Bible as an error-prone product of men rather than God, often questioned the divinity of Christ, and envisioned a universe governed by natural laws without divine interference. Tom Paine summarized this world-view in *The Age of Reason* (1796), and his gift for pithy expression won new adherents to the creed. On the other hand, to the orthodox these views enshrined science and reason at the expense of faith and piety and therefore struck at the very roots of religion. Though professed deists were never more than a handful, religious rationalism simmered in every major Protestant church. In Calvinist New England it blended nicely with Arminianism, a liberal strain of Puritan thought dating from the seventeenth century. Arminianism questioned the basic presumptions of Calvinism by presupposing a benevolent deity capable of granting universal salvation to all who led an upright life.

The latent contest between Arminian rationalists and orthodox Calvinists burst into the open in 1805 when the liberals succeeded in appointing their candidate to the Hollis Chair of Divinity at Harvard. Three years later a group of conservative ministers seceded from Harvard and founded Andover Theological Seminary, intended as a new citadel of orthodoxy. A decade of vicious pamphlet warfare followed, in which the liberals were denounced as "unitarians" who rejected the very foundation of Christianity by denying the divinity of Christ. The liberals at first heatedly denied the imputation and then gradually accepted it. In 1819, William Ellery Channing, minister of the Federal Street Church in Boston, delivered a sermon in Baltimore that outlined the Unitarian creed and earned him a national reputation. A year later he summoned a conference of liberal ministers, which in 1826 became the American Unitarian Association.

Just as deism and religious liberalism eventually took institutional form in the Unitarian Church, the evangelical thread of eighteenth-century Protestantism solidified institutionally into the Methodist and Baptist churches. The religious fervor that began as the Great Awakening continued to bubble forth in a series of revivals throughout the revolutionary decades. The stress on the emotion-packed conversion experience, in which the evildoer confessed his sins and accepted salvation through Christ, elevated faith over knowledge, emotion over reason. It led to a widespread practice of lay preaching, as those who had seen the light took to the road to spread the Gospel. Most of these migrated into the Baptist Church because adult baptism was the most obvious symbol of a new beginning in life, but the Methodist Church sent its own itinerant missionaries to America. Together these Baptist and Methodist circuit riders created dozens of churches and sponsored innumerable revivals through the latter decades of the century. Elimination of the religious establishment in the southern states after the war immensely benefited the evangelicals. With all churches on an equal footing and forced to compete for members, the most enthusiastic were, at least in the short term, the most successful.

The success of Methodists and Baptists in making converts encouraged "new light" Presbyterians to imitate their methods. Indeed, it was a conjunction of evangelical faiths that produced the largest religious revival of the post-revolutionary years—the frontier where the emotional appeal of evangelism captivated a rude, naive, isolated people who lived under the constant shadow of violent death. In 1796, a Scots-Irish Presbyterian named James McCready appeared in the Blue Grass region of Kentucky, and his preaching attracted vast crowds of all denominations. Other exhorters adopted McCready's techniques, and a wave of religious revivalism swept the entire Appalachian plateau, from Pennsylvania to Georgia. A unique feature of this western revival was the camp meeting which lasted for days on end while thousands were exhorted by itinerant preachers, rotating in shifts, for twenty-four hours a day. Mass hysteria led individuals to collapse with the "jerks," bark like dogs after the devil, or dance themselves into exhaustion. One meeting at Cane Ridge, Kentucky, in 1801 attracted more than ten thousand people. Forty ministers conducted services day and night without intermission for a week; at one point more than a hundred "sinners" were laid out unconscious in orderly rows. This meeting climaxed the Second Great Awakening; thereafter it burnt itself out. Yet visitors reported a noticeable improvement in frontier morality, and church membership leaped. The Baptist and Methodist churches emerged among the nation's largest, with a grip on the people of the Appalachian plateau that remains virtually unshaken at the end of the twentieth century.

The Pursuit of Science

With the Revolution, scientific endeavor became intermingled with American nationalism. The atmosphere of political freedom attracted a number of prominent European scientists, such as Joseph Priestley (discoverer of oxygen), and many felt that America was destined to become a haven for free inquiry. Only in America, where liberty "unfetters and expands the human mind," wrote one European emigre, "can science flourish." The new temper of American science was directed initially at disproving the popular European conception that everything in America was necessarily inferior. For a half-century European scientists had argued that the New World was in a lesser stage of development, savage, unformed, shriveled for want of nourishment. All things in America, wrote one European who had never crossed the Atlantic, "shrink and diminish under a niggardly sky and in an unprolific land, peopled with wandering savages." It was to counteract such uninformed prejudice that Jefferson wrote his *Notes on Virginia* (1784), and in so doing he managed to compile an impressive amount of data on American flora and fauna, society and customs, geography and land forms. European criticism thus provided a great impetus to the improvement of American science, and in the decades after the Revolution scientific societies proliferated, and courses in science and medicine crept into the educational curriculum.

Even so, Americans made few discoveries and contributed little to the growing body of scientific theory. They quickly absorbed and communicated the latest European discoveries, but their primary achievements were in the realm of practical application. Nathaniel Bowditch, an insurance actuary by profession, applied sophisticated mathematical theory to problems of navigation. In 1802, he published *The New American Practical Navigator,* which ran through fifty-six editions over the next century and became the standard navigational handbook for the Atlantic world. Bowditch also developed a system of actuarial tables, which contributed to the evolution of the modern insurance industry, and published a series of papers on astronomy and meteorology.

In the fields of botany and zoology, Americans carried on the colonial tradition of collecting and identifying species. The new nation's most noted botanist was Benjamin Smith Barton, professor of natural history, botany, and medicine at the University of Pennsylvania. Utilizing the Linnaean system of classification, he produced the first comprehensive American textbook in the field, *Elements of Botany* (1800).

The rapid expansion of scientific knowledge led to increased specialization in the university curriculum. Natural history or natural philosophy gave way to select courses in chemistry, botany, zoology, astronomy, and medicine. Yet American scientists often resisted professional specialization; most preferred to satisfy their amateur curiosity by dabbling in the whole spectrum of scientific inquiry. Samuel Latham Mitchill, professor of chemistry at Columbia University and Jeffersonian member of Congress, was a man of catholic interests who published papers in mathematics, geology, medicine, and botany. His most important contribution was to acquaint Americans with the role of oxygen in combustion, a revolutionary discovery made by the French chemist Antoine Laurent Lavoisier in 1789. It had been assumed by western scientists that combustible substances contained an element called phlogiston, which was freed in the burning process. Lavoisier's demonstration that combustion was actually a chemical combination of substances with oxygen forced a complete revision of chemical nomenclature and theory. Irreducible elements could then be distinguished from compounds, and each element could ultimately be assigned a place in a periodic table of atomic weights (a discovery of the English chemist John Dalton in 1808). Imported into America by men like Samuel Latham Mitchill, these revolutionary discoveries laid the basis for a flowering of American science in the next generation.

Medicine, in both Europe and America, lingered at the end of the eighteenth century in a twilight between medieval and modern practice, still lacking a theory that explained the cause, nature, or cure of disease. American physicians gained their medical knowledge by serving a brief apprenticeship to a practicing doctor; of approximately 3,500 persons practicing medicine at the outbreak of the Revolution only about 200 had medical degrees. Lack of professional training had its advantages, for American doctors often prescribed such commonsense remedies as rest and fresh air. Yet the limits of American medicine were illustrated by the career of Benjamin Rush, foremost physician of the age. A native of Philadelphia who was trained at Edinburgh in the 1760s, Rush held a chair of medicine at the University of Pennsylvania. He achieved national prominence as a result of his heroic work during the terrible Philadelphia yellow fever epidemic of 1793, and students flocked to his lectures. As the primary cause of illness, Rush stressed "excessive action" in the blood veins and recommended bleeding and purging as the most effective remedy. Tragically, the system passed the test of clinical observation, for the short-term effect of bleeding was to reduce a fever. So the system seemed to work. That it weakened a patient in the long run was not so readily evident. Rush's students carried his system into every part of the nation, and until discredited in the

1820s, bleeding was the standard weapon used to combat fevers. George Washington's death in 1799 may have been hastened by the excessive bleeding prescribed by his physician. So too, ironically, was Rush's. As he lay on his death bed ill with pneumonia in 1813, his last request was for a bleeder.

An American Style in Literature and the Arts

"Every engine should be employed to render the people of the country national," wrote Noah Webster shortly after the Revolution, "to call their attachment home to their country; and to inspire them with the pride of national character." Despite political independence, many Americans were painfully aware that they remained a cultural colony of Great Britain. English literary works were inexpensively imported and easily pirated; American readers commonly preferred the essays of Addison and Steele or the poetry of Alexander Pope to the hesitant productions of their own fledgling writers. Yet, as Noah Webster realized, if the new nation were to become a viable political entity, with an honored place in the family of nations, it must first develop a cultural identity capable of inspiring pride and unity.

To this end Webster published in 1783 his *American Spelling Book,* designed to replace English-made spellers in American elementary schools. He carefully distinguished American forms of spelling (reversing the "re" in *theatre* and *centre,* and dropping the "u" from *labour* and *favour*) and patriotically included peculiarly American words that were not found in English dictionaries (*prairie, tomahawk,* and *rattlesnake*). A few years later two more books issued from his pen—a grammar and a reader. The three works, combined as *The Grammatical Institute,* became the basic texts in American public schools for the next half-century. His reading primer contained passages on the lives of American heroes and events of the Revolution, designed to instill pride of nationality along with a measure of literacy. Webster devoted his remaining years to *The American Dictionary* (published finally in 1828), which contained some 12,000 new words of American origin, invented by an imaginative, mobile, miscellaneous people. Such efforts as Webster's laid the foundations for a distinctively American literature.

The literary productions of the new nation were self-conscious (and usually second-rate) efforts at cultural independence. The literary center of New England after the Revolution was Connecticut, the home of a group of poets known as the "Hartford Wits." Timothy Dwight, perhaps the ablest of the group, typified its Calvinist orthodoxy and conservative politics. He began his poetic career in 1785 by publishing a New England epic, *The Conquest of Canaan,* modelled closely on English forms. Though an unimaginative poet, Dwight was an inveterate traveler, and he kept elaborate notebooks on his journeys. His *Travels in New England and New York* remains a rich source of information on American society in this period. In 1795, Dwight became president of Yale University, where he quickly reversed the free-thinking policies of his predecessor, Ezra Stiles, and made Yale once again the citadel of Congregational orthodoxy, earning for himself the title of "Protestant Pope of New England."

Closely associated with Dwight was Jonathan Trumbull, another graduate of Yale who studied law in the office of John Adams in Boston before settling in Hartford. His poetic contribution was *M'Fingall* (1776), a biting satire on the revolutionary conflict between Whigs and Tories which proved to be the most popular poem for a half-century, passing through more than thirty editions.

The only member of the Hartford circle to escape the stifling atmosphere of Calvinist orthodoxy was Joel Barlow, politician, lawyer, and diplomat. On a journey to France in the 1790s, he came into contact with revolutionary political and religious thought, and made the acquaintance of Tom Paine. He returned a confirmed radical and completed his apostasy (in the eyes of Timothy Dwight) by supporting the presidency of Thomas Jefferson. While in France, he wrote one of the first good American poems, "The Hasty Pudding" (1793), which combined freshness of form with salty New England humor. Yet it was also Barlow who wrote *The Columbiad* (1807), a self-conscious effort at an American epic in the tradition of Virgil and Milton, which proved to be the poetic disaster of the century. Barlow died in 1812 while serving as President Madison's minister to France; he died in Poland while searching for Napoleon, who was then on his way to Moscow.

In the middle states, New York City vied with Philadelphia for cultural leadership. The Quaker city, still profiting from the energizing influence of Benjamin Franklin's many-sided mind, could boast the nation's best poet and first novelist. Philip Freneau, a graduate of Princeton, where he had been James Madison's classmate, earned himself the title "poet of the Revolution" with his bitterly anti-British verses written while serving in the revolutionary army. Son of a wealthy merchant, Freneau inherited an estate in New Jersey where he worked as a country printer and wrote lyric poems, such as "To a Wild Honeysuckle" and "The Indian Burying Ground," which utilized distinctively American scenes. Unlike the "Hartford Wits," Freneau was able to break free from the stultifying conventions of British poetry, and he produced lyrical passages dealing with the beauties of nature that anticipated the romanticism of Wordsworth and Coleridge. In 1791, Madison induced him to move to Philadelphia and found an anti-administration newspaper, the *National Gazette.* Thereafter he excoriated Federalists in editorials and satirical poems with the same gusto with which he had flayed the British during the Revolution.

Another resident of Philadelphia, Charles Brockden Brown, has the distinction of being America's first professional writer and first important novelist. In a series of works published at the turn of the century, Brown adapted the Gothic novel, then sweeping fashionable literary circles in England, to an American environment. The Gothic novel was characterized by brooding castles, secret passageways, desperate villains, supernatural events, and screams of terror (perhaps best exemplified by Mary Shelley's 1818 artistic creation, *Frankenstein),* and Brown slavishly utilized all these devices. But the best of his novels, such as *Wieland* (1798) and *Ormonde* (1799), reflected such originality, imagination, and lyric style that Keats considered him a "powerful genius."

New York, lagging behind Philadelphia in population, commerce, and artistic achievements, toward the end of this period managed to produce America's first literary giant, Washington Irving. Son of a wealthy Scottish merchant, he was brought up on Calvinist theology and Federalist politics. But in urbane New York both disciplines were more relaxed than in stern New England, and Irving had leisure to absorb the color of the city's docks and travel among the legend-filled Dutch settlements on the Hudson. In 1809, he brought out his *Knickerbocker's History of New York,* based on a fictionalized Dutch antiquarian Dietrich Knickerbocker, who recounted the legends of the province and jabbed wealthy and pompous Dutch families with satirical wit. The work brought Irving instant fame on both sides of the Atlantic, and six years later he toured the European continent. He remained there for the next seventeen years, a period that embraced most of his productive career. His most important work, *The Sketchbook* (1819–20), was written in England, though the scene for most of the stories, such as "Rip Van Winkle" and "The Legend of Sleepy Hollow," was set in the atmosphere of the old Dutch farms in the Hudson Valley. Yet Irving symbolized the paradox of American letters. He was lionized in Europe precisely because he was an oddity; people read his works because they marvelled at how a "colonial" culture could produce such a cosmopolitan genius.

Painting, like literature, revealed a self-concious effort to develop a national style. Pre-revolutionary American painters were London-oriented and dominated by the expatriate genius Benjamin West. John Singleton Copley, the first of West's protegés, remained in England through the Revolution, rejecting what he felt was the artistic wasteland of America.

But other students of West, after absorbing the atmosphere of the cultural center of the Atlantic community, returned home to lay the foundations for a native American style. John Trumbull was a Connecticut Yankee, a cousin to the "Hartford Wit," and brother to the governor of the state. At Harvard he encountered Copley, who taught him the rudiments of painting, but when his tutor departed for London, Trumbull joined the revolutionary forces, eventually obtaining a place on Washington's staff. Truculent and irascible, he eventually resigned over a fancied slight and departed for London to study under West. His imagination stirred by the deeds of arms he had witnessed during the war, Trumbull easily blended with West's own interest in historical paintings. Over the new few years he completed a number of grandiose canvases depicting such dramatic events as *The Surrender of Cornwallis,* which earned him the sobriquet "painter of the Revolution."

Trumbull was not a great artist, but he was a good one, and the same might be said for Charles Willson Peale. A Maryland lad of obscure lineage, Peale worked as a saddler, coachmaker, and silversmith before demonstrating a flair with a brush while painting family arms on the coaches of Maryland gentry. Convinced that he had a talent for limning, a group of planters sent him to London to study with West. After a brief stay, he returned to America to enlist in the revolutionary army. He spent the war years painting the portraits of American and French officers, as well as members of the Continental Congress. He painted Washington four times, once before the Revolution, twice during it, and once as president.

A confirmed patriot, Peale propagandized tirelessly for an American style in painting and hoped to awaken a popular interest in art. In 1786, he founded the first museum in the United States at Philadelphia, and kicked it off with an exhibition of 130 Italian paintings sent to him for sale. To promote patriotism among those who visited his museum he decorated the walls with portraits of revolutionary heroes. The museum also reflected Peale's catholic interests in botany, natural history, and taxidermy. He originated the idea of habitat-arrangement for his specimens, creating pools, grassy turfs, and branches as background for his stuffed animals. His scientific interests were shared by his close friend, Thomas Jefferson, who supplied him with specimens brought back by Lewis and Clark from their transcontinental expedition. To improve the standards of American painting Peale helped to establish the Pennsylvania Academy of Fine Arts (1805), the first such institution in America. He sired seven children with an artistic bent, at least one of whom, Rembrandt Peale, became a first-class portrait painter in his own right.

The ablest of Benjamin West's students was Gilbert Stuart, who so impressed the mentor that he provided Stuart with room, board, and free instruction. A native of Rhode Island, Stuart decided at the age of twenty that the colonies were an infertile environment for a budding artist, and in 1775 he joined West in London. In 1782, he opened his own studio in London and met instant success. Influenced also by Reynolds and Gainsborough, Stuart specialized in portrait painting, but he retained a fresh, independent style of his own. Stuart was popular among the court circle, but his living expenses eventually outran his income, and in 1792 he returned to the United States with the avowed purpose of recouping his fortunes by painting Washington. The famous bust portrait, done from life in 1795, brought him dozens of orders for copies. Stuart obligingly reproduced a number of copies, some with the aid of his students, so it is now virtually impossible to determine the original. Placed in nearly every elementary school classroom over the next century and a half, Washington's bust has stared grimly down at generations of school children (the pursed lips due to ill-fitting false teeth) indelibly etched the image of "the founding father" on the American mind.

American architects were, if anything, even more conscientious in their search for a distinctive national style. Colonial builders who erected magnificent mansions for the gentry were master carpenters, rather than architects, and they closely imitated the "Georgian" style fashionable among the country houses of English nobility. But the young republic was fortunate in possessing a number of talented, native-born architects who sought to express the aspirations of the American experiment through the medium of design. The classical designs of ancient Greece and Rome were perfectly suited for the purpose; the restrained elegance and mathematical proportion of their buildings were ready-made symbols of republican virtue. As it happened, the Americans' need for symbolic expression coincided with the rediscovery of classical architecture in Europe.

American builders' introduction to Roman forms was indirect at first, through the influence of the sixteenth-century Italian architect Andrea Palladio. Renaissance architects greatly admired Roman forms, and Palladio used the classic column and cornice for decoration as well as structural functions. Palladio's work, in turn, became popular in England in the mid-eighteenth century, and it crossed the Atlantic in English manuals used by American builders. Peter Harrison, the best of the colonial designers, used a Palladian sketch when he planned the Redwood Library in Newport (1750). Similarly, when Jefferson started on Monticello in the 1770s, he used a plan that he found in an English handbook, a plan that was an adaptation of Palladio's Villa Rotunda in Vicenza, Italy.

After 1750, French archeological discoveries, including the excavation of Pompeii, revived European interest in classical forms. Indeed, European designers began to bypass Renaissance classicism and turned to the original Roman and Greek models. For the first time they even distinguished between Roman and Greek; and some, particularly the French, argued that Greek forms were superior due to their simplicity and mathematical symmetry. When these new influences crossed the Atlantic, Americans eagerly subscribed because the classical style suited their need for symbols. When Jefferson remodeled Monticello in the 1790s, he added a Roman dome and portico, thereby changing the country home of a Virginia squire into a shrine for a prominent statesman of the republic.

Jefferson hoped to create a national architecture out of classical forms. His design for the state capitol at Richmond (1785) was a copy of a structure he saw at Nimes in southern France, the Maison Caree, which was a Roman copy of a Greek temple. The state legislature in the meantime had authorized another design, and construction of the capitol was already under way when Jefferson's plan reached Virginia. Jefferson nevertheless insisted that they start anew using his sketches. To Madison he explained: "How is a taste for this beautiful art to be formed in our countrymen unless we avail ourselves of every occasion when public buildings are erected, of presenting to them models for their study and imitation."

For Jefferson, independence was more than a severance of ties with the mother country. It was an opportunity to rebuild society on more rational lines. It was in this spirit that he rejected the Georgian Baroque that reminded him of monarchy and empire and embraced the Doric simplicity of the ancients. As secretary of state under President Washington, he had general supervision over the construction of the nation's capital, and the result was almost a resurrection of Rome on the banks of the Potomac. Jefferson did not design any of the public buildings in the federal city (though he submitted anonymously a design for the capitol which lost out in the competition), but he carefully scrutinized the sketches submitted. Both William Thornton's plan for the capitol and James Hoban's design for the president's mansion were essentially Roman in character. Jefferson's alterations made them more Roman still.

The Capitol was still unfinished when Jefferson became president in 1801, and he brought to Washington the outstanding classicist in the nation, Benjamin H. Latrobe, to finish the job. Born in England and educated in Germany, Latrobe arrived in the United States in 1795 to take up an architectural career. Four years later he was commissioned to design the Bank of Pennsylvania, and to the amazement of interested Philadelphians he modeled it on Greek, rather than Roman forms. A masonry vault dominated the massive interior, and on the front he placed huge Ionic columns supporting an Athenian portico. Greek democracy and Greek art, he explained to the Philadelphia Society of Artists, were the only proper models for the American experiment. "The days of Greece may be revived in the woods of America; and Philadelphia may become the Athens of the Western world." Latrobe was a bit ahead of his time, for the Greek Revival in architecture did not come until the 1820s, but he did alter the Capitol in significant ways. He remodeled both the east and west fronts and added Corinthian columns to the interior of the House of Representatives. In the columns he put in the Senate chamber, he changed the traditional leaf-clusters in the capitals to shocks of corn, evidently in an effort to adapt Greek design to the American environment. Artists howled in derision at the "corn cob capitals," but Congress, less meticulous and more patriotic, approved heartily.

Latrobe finished his work on the Capitol in 1811 and turned to other projects, but when the British burned the city in 1814, Madison asked him to supervise reconstruction. He made no further changes of importance, except to cover the burn scars of the president's house by painting it white (from which it derives its present name). Latrobe's successor as capital architect was Charles Bulfinch, who was probably the nation's first professional architect. Jefferson was only an able amateur, and Latrobe spread his creative energies among canals and steamboats in addition to buildings. Bulfinch made his living by his art, and his originality, knowledge of engineering capabilities, and insistence on supervising every detail of construction, all suggest professional maturity.

By 1817, the duties of capital architect were more honorary than onerous, and Bulfinch brought to the post an established reputation. A Bostonian by birth and a Harvard graduate, he spent several years in England in the 1780s before returning to Boston to take up an architectural career. During his stay abroad he came under the influence of the Scottish designer Robert Adam (1728–1792), who was the leading British exponent of neoclassicism. Adam embellished the rather plain exteriors of English "Georgian" houses by adding three-dimensional doorfronts, slender columns, and iron railings, but his main innovations were on the interiors. There his trade marks were the use of oval or octagonal rooms, arches supported by pilasters, and vaulted ceilings painted in minute detail and lit by spectacular chandeliers. Adam's inspiration was both Palladian and Roman, but the result was quite different from the purer classicism practiced by Jefferson and Latrobe.

On his return to America in 1790, Bulfinch became the leading proponent of Adamesque design, which, because its introduction coincided with the establishment of the federal government, became known as the Federal Style. The Adamesque also suited the tastes of the Federalist merchants of New England, and it received its finest American statement in Bulfinch's Boston. Jefferson, though he made extensive use of octagonal rooms in his designs, ignored the Adamesque vogue, perhaps because it was British-inspired and ornate.

Bulfinch's initial venture in design was an experiment in urban planning. He designed a self-contained unit of row houses in the shape of an open-ended oval, and the individual houses were to be differentiated by Adamesque features, such as octagonal bay windows and columned doorfronts. Facilities for marketing and entertainment were built into the plan. Unfortunately only half of the Tontine Crescent was completed before Bulfinch and his associates ran out of money. The project nonetheless had a profound influence on the postwar reconstruction of Boston, and though the Crescent itself burned in the mid-nineteenth century, its influence can still be seen today in the row houses of Beacon Hill.

Bulfinch's state house for Massachusetts, completed in 1798, established his reputation as a designer. Its use of Roman arches, the alternation of square and semicircular windows, and its gracefully slender columns set the tone for the Federal Style. Most noted for his private dwellings, Bulfinch revised the simple colonial pattern of four rooms to a floor by adding open staircases, entrance halls, and oval-shaped rooms. Like Adam, he specialized in intricately decorated interiors but usually left the outside an unadorned multi-story box. That mode suited the wealthy merchants of puritanical Boston where ostentation was still viewed with suspicion.

Bulfinch viewed Latrobe's work on the Capitol with distaste, but he had the good sense to confine himself to minor changes. By 1817, his architectural style was as outmoded as the Federalist merchants to whom it appealed. A sign of the changing times was the acceptance, a year later, of a plan for a second Bank of the United States to be erected on Fifth and Chestnut streets in Philadelphia. The architect was young William Strickland, and his inspiration was neither Georgian, nor Palladian, nor even Roman, but Greek. The design, particularly the front, was as close to the Parthenon as Strickland could make it and still preserve the functional difference between a temple and a bank. Completion of the edifice in 1824 coincided with a popular outburst of sentiment in behalf of the Greeks in their struggle for freedom against the Turks. For the next few decades Grecian columns were slapped on everything from dry goods stores to plantation mansions. Yet the Greek Revival movement expressed a different mood, a mood of Romantic escapism, of splendor and opulence. Gone was the eighteenth century's concern for mathematical proportion that had characterized the neoclassical styles of Jefferson and Bulfinch. Gone, too, was the search for republican simplicity.

Architecture, perhaps more than any other craft, is the sport of the wealthy elite. Public buildings and distinctive houses might symbolize the nation's aspirations, but they hardly represented the artistic tastes or capabilities of the average American. The "middling sort" of folk continued to live in boxlike structures without design or artistry. There was, however, considerable regional variation in plan. New Englanders favored multi-story square houses (adding gables to accommodate additions to the family) built around a central fireplace and chimney for maximum heating efficiency. The middle states still showed German and Dutch influence, building two-story brick houses with a massive fireplace and chimney at one end. In Virginia and the Southwest farmers of moderate means generally constructed rectangular houses, four rooms to a floor, with chimneys at each end so that each room possessed a small fireplace. To meet the needs of an expanding family wings could be added almost indefinitely.

In home furnishings, the gap between rich and poor was often the difference between European styles, either imported or copied, and various indigenous designs, some of surpassing beauty. In the mid-eighteenth century the wealthy often imported copies of Chippendale masterpieces, whose robust form and free-flowing curves complemented the Baroque or "Georgian" style of architecture. In the late-eighteenth century the neoclassical revival had its impact on furnishings. Robert Adam designed chairs and cabinets that complemented his imaginative doorways and ceilings, but George Heppelwhite and Thomas Sheraton had a greater influence on America. Both published manuals of furniture design that were widely used in America, and English copies of their pieces were a staple of the export trade. The Federal Style in furniture featured light. slender lines and a general tone of austerity. Chair backs were often oval or hooped, legs were usually straight, tapered, and footless. Inlays and veneers of exotic woods, such as rosewood or ebony, were common in cabinets, sideboards, and tables.

American furniture-makers imitated these English fashions with varying degrees of skill, and a few evidenced genuine originality. Samuel McIntyre of Salem, Massachusetts, designed townhouses for the wealthy in the Adamesque style like Bulfinch, but he was better known for his woodcarving. Whether demonstrated in an elegantly carved mantelpiece or an intricate freize on the arms and back of a Sheraton-style sofa, McIntyre was a genius with wood.

The leading American furniture designer of the period was Duncan Phyfe of New York City, and his specialty was the French mode, or *Directoire,* which appeared in the 1790s and evolved after 1800 into the Napoleonic or Empire Style. This fashion gives an impression of solidity and mass, in contrast to the light, almost ethereal Adamesque. Curved lines and scrolls were common features. On chairs the back curved gracefully into the seat; legs were often concave. Chair arms coiled around into themselves, and sofas had roll-over arms and serpentine backs. In France, the Empire Style eventually degenerated into ornate fixtures decorated with ponderous Roman scrolls, but in Phyfe's hands the same inspiration retained its subtle curves, graceful lines, and restrained decoration. Phyfe operated on a large scale; his factory on Fulton Street in New York eventually employed over a hundred men.

Indeed, the growth of Phyfe's operation was a good example of the profound changes taking place in American work patterns after 1800. In colonial times master craftsmen, journeymen, and apprentices worked side by side in the same shop. They shared the same hours, took the same breaks, drank in the same tavern. Duncan Phyfe, by contrast was a businessman, who concentrated on buying raw materials and marketing the finished product. He seldom saw his workers and left their supervision to shop foremen. This division of function had profound implications for the future of American labor and the concept of work. Tradesmen began forming unions shortly after 1800, and by the 1820s they were beginning to think of themselves as a working class, bound to their machines and held in their servile station by low wages and long hours.

Despite his innovations in work routine and his search for a national market, Duncan Phyfe still designed his furnishings for the wealthy. The middle classes, occasionally able to grace their living rooms with Duncan Phyfe's sofas, more often depended on the ubiquitous Windsor chair. Invented in Philadelphia about 1725, the wooden Windsor chair remained the most common furnishing in American homes for the next century. Long after it was abandoned in favor of more plush and comfortable pieces, it remained the standard seat in taverns and waiting rooms until the end of the nineteenth century. In the mid-twentieth century it once again appeared in the homes of many, this time in the guise of "Early American."

More than any other art, furniture styling remained dependent upon Europe for its inspiration. Yet there were some American innovations, and ironically they appeared first in the houses of the poor. Like folk music they were spontaneous and anonymous, spare of ornament, yet elegant in their functional simplicity. The most common example of this kind of furniture was the ladder chair, which derived its name from a high straight back with a number of cross-pieces that resembled a ladder. Simple yet sturdy, they required no artistic skill and only a modicum of carpentry. When not in use, they could easily be hung on the wall, for space was at a premium in the cottages of the poor.

This feature may also have recommended the ladder chair to the early communal settlements, such as the Shakers, because community dining rooms had to be cleared of tables and chairs for dancing and religious ceremonies. In the hands of meticulous Shaker craftsmen these stark, functional pieces became a genuine folk art. Pietist sects such as Shakers and Mennonites rejected worldly adornment. Their cabinets and tables were simple and utilitarian, straight of line and square in form. Yet the judicious selection of certain hardwoods—birch, maple, or oak—produced striking effects, and a process of hand-rubbing them with hot oil and turpentine produced a patina that conveyed a quiet elegance of its own. Perhaps this was the first genuine "Early American" style.

The Search for National Identity

The cultural strivings of Americans were only one aspect of their search for a national place in the sun. Unifying symbols were hard to appropriate in a young republic. The elimination of the monarchy meant that Americans could not look to a crown as a symbol of nationhood, and the Constitution, subject as it was to conflicting interpretations, did not serve as a valid replacement until after the Civil War. The flag (designed during the Revolution by the versatile Francis Hopkinson—scientist, musician, and playwright) was a natural rallying point, but the makeup of stars and bars was subject to constant fluctuation with the admission of new states. The flag, which Francis Scott Key saw at dawn on September 14, 1814, contained fifteen stripes and fifteen stars, and his poem (put to the music of an English drinking song) did not become the national anthem until 1931. July 4 was already celebrated annually in many places by a reading of the Declaration of Independence, but neither had yet achieved the symbolic stature that they would for later generations.

Faced with such a paucity of national symbols, Americans turned to classical Greece and Rome for models. Classical place names abounded as Americans sought to recall the glories of the ancients in the wilderness of America (New York state alone possessed Syracuse, Rome, Athens, Troy, Utica, and Carthage). Republican Rome was for the moment the most useful, and the conscious adaptation of Roman architectural forms in the nation's capital was only one example. The Roman eagle became the national emblem, and the upper houses in most American legislatures were termed senates. But such synthetic symbolism was temporary at best, and in the long run Americans turned to their revolutionary heroes for patriotic sustenance.

A good deal of American literature throughout this period was devoted to refurbishing the lives of Samuel Adams, Benjamin Franklin, Patrick Henry and other patriots of '76. As soon as the war was over, participants took up their quills to present the American side of the conflict. Much of it was "patriotic gore," but some lasting history also emerged—especially the works by the South Carolina physician David Ramsey and Plymouth's Mercy Otis Warren. Warren's four-volume opus was the first complete history of the Revolution. Unfortunately, its publication terminated a lifelong friendship with John and Abigail Adams. It seems that Mercy Warren's historical objectivity led to an assessment of Adams's role in the Revolution that was less important than Adams felt he deserved.

Those who played important roles in the founding of the republic had a keen sense of history and were eager to see that posterity accurately portrayed the event. Jefferson meticulously copied all his letters, and Madison late in life retrieved his letters from all his correspondents so they could be collected in one complete and coherent body. Americans thus had a wealth of material from which to fabricate their national self-image.

The most useful, and the most enduring, symbol of all was George Washington, who arose into the American pantheon almost immediately upon his death in 1799. Henry Lee's eulogy, "First in war, first in peace, and first in the hearts of his countrymen" became a national tribute (indeed, it is the only thing many people remember about "Light Horse Harry," along with the fact that he was the father of Robert E. Lee). John Marshall, a lifelong admirer of Washington, promptly made plans for an extensive biography. The first installment, of what eventually became five volumes, appeared in 1804, and it quickly established itself as more mausoleum than monument. Dull, rambling, desultory, Washington (who is born in volume II) stalks through the turgid pages in military regalia, cool, aloof, and distant. Yet the image of reserved detachment which appeared in Marshall's pages seemed to fit best the popular image of a hero, and Gilbert Stuart's likeness, which effused firmness and integrity, completed the conversion of a man into a symbol.

Washington was the stuff of which heroes are made. Tall, well-proportioned, a magnificent horseman, he led a life of republican virtue, exchanging plowshare for sword at the beginning of the Revolution and rejecting a proffered crown for a plowshare at the end. Even so, the fundamental humanity of the man might have shown through the crust of symbolism had it not been completely obscured by Parson Weems. Mason Locke Weems of Dumfries, Virginia, was an Episcopal minister turned book peddler and author. He traveled throughout Virginia with a wagonload of wares, dispensing nostrums, hardware, books, or sermons as the occasion (and the audience) demanded. Even before Washington's death he recognized the market potential of a popular, anecdotal life of the hero and began collecting materials. One recent historian calls him "a one-man market-research enterprise" who pre-tested his product before rural audiences across the country. He knew exactly what these people wanted and anticipated that his book would "sell like flaxseed at a quarter of a dollar."

Weems thus had his product ready for market when Washington's death created the popular demand; the first edition of his eighty-page booklet appeared in 1800. Most of the anecdotes stressed Washington's patriotism, virtue, and godliness, recounted in a sprightly style that entertained adults and provided a model for children. Undaunted by Marshall's extended biography, Weems merely revised his pamphlet, extending it to two hundred pages by including a number of appealing new anecdotes (including the cherry tree story), most of which he fabricated himself. Weems's *Life of George Washington* went through twenty-five editions before his death in 1825, selling more than 50,000 copies. Profitable as it was for the author, it imprisoned Washington-the-man behind the bars of myth. The hero emerges, even as a youth, with a fully developed code of ethics (e.g., the cherry tree story) and remains a model of all the virtues most admired by Americans—a stone idol devoid of emotion, ambition, temper, and humanity.

Yet, whatever Weems's biography did for Washington, it undeniably answered a need felt by Americans. It provided them with a hero who could rally the nation and counter all the centrifugal forces that threatened to tear apart the republican experiment. Geographical, ethnic, religious, and political rivalries were all submerged in this unifying symbol of republican virtue. The secular canonization of Washington was an integral part of the self-conscious search for cultural independence. The political reflection of this drive was the effort after 1789 to breathe life into the newborn Constitution, to prove that the men who assembled at Philadelphia two years before erected not just a frame of government—they created a nation.

6

The Federal Experiment

WHEN PRESIDENT WASHINGTON, IN HIS INAUGURAL ADDRESS, referred to the undertaking of a federated republic on a continental scale as a "great experiment," he was expressing both the hopes and the fears of many Americans. It was an axiom of eighteenth-century political theory that a republican form of government was weak and easily disrupted by the passions of factionalism; to endure, it would have to be confined to a small geographical area. To counter such doctrine Madison tried to demonstrate in the tenth essay of *The Federalist* that a republic of continental scope was actually more stable than a tiny one because jealousies would be dissipated in the welter of conflicting interests—regional, social, economic, religious—in which no single group would be strong enough to dominate or overthrow the government.

Despite Madison's reassuring philosophy, scarcely a man who participated in the making of the Constitution genuinely felt it would long endure. Indeed, the imminent collapse of the republic lingered as an undercurrent for the next two decades; not until after the War of 1812 did American political leaders relax their vigil and look to the future with optimism. This fact alone explains much of the hyperemotionalism and violence that characterized American politics in the 1790s. The cries of "monarchy," "faction," "tyranny," and constant pleas for men of virtue in public affairs were more than just propaganda; they reflected a genuine concern for the durability of the republic. Nor were American statesmen reassured by the contemporary experience of the French republic, which experienced a reign of terror, a committee of corrupt politicians (the Directory), and finally a *coup d'etat* by a military hero, Napoleon. It was thus with a strong undercurrent of doubt and fear that members of the first Congress gathered in New York City (the capital since 1784) to attend the inaugural ceremonies for the first president. Their task was to breathe life into the Constitution, to convert a piece of parchment into a stable government, and in their success lies their enduring monument.

Launching the Vessel of State

Elections for the new government were held during the fall of 1788, and the electoral college met in February 1789. With each elector casting two ballots, Washington was elected president and John Adams, with the second highest-vote, was chosen vice president. The initial session of the first Congress failed to remove the apprehensions of the fearful, for members straggled in slowly from the far reaches of the continent. It took Congress a month to obtain a quorum, and many eager Federalists, such as James Madison, who had secured a seat in the House of Representatives, fretted that the new regime would be as hampered by absenteeism as the old Continental Congress.

Washington, who conducted a leisurely and much-celebrated tour northward from Mount Vernon, was not inaugurated until April 30, and in the interim Congress became bogged down in a comic-opera debate over what to call the new president. Vice President John Adams, presiding over the Senate, led to the debate over the proper title for the President. Concerned that the new government be dignified and respected, Adams felt that to address Washington merely as "Mr. President" might put him on a level with the governor of Bermuda. Yet such titles as "His Excellency" or "His Elective Highness," suggested in the Senate, raised the specter of monarchy. Fortunately, the dilemma was resolved in commonsense fashion when the House of Representatives, at the suggestion of Madison, ruled that the Constitution conferred the only proper title: "President of the United States." The vice president received the nickname "His Rotundity," but beneath the surface hilarity lingered an undercurrent of apprehension.

The supporters of the Constitution had worked frantically in the fall elections to prevent their enemies from gaining control of the new Congress, and their efforts met with total success. When first Senate assembled there were only two Antifederalists (both from Virginia), and in the House only eight. Even voters who were skeptical of the Constitution evidently felt that the new government ought to be given a trial.

Armed with substantial majorities in both houses, the Federalists moved to exercise the new powers conferred by the Constitution. In May, Madison (who was immediately recognized as the administration spokesman, both by virtue of his role in the federal Convention and his intimate association with Washington) introduced the nation's first revenue bill levying customs duties on imports. Final action on the bill was delayed until July, at the request of merchants who wanted to get their ships and cargoes into port before the duties went into effect. The general level of rates was 5 percent ad valorem, but a protective duty of 50 percent (high enough to discourage imports) was granted to a few products, such as steel and cloth, the domestic manufacture of which Congress wished to encourage.

The problem of revenue solved, Congress turned next to filling out the constitutional outlines for the executive and judiciary. The Constitution wisely left to Congress the organization of executive departments under the president. Of these the Treasury gave the most trouble because many congressmen feared losing "the power of the purse" should the agency become too independent. Moreover, in England the First Lord of the Treasury had evolved into the prime minister in the course of the eighteenth century, a precedent not forgotten by wary Americans. After much debate Congress decided to reserve the right to examine the accounts of the Treasury and require information of its secretary without consulting the president. Although subject to special supervision by Congress, the Treasury was authorized to have the largest staff of any executive department—some thirty clerks and more than a thousand revenue agents and customs house collectors.

The State Department, which governed diplomacy and such interior affairs as weights and measures, patents, and coinage, was authorized a secretary, four clerks, and a part-time translator. Its annual budget was $7,000, about half earmarked for the secretary's salary. The War Department was carried over intact from the confederation government and consisted of a secretary (General Henry Knox), five clerks, and a standing army of about three thousand, most of which was posted on the frontier.

Washington's appointment of Alexander Hamilton to the treasury post was greeted with mild surprise. Born in the West Indies and educated at King's College (Columbia), Hamilton had served in the Revolution as aide-de-camp to Washington and participated in the siege of Yorktown with considerable valor. Afterwards, he helped organize the Bank of New York and collaborated with Madison and Jay on *The Federalist.* He thus brought to his new position both financial experience and a devotion to central government. The appointment of Thomas Jefferson to head the State Department, on the other hand, occasioned no surprise, for he was a fellow Virginian widely respected for his authorship of the Declaration of Independence. Moreover, he possessed experience in the art of diplomacy, having served as minister to France since 1784.

In contrast to the executive departments, the judiciary created a mild political storm. The issue had even troubled the federal Convention, for critics of the Constitution at Philadelphia had argued that a national judiciary was at best superfluous and at worst would supersede the state courts. As a result, the Constitution contained only a vaguely worded authorization vesting the judicial power of the United States in "one Supreme Court, and in such inferior Courts as the Congress may from time to time ordain and establish." This, in effect, dumped the problem into the lap of Congress, and a special Senate committee headed by Oliver Ellsworth of Connecticut reported in May 1789, a bill creating a hierarchy of federal courts under the Supreme Court.

Adopted in September, the Judiciary Act of 1789 represented a compromise between the demands of the nationalists and the fears of the Antifederalists. The act authorized a Supreme Court with a chief justice (Washington appointed New York lawyer John Jay) and five associate justices. Beneath the Supreme Court were three circuit courts (presided over by two Supreme Court justices and one district judge) and thirteen district courts, one for each state except two for Massachusetts and Virginia (North Carolina and Rhode Island were not yet in the Union). The act also authorized an attorney general to act as the president's legal adviser; to this post Washington appointed another friend from Virginia, Edmund Randolph. Creation of a federal judicial hierarchy was a victory for the nationalists, but the jurisdiction of these courts was limited to cases arising under the Constitution or laws and treaties of the federal government; thus ordinary civil and criminal jurisdiction was reserved for the state courts. Section 25, however, provided for appeal from state supreme courts to the federal Supreme Court in cases involving the Constitution or laws of the national government, in effect, making the federal courts supreme.

The Bill of Rights

Throughout the summer of 1789, Congress conducted a sporadic debate on the problem of amending the document so recently ratified. The lack of a specific list of guarantees for the rights of citizens had occasioned some criticism at the Philadelphia Convention, and it became the prime target of Antifederalists in the great debate over ratification. A generation that had just concluded a war in defense of its rights was naturally concerned that they be forever guaranteed, and the Antifederalist argument enlisted broad support. Seven of the state ratifying convention suggested changes in the Constitution. Some were designed to protect basic freedoms, others were attempts to change the structure of the federal government, while others were mere efforts to weaken the powers of the central government, especially in the areas of taxation and trade. In Virginia, Madison steered the Constitution through a closely divided ratifying convention largely on the promise that he would work for a bill of rights.

During the spring of 1789, Madison redeemed his promise by consolidating the two hundred or more amendments suggested by various ratifying conventions, ignoring the recommendations for substantive changes, and focusing on the ones dealing with rights. He submitted seventeen proposed amendments to the House in June, but the House postponed action while it completed what it felt was more urgent business. Finally, in September, Congress submitted twelve amendments to the states, ten of which were ratified over the next two years. These amendments, called the Bill of Rights, provided guarantees for such elementary freedoms as speech, press, and religion; but they did not weaken the fundamental powers of the central government. Politically, they silenced critics of the Constitution, and Antifederalism withered away. Their constitutional significance was overlooked for many years, for the Founding Fathers realistically regarded a "paper barrier" (as Madison called it) as a weak defense against the passions of the majority. Only in the twentieth century, amidst the growth of omnipresent government, has the Bill of Rights become an important bulwark for individual rights.

Public Finance: Hamilton vs. Madison

Exhausted, the First Congress departed for home in September 1789, leaving one crucial problem—government credit—unresolved. Chronic bankruptcy had greatly hampered the Confederation Congress, but now that the central government had the power to tax it could provide for the payment of its debts and restore its credit. The public debt in 1789 stood at roughly $52 million. About $12 million was owed to foreign creditors (the governments of France and Spain and Dutch bankers); the remainder was owed to American citizens. The domestic debt was represented in a variety of negotiable securities, issued during the Revolution by Congress, by the Office of Finance, and even by the army. Because the Continental Congress lacked the power to tax, the securities had depreciated, and most were purchased by speculators at a fraction of their face value. The speculators bet wisely that the central government would be strengthened, and they now eagerly looked to Congress for their reward.

The issue was bristling with political thorns, so the weary Congress turned it over to Hamilton, asking the treasury secretary to investigate ways of reviving the public credit. Hamilton worked on the subject through the fall of 1789, and when Congress reassembled in January he submitted his First Report on the public credit. His solution was both shrewd and deceptively simple. He proposed to refund the public debt by offering to exchange government bonds for the outstanding securities. The bonds would hold their value because they would bear a fixed interest and would be redeemed at regular intervals; thus the government's credit would be restored. Moreover, he would exchange the outstanding securities at their face value, which would reward the speculators with a handsome profit. Hamilton realized that only by dealing fairly with its past creditors could the government hope to restore faith among moneyed men and borrow from them in the future. He also hoped to tie these wealthy merchants and landowners to the new government, thereby giving it added strength and stability. He was aiming at a relatively small group of men. By 1790 only 2 percent of the adult white men in the country held securities. But these were also the richest people in the country, and to Hamilton wealth meant power.

Since most of these men were northern merchants, Hamilton's scheme blended political, financial, and sectional interests. But it also evoked criticism from those who did not benefit. Madison, whose constituency was southern and rural, objected that the plan gave an unreasonable profit to a wealthy few. He suggested that the government discriminate among its creditors, paying the present holders of securities only the current market value (then about 50 percent of the face value), and giving the remainder to the original holders who had been forced to sell out. The suggestion was eminently fair, but it was also impractical since the securities had changed hands many times, and most records had been lost. Congress accepted Hamilton's funding plan in the spring of 1790.

The other feature of Hamilton's report created more trouble. In addition to funding the national debt at face value, he proposed that the central government assume the war debts of the states, which would increase the national debt by another $25 million. Since these debts had been incurred in the common fight, he reasoned, it was only fair that they be paid off by the general government. The politics of the matter was that state creditors would thereafter look to the central government for relief. The federal government would gain added strength at the expense of the states, and it would win new adherents among men of wealth and power.

This proposal also had important sectional implications, for the treasury records of the southern states were in disarray. Virginia and the Carolinas were swept by fighting in the last years of the war, their governments constantly on the move. Southern congressmen feared, therefore, that their state treasurers would not be able to document all their obligations, and they would come up short on the exchange. Again Madison assumed leadership of the opposition, and the proposal for assumption of state debts was defeated in four successive votes during the spring of 1790. The contest marked the first sign of a division of opinion among the supporters of the Constitution, and it signaled the rise of a political opposition led by James Madison. A principal author of the Constitution, Madison was a consistent nationalist who favored strong stable government. But he objected to the ways in which Hamilton was using the new-found powers of government; specifically he distrusted the emerging alliance between the administration and northern merchant-speculators.

Assumption of state debts, however, was not the only issue before Congress that had sectional implications. Since the end of the war, Congress had debated sporadically the establishment of a permanent seat of government. The question was enmeshed in local rivalries, for it was widely assumed that the region which possessed the capital would have the strongest influence on the government. New York had held the honor since 1784, but that site was never satisfactory to southerners, who objected to its distant location and shivered through its winters. The debates over Hamilton's program, which were attended by noisy speculators, only reinforced Madison's distaste for New York's atmosphere of money-hungry chicanery. Both Maryland and Virginia offered to cede Congress districts for the erection of a new national capital, but a southerly move was complicated by the desire of Pennsylvanians for a return to Philadelphia. Nonetheless, in this welter of conflicting regional interests were the elements of a compromise.

Jefferson later explained how it came about. He had returned from France at the end of 1789, and in March of 1790 he moved to New York to take up his duties at the State Department. Although he undoubtedly conversed with Madison, he was not deeply involved in Madison's opposition to the funding system. In addition, he was flattened by a migraine headache that lasted almost a month. In early May, while preparing to make a social call on the president, Jefferson was accosted by Hamilton, who asked for his help on the passage of the assumption bill. Having spent much of his diplomatic service trying to borrow money abroad, Jefferson was deeply concerned about the nation's credit. Hamilton convinced him (to Jefferson's subsequent regret) that assumption was essential to his entire system. Jefferson agreed to bring the parties together at a dinner party, and there an informal bargain was struck. The capital would be moved to Philadelphia, where it would remain for ten years while a new federal city was erected on the banks of the Potomac, the ultimate site to be chosen by President Washington. In return a few southern votes were switched, and Congress approved the plan for assumption of state debts.

When Congress assembled in Philadelphia for its third session in December 1790, Hamilton was ready with two more reports. His Second Report on the Public Credit dealt with the need for additional revenue to support the government and pay off the newly enlarged debt. He recommended a series of excises, mostly on luxuries and distilled spirits. Madison, who had long felt that duties on luxuries were the most painless form of taxation, had no objection, and the excise bill passed Congress with relative ease. Congressmen from frontier districts, however, voted against it, predicting that the tax on whiskey would cause trouble in the West. Pennsylvania had experimented with a whiskey tax since 1783 and had found it impossible to collect in the counties along the Allegheny and Monongahela rivers west of the mountains. For the moment, however, Congress, firmly under Hamilton's control, ignored these portents of trouble.

Hamilton's third major recommendation, submitted to Congress in December 1790, was a Report on a National Bank. Conceived as an alliance between business and government, this Bank of the United States, as it came to be called, would serve as the fiscal agent of the Treasury in collecting and dispersing funds, and its notes would be legal tender in payment of all obligations to the government. Four-fifths of its capital would be obtained by private subscription, the government would furnish the other fifth; and the president would appoint five of the twenty-five directors. Chartered for twenty years, the bank would be authorized a capital of $10 million, divided into 25,000 shares of stock. Three-quarters of the private subscriptions would be in government bonds created by the funding system; the remainder would be in specie. That alone would draw $6 million in bonds out of the speculative market and boost prices, further restoring the credit of the government.

When the bill chartering the bank came before the House of Representatives in early 1791, Madison again took the lead in opposition. He feared that the bank would further solidify the alliance between northern speculators and the government. Madison had long been an advocate of strong, effective central government, but he disliked the direction in which Hamilton was warping the government's powers. Rather than attack Hamilton's policy of catering to business interests directly, Madison objected to the bank's constitutionality. Authority to erect a private corporation, he pointed out, was not among the delegated powers of Congress. The bill passed anyway, but Madison's argument did raise some doubts in the mind of President Washington, who consulted his cabinet on the issue. Secretary of State Jefferson followed Madison's reasoning and argued for a narrow construction of the Constitution. Hamilton instead pointed to the clause that gave Congress power to pass any laws that were "necessary and proper" to carrying out its other powers. This phrase meant, he suggested, that in addition to its specifically mentioned powers Congress had certain "implied powers" to carry out its duties effectively. Implied in the power to print money and pay its debts, for instance, was the power to create a bank for that purpose. The argument dispelled Washington's doubts, and he signed the bank bill into law. But the cabinet split over the meaning of the Constitution also spelled the difference between Hamilton and his opponents.

Hamilton's final reports raised comparatively little partisan opposition. His Report on the Establishment of a Mint (January 1791) resurrected a plan adopted by the Continental Congress in the 1780s. It was written into law as the Coinage Act of 1792. The act provided for the coinage of both gold and silver, and abandoned the English system of pounds and shillings in favor of a more rational decimal system. Because most metallic currency in circulation came from the West Indian trade, the American dollar was given the same number of grains of silver as the Spanish dollar (or "piece of eight"). The mint was opened at Philadelphia in 1794, but it turned out few coins because of the chronic shortage of bullion. Foreign coins were legal tender in the United States until 1857.

Hamilton's final proposal—the Report on Manufactures of December

1791—was never enacted into law. Hamilton's followers were merchants, not manufacturers. The "manufacturers" of the country, at this point in time, were small, independent craftsmen for whom Hamilton had little interest. Thus, although the report appeared to be a comprehensive scheme for the promotion of domestic industries through bounties and patent laws, its main purpose in Hamilton's mind was to promote a single project in which Hamilton was interested, the Society for Establishing Useful Manufactures. The society was to be another alliance of business and government, like the Bank of the United States. Capitalized at $500,000, the society planned to construct a huge cotton mill in northern New Jersey. Ninety percent of the society's capital was to be in government bonds, and therein lay the rub. Cotton production was only an incidental function of the society; its main function, in Hamilton's view, was to soak up more of the public debt. In any case, Hamilton sealed the fate of the Society for Manufactures when he placed it in the care of William Duer, a stock speculator and a rogue, even by eighteenth-century standards. The mania of speculation triggered by Hamilton's funding system climaxed in the spring of 1792, and then the market crashed carrying Duer with it. It developed that he had diverted $80,000 of the society's funds to support his speculations, and with Duer in debtor's prison, the society slipped into oblivion. When the House of Representatives tabled Hamilton's report, he uttered not a word of protest.

Paradoxically, the apparent strength of the Hamiltonian system was also its fatal flaw. His centralization of power provoked fears of tyranny and incipient monarchy. His frank appeal to northern commercial interests, whose wealth and influence enhanced Federalist prestige, awakened sectional jealousies in the South and West and disturbed rural interests everywhere. By mid-1791 the opposition, which had crystallized around Madison in Congress, was calling itself the "republican interest." The choice of the name "Republican" was a shrewd one, for it identified them with the populace and implied that the Federalists were incipient monarchists.

Initially confined to Congress, the Republicans soon realized the necessity of organizing popular support. In the summer of 1791, Jefferson and Madison persuaded the poet Philip Freneau to come to Philadelphia and found an anti-administration newspaper, the *National Gazette.* That autumn the two Virginians made a "botanical tour" of New York and New England, ostensibly in pursuit of Jefferson's varied scientific interests. Many suspected, however, that their actual purpose was to seek political alliances in the North. New York, a hotbed of Antifederalism a few years earlier, was a natural target. Although Jefferson and Madison did not meet with Governor Clinton, they did converse with Robert R. Livingston, former Secretary for Foreign Affairs and now chancellor of New York, and a power in the state. There is no evidence that any political bargain was struck; but in the election of 1792, Clinton did receive Republican electoral votes for vice president. Washington was reelected unanimously, however, and John Adams remained for another term as vice president. The Republicans were still an unorganized faction, not a political party. Virginia, for instance, cast its vice presidential vote for another aging critic of the Constitution, Sam Adams. The whole concept of parties still seemed generally unacceptable; factions were universally denounced as disruptive elements that often contributed to the downfall of republics. Yet the clouds of political partisanship hung low on the horizon, and fresh winds from across the Atlantic told of approaching storm.

The Politics of Neutrality

Unable to fathom the complexities of Hamiltonian finance, most Americans remained indifferent to the political conflict taking place in the capital city. Only the whiskey tax imposed any immediate burden on many citizens, and that did not ripen into a political issue until 1794. The French Revolution and the outbreak of war in Europe, on the other hand, presented problems for the new nation that could easily be reduced to the symbols and stereotypes essential to political warfare.

Americans generally sympathized with the initial stage of the French Revolution as a step toward constitutional government, but the execution of the king and the Reign of Terror in 1793 alienated most Federalists. It confirmed their fears that republican government was inherently weak and prone to mob-rule. In the European contest their sympathies went to Britain as a symbol of stability and balanced government. Republicans, on the other hand, remained loyal to America's revolutionary ally and cheered France as a bastion of republican liberty. Should France fall to the coalition of monarchies, Jefferson feared, the American experiment in republican government might also be endangered. "The liberty of the whole earth was depending on the issue of the contest in Europe," he explained. "Rather than it should have failed, I would have seen half the earth desolated; were there but an Adam and an Eve left in every country, and left free, it would be better than it now is." Thus the ideological conflict between monarchy and republicanism in Europe provided the symbols that polarized American public opinion as well.

The outbreak of war in Europe in early 1793 presented an immediate problem for American diplomacy, for the nation was still tied to France by the old alliance of 1778. Benjamin Franklin's treaty did not commit the United States to enter the European war, but among its provisions was an obligation to aid in the defense of the French empire in the New World. Since Britain could be expected to use its sea power against the French colonies as it had throughout the century, a quick decision on American policy was essential. On April 19 Washington summoned a cabinet meeting at his house. It was the first use of the cabinet as a body of advisers; previously Washington had consulted the cabinet members individually. Hamilton argued that the overthrow of the French monarchy automatically voided the treaty; he felt that the United States should maintain close ties with Britain because it was dependent for the foreseeable future on British investment capital and British manufactures. Indeed, his entire fiscal system rested on the revenue from duties on British imports.

Jefferson agreed that we could not afford to become entangled with France, but he felt that, in exchange for not honoring our treaty obligations, we might at least demand trade concessions from Britain. From the moment he had taken over the State Department Jefferson had sought reciprocity in

Anglo-American trade, and when Britain had refused to negotiate, Jefferson had asked for laws that would discriminate against British shipping. He realized also that such laws would help shelter and thus encourage American manufactures. Hamilton, however, had blocked that policy because of his dependence on British imports. In the meeting of April 19 Washington stepped between his quarreling secretaries. He agreed with Jefferson that the treaty with France ought to be honored, but he also insisted on American neutrality without making any demands upon the British. Three days later on April 22, 1793, President Washington issued a proclamation that pledged the nation to impartial conduct.

That same day a new French minister, Edmond Genêt, landed in Charleston, South Carolina. Hoping to persuade the United States to honor the French alliance, Genêt was prepared to offer trade concessions in the French West Indies if the United States would help defend the islands. If Americans proved cooperative, he planned to organize expeditions against the British and Spanish islands and use American ports to harbor French privateers. Ignoring the president's proclamation, he issued letters of marque to American ship captains to enable them to prey on British commerce under the French flag and plotted expeditions against Florida and Louisiana. He then started for Philadelphia on a triumphant march that brought forth the pro-French sympathies of southern Republicans.

President Washington received the French emissary with understandable coolness. Secretary of State Jefferson was friendlier but determined to maintain American neutrality. He warned Genêt against dispatching any more privateers or plotting adventures against Spanish colonies. Unfortunately, Genêt, who was as excitable as he was naive, had let the public reception go to his head and concluded that the administration did not represent the people. "I am doing everything in my power," Jefferson wrote to Monroe in June, "to moderate the impetuosity of his movements and to destroy the dangerous opinion which has been excited in him, that the people of the U.S. will disown the acts of their government, and that he has an appeal from the Executive to Congress, and from both to the people." Jefferson's ebbing trust was quickly exhausted when Genêt took over a brig that had been brought into the Delaware River as a French prize and began arming it as a privateer. Genêt named it *La Petite Democrate* and prepared to send it to sea under the French flag. Philadelphia was ravaged by yellow fever that summer, and most of the government had fled into the countryside. Before Washington could be summoned back to the capital to render an official decision on the privateer, the brig slipped down the river and put to sea. "Never in my opinion, was so calamitous an appointment made as that of the present minister to France here," Jefferson exploded to Madison on July 7. On August 1, the cabinet took "family dinner" with the president and agreed on a message to the French government asking for Genêt's recall. In the meantime, a turn of the political wheel in France had brought the Jacobins to power, and they ordered Genêt sent home in chains. Rather than face the guillotine the Frenchman sought asylum in the United States, eventually settling in New York and marrying the daughter of Governor Clinton.

For the Republicans, Genêt's mission was a mixed blessing. The minister's defiance of the administration provoked popular sympathy for the president and embarrassed the friends of France. However, his whirlwind visit did help to spread the partisan conflict. In the summer and fall of 1793, Democratic Societies sprang up in cities and towns from New York southwards. Generally made up of middle-class artisans and shopkeepers, these organizations were pro-French and Republican. Alarmed Federalists considered them agents of French subversion and denounced them as "Jacobin Clubs." Although most of the societies were short-lived, they evidenced the growing polarization of public sentiment.

Western Lands and Border Warfare

Relations with Great Britain also stirred popular political passions. But here the story was complicated by Anglo-American land hunger and Native American hostilities in the West. The British were indirectly involved because they violated the peace treaty of 1783 by maintaining garrisons on American soil (at Oswego, Niagara, Detroit, and elsewhere along the Great Lakes). Americans suspected, with some justice, that British agents operating from these posts gave diplomatic support, clothing, blankets, and occasionally arms to the tribes of the Northwest, enabling them to resist the advance of the white frontier.

Actually the Native Americans had provocation enough to go to war without any encouragement from the British. For nearly two centuries the native inhabitants of the continent had been systematically pushed westward by the advance of European civilization. Native American resistance usually resulted in a skirmish or two, followed by further land cessions. The colonists justified their land hunger on the thesis that the West belonged to the people who could most effectively use and develop it. Most whites considered the Native Americans inferior, and even the most enlightened men, such as Thomas Jefferson, wanted them to abandon their nomadic tribal existence and settle onto farms side by side with their white neighbors. Few Native Americans had any desire to abandon their woodland environment for the competitive world of market agriculture, and, besides, they felt that land should be freely available to all—Native American and white alike—to be used by each according to his needs, much like water and air. In such a conflict of cultures a mutually satisfactory accommodation was beyond the talents of any living human.

Even in the seventeenth century, enlightened leaders such as Roger Williams and William Penn recognized the Native Americans' title to the land. Gradually the concept became generally accepted, and with the establishment of the federal government it became official policy. "The Indians, being the prior occupants, possess the right of soil," declared Secretary of War Knox in 1789. "It cannot be taken from them unless by their free consent or by right of conquest in case of a just war. To dispossess them on any other principle would be a gross violation of the fundamental laws of nature, and of that distributive justice which is the glory of a nation." Without even considering what a "just war" might be under the circumstances, it can be said that the government's policy involved certain practical difficulties. Among the problems was the fact that neither Indians nor whites knew for sure who owned what. With few exceptions (among them, for instance, the Black Warrior River in Alabama which marked the boundary between Creeks and Choctaws), tribal lands were only vaguely defined. Some tribes, such as the Shawnee, wandered between the Ohio valley and the South long before Europeans arrived on the continent, and hence had little concept of possessiveness about land. Others were early pushed out of their homes on the seacoast, ran into more belligerent tribes in the interior, and never did find a permanent residence. Among the most tragic of these were the Leni Lenape (which can be translated as "Human Beings" or "Best People"), a large, powerful, and sophisticated tribe that inhabited the Delaware Valley in the seventeenth century. The early Pennsylvania colonists conferred on them the English name "Delawares" and then pushed them westward into the mountains. Intelligent and peace-loving, they were valued as guides for exploring parties and scouts for military expeditions, but they never again found a tribal home. By the mid-nineteenth century their settlements were scattered from Ohio to Kansas to Texas.

A related problem was that Native Americans did not fully understand the European concept of contract and had little notion of permanent possession. Often they sold their lands without realizing that they could no longer hunt or fish on them. Moreover, they were seldom certain who in the tribe had authority to alienate lands. Sometimes minor chiefs would sell lands belonging to the whole tribe, or worse, one tribe would sell lands claimed by another. The most infamous example of this practice was the Treaty of Lancaster (1744, which was reaffirmed by the Treaty of Fort Stanwix in 1765) by which the Iroquois surrendered their claim to all lands south of the Ohio River. Iroquois war parties had occasionally passed through the region, but otherwise the Iroquois had no connection with the lands they sold. Nonetheless, political leaders in Virginia and Pennsylvania announced that the West was open to settlement, and pioneers began filtering into western Virginia and Kentucky, ignoring the claims of the Ohio tribes who had long hunted there.

The French wars and royal restrictions on the colonists' westward advance inhibited settlement of the region until the eve of the Revolution when Daniel Boone blazed the Wilderness Road into Kentucky. When the Ohio Indians raided the first settlements west of the mountains, Virginia's governor, Lord Dunmore, personally led a punitive expedition into the Ohio country in 1774. One branch of his army was attacked at Point Pleasant at the mouth of the Kanawha River by a force under the Shawnee chief Cornstalk. The attack was beaten off, and when Dunmore marched on the Shawnee villages on the Scioto River, Cornstalk sued for peace. In the ensuing settlement the Shawnee had to surrender their claims to Kentucky.

A short while later a band of frontiersmen broke into Cornstalk's cabin and fatally shot him, and the Shawnee went on the offensive again. There were sporadic attacks on the Kentucky settlements throughout the Revolution, including a major assault on Boonesborough in 1778 when Daniel Boone escaped from Indian captivity and traveled 160 miles in four days to sound the alarm. Border warfare continued throughout the Revolution and even extended to the South where the early settlements in Tennessee alarmed the Creeks and Cherokees.

After the Revolution the state cessions in the Northwest placed the Native American question in the hands of Congress. In 1785, Congress negotiated the cession of southern Ohio from the Delaware, Wyandot, Chippewa (who lived in Wisconsin) and Ottawa (who lived in Canada) tribes. But the sale was worthless since the Shawnees and Miamis, who inhabited most of the region, were not involved. Worse yet, the cession encouraged frontiersmen to swarm into the country north of the Ohio. General Josiah Harmar, sent to investigate, discovered several thousand "banditti whose actions are a disgrace to human nature" squatting on the national domain, organized under an elected governor, and convinced that every American had "an undoubted right to pass into every vacant country, and there to form their constitution." The following year continuing Shawnee intransigence brought a punitive expedition led by George Rogers Clark, who destroyed their villages at Piqua and Chillicothe and burned their cornfields. But the Native Americans refused either to surrender or to fight a pitched battle, and the result was stalemate in the West, while Anglo-American civilization in the East occupied itself with strengthening its governmental institutions.

President Washington's policy was to subdue the Ohio tribes militarily, while conciliating the southern tribes. The focus of Native American resistance in the South was the numerous and warlike Creek tribe of Alabama, which looked for leadership to the wealthy, slaveowning biracial Alexander McGillivray. The son of a Tory merchant of Charleston, who had lost his property in the Revolution, McGillivray was a master of international diplomacy. He received arms and supplies from the Spanish authorities in Florida, and permitted enough horse-stealing on the Georgia and Tennessee frontiers to keep the border tense without inviting retaliation. The government had to handle McGillivray with prudence because it could not afford to irritate his Spanish friends, who controlled the lifeline of the West, the Mississippi. The problem had to be solved quickly, however, for Georgia had refused to surrender its western claims and was busy trying to sell the region to land speculators. Settlement would surely bring on a full-scale clash between cultures.

In the summer of 1790, Washington invited McGillivray to New York City, where they signed a treaty of mutual benefit. The Creeks ceded their claims to eastern Georgia and received in return a perpetual guarantee of their remaining hunting lands from the Oconee River westward, including lands which speculators had bought from Georgia. The Native Americans also recognized the federal government as the ultimate sovereign over their lands, thereby effectively excluding the claims of Georgia. To seal the bargain McGillivray was commissioned a brigadier general in the American army at a salary of $1,200 a year. The Treaty of New York brought peace to the southern frontier; but it drove Georgia, which had unanimously favored the Constitution, into the arms of the Jeffersonian Republicans.

While the president was giving McGillivray and his entourage a royal welcome in New York (including a parade led by the Sons of St. Tammany in full regalia), General Harmar was preparing to attack the Native American villages on the Maumee River in northwestern Ohio. A Miami chief, Little Turtle, had united the Ohio tribes to an extent unknown since the death of Cornstalk. Harmar started north from Fort Washington (Cincinnati) in the summer of 1790, but his march was so slow that the Native Americans were alerted and melted into the woods. In an effort to find the enemy he divided his army, whereupon the tribe fell on one of the detachments and killed 183 troops.

The following year General Arthur St. Clair, governor of the Northwest Territory, personally led an army of 3,000 into hostile territory. Cheated by military contractors, the army was woefully short of everything—tents, knapsacks, food, cartridges, and pack-saddles. Sick and hungry men drifted away, and by November 3 St. Clair had only 1,400 men when he camped on the upper reaches of the Wabash River. The tribes pounced on him at dawn. St. Clair's demoralized army broke and fled, abandoning its artillery and equipment. By sunset the remnants staggered into Fort Jefferson, twenty-nine miles away, having left 913 dead on the field—the worst defeat in the annals of the frontier.

The disaster encouraged both the Native Americans and their British supporters in Canada. The tribes recovered the Ohio countryside, while the settlers huddled in the beleaguered outposts of Cincinnati and Marietta. In Canada, Governor General Lord Dorchester decided it was time to unveil his scheme to establish an independent Native American buffer state in the region north of the Ohio River. Simultaneously, the Indian agency at Malden at the mouth of the Detroit River began stockpiling arms and blankets, so a sizable Native American army could be maintained in the field. In the summer of 1793, a conference at Malden attended by representatives from all the Great Lakes tribes issued a declaration of war against the United States, demanding as the price of peace a permanent frontier at the Ohio River. In February 1794, Lord Dorchester took note of the worsening relations between the United States and Great Britain, and informed the tribes, "I shall not be surprised if we are at war with them in the course of the present year; and if so, a Line must then be drawn by the Warriors." That spring the British constructed Fort Miami on the Maumee River in northwestern Ohio and garrisoned it with British soldiers. If war came, the Native Americans had every right to expect that the British would aid them.

The American government too was making preparations for an ultimate showdown. In 1792, President Washington appointed General Anthony Wayne commander in the West. It was a good choice, for Wayne had shown himself an able brigade commander during the Revolution. Wayne collected a new army of regulars at Pittsburgh, named it the "Legion," and subjected it to intensive training and rigid discipline. In the spring of 1793, he moved downriver to Cincinnati, but the campaigning season that year was spent in fruitless negotiations that broke down with a Native American declaration of war. In the fall he marched seventy miles up the Miami River and built Fort Greenville. When spring opened the forest trails and provided forage for his horses, Wayne resumed his deliberate advance into northwestern Ohio.

In the interval since St. Clair's defeat, Miami chief Little Turtle had lost

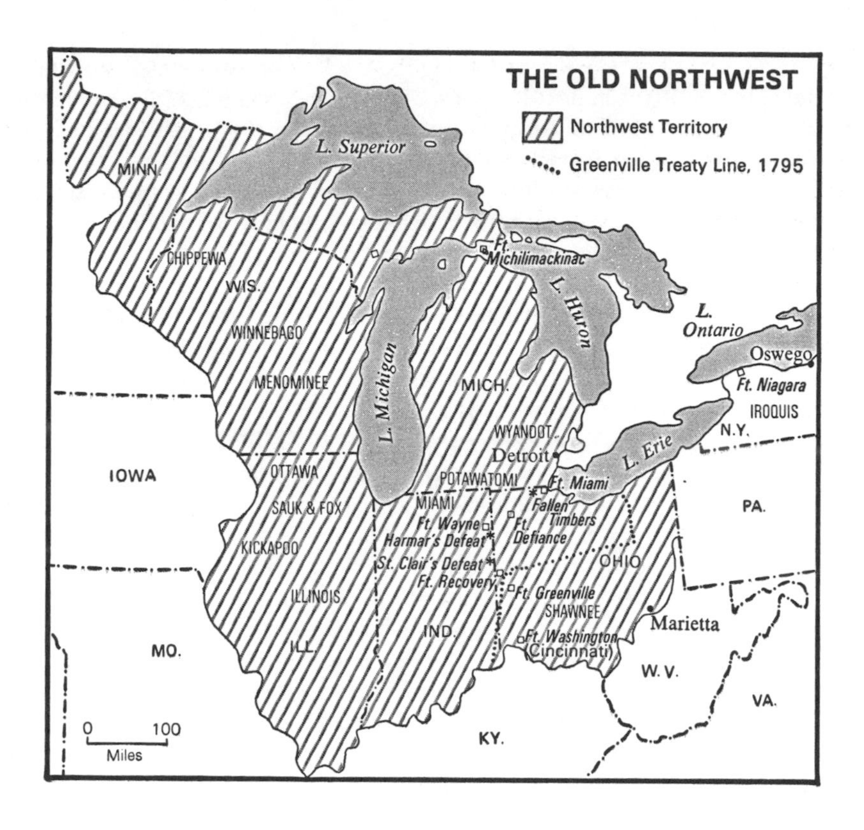

his military ardor. He counseled peace while his son actually became a scout for the Americans. Tribal leadership thus devolved upon the Shawnee chief Blue Jacket, who elected to make a stand in a tangle of fallen trees along the Maumee near the British Fort Miami. Knowing of the Native American habit of fasting before a battle, Wayne delayed his attack for three days, until nearly half the Native American force straggled into the British post for food. On August 20, 1794, he attacked in columns from the front and flank; after two hours the Native Americans broke and fled toward the British fort. The British commander closed his gates and refused any overt aid to the tribes. His outpost, after all, was on American soil, and in the inflamed state of Anglo-American relations the tiniest spark could start another transatlantic war. Betrayed by their British allies, the tribes scattered into the forest. The Battle of Fallen Timbers, though small in scale (about fifty casualties on each side), brought peace to the frontier for the first time in twenty years. Defeated and disillusioned, the Native Americans kept the peace for over a decade until pressures for further land cessions goaded them into another war.

In the summer of 1795, General Wayne summoned the chiefs from all the northwestern tribes to a gigantic conference at Fort Greenville. After fifty days of feasting the Native Americans signed the Treaty of Greenville under which they ceded all of Ohio, except the northwest corner, and a strip of eastern Indiana for $20,000 in goods. The line drawn across western Ohio from Lake

Erie to the Ohio River was the first attempt to draw a permanent boundary line between white and Native American territory. To police the border (and doubtless to keep an eye on the tribes), Wayne also obtained permission to establish outposts in the Native American country—Fort Wayne on the headwaters of the Maumee and Fort Dearborn at the southern tip of Lake Michigan. Though technically a purchase of land, the Greenville settlement was actually a matter of the victor dictating terms to the vanquished.

Among the very few chiefs who refused to sign the treaty was a Shawnee warrior who had served as Blue Jacket's chief scout during the campaign—Tecumseh. A man with an inveterate hatred of whites after two Virginians shot his father for refusing to carry a slain deer for them, Tecumseh had mastered the terms of every treaty signed between whites and Native Americans. His refusal to sign the Greenville Treaty gave him stature among the tribes of the Northwest, and when a new crisis arose on the western border he would stand ready to unite the scattered tribes once again.

The Whiskey Rebellion

Although the center of conflict in the war was western Ohio, tribal war parties ranged as far east as Pennsylvania massacreing isolated families of settlers. Between 1783 and 1790, Native Americans killed, wounded, or took prisoner an estimated 1,500 whites, while stealing about 2,000 horses. Tribal depredations combined with settlers' inability to market their crops, so long as the Mississippi remained closed, severely retarded the development of the West. Indeed, farmers in western Pennsylvania actually lost ground in the 1780s and early 1790s, as they sank into debt and were forced to sell their lands to eastern landlords. In 1790, about one-quarter of the farmers in western Pennsylvania were "croppers," men who worked the land of others and paid their rent in crops. The national government's inability to pacify the Native Americans or secure free navigation of the Mississippi left them unwilling to pay for a government that delivered no visible services. The whiskey excise, imposed by Congress in 1791, was perceived as an added burden to the impoverished frontier. It triggered the most serious rebellion in America prior to the Civil War.

Whiskey was the centerpiece of the western economy. It was not commercially feasible to transport flour or grain across the mountains to market. Hence the only way western farmers could get their grain to market was to convert it to whiskey. Whiskey even served as a medium of exchange in the currency-shy West. In Washington County, Pennsylvania, for example, there were about five hundred stills in 1790, one for every ten farm families, and nearly every farmer reckoned his wealth in "Monongahela rye." The whiskey excise fell with brutal force on these people because they had no money to pay it; they lived in self-sufficiency, bartering with neighbors for whatever they could not fashion themselves. Tax collectors would be forced to confiscate what little land they had left. Nor was it lost upon them that the collectors appointed by the government were the wealthiest men in the district. John Neville, at whom the initial protest was directed, had more than a thousand acres of land and eighteen slaves in addition to a herd of cattle and horses. Common farmers, who were lucky to possess one cow, viewed the tax in terms of class conflict; they saw Neville as the lackey of a wealthy eastern elite. They also viewed the excise as an "internal tax" imposed by a distant authority in which they had no voice. That invoked memories of the resistance to the Stamp Act and the "Spirit of '76." One recent student of the rebellion has called it an "epilogue to the American Revolution."

The resistance was by no means confined to western Pennsylvania. The legislatures of Maryland, Virginia, North Carolina, and Georgia voiced opposition to the excise. Collectors sent onto the frontier could find no one willing to rent them property for an office. Not a penny was ever collected in Kentucky or Tennessee. Attention focused on western Pennsylvania primarily because Hamilton determined to make an example of it. Hamilton argued, and Washington eventually agreed, that the authority of the government depended on "prosecuting with vigor delinquents and offenders." Of all the pockets of resistance, western Pennsylvania was the most accessible. Hamilton even suppressed evidence of resistance in western Virginia and North Carolina lest the public realize how widespread the "rebellion" was.

In the summer of 1794, the government forced the issue by securing processes from the federal court in Philadelphia ordering the appearance of sixty western distillers. The processes were served by federal marshals in July. One farmer described his reaction: "I felt myself mad with passion. I thought $250 would ruin me; and to have to go [to] the federal court at Philadelphia would keep me from going to Kentucky this fall after I had sold my plantation and was getting ready. I felt my blood boil at seeing General Neville [the tax collector] along to pilot the sheriff to my very door." Early one evening in mid-July, between 500 and 700 men paraded to the cadence of drums in front of Neville's mansion. Neville escaped, leaving a few soldiers and his slaves to defend the house. A brief skirmish ensued with perhaps a half dozen casualties. The militia then sacked and burned the house and its outbuildings.

On August 1, a mob of seven thousand farmers, most of them propertyless and only a third of whom owned stills, assembled at the field where General Edward Braddock had been defeated and vowed to march on Pittsburgh. Town residents turned them back at the edge of town with casks of whiskey and expressions of sympathy for the cause. The march turned into a meeting dominated by moderates, most important of which was Albert Gallatin, a member of the state assembly. The meeting adopted resolutions and agreed to negotiate with commissioners of the federal government.

Even before the commissioners arrived in the West, Washington and Hamilton had decided to send in an army. On September 24, Washington issued a proclamation calling on the states of Pennsylvania, Maryland, and Virginia to furnish troops to suppress the rebellion. An army commanded by Virginia's "Light Horse Harry" Lee marched into western Pennsylvania. Hamilton went along to interrogate captives and determine who were the leaders of the insurrection. When no resistance materialized, cavalrymen began scouring the countryside for suspects, in some cases literally dragging men from bed. The real leaders of the resistance had escaped into the wilderness; moderates such as

Gallatin had done nothing illegal. The army was left with about twenty obscure characters in custody to shoulder blame for the rebellion. It paraded these, bound together by ropes, all the way back to Philadelphia. Two were eventually convicted of treason, but Washington pardoned them lest they become martyrs.

The aftermath of the rebellion and its absurd repression was the politicization of the frontier. The West thereafter was Jefferson's country. Ironically, the army sent to the Monongahela made its own unintended contributions to the western economy. The government sent large sums of money into western Pennsylvania to keep its soldiers supplied with food and whiskey. It was the largest injection of money the frontier had ever experienced, and cash-poor farmers, with money to spend, bought land. President Washington, one of the largest landholders in the region, sensed a sudden demand for property that had been selling listlessly. He was not sure of the cause, but he was pleased nonethless. History works in mysterious ways.

Jay's Treaty

Unwilling to look for the real causes of their troubles with western tribes, Americans blamed British agents and British diplomacy. And it is true that the continued presence of British troops on American soil south of the Great Lakes was a humiliating imposition. When Secretary of State Jefferson objected to this violation of the peace treaty, Britain replied that Americans had violated the treaty first by failing to pay their prewar debts. Most of these debts were owed by southern planters to British merchants, and the Revolution had provided an opportunity to delay payment. Several southern states even closed their courts to suits by British creditors, justifying the action as retaliation for slaves carried off by British armies. The peace treaty largely evaded the debt question, and the failure of Britain to dispatch a fully accredited minister to the United States for nearly a decade after the Revolution gave southern debtors additional opportunity to procrastinate. Relations between the two countries deteriorated steadily amidst mutual recriminations over the peace treaty and British intrigues among the Ohio tribes. The outbreak of war in Europe and a dispute over American neutral rights quickly brought matters to a head.

Neutrality for the United States meant not only freedom from war but freedom to trade with both sides. And America profited immensely from the European conflict. The Royal Navy swept French merchant shipping from the seas. At the same time its demand for sailors crippled British merchant shipping. Americans moved into the vacuum. Between 1793 and 1795, American tonnage increased 150 percent. France opened its West Indian colonies to American ships, which began carrying French sugar and molasses to American ports and then reexporting them to France. This "carrying trade," as it was called, became the nation's primary source of international income. But from the British point of view it largely negated the effect of their naval blockade. They felt it had to be stopped.

When the war began the British ministry issued an order-in-council prohibiting neutral vessels from carrying foodstuffs to France. Jefferson protested the blockage of nonmilitary goods as contrary to international law. He also pointed out that the measure violated American neutrality by confining its trade to Britain alone. Britain greeted these protests with a new order-in-council of November 1793, which invoked the old Rule of 1756. Instituted during the French and Indian War, this regulation had inhibited the trade between America and the French West Indies by announcing that a trade illegal in time of peace was also illegal in time of war. Since France ordinarily restricted trade in her empire with navigation acts, it could not throw open her colonies in wartime merely to evade the British blockade. Enforcing this new decree in the winter of 1793, the Royal Navy seized more than 250 American ships that were carrying French cargoes and brought them into British ports. Over half were condemned as wartime prizes by British admiralty courts.

When news of the British seizures reached Philadelphia early in 1794, Madison sponsored in Congress a nonintercourse resolution that sought to cut off all trade with England. His purpose was to revive the policy of commercial retaliation that had proved effective in defending American rights before the Revolution. Federalists objected that such a move would be a disastrous blow to the federal treasury, since British imports still constituted two-thirds of its revenue. In the end, however, they compromised on a thirty-day embargo. The war had furthered a developing rift in mercantile ranks, which had previously been solidly Federalist. Traders who did their principal business with Britain remained Federalist, but those who were growing rich on the emerging trade with the West Indies and southern Europe—men such as the Crowninshields of Massachusetts, Stephen Girard of Philadelphia, and Samuel Smith of Baltimore—were shifting to the Republican ranks.

Hamilton spearheaded the effort to undercut Madison's congressional sanctions by appointing a special envoy to negotiate a settlement. Washington agreed and sent to London Chief Justice John Jay. Jay's prominent position in the American government and his prior service as Secretary for Foreign Affairs underscored the importance of the mission. Arriving in London in June 1794, Jay found the Pitt ministry desirous of peace but not disposed to grant concessions. In order to reach any sort of agreement, he had to omit any mention of America's neutral rights, and that, in effect, meant a tacit acceptance of the British position on blockades and contraband.

The treaty signed in November created an international commission to supervise the payment of colonial debts, and Britain promised to surrender the Northwest posts by June 1796. A commercial agreement gave Americans limited trading privileges in India and the British West Indies, but only on the stipulation that products of all the West Indian colonies (French and Spanish included) were carried only to the United States. This would have meant acquiescence in the Rule of 1756, and the Senate subsequently deleted the provision. Direct trade between Britain and the United States was placed on a "most favored nation" basis, which meant, in effect, commercial equality.

Considering Britain's strong military and diplomatic position in Europe and Jay's lack of bargaining leverage, the settlement probably represented the best terms possible. Significantly, the British government considered it an equitable settlement, and Pitt even had to defend himself in the House of Commons against charges of being pro-American. Moreover, the treaty did resolve most of the outstanding disputes between the two nations and helped bring about a decade of comparative Anglo-American friendship. But it had an explosive impact on America's domestic political conflict. Jefferson and Madison objected to the omission of neutral rights and noted that the commercial equality granted Britain prevented the sort of retaliation that Madison had advocated in Congress. It also meant that any favors that the United States granted another country in return for a reciprocal favor automatically applied to Britain. Madison concluded that the "whole Treaty . . . assassinates the interest" of American merchants. The surrender of the Northwest posts was a hollow benefit, since Britain had been retaining them illegally anyway. Nor did it escape Republican leaders that the British concessions principally benefited the North while southerners were once again asked to bear the cost—this time by being obliged to pay their British debts.

Federalists were not happy with the treaty. President Washington himself admitted that it was "damned bad." But it did promise peace. And it did mend relations with Great Britain, which benefited both Federalist merchants and Hamilton's Treasury.

Aware of its political implications, the Senate voted to keep the treaty secret until it was ratified. Inevitably it leaked to the Republican press, which set up a howl of indignation. Taking advantage of the popular furor, Republican leaders hastily summoned mass meetings which mailed gigantic petitions to the president and lit bonfires to "damn John Jay." Jay himself ruefully observed that he could have found his way across the country at night by the light of his burning effigies.

Amidst the uproar, the outlines of a national party system emerged. Well-organized popular meetings and the systematic adoption of carefully prepared resolutions evidenced the extent of party organization at the local level. Federalists abandoned their elitist notion that public opinion was irrelevant, and organized their own popular assemblies and mass petitions. As popular sentiment polarized, members of Congress (of which previously a third had voted with neither party) were forced to choose sides. When in early 1796, Madison led a move to undermine the treaty by denying funds to carry it out, Republicans in the House of Representatives held the first party caucus in order to ensure a united stand. Madison's move failed, but thereafter no more than a handful of congressmen remained politically uncommitted.

Washington's Farewell

Among those driven into party ranks was President Washington himself. Though more inclined to accept Hamilton's advice than Jefferson's, Washington remained neutral in the party contest until Jefferson retired from the State Department at the end of 1793. Thereafter the shocking tactics of Genêt, the subversive appearance of the Democratic Societies, and the criticism of his foreign policies in the Republican press drove him relentlessly into the arms of the Federalists. Jefferson was replaced by Edmund Randolph, a middle-of-the-road Virginian, but Randolph lasted only a year. An indiscreet communication with the French Minister to the United States, Jean Antoine Joseph Baron Fauchet, which the Frenchman misinterpreted as a request for a bribe, was intercepted and turned over to the President. Washington angrily demanded an explanation, whereupon Randolph resigned and published a vindication of his actions.

In early 1795, Hamilton and General Henry Knox both left the government, the former for financial reasons and the latter from ill health, and Washington spent a substantial part of his last year searching for replacements. His search was hampered by the meagre pay afforded executive officials and the reluctance of able men to leave prominent positions in their home states. The Treasury post went to Oliver Wolcott of Connecticut, who had served in minor positions in the department since 1789; and the State Department ended up in the hands of Timothy Pickering, a strong Federalist partisan from western Massachusetts. The War Department was offered as a political plum to several veterans of the political wars, among them Patrick Henry, before it was finally accepted by James McHenry of Maryland, whose only recommendations were that he was a southerner and a friend of Hamilton. Thus by 1796, the administration had taken on a distinctly partisan character. Equally important, the new members, particularly McHenry, were inclined to look to Hamilton for advice and guidance. Though engaged in private law practice in New York, Hamilton was kept informed of administration decisions and lent his voice to executive councils.

As the nation's third presidential election approached, Federalist leaders begged Washington to run for a third term. He would doubtless have been reelected, but the aging hero decided that eight years in office were enough. In September 1796, he issued a farewell address to the nation, drawn up with considerable help from Hamilton. Two-thirds of the message was devoted to domestic matters and the problems caused by political parties. Washington, true to eighteenth-century political theory, failed to understand the nature of a party system and felt that factions contributed only to division and instability. Factions, moreover, were particularly pernicious when they represented sympathies for rival foreign governments. Similarly, in its foreign affairs he felt the nation should pursue a policy of pure neutrality, maintaining friendship and commerce with all. Though he hoped the nation would avoid alliances of the sort that embarrassed our relations with France, he did recognize the advantages of short-term alliances under certain circumstances. Primarily he wished the nation to stay aloof from the conflicts of Europe and confine its attention to its own sphere of interest, the New World.

Both parties selected presidential candidates by a caucus of members of Congress. Republicans formalized a New York-Virginia alliance by choosing Jefferson and Aaron Burr; Federalists picked John Adams and Thomas Pinckney of South Carolina. Jefferson, in retirement at Monticello, did not seek the presidency and did not even consent to run. Madison, fearing a refusal, did not even consult Jefferson's wishes and treated his friend's silence as acquiescence. The Republicans seemed to have a good chance of winning because they had scored impressive gains in the congressional elections two years before, but the Federalists had the immense advantage of Washington's favor. Actually, popular opinion had relatively little effect because presidential electors in several key states were chosen by the legislatures.

The French Minister Pierre Adet seemed unaware of this, however, as he intervened in the election in an attempt to sway public sentiment. Hoping to benefit Jefferson's candidacy, he announced that the president's recent appointment to Paris, Charles Cotesworth Pinckney (a brother of Thomas Pinckney) would not be received by the French government. This virtual break in diplomatic relations was followed by a tougher French policy on neutral shipping, the purpose of which was to discredit the Federalists by demonstrating the extent to which their policies had alienated France. Though he favored Jefferson, Adet knew that Jefferson would never be the tool of France. "Mr. Jefferson likes us because he detests Britain . . . ," the Minister explained to his government, "but tomorrow he might change his opinion of us if tomorrow Britain should cease to inspire his fears. Jefferson, though a friend of liberty and enlightenment, an admirer of the efforts we have made to break the bonds and dispel the ignorance which burden the human race, Jefferson, I say, is an American and, as such, he cannot be sincerely our friend. An American is the born enemy of all the peoples of Europe." Adet nevertheless felt that Jefferson was a better bet than Adams.

Adet's heavy-handed moves probably influenced few voters, but they embarrassed Republicans by exposing them to the charge of foreign influence. Whatever advantage Federalists might have gained from this, however, was nearly thrown away by Hamilton, who sought to supplant Adams with the Federalist vice presidential candidate Pinckney. The scheme turned on the method of voting in the electoral college. The Federalist electors, Hamilton suggested, should all cast their initial votes for Pinckney. Then by wasting a few of their second votes, instead of giving them to Adams, they might ensure that Pinckney would be elected president. The idea failed when Adams's supporters, learning of the plot, cast away their Pinckney ballots, and the Republicans made an unexpectedly good showing in the election. In the end, Adams beat Jefferson by a margin of only three electoral votes, and Jefferson emerged as the new vice president. The only effect of Hamilton's intrigue was to leave a legacy of bitterness in Federalist ranks that divided the party and hastened its downfall. Ironically, the Republican party was also weakened by the voting in the electoral college. When the Virginia electors wasted their second ballots in order to ensure that Burr ranked behind Jefferson, Burr felt betrayed. He would remember the betrayal four years later.

Jefferson remained at Monticello aloof from the contest until the balloting in the states was nearly completed. In December 1796, when it appeared that the electoral vote would be uncomfortably close, he wrote to Madison that if the election should end in a tie, he wished the choice to go to Adams. He had always been Adams's junior in their political careers, and he could accept second place more gracefully than the New Englander. Madison quietly circulated the letter in Philadelphia, and, though it alarmed the Hamiltonians, it laid the foundation for a reconciliation between Adams and Jefferson. After the electoral college completed its balloting, the two old friends called upon one another, and the new administration began, at least, on a note of cordiality.

The Troubles of John Adams

The inauguration of John Adams foretold no important shift in Federalist policies. He retained intact his predecessor's cabinet, seeing, for the moment, no reason to remove any of them, and in foreign affairs he hoped to maintain a strict neutrality. That stance was becoming increasingly difficult to maintain because all Europe assumed that the Jay Treaty meant a virtual alliance between the United States and England. This conclusion had a happy effect on our relations with Spain, but it also produced a crisis with France that ruined the president and his party.

By 1795, Spain desperately wanted to get out of the war. Its armies had met with little success and its treasury was empty. For almost a century it had been an ally of France, and it had only reluctantly joined the coalition of monarchies organized by Britain. Yet it feared British reprisals if it made peace with France. In this context Spain viewed the Jay Treaty as an Anglo-American threat to Spain's New World empire. As a result, the head of the Spanish government, Prince Godoy, hastened to mend fences with the United States. He summoned the American minister, Thomas Pinckney, and offered a formal alliance. Pinckney had no authority to undertake such a union, but he was armed with a list of American grievances dating back to the Revolution. Spain had acquired the Floridas (including the Gulf Coast from the present state of Florida west to the mouth of the Mississippi River) but had never recognized the thirty-first parallel as the boundary, claiming instead territory as far north as Tennessee. In addition, Spain had refused Americans permission to use the lower Mississippi or the port of New Orleans and had encouraged southern Indians, Creeks and Cherokees, to resist the advancing frontier.

On all these matters Godoy proved tractable, and the treaty that was signed at the Royal Palace of San Lorenzo in October 1795 was a diplomatic triumph for Pinckney. Spain settled on the thirty-first parallel as the northern boundary of Florida and agreed to open New Orleans for the deposit and transshipment of American goods for three years. The settlement also gave Godoy leverage in Europe, which enabled him to switch sides. Safely in the arms of France by 1798, Godoy lived up to the American bargain and opened New Orleans to the products of western farmers.

France, too, assumed that the Jay Treaty amounted to an alliance between the United States and Britain, but the French reaction was anger rather than fright. Shortly after Jay arrived in England, the French republic went through one of its periodic upheavals. In the summer of 1794, the Reign of Terror came to an end, and the Jacobins were replaced by a committee of corrupt politicians called the Directory. About the same time French armies began to win striking victories, and Britain's coalition of monarchies crumbled. With victory came a change of mood in France, as the initial idealism of the Revolution degenerated into rank imperialism. Within a few years France surrounded itself with satellite republics—in northern Italy, western Germany, and the Netherlands—and the Directory even expressed some interest in New World empire when it obtained the island of Santo Domingo from Spain.

In retaliation for the Jay Treaty, France refused to receive the minister Washington had sent to Paris, Charles Cotesworth Pinckney; and it announced a tougher policy on neutral shipping. A decree of March 1797 (coinciding with Adams's inauguration) authorized the seizure of American vessels found carrying British goods. By June, the French had confiscated some 316 American vessels and the two nations were on the brink of war. Or at least Secretary of State Pickering thought the seizures a cause for war. Adams instead decided to make a final effort at negotiation. To reinforce Pinckney, who had been expelled from Paris and was waiting nervously in the Netherlands for further instructions, Adams nominated John Marshall, a fast-rising Virginia Federalist, and Elbridge Gerry, an old friend from Massachusetts.

When the three commissioners assembled in Paris in the fall of 1797, they found that Talleyrand, foreign minister for the Directory, refused to treat with them officially. Instead he sent three agents (subsequently described in the American report as X, Y, and Z), who suggested that the wheels of diplomacy might be greased with a gift of $250,000 to the Directory and an official loan to France of $12 million. Humiliating though the proposal was, the Americans were not averse to tendering the bribe, since that was almost standard procedure in European diplomacy; but they felt that the loan would be a serious violation of American neutrality. What Talleyrand desired, in short, was a reversal in American policy. He hoped to undo the Jay Treaty and tie the American republic to France by financial strings. The American envoys carried on informal discussions for several weeks hoping to modify Talleyrand's stand and then sent a blistering note to the president describing the humiliating treatment they had received. In March 1798, Marshall and Pinckney left for home, but Gerry, who had been courted by Talleyrand with intent to divide the commission, remained in Paris in the hope of achieving a settlement without war.

When President Adams published the XYZ dispatches in the spring of 1798, the public responded angrily to the humiliating treatment accorded the nation's envoys. While newspapers shrilled "Millions for Defense, but not one cent for Tribute," Congress prepared for war. It tripled the army, created a Navy Department (to supervise a squadron of six frigates authorized in 1794), and permitted privateers to capture armed French vessels. It never formally declared war, however, and the crisis gradually eased. Fighting was confined to a few minor naval engagements, as the young American navy drove French vessels out of the hemisphere.

More important was its domestic political impact, for the "quasi-war" divided the Federalists and decimated the Republicans. Adams's failure to recommend a declaration of war heightened the differences between him and the more belligerent members of the cabinet, Pickering and McHenry. In Congress a handful of moderate Federalists supported the president, but they were increasingly alienated from the "High Federalists" who desired war with France and an alliance with England. The latter looked to Hamilton for leadership, though the New Yorker was equivocal on the war issue. For the moment, however, the Federalist schism was obscured by the decline of the Republicans' fortunes. Under a cloud in the popular mind for their supposed associations with France, the Jeffersonians found themselves helpless to resist the military preparations in the spring of 1798. Jefferson, who had to preside over the Senate, found himself politically isolated and socially ostracized. Madison had left Congress the previous year, and Republican leadership in the House devolved upon Albert Gallatin, a Swiss-born expert in government finance who had been elected four years before from turbulent western Pennsylvania. With a dwindling band of followers, Gallatin could do little but conduct a holding action, voting against every Federalist proposal that smacked of war. It was in this crucible of negativism that the basic tenets of Jeffersonian Democracy were forged—opposition to armies, navies, taxes, and every other form of centralized power.

Federalist Repression

After completing preparations for a military contest with the French foe abroad, the Federalists turned on their domestic enemies. Unable to comprehend the purposes of parties or the function of an opposition, they viewed criticism of their policies as factious and divisive. In the context of the ideological conflict posed by the French Revolution, such criticism was viewed as subversive, or worse, treasonable. Objects of particular suspicion were the French and Irish immigrants who had entered the country in the course of the decade, many of them refugees from revolutions in Europe and the West Indies. Being fervently anti-British, they naturally gravitated to the Republican party. In addition, there was a small but vocal collection of English radicals, such as Dr. Joseph Priestley, who had despaired of ever reforming the British government and had come to observe the American experiment. Before long they could be found in an intellectual circle that gathered around Vice President Jefferson. To an orthodox, God-fearing New England Federalist such a union of alien, ideological, and sectional interests was sinister indeed!

In June 1798, Federalist leaders pushed through Congress a series of laws designed to dampen foreign influence in American politics. The Naturalization Act extended from five to fourteen years the waiting period before an alien could become a citizen with the right to vote and hold office. Two Alien acts, which Jefferson thought "worthy of the eighth or ninth century," gave the President power to imprison or deport any foreigners whom he regarded as dangerous. Although Adams, to his credit, did not enforce the law (he signed only one warrant for deportation), the atmosphere of nativist hostility and the fear of further reprisals induced several hundred Frenchmen to flee the country.

In July 1798, Federalist leaders struck directly at their domestic critics by passing the Sedition Act, making it a crime to publish anything of a false, malicious, or scandalous nature against the government or any public official. The one official exempted from the protection of the act was the vice president, and that in itself revealed the partisanship behind it. The measure did include various rights initially established by the *Zenger* case of 1735. It allowed the accused a trial by jury, and it required the government to prove that the statement in question was in fact false. Even so, Federalist judges ignored or evaded these rights. They often considered the fact of publication itself to be evidence of malicious intent, and in some cases the only function of the jury was to determine the amount of punishment. The act expired after two years, which suggests that it was intended to suppress debate during the presidential election of 1800. In all, twenty-five newspaper editors (all Republicans) were arrested, seventeen indicted, and ten convicted. It hardly constituted a "reign of terror" in the French style, but neither was it the brightest hour for American civil liberties.

Jefferson fled from the political madness even before the Sedition Act was passed, arriving at Monticello on the third of July. Unable to trust the mails, he corresponded with no one for seven weeks, and when he commenced writing he relied on messengers, rather than the government post. He had always shunned controversy, and in this season of madness he found the time and wit to write an essay on Anglo-Saxon grammar. When the republican theorist John Taylor of Caroline wrote him to suggest that it was time to consider Virginia's secession from the Union, Jefferson replied: "A little patience, and we shall see the reign of witches pass over, their spells dissolved, and the people recovering their true sight, restoring their government to its true principles."

Even so, he could not escape the conclusion that the Federalists had overstepped the Constitution. The Alien acts were unconstitutional in his view because of the discretionary power conferred on the president, and the sedition law violated the First Amendment guarantees for freedom of speech and press. The problem was how to attack the laws. It was widely assumed that the Supreme Court could review acts of Congress, though it had not yet declared one unconstitutional, but the Federalist complexion of the Court made it an unlikely ally. Instead, he decided to counteract arbitrary federal power by appealing to the sovereign states. Early in the fall he penned a series of resolutions intended for the North Carolina legislature and turned them over to his friend Wilson Cary Nicholas for disposition. Jefferson wanted the resolutions to appear to be the sentiment of a state; he did not want his authorship known (and indeed it was not known for many years). Nicholas decided that the Kentucky legislature was more fertile ground for Jefferson's seed and gave them to a friend in that state. A week later Madison visited Monticello, saw a copy of Jefferson's resolutions, and decided to draft some of his own for adoption by the Virginia assembly.

The Virginia and Kentucky resolutions, adopted in November and December 1798 represented the first extended statement of the doctrine of states' rights. Adapting Lockean social contract theory to the American federation, Jefferson claimed that the Constitution was a compact among the states that delegated certain specific powers to a central authority. The federal government was only the agent of the states, set up to handle certain mutual problems, but the states retained ultimate sovereignty. Should the central government exceed its prescribed powers, the states had the right to intervene. Jefferson then went on to demonstrate that the alien and sedition laws were unconstitutional usurpations of power and declared that a "nullification" of them was "the rightful remedy." This was too stark a challenge to federal power for the

Kentuckians, who deleted the term "nullification" before approving the resolutions.

Madison's resolutions, reflecting his judicious temperament, were more cautiously worded. They too were founded on the compact theory, but instead of using the word "nullify" (which invites the chaos of minority rule), Madison asserted the power of Virginia to "interpose" itself for the protection of its citizens against the arbitrary actions of the federal government. The Virginia and Kentucky resolutions were thus an early attempt to conceptualize the American federation, and as a theory of limited government they provided a philosophical foundation for the Republican party. But their immediate political impact was marginal. They did call attention to Federalist repression and occasioned considerable debate in several states, but not one state legislature responded favorably to the circularized resolutions. The Federalist legislation was ostensibly directed against aliens and subversives, and Americans seldom rally to the defense of those two groups. More important in undermining Federalist popularity was the impression of militarism conveyed by their efforts to enlarge the army and the burden of taxes necessitated by the war preparations. The final blow was a split in the party brought into the open by President Adams's attitude toward the army and his efforts to make peace with France.

The Politics of Peace

The French crisis widened the schism in Federalist ranks that had made its appearance during the election of 1796. In the summer of 1798, Federalist war hawks in Congress came within a few votes of adopting a declaration of war against the wishes of both the president and the cabinet's mentor, Hamilton. To head the newly enlarged army, Washington was asked to come out of retirement; he agreed only on the condition that Hamilton be made second in command and given the post of inspector general. Adams objected that the elevation of Hamilton over officers who outranked him would cause trouble, but he relented when Washington insisted. Adams was never enthusiastic about the army, anyway, anticipating that fighting would be confined to the high seas. He was slow in issuing recruiting orders, and consequently the ranks were never filled. Hamilton, who grossly overworked himself organizing the army, never forgave the president for thwarting his military ambitions. But there was more at stake than personal differences between Adams and Hamilton. The extreme wing of the party, or "High Federalists," demanded an outright declaration of war and an alliance with Great Britain. They were bitterly disappointed when the president, backed by moderate "Adams Federalists," moved in the direction of a peace settlement.

When President Adams sent to Congress the XYZ dispatches in the spring of 1798, he warned that he would not send another envoy to France until he had prior assurances "that he will be received, respected, and honored, as a representative of a great, free, powerful, and independent nation." By early 1799, Adams believed that the French were prepared to meet this condition. Talleyrand was both surprised and distressed at the belligerence of the American response. He was accustomed to shaking down European governments without causing a diplomatic ripple, but his position in the Directory would be jeopardized if his greed caused an American war. By midsummer he was backpedalling rapidly in the face of American military and naval preparations, and Elbridge Gerry returned home certain that France wanted peace. Formal assurances of Talleyrand's pacific disposition were conveyed through William Vans Murray, the American minister to the Netherlands, and in the spring of 1799 Adams decided to nominate another three-man commission. Murray, already on the continent, was a natural choice, and to aid him Adams appointed a moderate North Carolina Federalist, William R. Davie, and the chief justice of the Supreme Court, Oliver Ellsworth.

Dispatch of the new commission was deferred, however, by the procrastination of Timothy Pickering, loudest war advocate in the cabinet. Hoping that his allies in Congress might yet push through a declaration of war, Pickering delayed issuing instructions to the commissioners through the summer of 1799. In the meantime the government was disrupted by the annual yellow fever epidemic; Pickering and several other officials ended up in Trenton, while the president hurried home to Quincy to nurse a very sick wife. At last, in October, he returned to Trenton and found the commissioners still waiting for instructions. In a burst of anger (not surprising for a man who had already yielded too often) he sent the commission off to France, and six months later he summarily dismissed Pickering from office. His new secretary of state was John Marshall, hero of the XYZ Affair and a moderate.

By the time the new commission arrived in Paris there had been another governmental turnover in the turbulent French republic. General Napoleon Bonaparte, fresh from a victorious campaign in Italy, chased out the corrupt and inept Directory in November 1799, and made himself First Consul. The *coup d'etat* proved fortunate for the United States, however, for Napoleon wanted peace. He was already nursing imperial ambitions in the New World (he was simultaneously negotiating with Spain for the retrocession of Louisiana), and this required friendly relations with the United States. The negotiations were periodically interrupted by Napoleon's military expeditions, but an agreement was at last signed in the fall of 1800. The convention terminated the alliance of 1778 and the American commitment to defend the French West Indies. Although Napoleon would not pay reparations for the spoilation of American shipping, he did agree to commercial equality between the two nations.

John Adams's peace initiative was statesmanship of the highest order, and it was undertaken at considerable personal cost. It meant that the presidential contest of 1800 would not be a wartime election, and Adams thereby deprived the Federalists of the popularity that often redounds to the party in power during a war. This factor had brought the Federalists substantial gains in the congressional elections just two years before. In addition, the settlement with France completed the division of his party, for the Hamiltonian Federalists never forgave him and worked openly for his defeat in 1800. Yet the settlement of the French imbroglio paved the way for a vast expansion of American territory by the purchase of Louisiana. Ironically, it was Adams's old friend, recent rival, and immediate successor Thomas Jefferson who earned the credit for that. At the moment Adams was frustrated by the carping from within his own party and bitter over his defeat in the election of 1800. But he eventually concluded that the final diplomatic moves of his administration were his finest hour. And rightly so.

"The Revolution of 1800"

In his later years Thomas Jefferson habitually referred to his elevation to the presidency as the "Revolution of 1800." He actually considered it "as real a revolution in the principles of our government as that of 1776 was in its form." Reflecting the preoccupation of the times with the durability of the republic, he felt that the Republican victory had saved the nation from tyranny and incipient monarchy.

Jefferson was correct in his assessment that a "revolution" occurred in 1800; he erred only in framing the issue as one of republicanism versus tyranny. John Adams was no monarchist, but he did have an antiquated view of society and politics. Adams's political science was grounded on the assumption—common among the Founding Fathers—that all men are created evil. He thus saw the American republic beset by political factionalism and social anarchy. "The great division of our country into a northern and southern interest," he wrote in 1790, "will be a perpetual source of Parties and Struggles." In addition, he wailed, "We have the great divisions of the rich and poor, Creditors and Debtors." Adams felt—again in common with most of the framers of the Constitution—that the future of the republic lay in discovering and rewarding men of public spirit and virtue. His solution was balanced government linked to social orders: the Aristotelian concept of the one, the few, and the many, each with its arm of government. In Adams view the few—that is, the rich, the wise, and the wellborn—were most likely to be endowed with public spirit and virtue, and were thus the saviors of the republic.

The Jeffersonians initially objected to this philosophy as English-style "court" politics, and they railed against the mercantile favoritism of Hamilton's financial system. But by 1800 their ideology had undergone a subtle change. They started with the same assumption—that mankind is driven by its baser "passions," the drive for self-gratification. But, unlike Adams, they concluded—as Adam Smith had a quarter century before—that the pursuit of self-interest can result in broad social benefit. To Adams the pursuit of wealth was a zero-sum game, for every winner there was a loser, for every creditor, a debtor. The insight of Adam Smith (and Madison was so well acquainted with the *Wealth of Nations* that a number of phrases in his writings and speeches were inadvertant plagiarisms of Smith) was that an individual, by investing his capital and subdividing the burdens of labor, would actually add to the available total of useful goods or services and thus benefit society as a whole. Far from behaving immorally, that person was the public-spirited "man of virtue" so necessary to the future of the republic. The Jeffersonians, to be sure, had not fully worked out this philosophy by 1800, but in word and deed they were in the process of forging a social and political mind-set that fused public good with private interest, permitting individual differences to be expressed through organized factionalism. In short, they were in the process of establishing the liberal framework for modern American development.

Little of this, admittedly, was apparent to the electorate in 1800. The contest between Jefferson and Adams was one of the closest in our history. A look at the electoral map, moreover—Adams carried New England, Jefferson the South, and they split the middle states—suggests that regionalism was a bigger factor than ideology, just as Adams had predicted in 1790.

The most important factors in Jefferson's electoral victory were the rift in Federalist ranks and the sophistication of Republican organizational techniques and propaganda. In a decade of partisan warfare, the Jeffersonians became adept in political journalism, and they generally succeeded in identifying themselves with the interests, passions, and prejudices of the average citizen—small farmers and urban artisans. During the crisis with France when congressional Republicans were discouraged and impotent, the party press found political capital in every Federalist measure. Against the array of administration military preparations, Jeffersonian newspapers evoked the ancient specter of militarism and the fear of standing armies. New excises imposed by Congress to finance the armaments were greeted with a carefully organized popular protest that verged on open resistance in eastern Pennsylvania.

What happened in Pennsylvania was symptomatic of Adams's problems in the country as a whole. The counties along the lower Delaware—Montgomery, Bucks, and Northampton—were predominantly German in population and Federalist in sentiment. The war taxes of 1798–99 were received with glum hostility by the thrifty farmers of the area, and a Republican-inspired rumor that President Adams planned to marry his daughter to the son of George III and establish an American dynasty increased tensions. The climax came when a federal marshal entered Northampton County, arrested two tax dodgers, and jailed them in Bethlehem. Thereupon John Fries, who had always voted Federalist and was an auctioneer by profession, led a band of armed vigilantes to Bethlehem and released the prisoners. Adams promptly sent the army into Northampton County to suppress the "insurrection." Although it scoured the countryside for three weeks, it found nothing but sullen farmers harvesting their crops. Fries was arrested while conducting an auction, taken to Philadelphia for trial, and convicted of treason. Adams wisely pardoned him to avoid another political martyr, but the damage was done. A panicky figurehead, closeted in his Philadelphia mansion, reacting to every popular movement as a threat to the government's authority, hardly seemed the proper person to head a republic that was dependent on "the just consent of the governed."

Adams's tendency to overreact offered numerous propaganda opportunities to the Jeffersonian press, but the Republicans were also adept at manipulating the political system. Their tactics in Virginia were masterly. Virginia was Jefferson's home state, but it was also Washington's, and the Federalists could still command sizable support. Presidential electors were chosen by popular ballot in districts; and, in 1796 Adams had picked up one electoral vote in the state. The contest that year was decided by a margin of only three electoral votes, and all agreed that the election of 1800 would be just as close. It was thus essential that Virginia's vote be unanimous. In the winter of 1799, the Republican majority in the legislature modified the electoral law, abolishing the district system and awarding the state's entire electoral vote to the candidate with the most popular votes. They then, in what appeared to be a democratic reform, eliminated oral voting in the choice of presidential electors, so that each voter had to write in the name of each of the twenty-one electors allotted to the state. The purpose of all these maneuvers became evident a few weeks later when the Republican central committee distributed printed ballots containing the names of the Republican electors. It even suggested that county committees might hand them out to voters to be used as genuine ballots on election day.

The Federalists made sporadic efforts to mobilize the electorate, but they had neither the talent nor the will for mass appeals. Jefferson's religious skepticism afforded them some political capital in New England, where it was assumed that God would not "permit a howling atheist to sit at the head of the nation," but elsewhere their accusations of Jacobinism, sedition, miscegenation, and even animal vivisection made little headway. In the end, the South, with the exception of South Carolina, was solidly Jeffersonian, while Adams was dominant in New England. As a result, the election was decided in the middle states, and there the split in Federalist ranks was of crucial importance.

In New York everything depended on the state election in May 1800, since the assembly would choose the state's presidential electors. Republicans presented a formidable alliance of Clinton and Livingston interests, plus a smooth political machine in New York City headed by Aaron Burr (Jefferson's running mate). Clearly losing touch with political reality, Hamilton revived his scheme of 1796—this time dumping Adams in favor of Charles Cotesworth Pinckney, the Federalist vice presidential candidate. To further this plot Hamilton wrote a scathing indictment of Adams's treatment of the army and criticized the president's peace initiatives. Though intended for private circulation among Federalist leaders, the pamphlet (which Hamilton signed and printed) inevitably fell into Republican hands, and Jeffersonian editors printed excerpts with glee. Republicans won New York's vote, and with that went the election.

Republican organization and Federalist errors, however, were not the entire story. The most surprising feature of the electoral map of that contest is that Jefferson won the vote of every eastern city, from Boston to Baltimore. This meant that he got the support of merchants and artisans, in addition to his traditional power base of farmers and planters. The reason is that the *petite bourgeois* of the cities had been offended by Hamilton's alliance with great merchants and speculators and had found the Republicans more compatible. Artisans and shopkeepers had founded the Democratic Societies of the mid-1790s out of a sympathy for the French Revolution and in an effort to rekindle the "Spirit of '76." They moved into the Republican party because they detested elitism and sensed that Jefferson stood for individual enterprise.

As the election approached in early 1801, the Republicans possessed 73 electors and the Federalists 65, but so rigid was Republican unity that every

Jeffersonian elector cast one vote for Jefferson and one for Burr. As a result of the tie the election went to the House of Representatives which, under the Constitution, chose a president by states, with each state having one vote. Ironically, the House that met in December 1800, was a "lame duck" Congress controlled by Federalists elected in 1798. Although the Republicans had clearly intended Jefferson to be their presidential candidate Burr refused to withdraw from the contest, remaining silent in his New York home, a political enigma to all concerned. Federalist congressmen promptly seized this opportunity to promote Burr over Jefferson, hoping to profit from the New Yorker's gratitude once he attained office. This intrigue was undertaken against the wishes of Hamilton, who knew both Republicans well, having battled them for years. Jefferson, he knew, was no wild-eyed radical, despite all the Federalist rhetoric in the campaign. Burr, on the other hand, Hamilton considered "as true a Cataline as ever met in midnight conclave." Hamilton's sensible advice went unheeded, so completely had he alienated his party by his antics in the spring elections.

The House began balloting on February 16, just three weeks before the anticipated inauguration. With sixteen states in the Union nine was the requisite majority; Jefferson received the votes of eight states, Burr seven, and one was divided. Through thirty-five ballots over the next week the division held firm. The impasse was broken when several moderate Federalists having received indirect assurances that Jefferson would not totally scrap the Federalist system, reversed their votes or cast blanks. Jefferson won by ten states to four for Burr, two divided. Jefferson was president, and Burr, though nominally vice president, was politically dead.

The Experiment Confirmed

The election of 1800 was not a great popular upheaval. It was not a matter of the common man rising up in righteous wrath to evict his aristocratic oppressors, the Federalists. It was not an upheaval, if only because it was extremely close. If either of two states where the parties were in even balance—New York or South Carolina—had gone Federalist, Adams would have won. Moreover, the sectional character of party support suggests that regional jealousies were more important in determining voter behavior than ideology or image.

In addition, the presidency was carefully hedged from popular control. Most states had property qualifications that limited the number of voters who could participate in the political process, and in several key states—notably New York, Pennsylvania, and South Carolina—presidential electors were chosen by the legislatures. On the other hand, in the one national contest where the voters did have a direct influence—the balloting for the House of Representatives—the Republicans won a tremendous victory, capturing two-thirds of the seats and totally reversing the Federalist victories of two years before.

The election, nonetheless, marked a major shift in American political ideology. The Jeffersonians—although they were not fully aware of it in 1800—would lay the foundations for modern American free-enterprise capitalism. The election was also significant for its impact on the party system. It marked the final stage in the evolution of a two-party system, and the local machinery developed by Republicans for the campaign insured their supremacy for years to come. Although the Federalists ultimately imitated the organizational techniques and propaganda devices of the Republicans, they were never again able to control the government. During the 1790s, Republican efforts had been continually hampered by the ideological stigma attached to "factions" and by the Federalist tendency to view criticism as subversive. Although the phrase "loyal opposition" was not coined in Britain until 1820, Americans clearly understood the concept in 1800. Jefferson's election marked the first change in the ruling elite since the Constitution, and its peaceful nature meant that Americans recognized that an opposition could criticize executive policies without desiring to overthrow the government. The relative stability of the republican process in America displayed considerable political sophistication for so young a republic, and marked a favorable contrast to the simultaneous rise of Napoleon in France.

7

Jefferson's "Empire for Liberty"

THROUGH THE FALL OF 1800, WHILE THE NATION CONDUCTED its presidential canvass, the government was moving from Philadelphia to the new "federal city" on the banks of the Potomac. Relocation of the nation's capital had been part of the sectional compromise of 1790. The exact location of the capital had been left to President Washington, in part to gain the support of the Pennsylvania congressmen who were still hoping that the president might choose a location in their state. To the surprise of everyone—except perhaps the Virginians—Washington chose a site just below the falls of the Potomac, a few miles from Mount Vernon.

By 1800, there were perhaps 3,000 people in scattered settlements in the rolling woodland between Georgetown and the Anacostia River. On the highest hill in the district that had been ceded by Maryland stood the still unfinished Capitol. A mile and a half away, down a woodland path called Pennsylvania Avenue, stood the president's house, also unfinished, but gleaming in the sunlight from a new coat of whitewash. Around the Capitol a cluster of buildings had appeared, the largest of which would house the departments of State, War, and Treasury. There were shops in which a tailor, shoemaker, printer, and grocer plied their trades, and seven or eight boardinghouses accommodated the members of Congress, usually two or more to a room. In the best of these, the hostelry of Conrad and McMun, Jefferson resided while he waited to move into the house on Pennsylvania Avenue. Jefferson had a parlor and a bedroom to himself, but in the common dining room he "occupied during the whole winter the lowest and coldest seat at a long table at which a company of more than thirty sat down."

"A Wise and Frugal Government . . ."

The Adamses had moved into the new executive mansion in November 1800. Abigail reported that it was "a castle of a house" on a small hill that commanded a splendid view of the Potomac. The area around it was "romantic but wild, a wilderness at present." Although the exterior of the house was finished the inside was in rough shape. Indeed, the hammering and painting continued through much of Jefferson's first term. Not a single room was completely furnished, and the place was so drafty that the Adamses had to keep thirteen fires going constantly to stay warm. Their discomfort was short-lived, however, for as soon as the election results were known they began packing. Abigail departed early in the new year, and at 4:00 a.m. on the morning of Jefferson's inauguration, Adams himself set off for Quincy.

At noon on March 4, 1801, the 57-year-old statesman left his boarding-house and walked over to the Capitol where John Marshall, appointed chief justice by Adams only a few weeks earlier, was waiting to administer the oath of office. Knowing the chief justice's habits, Jefferson had written him a suggestion that he be on time, and Marshall had obligingly agreed to do so. As Jefferson mounted the Capitol steps a company of Alexandria militia fired a salute. The procession was otherwise without pomp or ceremony as befitted the man and the occasion. A Washington lady caught the significance of the peaceful transfer of power. "The changes in administration," she noted in her diary, "which in every government and in every age have most generally been epochs of confusion, villany, and bloodshed, in this our happy country take place without any species of distraction or disorder."

After taking the oath of office, the lanky Virginian, indistinguishable in dress or manner from the crowd below, rose to give his inaugural address. He had spent considerable time on the speech, revising it down to the last minute (the draft he gave to the press differed in minor ways from the one he read that day), and it was certainly one of his finest compositions. He was concerned first of all to allay the passions that had divided the nation for the past three years and reassure his worried opponents that he was no political fanatic. This he did by pointing out that Americans, whatever their party differences, were in agreement on fundamental principles. "We are all Republicans—we are all Federalists. If there be any among us who would wish to dissolve this Union or to change its republican form, let them stand undisturbed as monuments of the safety with which error of opinion may be tolerated where reason is left free to combat it." Amidst his reassurances Jefferson could not resist a gentle gibe at the Federalist Sedition Act.

He then assailed the ideological apprehensions of the Federalists.

> I know, indeed, that some honest men fear that a republican government cannot be strong; that this government is not strong enough. But would the honest patriot, in the full tide of successful experiment, abandon a government which has so far kept us free and firm, on the theoretic and visionary fear that this government, the world's best hope, may by possibility want energy to preserve itself? I trust not. . . . Sometimes it is said that man cannot be trusted with the government of himself. Can he, then, be trusted with the government of others? Or have we found angels in the forms of kings to govern him? Let history answer this question.

Here indeed was a radical notion! Governments did not require for survival royal majesty and ministerial pomp, the support of armies and navies, or an alliance with the rich and wellborn. Government, suggested Jefferson, can be strong only when it has the affections of the people. And it can win those only by being attentive to the people's interests.

Jefferson's second concern was to outline his own political program, and here he succeeded in elevating the Republican creed into an American creed. It was the first important statement of American Liberalism: "Equal and exact justice to all men, of whatever state or persuasion, religious or political; peace, commerce, and honest friendship with all nations—entangling alliances with none." What Jefferson envisioned was an evenhanded, unobtrusive government that would concern itself with protecting law and order at home and the peaceful pursuit of free trade abroad. This concept of political liberty easily blended with the economic liberalism expounded by Adam Smith in *The Wealth of Nations* (1776). Jefferson summarized it as "a wise and frugal government which shall restrain men from injuring one another, which shall leave them otherwise free to regulate their own pursuits of industry and improvement, and shall not take from the mouth of labor the bread it has earned. This is the sum of good government. . . ." In Europe, where the message did not pass unnoticed, people could not believe that the chief magistrate of a country would voluntarily renounce patronage and power. It promised, said an English journal, "a sort of Millennium in government."

Jefferson followed his inaugural reassurances with a refusal to dismiss Federalist officeholders. He announced that government servants appointed by Washington or Adams would be discharged only on proof of malfeasance in office. Under pressure from jobseekers in his party, Jefferson modified this stand and agreed to dismiss all Federalists appointed by Adams after December 12, the day that Adams knew he had been defeated. The ex-president had in fact tried to pack the government with Federalists in his last hours. Jefferson regarded such appointments as "nullities" and therefore not chargeable as removals; he simply replaced them with Republicans. He also adopted a policy of naming only Republicans to fill vacancies in order to achieve a balance between the parties in officeholding. Even so, at the end of his first term Federalists still held almost half of the clerical offices in the federal civil service.

His policies generally reflected the same pragmatic moderation. Although several of his more ardent followers demanded constitutional amendments that would prevent a reenactment of the Federalist program of 1798, Jefferson saw no point in tilting with windmills. Most of the alien and sedition laws expired in 1800, and the new Congress quickly repealed the naturalization law. Jefferson had no intention of reinstituting such a program, so amendments seemed unnecessary. The "reign of witches" was over, and the people had nothing to fear from him. Similarly, the Federalist financial system, merchant-oriented though it was, had established the fiscal integrity of the government; to assault it head-on might disrupt the entire economy. Instead, he hoped to chip away at some of its more exposed edges.

Although the change in ruling elite from Federalists to Republicans hardly constituted the "revolution" that Jefferson later recalled, there was, nonetheless, a genuine shift in direction. Where Federalist ideology had stressed the depravity of man and the need for powerful rulers closely connected with institutionalized religion, Jefferson affirmed a faith in an enlightened populace that needed no overt guidance in matters political or religious. One measure of the difference was in their respective attitudes toward the civil service. John Adams believed in government by the wealthy, the wise, and the wellborn, and the men he appointed to office generally reflected these criteria. Jefferson felt that status and pedigree were no measure of worth; he looked only for men of talent and training. As a result, his choices began a gradual democratization of the governmental elite.

Both Jefferson and Madison desired some legal changes in the direction of broader suffrage and a more equitable system of representation. Such reforms were matters of state, rather than national, concern, however. And it was not in Jefferson's philosophy or makeup to interfere in local matters. His followers at the state level, moreover, evinced little interest in democratic progress. Even those "radicals" who demanded that every vestige of Federalism be purged from the government said nothing about universal white male suffrage. Though they were short on deeds, the Republicans talked much about the virtue of the common man, and their newspaper propaganda made frank appeals to him for support. Thus their rhetoric alone enhanced the importance of the average citizen. Even the Federalists had to recognize that he was an integral part of the political process. As the parties competed for votes, they developed evermore sophisticated machinery for mobilizing the electorate. The result was a dramatic rise in voter turnout, reaching in some states as high as 80 percent of the eligibles by the eve of the War of 1812. This level of participation can be achieved only if voters feel that the system is working, that it is responding to their needs. That was the rhetorical triumph of the Jeffersonians.

Jeffersonian democratization was thus, in large measure, a matter of image-making, and the president himself was a master at it. His own tastes were simple enough (except for his dinner table, which was always elegantly furnished), and he had little difficulty in surrounding himself with an aura of republican simplicity. His predecessors' practice of addressing Congress in person appeared to him a vestige of monarchy. Since he was a wretched public speaker anyway, he initiated a practice of sending his annual messages to be read by the clerk of the House. The custom reemphasized the constitutional separation of executive and legislature, and remained standard until the time of Woodrow Wilson. He also made himself accessible to all, though he was driven to distraction by the frequent interruptions of business. The studied effort to avoid European protocol even extended to Jefferson's dinner parties, where seating was "pell mell" rather than by rank, a practice that offended the snobbish British Ambassador Anthony Merry.

Even the President's bowels became indirectly involved. He was much troubled by diarrhea at the time of the election, and a doctor suggested horseback riding as a possible cure. Jefferson never had much faith in physicians, but he took the advice since he enjoyed riding anyway. His solitary rides around the federal district excited considerable attention, and observers compared his frugal habits with the ostentatious coach-and-six in which his predecessors had pranced around the capital city. Before long even his intestinal difficulties cleared up.

But there was substance, as well as imagery, in the notion of Jeffersonian Democracy. His "wise and frugal government" contrasted sharply with the neo-mercantilism that had characterized Federalist economic policies. He desired a light-handed regime that neither burdened commerce with regulations nor the citizen with taxes. Implementation of this ideal fell to Secretary of the Treasury Albert Gallatin, whose fiscal policies were as central to the Jeffersonian system as Hamilton's had been to Federalism.

Gallatin at the Treasury

To this uncomplicated republican from western Pennsylvania, a national debt was not a blessing but a national curse—one to be relieved as rapidly as possible. Repudiating Hamilton's funded debt never entered his mind; instead he devised a program for retiring it over a period of sixteen years at the rate of seven millions a year (two presidential terms for Jefferson and two for Madison would suffice). Since Gallatin estimated his annual receipts at only $9 million (after the Federalists' internal taxes were repealed), his program of debt retirement consumed 80 percent of the revenue and left only $2 million annually for the operation of the government. That meant cutting expenses and reducing the size of the federal payroll. The civil list could not be appreciably reduced, for the Federalists had not been extravagant there. Indeed, the entire civil service resident in Washington, D. C., when Jefferson took office numbered only 127 persons. The best the Jeffersonians could do was see to it that this did not increase, and there they were successful. When Jefferson left office in 1809, despite having doubled the size of the country with the purchase of Louisiana, the federal bureaucracy in Washington numbered 123.

But the military was something else. With the French crisis ended, the Federalists had moved to cut the navy even before they left office. An act signed by Adams on March 3, 1801, authorized the president to sell or take out of service all but six of the navy's frigates. Jefferson went even further, decommissioning all of the navy's ships, except for a small force that he sent to the Mediterranean to battle the Barbary pirates. In 1802, Congress fixed the army at one regiment of artillery, two regiments of infantry, and a corps of engineers, totaling 3,312 officers and men. Most of the army was scattered in frontier outposts. However, the corps of engineers was stationed at West Point, where the corps became a military academy with the principal engineer acting as superintendent. The founding of a military academy, at first blush, might seem to run counter to the well-known antipathy of the Jeffersonians for the military. However, if there was one thing they feared more than a standing army, it was a Federalist army. The evidence is scant, but West Point may well have been designed to produce a Republican, or at least a politically neutral, officer corps.

These economy measures enabled Congress to repeal most of the Federalist excises; thereafter, the government would subsist almost exclusively on the revenue from customs duties and the sale of public lands.

Gallatin had more in mind, however, than the negative goal of reducing the national debt. By freeing his countrymen of taxes and other restraints he hoped to harness their crude vitality for the public good. He saw his fellow Americans, not as yeomen farmers, but as potential entrepreneurs. "Go into the interior of the country," he had told the House of Representatives in 1799, "and you will scarcely find a farmer who is not, in some degree a trader. In a grazing part of the country, you will find them buying and selling cattle; in other parts you will find them distillers, tanners, or brick-makers." Some years later he described to Congress what he perceived to be the effect of his fiscal policies. "No law exists here, directly or indirectly, confining man to a particular occupation or place," he exulted. "Industry is, in every effect, perfectly free and unfettered; every species of trade, commerce, art, profession, and manufacture being equally opened to all. . . . Hence the progress of America has not been confined to her agriculture." Adam Smith, with whose writings Gallatin was well acquainted, must have given a silent cheer from the grave, for this was a distillation of his Liberal thought.

Adam Smith, contrary to popular supposition, was not totally opposed to government activity. He was willing to concede that there were a number of ways in which government intervention might be beneficial—with protective tariffs, for instance, and commercial retaliation. Gallatin, too, was willing to accept government agencies that he found useful, including the arch-symbol of Federalist mercantilism, the Bank of the United States. Through the 1790s the bank was well-managed and proved to be a useful adjunct to the Treasury. It was a convenient place of deposit for government funds, and its various branches enabled the Treasury to pay its obligations without carting funds from one end of the country to the other.

Jefferson remained hostile to the bank, but Gallatin managed to deflect that by severing the bank's ties with the government. In 1802, he sold the government's bank stock to the House of Baring in London and used the proceeds to make a payment on the debt owed the Dutch. The tactic also enabled him to avoid having to borrow in the domestic money market in order to pay the foreign debt. To the bank's president, Thomas Willing, he explained that "I have been less guided by the facility thereby given to the Government operations, than by the general relief it will afford to the commercial interest." In closing, he expressed the hope that liquidation of the government's stock would "in no degree affect the friendly & liberal relations which have heretofore subsisted between Government & Bank, which it will ever be my duty to promote & increase."

Such a drastic reduction in the national debt in so short a time would disrupt a modern economy; that Gallatin got away with it is perhaps an indication of the importance of the public sector in his day. Even so, he might have been in trouble but for an unparalleled economic boom occasioned by the war in Europe. After the French difficulties ended, Americans were free to trade with both sides, and they found new markets in the French and Spanish possessions in the West Indies. American exports leaped from $56 million in 1802 to $95 million in 1805, and exceeded $100 million for the first time in 1806. Ultimately the neutral commerce would embroil the nation in new problems with Europe; but, for the moment the proceeds relieved the chronic shortage of capital and financed a spurt of economic growth.

The customs receipts, in turn, exceeded Gallatin's expectations by several million dollars annually, enabling him to pay off the debt much faster than anticipated. Indeed, as early as 1806 the administration was faced with the prospect of an annual surplus. The president's annual message of that year proposed to solve this embarrassment of riches by building a national transportation network. Gallatin, unconcerned for the constitutional and political implications of such government largesse, promptly set to work on a scheme for federally financed internal improvements. The only result, unfortunately, was the survey of a "national road" from Washington to Cumberland, Maryland, thence across the mountains to Wheeling, Virginia, on the Ohio River. This project was barely under way when the Embargo and the War of 1812 blasted away Gallatin's whole fiscal system. Not until 1835 did the government again face the prospect of being completely debt free.

In their fiscal policies, Jefferson and Gallatin departed in both theory and practice from the Federalist methods developed by Hamilton. But their innovations were tempered by a pragmatic awareness of political realities. They retained those Federalist devices that suited their purposes, and they demonstrated an ideological flexibility toward the role of government in the economy. A similar pragmatism characterized the other feature of the Jeffersonian "revolution"—the attack on the judiciary.

Assault on the Courts

The attack on the federal judiciary bespoke the Antifederalist origins of Republican ideology. The critics of the Constitution had focused on the provision for a judiciary, calling it both redundant and dangerous. The federal judiciary, they insisted, would compete with the state courts for business, enforce the decrees of a remote and indifferent authority, and expose Americans to suits by foreign citizens and foreign governments. During the 1790s the Supreme Court did nothing to relieve the apprehensions of its critics. In *Chisholm* v. *Georgia* (1793), the court upheld the right of a private citizen to sue a state against its will. This was a blow to the whole concept of state sovereignty, and it subjected the states to a barrage of lawsuits for the recovery of confiscated Loyalist property. New York, which had appropriated Loyalist property after the peace treaty was signed, and Virginia whose citizens still owed millions to British merchants, were both endangered by the decision. The two states were also the geographical axis of the Republican party. Such suits were subsequently barred by the Eleventh Amendment to the Constitution. Republican hostility to the judiciary increased with the blatantly political enforcement of the Sedition Act in 1799–1800, which indicated that the judiciary was nothing more than the creature of the Federalist party. The final straw was the dramatic expansion of the court system undertaken by the "lame duck" Federalist Congress after Jefferson's election.

The federal judiciary created by Congress in 1789 was imperfect at the time, and it became increasingly outmoded with the addition of new states in the 1790s. Special circuit judges were needed to relieve Supreme Court justices of the onerous duty of riding circuit, and additional lower courts were required in the new states of the West. After Jefferson's electoral victory, the Federalists hurried through these needed reforms so Adams would have the opportunity of making the new appointments before leaving office. The Judiciary Act of 1801 not only created a host of new circuit and district courts, as well as judicial offices for the District of Columbia, but it also reduced the number of Supreme Court judges from six to five upon death or retirement. This effectively prevented Jefferson from making an early appointment to the nation's highest court. With a host of new offices to fill, Adams quickly set about making his nominations; indeed, rumor had it that he was up until midnight on the eve of the inauguration flooding the judiciary with Federalists. This lack of political sportsmanship shocked the Republicans, who feared that the Federalists, having been defeated at the polls, would use their judicial citadel to block the entire Jeffersonian program.

Among the first measures of the new Republican Congress was the repeal of the Federalist law, although their Judiciary Act of 1802 did retain a few lower courts in the western states. In the debate on this measure, Federalists argued that the repeal violated the life tenure of judges guaranteed by the Constitution. Republicans responded that they were not dismissing judges, they were abolishing courts, and if a judge lost his job that was incidental. Federalists warned that the Supreme Court would find the new law unconstitutional, and Republicans answered by denying the power of judicial review. Relying on the Virginia and Kentucky Resolutions, they argued that only states could review the constitutionality of acts of Congress. At this juncture John Marshall (himself a last-minute appointment, having been nominated to the post of chief justice in January 1801) intervened with his decision in the case of *Marbury* v. *Madison* (February 1803).

William Marbury was one of Adams's "midnight appointments," named a justice of the peace for the newly formed District of Columbia. But so late was the nomination made that James Madison found the undelivered commission on his desk when he took up his duties at the State Department. Under instructions from the president, who hoped to nominate a Republican for the office, Madison refused to deliver the commission. Marbury promptly sued him, seeking a *writ of mandamus* (if issued, the court would command the official to do his duty and surrender the commission). To avoid delay Marbury instituted his suit in the Supreme Court, relying on a provision of the Judiciary Act of 1789 that gave the court original jurisdiction in cases involving a *writ of mandamus* against executive officials. In deciding the case, John Marshall ruled that the court did have power to issue orders to executive officials, even when they were operating under the expressed instructions of the president. The only question in Marshall's mind was whether Marbury had followed the correct procedure. Article III of the Constitution listed the circumstances under which the Supreme Court could take original jurisdiction (cases involving foreign emissaries, and suits in which a state is a party), but nowhere could he find any mention of the *writ of mandamus*. Marshall concluded that Congress had exceeded its authority by adding to the jurisdiction of the court, and he declared that particular section of the Judiciary Act of 1789 unconstitutional. The case was therefore dismissed for lack of jurisdiction. Like many of Marshall's later decisions, the case was a political coup, for Marshall established his doctrine of judicial supremacy and let the Republicans win the case; Marbury never received his commission.

Despite their concept of state review expressed in the Virginia and Kentucky Resolutions, the Jeffersonians were generally able to swallow Marshall's doctrine of judicial review. Most lawyers accepted the notion in the 1790s; Jefferson had denied it only when faced with a partisan judiciary. What the Republicans seriously objected to, instead, was Marshall's *obiter dictum.* After dismissing the case for lack of jurisdiction, Marshall went on unnecessarily to say what he would have done if he had jurisdiction. The chief justice upheld the power of courts to issue orders to executive officials; even the president must be subject to the law. This declaration confirmed all the Republican suspicions that the Federalists intended to use their judicial bastion to block everything the Republicans attempted to do. Even so, Jefferson could not publicly object to Marshall's dictum because to do so would have involved taking the position that the president is above the law. This he could not do, having inveighed against executive power throughout the 1790s. Thus Marshall's shrewdly calculated political gambit became a constitutional landmark. By declaring an act of Congress void on the one hand, and establishing his authority over executive officials, on the other, Marshall in one grand stroke promoted the Supreme Court as the highest of the three branches of the government.

Chagrined, the Republicans sought ways of cracking the Federalist hold on the judiciary. The attack had popular appeal because courts and lawyers were never popular in early America. The populace regarded them as agents of the wealthy. Whether the matter at issue was a conflict over land titles, a suit for debt, or a stray cow, the wealthy could better afford to hire attorneys, transport witnesses, and impress the jury. Any decision reached by the court was then enforced with the full powers of the government.

By 1803, the radical element in Jefferson's party was in full cry against the judiciary. The Pennsylvania assembly removed one state judge who had openly flaunted his Federalism, and then instituted impeachment proceedings against the entire supreme court of the state. In Congress various Republican leaders were likewise discussing the use of impeachment as a means of bringing the federal judiciary in tune with the new political order. "We shall see who is master of the ship," said one. "Whether men appointed for life or the immediate representatives of the people . . . are to give laws to the community."

The procedure for removing such officials was outlined in the Constitution. The House of Representatives voted the impeachment (indictment), and the trial was conducted before the Senate, with members from the House serving as the prosecution. A vote of two-thirds of the Senate was required for conviction and removal from office. Unfortunately the procedure, when applied to judges, contained a glaring loophole. The Constitution provided federal judges with life tenure during good behavior, but removal by impeachment required conviction of "Treason, Bribery, or other high Crimes and Misdemeanors." And therein lay the gap. What if a judge misbehaved but could not be convicted of a crime? Or, put another way, did the misuse of judicial authority constitute a misdemeanor within the meaning of the Constitution, or did the indicted judge have to be convicted of a crime with due legal process?

Despite the ambiguity of the Constitution, the Republicans decided to test the impeachment process, though it now seems that legislation curtailing the jurisdiction of the courts or an effort to pack them with Republicans would have been more effective alternatives. Their first target was an easy mark—a hapless, alcoholic, mentally ill district judge in New Hampshire named John Pickering. In February 1803, three weeks before Marshall rendered his decision in *Marbury* v. *Madison,* Jefferson referred the complaints against Pickering to the House of Representatives. A heated political controversy ensued. Republican leaders, lacking any evidence of a crime, were forced to admit that Pickering should be removed for misbehavior. They argued that, since the Constitution mentioned no other means for dismissing judges, it must have intended that impeachment include misbehavior as well as misdemeanors. Federalists demanded a strict interpretation of the Constitution and accused the administration of launching a reign of terror against the courts. To get a conviction the prosecution had to compromise, and Pickering was voted "guilty as charged." Such a decision merely sidestepped the basic issue, and Pickering's removal was neither a victory for reform nor a useful precedent.

Undaunted, Jefferson in May 1803 called the attention of Republican congressional leaders to a viciously partisan address made by Samuel Chase, one of the justices of the Supreme Court, to a Baltimore grand jury. Chase had been a thorn in the side of Republicans for years. He had conducted several of the sedition trials in a grossly injudicious manner; and it was he who had convicted poor John Fries of treason for resisting federal taxes in 1799. His Baltimore address, which denounced the democratic tendencies of the government and predicted mob rule, was more than Republicans could tolerate. In the 1804 session, the House of Representatives approved some eight articles of impeachment, drawn up by the administration's floor leader John Randolph. Randolph was a brilliant orator, who terrorized the House with a rapier wit and a razor-sharp tongue, but he was no lawyer. The allegations listed only Chase's highly partisan conduct on the bench, but the question remained whether his lack of judicial restraint constituted a crime.

The prosecution itself seemed uncertain when the trial opened before the Senate in February 1805. Joseph H. Nicholson (Gallatin's brother-in-law) argued that misbehavior was sufficient grounds for removal, and proof of a crime was unnecessary. Randolph followed with a rambling speech, the gist of which seemed to be that Chase was guilty of criminal misbehavior. The attorneys for the justice quickly pointed out that this allegation, in effect, made the Senate a court of law. Hence a crime would have to be proved under the normal procedures of criminal law. The Senate agreed, and the judge was saved. The Republicans failed to get the necessary two-thirds vote on any of the eight articles; they mustered a bare majority on only two.

The failure of the Chase impeachment ended the "war on the judiciary." On the surface it seemed that little had been accomplished, but the battle was of considerable importance. In the 1780s, the overriding political issue was the power of Congress; in the 1790s, executive authority was a central issue in the Federalist-Republican contest. Each issue was eventually resolved, through the adoption of the Constitution, and through practice and precedent. It was thus almost natural, if not inevitable, that the judiciary would be a major bone of contention after 1800. The radicals in the Republican party were not internally united, but it is clear that if they had succeeded the court system would have been seriously weakened. Jefferson gave them a good deal of verbal support, but his actions were moderate. The Chase impeachment, for instance, was a congressional show; except for some initial encouragement, the administration made no effort to influence the outcome.

The result of the conflict was a pragmatic stalemate, of the sort reached earlier in regard to legislative and executive powers. The federal judiciary retained its jurisdictional powers and independence, but never again would it become the partisan tool of one political interest. There is no better evidence of Jefferson's pragmatism, of his recognition, as he himself put it, "that no more good must be attempted than the nation can bear." John Randolph, the political doctrinaire, also recognized this; he blamed, not the Federalists, but Jefferson and Madison for his failure to remove Chase and purge the Supreme Court. Bitter and vindictive, temperamentally unstable and suffering from chronic internal disorders, he plotted revenge. Foreign affairs, which were demanding increasing attention as Jefferson's first term neared an end, gave him his opportunity.

National Honor and National Interest

The emergence of American nationalism is one of the most important themes of the early republic. In its political character nationalism provides a thread of continuity from the Federalist regime to the Jeffersonians. Federalist nationalism was most evident in their domestic policies, in their efforts to strengthen the central government. The Jeffersonians were also nationalists, but with them it was more apparent in their foreign policies. In the field of foreign affairs, early American nationalism took two forms—it involved a sensitivity to the nation's honor and prestige abroad, and, secondly, it led to an aggressive expansion of American territory. The first was evident in the American resistance to British transgressions on the high seas, which led ultimately to the War of 1812; but, it could also be detected at the very beginning of Jefferson's administration when the new president found himself at war with pirates in the Mediterranean.

The Muslim city-states along the Barbary Coast of North Africa (Algiers, Tunis, and Tripoli) made their living by preying on the commerce of the Mediterranean. Through the latter half of the eighteenth century every major seafaring nation paid them an annual tribute to avoid having its commerce plundered. When independence deprived American ships of the protective umbrella of the Royal Navy, the Continental Congress decided to buy off the pirates in order to keep open American commerce in the Mediterranean. Having no alternative for lack of a navy, the Federalist administrations continued the same policy.

In May 1801, the pasha of Tripoli, unhappy with the meager sums he was getting in tribute, cut down the flagpole of the American consulate, which turned out to be his method of declaring war. Jefferson's response revealed his commitment to national security, and it also affords an insight into his executive decision-making. He summoned his cabinet and put the question: "Shall the squadron now at Norfolk be ordered to cruise the Mediterranean?" And, if so, "what shall be the object of the cruise?" For the second time in three years the nation found itself on the edge of a fight without a declaration of war by Congress. The question was how far the president's power extended when it came to taking military action on his own authority. The cabinet decided that the cruise should be undertaken and that American ship captains could be authorized to search for and destroy enemy vessels. This conclusion revealed the Republicans' willingness to use executive power, especially when the issue was the country's honor abroad.

This meeting also set the standard for Jefferson's relations with his cabinet. Far more than his predecessors he treated the cabinet as a body of advisors and frequently submitted ticklish questions to a cabinet vote. With Jefferson's talent for persuasion and compromise, he was more often than not able to achieve a unanimous decision. Jefferson's administration was far more united than either of his Federalist predecessors; and, indeed, it set a standard for harmony that rarely, if ever, has been equaled. It also set a record for longevity. In Jefferson's eight years in office only one cabinet member resigned, Attorney General Levi Lincoln, and that was due to his ill health.

In reporting the decision with respect to the Barbary pirates to the Congress, Jefferson emphasized the defensive nature of the naval mission. Nevertheless, having decided to commit the navy, he prosecuted the war with vigor. Several of the recently completed frigates were recommissioned, and by 1803, a squadron commanded by Commodore Edward Preble was blockading the port of Tripoli. When one small frigate, the *Philadelphia,* ran aground and was captured by the pirates early in 1804, a gallant band of men under Lieutenant Stephen Decatur sailed into the harbor at night and burned it.

Decatur's adventure kindled public interest in this romantically distant conflict, but more was to come. The American consul at Tunis, William Eaton, was a Connecticut Yankee with a gift for international intrigue. Among his acquaintances at Tunis was a potential rival to the throne of Tripoli. Hamet Caramelli, the rightful pasha, had been driven into exile some years before by his younger brother Yusef. Eaton's scheme was to place Hamet on the throne, sign a favorable treaty with him, and impress both North Africa and Europe with the might of American power. In 1803 he returned to Washington to push his scheme, but found the administration noncommittal. Jefferson was understandably adverse to putting American policy in the hands of such an adventurer, but he did recommend Eaton to the naval commanders in the Mediterranean as a potentially useful agent.

Armed with no other authority than this vague recommendation, Eaton returned to the Mediterranean and tracked down Hamet, who by this time had taken refuge in Cairo. The two struck a bargain and went to Alexandria where they recruited an army of several hundred men, a motley assortment of American and Greek adventurers, Tripolitan followers of Hamet, and Egyptian camel drivers. With neither organization nor discipline, nor supplies, nor water for days at a time, this force marched across five hundred miles of desert in six weeks. It appeared outside Derne, a town on the Tripolitan frontier, in April 1805. With the help of three ships from the American fleet blockading Tripoli, Eaton subdued the garrison and captured the town. Yusef sent a large force out to dislodge him, but this was beaten back with the help of naval artillery. In May 1805, Pasha Yusef opened peace negotiations with Tobias Lear, consul-general at Algiers, who had gone to Tripoli for that purpose.

At Derne, Eaton was still seven hundred miles from Tripoli, so it is unlikely that Yusef regarded him as much of a threat. Even so, his presence with a potential rival for the throne was an acute embarrassment. In addition, the American blockade was cutting off his normal sources of revenue, piracy and ransom. He quickly came to terms with Lear, and the treaty signed on June 3 terminated the war and the tribute. In return, the United States paid $60,000 ransom for the crew of the *Philadelphia.* Hamet was ensconced in Sicily with a well-financed harem, and Eaton spent the rest of his life trying to collect from Congress the $20,000 he spent on the expedition.

Jefferson viewed the result with understandable pride. When Commodore Preble negotiated similar treaties with Algiers and Tunis, the United States, alone among the major commercial nations of the world, could traffic in the Mediterranean without harassment or tribute. The conflict also provided both training and tradition for the young navy. When the nation again went to war, in 1812, it would give a good account of itself. Together with the Louisiana Purchase, the war with Tripoli marked the successful union of national honor and national interest in Jefferson's foreign policy.

The Rising Empire

Spain's possession of the Gulf Coast and the mouth of the Mississippi was an obstacle to American expansionism, but the nation's initial interest in the region was far more than mere land hunger. Instead, it was essentially commercial. Every river of the lower South flowed through Spanish territory before emptying into the Gulf of Mexico, and the rest of the trans-Appalachian West was dependent on the Mississippi River for access to world markets. In possession of West Florida (the coastline south of the thirty-first parallel extending from the Perdido River west to the mouth of the Mississippi), Spain had an economic stranglehold on the entire American West. Throughout the 1780s and 1790s, the West simmered with discontent over its intolerable position, alternating between plots to seize New Orleans by force and secessionist intrigues aimed at creating an independent republic that could negotiate a bargain with Spain. The opening of the Mississippi under the Pinckney Treaty cooled western tempers temporarily, but French imperial designs on the New World set the pot boiling again. After New Orleans was opened, the port handled more than a third of all American exports, a measure of the commercial stakes involved.

Despite its strategic advantage, Spain was not comfortable. The revenue from Louisiana and Florida never equalled the costs of administration. The region's only value to Spain was that it served as a buffer between the expansive United States and Spanish Mexico. By 1800, Spain was firmly allied to France, and Napoleon offered the prospect of an even stronger buffer. Napoleon, in turn, dreamt of recreating the New World empire that France had lost in 1763, and a deal was quickly consummated. By the Treaty of San Ildefonso, Napoleon promised the throne of Italy to the brother-in-law of the Spanish king, and received in return an empire that included the mouth of the Mississippi and the entire basin from the river west to the Continental Divide. Anticipating an adverse American reaction to the presence of a powerful and militant neighbor on its western border, the two European powers agreed to keep the treaty secret. Spanish officials continued to administer New Orleans, and they even kept the port open to American traders after the right of deposit expired.

Within a year the provisions of the treaty leaked out among the diplomatic circles in Europe, and Jefferson learned of it shortly after his inauguration in May 1801. His reaction was restrained since for the moment there was no overt threat to American interests in the area. His new minister to France, Robert R. Livingston, was instructed only to seek assurances for continued American use of the Mississippi. Madison later asked him to determine whether the French might be willing to sell New Orleans and the Gulf Coast, but Livingston was unable to find out from Talleyrand whether West Florida was even included in the Spanish cession.

In the spring of 1802, Jefferson decided to turn the screws. He informed Livingston, in a letter that was left open for French officials to inspect, "The day that France takes possession of New Orleans fixes the sentence which is to restrain her forever within her low water mark. It seals the union of the two nations who in conjunction can maintain exclusive possession of the ocean. From that moment we must marry ourselves to the British fleet and nation." In his single-minded pursuit of American national interests, Jefferson was quite willing to reach a temporary understanding with Great Britain in order to prevent a French takeover in Louisiana.

As it turned out, Jefferson did not have to carry out his threat of playing one European power off against the other, for within a year Napoleon's imperial plans were dead, stung to death by a mosquito. The disaster began with a slave rebellion on the island of Santo Domingo, acquired by the Directory from Spain in 1795. Taking to heart the French revolutionary slogan "Liberty, Equality, and Fraternity" the Haitian slaves rose up against their masters and created a republic under their black leader Toussaint L'Ouverture. For a time Toussaint's republic coexisted in an uneasy truce with the French colonial regime on the island; but, fear that the rebellion might spread to neighboring islands induced France to crush it as soon as it could disentangle itself from the European war. Taking advantage of a temporary lull in the struggle with England (the Peace of Amiens), Napoleon in 1802 dispatched an army of 30,000 to the West Indies. The commanding general, Victor Emmanuel Leclerc, was instructed to subdue the slave rebellion and then proceed to New Orleans where he was to take control of Louisiana. Leclerc's army suffered heavy losses in its contest with Toussaint, and it was further decimated by a plague of yellow fever. By September 1802, it was down to four thousand effective soldiers, and Leclerc himself was dead.

When news of this disaster reached Napoleon's ears, the First Consul realized that his imperial dreams had vanished. It would now be impossible to occupy New Orleans and hold it against an Anglo-American attack. Moreover, he anticipated a renewal of the struggle with England, and in that event New Orleans was a hostage to the British navy. In chronic need of funds to feed his war machine, Napoleon decided to sell his New World real estate to the Americans. In early 1803, he summoned Livingston and offered to sell, not only New Orleans, but all of Louisiana (after all, the Mississippi basin was useless without the mouth of the river) for $15 million. Lacking authority to buy an empire, Livingston rejected the offer.

In the fall of 1802, Spanish authorities in New Orleans, in retaliation for American abuses of their treaty privileges, closed the Mississippi River to American traffic. War fever swept across the West, and Congress contemplated resolutions that would authorize the president to seize New Orleans. To allay the war sentiment and put new pressure on France, Jefferson sent to Paris a special commissioner to aid Livingston. His choice was James Monroe, trusted associate from Virginia, and an old friend of the French. Monroe was instructed to purchase New Orleans and West Florida, paying no more than $10 million, or at least secure the use of the Mississippi if Napoleon proved unwilling to sell out. Failing both, he was to journey to London and sign a defensive alliance with the British. By the time Monroe arrived in Paris in April 1803, Livingston was beginning to sense the opportunity in Napoleon's offer. He was on the verge of coming to terms with the French minister of finance, Marbois, and Monroe promptly ratified their agreements. The treaty, signed in May, gave the United States New Orleans and the Louisiana territory, from the Mississippi River to the Rocky Mountains, for $15 million. That worked out to approximately thirteen cents an acre.

Despite the fact that the American commissioners had violated their instructions (told to buy the Gulf Coast, they bought the Great Plains instead and paid 50 percent more than authorized), President Jefferson leapt at the opportunity to double the size of the nation. What concerned him more than the price was the legality of the agreement. A quick check of the Constitution revealed that there was indeed no delegated power given the federal government to buy an empire. Jefferson himself drafted a tentative amendment that would retroactively legalize the purchase; but he was dissuaded from the idea by his cabinet members, who pointed out that there were no limitations on the government's treaty-making power under the Constitution.

In the Senate debate on ratification both sides agreed with this view; the only contest was over the disposition of the territory. Federalists, fearing the further dilution of New England influence, demanded that it be governed as a permanent colony. Since it was not part of the original constitutional compact, they argued that no new states could be created in the region without the

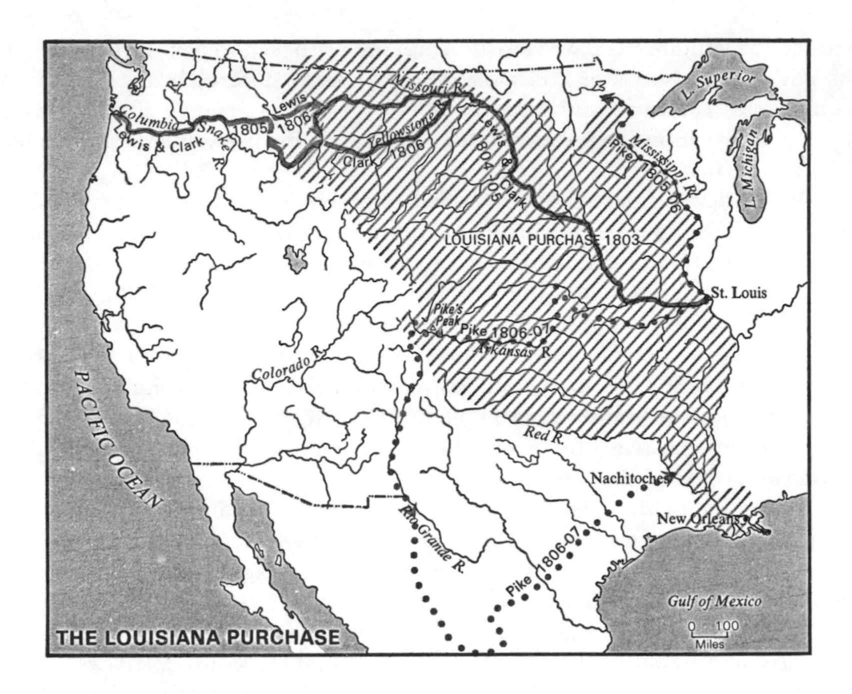

consent of the original thirteen. The Republican majority rejected this bit of legal sophistry, ratified the treaty, and then erected the southernmost part of the purchase into the Orleans Territory, leaving the remainder a military district under the general supervision of the Indiana Territory. This scene of Federalists appealing to states' rights and Republicans exercising broad constitutional powers might seem odd in view of their relative political positions just a few years before. But it illustrates the fact that the doctrine of states' rights, far from being an eternal verity, is more often a defense mechanism for those who are out of power, to be shed like a well-worn coat when the "outs" become the "ins."

Exploration of Louisiana

The first problem presented by the Louisiana Purchase was what had the United States bought—mountains, deserts, plains, or trackless forests? Jefferson had long evidenced an interest in the scientific exploration of the continent. While serving as minister to France in the 1780s he had inspired an eccentric American adventurer named John Ledyard to explore the Pacific Northwest by way of Siberia. Reinforced with letters from Jefferson and Lafayette, Ledyard proceeded eastward across Russia, and nearly reached the Kamchatka peninsula before being intercepted by agents of Empress Catherine.

Shortly after Jefferson's inauguration as president, he formed plans with his plantation neighbor and private secretary, Meriwether Lewis, to conduct an expedition up the Missouri River and across the mountains. Besides the gathering of scientific data, the object of the expedition in Jefferson's mind was to find "the most direct and practicable water communication across this continent, for the purposes of commerce." The president asked Congress to appropriate funds in January 1803, and commissioned Lewis a captain in the army. The subsequent purchase of the region provided a color of legitimacy to what otherwise might have been a military invasion of French soil. Lieutenant William Clark (younger brother of George Rogers Clark) was made second-in-command, and the expedition, recruited from the ranks of the army, was organized at St. Louis in the winter of 1803–04.

In May 1804, a total of forty-five soldiers departed St. Louis in two keelboats and a batteau, and for the next four months they sailed, rowed, poled, and even waded their vessels up the Missouri River. Well-planned and organized, the expedition fed itself by sending horsemen to hunt deer and buffalo along the river bank, and the military discipline with which it functioned intimidated even the belligerent Sioux. They spent the winter at the main village of the Mandan Indians (present-day Bismarck, North Dakota), a comparatively sedentary agricultural tribe. There they encountered Sacajawea, or "Bird Woman," a captive of the Mandans who had been kidnapped from one of the mountain tribes. Though burdened with an infant (fathered by the expedition's French interpreter), she proved to be a durable and uncomplaining guide when the expedition reached the mountains the following summer. Sacajawea turned out to be the sister of the chief of one of the mountain clans, and her relatives provided the expedition with guides in crossing the rugged Bitteroot Mountains of southern Idaho. At the village of the Nez Perce on the Snake River west of the Continental Divide, they left their horses and borrowed canoes for the journey down the Snake and the Columbia.

The expedition arrived at last at the mouth of the Columbia River on November 7, 1805. There they built a rude fort to protect their belongings from the local Clatsop tribe, who were mischievous thieves, and settled in for the winter. They traded with Native Americans for food (mostly beaver and dog meat, which Lewis concluded was better than roast beef) and weathered their second winter. The following spring they found the Columbia too rapid for paddling, so they returned on foot to the Nez Perce villages where they recovered their horses. At the Continental Divide they divided forces to cover more territory, Lewis returning by the original route and Clark heading south to explore the Yellowstone. Reassembling at the Mandan village in midsummer, they swept down the Missouri and were back in St. Louis by September 1806, having covered nearly three thousand miles in two and a half years. It was a feat virtually without parallel in the history of exploration. In the whole voyage of hardship and danger among nomadic Indians, only one person died (an Indian killed by Lewis for stealing horses). And they returned with priceless geographical and scientific information about the interior of the continent. Jefferson personally experimented with the Indian corn sent home by the explorers, filed the Native American vocabularies that Lewis had compiled in his library, and mounted the great horns of an elk in the entrance hall at Monticello. The rest of the specimens were sent on to scientists in Philadelphia.

The other important early explorations of the Louisiana Purchase were undertaken by an army lieutenant, Zebulon Montgomery Pike, "the lost pathfinder." In the fall of 1805, Pike was ordered by the military commander of Louisiana, General James Wilkinson, to explore the headwaters of the Mississippi. Knowing the source of the Mississippi was important, for it would mark the boundary between the United States and British Canada west of Lake Superior. Pike departed at the wrong time of year for tours of northern Minnesota, and he became lost in the maze of lakes and snowbound forests. He would have starved or frozen to death had he not been rescued by British fur trappers, who were interloping on American soil.

Undismayed by this failure, General Wilkinson gave his young lieutenant a few months to rest and then dispatched him in August 1806, on another expedition—this time to explore the headwaters of the Arkansas River. The assignment coincided with a sharp clash in Spanish-American relations that verged on war, and Pike's purpose may have been to investigate Spanish garrisons in New Mexico. One scholar has suggested that the expedition might be called "Pike's Peek." After meandering across Kansas, Pike struck the Arkansas near present-day Dodge City and followed the river westward to its source in the mountains of southern Colorado.

At this point the expedition becomes shrouded in mystery, for Pike unaccountably turned southwestward to the headwaters of the Rio Grande. An explorer of Pike's experience must have known that he was on waters that flowed directly into the gulf and were therefore not part of American Louisiana. He was subsequently found by Spanish soldiers wandering around in the desert near Santa Fe. (Was he lost again or was it espionage?) The Spanish conducted him across Texas to the Louisiana frontier, where he was released to a mildly embarrassed General Wilkinson. Pike subsequently published memoirs of his deeds and earned a contemporary fame that overshadowed even that of Lewis and Clark. Whatever the motives for his expedition, it marked the first real white penetration of the southern Rockies; and the map he drew of his travels proved useful some years later when the trail to Santa Fe was opened.

The West Florida Controversy

The major diplomatic result of the Louisiana Purchase was a conflict with Spain that preoccupied the Jefferson administration for the next few years. The problem originated in the undefined boundaries of Louisiana. The treaty defined the purchase as "Louisiana with the same extent as it now has in the hands of Spain, and that it had when France possessed it." But these were two different things. As part of the old French empire prior to 1763 Louisiana embraced the entire Mississippi basin, from the Appalachians to the Rockies. By the peace settlement of that year the territory east of the Mississippi was surrendered to Britain, and the area west of the Mississippi went to Spain. At the same time Britain acquired Florida from Spain, and subsequently united East Florida (which had been Spanish) to West Florida (which had been French, part of Louisiana) into one colony; then in 1783 Britain was forced to surrender both the Floridas to Spain. The question was this: was West Florida included in the

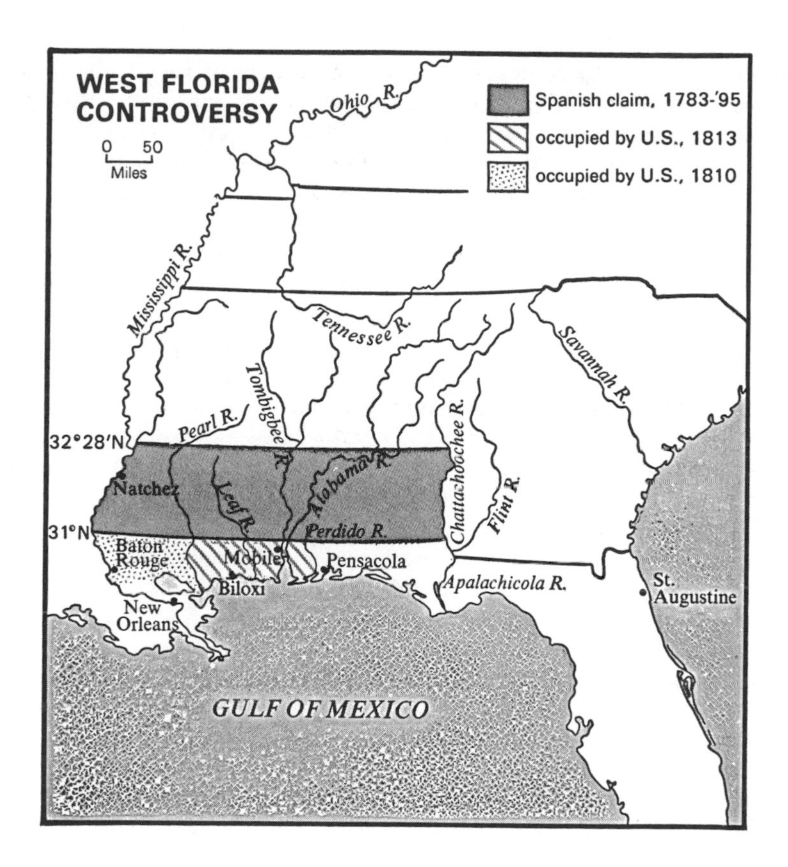

retrocession of Louisiana to France in 1800, and, if so, did the United States purchase it in 1803?

The question was important, for the Gulf Coast, which held the commercial key to the American South, was more important at the time than the whole expanse of grassland west of the Mississippi. Monroe and Livingston were both in France with orders to buy it if possible, and they naturally asked foreign minister Talleyrand if West Florida was included in the Louisiana deal. Talleyrand, hoping to keep Spain dependent upon France in Europe by causing friction between Spain and the United States in the New World, replied enigmatically: "Gentlemen, you have made a noble bargain for yourselves, and I suppose you will make the most of it." Taking the hint, Monroe and Livingston informed the president that they considered West Florida part of the Louisiana Purchase. Jefferson and Madison agreed, and it became official administration policy that West Florida was American soil, although that stance was coupled with periodic offers to buy it from Spain.

Surrounded by apparent duplicity, Spain reacted violently. The Spanish regarded the Louisiana Purchase as illegal, since their agreement with Napoleon stipulated that it was not to be sold, and they had no intention of surrendering West Florida. Encouraged by the French, they began plundering American commerce on the high seas, and the deterioration in Spanish-American relations was punctuated by periodic armed conflicts on both the West Florida and the Texas frontiers. In the summer of 1805, Napoleon, motivated by his chronic need for funds, decided to fish in the troubled West Florida waters. Summoning the American minister (Livingston had been replaced in Paris by his New York brother-in-law, John Armstrong, while Monroe had gone to the London embassy), Napoleon suggested that if the United States would submit its dispute with Spain to his arbitration, he would induce his Spanish ally to part with West Florida and a portion of Texas for $10 million. The sum coincided with the amount which Spain annually paid to France as a war subsidy, and it was clear that the money would wind up in French coffers. Armstrong noted that French speculators in American securities were already swarming around the foreign office.

Even though it might have seemed that Napoleon was beginning to make a habit of selling Spanish real estate, Jefferson and Madison decided to accept the offer. Recognizing that such devious diplomacy required secrecy and speed, they formed a plan that was both ingenious and disingenuous. In his annual message of December 1805, the president sounded a highly belligerent note, reviewing the difficulties with Spain and requesting additional troops. Three days later he informed Congress secretly that the whole matter could be settled peacefully if the administration were given the means. When the House leader, John Randolph, called on the president to get the details, he was told that the administration needed $2 million as a starter.

Still smarting from the president's aloof stand in the Chase impeachment, Randolph flatly refused to participate in any such underhanded scheme. To him the whole arrangement had the unsavory aroma of the XYZ Affair; it smacked of the speculative chicanery of Federalism. Already unhappy with Jefferson's compromises in failing to amend the Constitution or dismiss Federalist officeholders, Randolph viewed this plot as final evidence that the president had lost his out-of-power purity. In addition, Randolph had become suspicious of executive influence in Congress. Jefferson enjoyed excellent relations with Congress; he entertained a handful of congressmen at dinner on an average of three nights a week when Congress was in session. Jefferson on occasion personally drafted laws that he desired; and, members of his cabinet frequently testified before congressional committees. Jefferson exerted more power over Congress than either his predecessors or his immediate successors, and it was precisely this that made Randolph suspicious. He broke with the president and caused the first serious rift in the ranks of the Republican party.

Although Randolph carried into opposition only a dozen southern Republicans (nicknamed "Tertium Quids," though they hardly constituted a third party), the administration ranks generally held firm, and the Two Million Act was passed in the spring of 1806. Randolph's schism, however, doomed for the moment the effort to acquire West Florida. By the time Congress appropriated the money, Napoleon had departed for a campaign in central Europe and had lost all interest in Florida.

The Gulf Coast was subsequently acquired, not by bribery, but by revolution. Southern pioneers, attracted by the rich coastal plain, moved into West Florida in increasing numbers after 1806. Becoming unhappy with the corrupt and inefficient rule provided by the Spanish military garrisons, they rebelled in the summer of 1810 and captured the arsenal at Baton Rouge. President Madison promptly ordered the American army to occupy the forts at Mobile and Baton Rouge, on the pretext that West Florida had been American soil all along. Spain, distracted by her own civil war and the presence of a British army under Wellington, was helpless to intervene. Congress then calmly added the Baton Rouge region to the Orleans Territory (which became the state of Louisiana in 1812) and divided the remainder of West Florida between the Alabama and Mississippi territories. Aggressive nationalism had triumphed.

The Conspiracy of Aaron Burr

While the West Florida controversy was the primary problem created by the Louisiana Purchase in the field of foreign affairs, its main domestic aftermath was the conspiracy of Aaron Burr. This plot was the climax of a long train of "Spanish intrigues" in the Southwest dating back to the 1780s. The initial leader of the "Spanish conspiracy" was a merchant of Louisville, Kentucky, named James Wilkinson, who had served as Washington's clothier general in the Revolution (the same Wilkinson who would later be Zebulon Pike's patron). In 1787, Wilkinson negotiated a contract with Spanish officials in New Orleans that gave him a monopoly on Kentucky tobacco shipped out through the port. Wilkinson was also provided an annual pension of $2,000 a year, and in return he was to further the Spanish interest in a secession of the American Southwest. Despite this favorable agreement, he went bankrupt and returned to a military career. During the war scare of 1798, Hamilton promoted him to the rank of major general and gave him command of the Southwest frontier (Spain promptly increased his secret pension to $16,000). This was the position he held when Jefferson took office. As military commander of the western army, Wilkinson would be a key figure in any conspiracy.

Despite Wilkinson's efforts, the secessionist intrigues evaporated in the 1790s on the admission of Kentucky and Tennessee as states, but the acquisition of Louisiana added a new problem. The Creole population of Louisiana (persons of French or Spanish descent) feared for the survival of their laws, customs, and religion under American rule. Their discontent was given political voice by a wealthy New Orleans merchant, Daniel Clark, who was a political foe of the governor of the Orleans Territory, William C. C. Claiborne. Clark helped the Creoles to form a secret society called the Mexican Association, ostensibly for the conquest of northern Mexico; but because of the Creole dissatisfaction it also had secessionist undertones. For several years after the Louisiana Purchase these various elements of intrigue simmered under the surface. The catalyst for a full-blown conspiracy was Aaron Burr.

Burr's failure to withdraw from the electoral contest with Jefferson in 1800 was the beginning of the end of his political career. Jefferson thereafter distrusted him and dispensed his political favors on Burr's archrivals in New York Republican politics, Clinton and Livingston. In the presidential election of 1804, Jefferson dropped Burr in favor of George Clinton as his running mate.

Seeking to recoup his political fortunes, Burr ran for governor of New York in 1804. To win he needed Federalist support, but this was frustrated by the opposition of his old enemy, Alexander Hamilton. Seizing upon Hamilton's criticism as a pretext, Burr challenged the ex-secretary to a duel. The two fought across the Hudson River at Weehawken, New Jersey, and Hamilton died of the wound he received. Public outrage over this act finished what was left of Burr's political career. In addition, he was forced to flee from possible arrest since dueling was illegal in both New York and New Jersey.

In Philadelphia, Burr encountered General James Wilkinson, who was back East visiting relatives. Though no one knows for sure, the first definite plans for the conspiracy seem to have been formulated at this meeting. It was apparently an open-ended plan that might have taken any of several directions. Under cover of the Spanish crisis over West Florida, they might seize Texas and northern Mexico. If western discontent seemed ripe, they might even be able to sever the Union, establishing an empire that extended from the Ohio River to the Rio Grande. The following winter Burr, though a "lame duck" vice president, persuaded Jefferson to appoint Wilkinson governor of the Louisiana Territory, thereby giving the general civil as well as military authority west of the Mississippi.

The primary requisites for a successful conspiracy were foreign aid and military opportunity. Neither materialized. On leaving office in March 1805, Burr visited the British ambassador, Anthony Merry, to request money and warships. Merry, who detested Americans in general and Jefferson in particular, expressed interest in the scheme; but, he naturally demanded time to consult London before he committed the British government to an intrigue to divide the United States. Communications with London would take months. In the meantime Burr departed on a tour of the West, visiting prominent politicians in Ohio, Kentucky, and Tennessee (including Henry Clay and Andrew Jackson) who naturally welcomed such a prominent figure as a former vice president. In New Orleans, he held a series of meetings with leaders of the discontented Creole faction before journeying back to St. Louis for another meeting with General Wilkinson.

Back in Washington in the fall of 1805, Burr received the disappointing news that the British government refused all aid to his plans. Simultaneously, Jefferson's decision to negotiate a purchase of West Florida cooled the crisis with Spain and deprived Burr of an excuse for military operations in the Southwest. Undaunted, Burr made a second tour of the West in the summer of 1806. From Pittsburgh in July, he sent a coded letter to Wilkinson which informed the general untruthfully that British naval support was on its way to New Orleans, and he himself was proceeding down-river with men and supplies.

The center of Burr's operations that summer was an island in the Ohio River owned by an Irish immigrant, Herman Blennerhassett, whom Burr had met the previous year. Blennerhassett was brought into the conspiracy and induced to collect men and supplies for a downriver expedition, while Burr departed for Kentucky to sign up additional recruits. The recruits were apparently told only that they were going to settle newly opened lands in Texas. Burr maintained, to the end of his life, that this was the only purpose of his expedition.

In the meantime, President Jefferson, warned by repeated rumors of a revival of the "Spanish intrigue" in the West, dispatched his private secretary, John Graham, to shadow Burr. After months of gathering information, this agent awakened the governor of Ohio to the suspicious preparations on Blennerhassett's island; and, in early December the governor ordered the state militia to raid the place. Blennerhassett escaped down the Ohio River with only one boatload of men and provisions.

General Wilkinson received Burr's July letter in September while he was on the Texas frontier carrying out the president's orders for a military demonstration against the Spanish. The general worked out a truce with the Spanish commander, and then covered his tracks by writing directly to the president. Wilkinson, after all, had little to gain from Burr's conspiracy and much to lose; by betraying Burr he could portray himself as savior of the Union and simultaneously reward his Spanish paymasters by thwarting an attack on Mexico. His letter to Jefferson, written on October 21, warned the president of an impending attack on Mexico, and he enclosed Burr's coded letter of July, carefully edited to omit all passages that incriminated himself. He then hastened to New Orleans where he declared martial law and arrested all the prominent leaders of the disaffected Creole element. All fronts secured, Wilkinson sat back to wait for the unsuspecting Burr to float downriver into his clutches.

President Jefferson's attitude, throughout a year of rumors and suspicions, was one of delay. Confident in the loyalty of the western people, Jefferson was evidently willing to give Burr enough rope to hang himself. Except for sending his secretary west to investigate, he did nothing until he received Wilkinson's letter on November 25. This was the first official word of a conspiracy from the military commander on the spot; and, the president had no choice but to issue a proclamation directing federal officials to arrest anyone conspiring to attack Spanish territory. Wilkinson had not specifically mentioned Burr, so neither did the president.

After leaving Blennerhassett's island, Burr's activities were hampered by rising suspicions in the West. A Kentucky grand jury investigated him, but when his attorney Henry Clay pointed out that he had broken no law, he was released. Burr then went to Nashville, Tennessee, where he gathered two boatloads of men and sailed down the Cumberland River for a rendezvous with Blennerhassett. The party stopped at Natchez early in January where Burr saw a newspaper containing the president's proclamation of November 27. Realizing that he had been betrayed, Burr surrendered to authorities of the Mississippi Territory, was released because he had done nothing illegal there, and started overland toward Florida disguised as a river boatman. Near Mobile, Alabama, he was recognized by an army lieutenant, arrested, and shipped back east for trial.

Burr was tried before the federal circuit court meeting in Richmond, Virginia, Chief Justice John Marshall presiding. The southern circuit had jurisdiction of the case because the locus of the conspiracy, Blennerhassett's island, was in Virginia. A grand jury, headed by Jefferson's foremost critic, John Randolph, assembled in May 1807 to hear testimony from the government's star witness, James Wilkinson. Under examination from Burr's shrewd defense counsel, the general was forced to admit that he had deleted parts of Burr's letter before sending it to the president and that the code between him and Burr was devised as early as 1794. The grand jury came within a few votes of indicting the government witness himself, and then voted to indict Burr and Blennerhassett for treason. When the trial opened on August 3, the president took an active part, maintaining almost daily communication with the prosecuting attorney and enclosing signed pardons for anyone willing to turn state's evidence. After his long procrastination amidst persistent rumors of conspiracy in the previous year, Jefferson's zeal for a conviction seems untimely at best, revengeful at worst.

The crime of treason as defined by the Constitution requires two witnesses to the same "overt act." The intention of the Framers was clearly to make conviction for treason difficult, for the crime had been a political weapon throughout much of English history, wielded by those in power against their enemies. After taking testimony for nearly a month, John Marshall read his opinion on August 31. Interpreting the key phrases in the Constitution as narrowly as possible, Marshall ruled that the mere assemblage of men, or the inoperative intention to divide the Union did not constitute an "overt act" of treason. Moreover, since Burr was not present on Blennerhassett's island during the preparations for the expedition, no two of the government's witnesses could testify to seeing him at the same moment, and Marshall held that he could not be there by "constructive presence." Since this ruling disposed of much of the testimony for the prosecution, the government dropped the case.

A free man, Burr departed for Europe, returning in 1810 to take up the practice of law in New York. Although the preponderance of historical evidence suggests that Burr and Wilkinson (who retained his rank and military position) were guilty of complicity in a plot, either to attack Mexico or divide the Union or perhaps both, Marshall's insistence on a strict interpretation of the Constitution seems a healthy one, for it removed treason from the realm of politics and preserved the fundamental right of Americans to voice opposition to the government.

Neutral Rights

The war which the United States declared on Great Britain in June 1812, was a direct product of the contest in Europe; it is safe to say that had the Napoleonic wars in Europe not existed, there would have been no War of 1812. Ever since the European war broke out in 1793 the United States had gingerly trod the tightrope of neutrality; but as the foreign war intensified, it became increasingly difficult to do so. Engaged in a mortal struggle, England and France both trampled on American rights and infringed the nation's sovereignty. Had Americans ignored these incursions (as the Federalists, for instance, desired), war with Britain might have been avoided. But adolescent nations have to prove themselves; they are often willing to fight to win the respect they feel they deserve. The Madison administration did everything it could to gain respect for the nation's rights, but after a long train of humiliations at the hands of both belligerents, it struck back. It ultimately concluded, as one Virginian expressed it, that "War alone can furnish a remedy . . . for insufferable insults daily heaped upon us by the enemy."

The year 1805 marked the end of the decade of relative Anglo-American goodwill that followed the Jay Treaty. In that year the war in Europe underwent a subtle but significant change. Napoleon embarked upon a magnificent campaign in central Europe which ultimately crushed the Third Coalition of monarchies raised up by British diplomacy. In October 1805, Britain thwarted a serious invasion threat by smashing the combined French and Spanish fleets off Cape Trafalgar. With England supreme on the sea and Napoleon impregnable on the Continent, the war for the time being settled down into a gigantic economic squeeze, and in the middle was the neutral United States, helplessly watching its ships seized by both sides.

Napoleon seized as many American vessels as the British did, but Americans directed most of their wrath at Britain. Most French seizures occurred in French ports, while Britain interfered with our commerce on the high seas in apparent violation of international law. In addition, Americans had special grievances against the British, the oldest of which was impressment.

Chronically short of men, the Royal Navy had long practiced a crude form of military conscription by sending "press gangs" through the streets of British seaports, kidnapping sailors, and the practice even extended to merchant vessels on the high seas. Because of wretched pay and low morale, a sizable portion of the crew went over the side whenever a British man o' war put into a foreign port, and many of these deserters wound up in the American merchant service where pay and working conditions were better. Indeed, it has been estimated that between one-half and one-third of America's merchant fleet was manned by foreign, mostly British, seamen. Without the deserters America's trade would have been crippled. The quarrel over impressment involved economics as well as national honor.

To recover these men, British captains adopted the practice of stopping American vessels on the sea, mustering the crew, and seizing suspected Englishmen. Though a slap at American sovereignty, the recovery of deserters alone might have been tolerable, but careless British officers dragged many native-born, as well as naturalized, Americans into the Royal Navy (a common newspaper estimate was six thousand by 1806). Not only did this practice endanger the lives of Americans, but it humiliated the government, which found itself helpless to protect its own citizens on the high seas. Though intensified after the war in Europe resumed in 1803, the problem of impressment remained a latent grievance, a source of continual diplomatic wrangling, but not an immediate cause for war.

Of more immediate consequence were the orders-in-council, which sought to employ British naval power to starve the French by blockade. This practice too dated from the beginning of the war, but it was vastly extended when Napoleon gained control of Spain, the Netherlands, and northern Germany. By an order-in-council of 1806, the British blockade was expanded to include the entire northwest coast of Europe, from Denmark to Brittany, though it was actually enforced only in the zone between the Seine River and Ostend. International law permitted blockades in time of war, provided each blockaded port was actually invested by ships. With respect to American traffic British captains found it easier to hover off American ports, stopping outgoing vessels and inspecting their papers to determine whether they were destined for blockaded ports. They then seized all "contraband" (which the British expanded to include food and raw materials, as well as munitions of war) and sometimes the vessel itself. Secretary of State Madison denounced this practice as a "paper blockade" which violated the strictures of international law. Moreover, the practice of search and seizure of American cargoes on the high seas was as much an affront to American sensitivities as the problem of impressment.

The British stranglehold on the Atlantic sea lanes, moreover, induced Napoleon to retaliate. In Napoleon's mind, Britain had to trade or die, and because much of Britain's trade was with the continent of Europe, he sought to cut Britain off in hopes of crushing its economy. His Berlin Decree of 1806 imposed a French blockade on Britain, to be enforced by seizing any neutral ship that stopped in England before coming to a Continental port. The British countered that with an order-in-council of November 1807, which required all neutral vessels destined for a Continental port to stop in England first. Napoleon promptly responded with his Milan Decree, which ordered the seizure of any neutral vessel which even submitted to a British search on the high seas. Thus no matter what American captains did they were liable to seizure. Even so, Americans saw a difference between Napoleon's confiscations, which occurred in French ports, and British seizures on the high seas, which were a flagrant violation of American rights.

It can be argued, of course, that Britain was struggling for its very existence. After the collapse of its allies on the Continent, Britain stood alone, the last bastion opposing the imperial ambitions of Napoleon, and the orders-in-council were its only available weapon. In such circumstances, the anger of a few impotent neutrals seemed a small price to pay. But less justified than the orders-in-council, and more selfish, was Britain's desire to retain a monopoly of the world's carrying trade. Throughout the eighteenth century, Britain had traditionally financed its wars by expanding its trade. When the Royal Navy cut off France and Spain from their New World empires, the British merchant fleet moved into the vacuum, and in the course of the eighteenth century became the world's carrier.

In the Napoleonic Wars, Britain was dismayed to find American ship captains threatening the British monopoly by offering cheaper rates and better service. It was with the dual purpose of depriving France of West Indian products and regaining the imperial trade for itself that Britain invoked the Rule of 1756, which sought to exclude American ships from the French and Spanish islands. Americans circumvented this regulation by bringing French and Spanish products to an American port and paying customs duties before reexporting them to the Continent. Ironically, it was mostly Republican merchants, such as the Crowninshields of Salem, who pioneered this trade. Federalists generally adhered to the traditional transatlantic trade with Britain, a trade with which

Britain did not interfere. The blend of politics and commerce was an explosive one indeed when Britain turned its attention to the "indirect trade."

The reexport trade was held legal by a British prize court in 1800, but the court reversed itself five years later in a decision involving the American ship *Essex*. The *Essex* had left Spain with a cargo destined for Cuba, and it had stopped and paid nominal duties in the United States before it was halted by a British warship. The prize court declared it to be in violation of the Rule of 1756 and ordered it condemned. With orders to enforce the *Essex* decision in the fall of 1805, the Royal Navy seized over two hundred American vessels found carrying French cargoes in the West Indies. This action precipitated the chain of events that led to war.

Eschewing for the moment the possibility of war on the grounds that the nation was unprepared, Jefferson and Madison decided to make a last effort at negotiation. To aid Monroe in London, they nominated a special emissary, a Maryland lawyer named William Pinkney. Secretary of State Madison instructed Pinkney to secure an agreement on impressment and a modification of the *Essex* decision that would permit Americans to engage in the colonial reexport trade. The principle which Madison prescribed was that neutrals ought to be free to enter any port that was not under effective blockade and trade in any goods except military contraband. Madison also desired some restraints on British cruisers which hovered off the American coasts inspecting cargoes and impressing seamen. This particular issue came to the fore only a few weeks earlier when the British frigate *Leander,* hovering at the entrance to New York harbor, fired a "warning" shot that hit an American vessel and killed a sailor.

While Pinkney was at sea, Congress decided to give him some bargaining leverage in the form of commercial retaliation. Though the administration seemed indifferent on the subject, various proposals were introduced and debated in the spring of 1806. After John Randolph's defection there was no effective leader in the House, and without administration guidance Congress floundered in a morass of factional bickering. Jefferson and Madison had no interest in a weak measure of coercion, and Congress had no stomach for a strong one. What finally emerged actually looked more like a bill to foster American manufactures. The Nonimportation Act of 1806 prohibited the import of a select list of British manufactured goods beginning on November 15, unless Britain came to terms in the meantime. Randolph, who had denounced the administration for catering to the interests of northern merchants, scornfully called it "A milk and water bill, a dose of chicken broth to be taken nine months hence."

It is doubtful that any form of coercion would have intimidated Britain at this juncture, but Monroe and Pinkney could well have used a weapon of some kind. They found the British still basking in the afterglow of Trafalgar and unwilling to budge. Their one hope was Charles James Fox, a pro-American Whig, who became prime minister on the death of Pitt in January 1806. But that glimmer vanished when Fox died in September. He was succeeded by a coalition misnamed "the ministry of all talents," which had neither the wit to be accommodating nor the strength in Parliament to offer concessions. As a result, Monroe and Pinkney had to ignore their instructions in order to secure any agreement at all. The treaty they signed in December 1806, made no mention of impressment; it did, however, permit the reexport trade in West Indian cargoes provided the goods paid a 2 percent customs duty in an American port before being shipped to Europe. In return, the United States would agree not to discriminate against British commerce for ten years.

Jefferson and Madison were dismayed with the result. In return for a niggling concession on the West Indian trade they had to surrender their trump card, the threat of commercial retaliation, for a decade. And the treaty ignored the most humiliating circumstance of all—the harassment of American commerce and the kidnapping of American seamen within sight of our own shores. It was not the fault of Monroe and Pinkney; they simply had nothing to offer that Britain wanted. Jefferson still felt that an agreement of this sort was worse than none at all. He did not even submit it to the Senate for ratification.

The Embargo Experiment

A few months later, Anglo-American relations took a decided turn for the worse as a result of the *Chesapeake* incident. The *Chesapeake* was a thirty-eight-gun frigate built by the Adams administration and decommissioned by the Jeffersonians. In the spring of 1807, the vessel was brought back into service as a result of the deteriorating international situation; and, it was being fitted out in the port of Norfolk, Virginia. Lying in the roadstead at the time was the British frigate *Leopard,* which had put in for food and water, and, as usual, the British crew had evaporated. Three of these deserters were accidentally signed on to the crew of the *Chesapeake,* and feeling secure in the American navy they even insulted their former British officers on the streets of the city. When the *Chesapeake* departed on a "shakedown" cruise on June 22, the *Leopard* followed her out of the harbor. At sea the *Leopard* came up to the American vessel and demanded to board. When the American captain, who had not even opened his gunports, refused, the *Leopard* proceeded to fire into the American ship for ten minutes killing three and wounding twenty more before the *Chesapeake* could strike its flag. Officers of the *Leopard* then boarded the American warship took off four of its crew, hanged them from a yardarm, and sailed off into the blue, leaving the *Chesapeake* to limp back to Norfolk.

News of this outrage sent a shock wave of indignation the length of the continent. War seemed inevitable even to those who had sought peace at any price. Jefferson issued a proclamation banning British warships from American waters and summoned Congress into early session. His recommendation was an expansion of commercial retaliation in the form of an embargo, which would confine American vessels to port and out of enemy hands while the nation girded for war. Congress hastily passed the Embargo Act in December 1807, and authorized an increase in the regular army. It made no effort to improve the navy, however, for that institution remained anathema to southern Republicans despite its gallant behavior in the Tripolitan war. Old Republicans like John Randolph, and even Albert Gallatin, considered the navy an expensive toy which northern merchants would use to embroil the nation in trade wars.

When the Congress inquired about the condition of the navy, the secretary could count only two frigates and eight smaller vessels that were actually in service. The army, moreover, never reached its assigned limits. In the absence of an overt military threat, it was difficult to create an army of volunteers. As the months passed the war fever evaporated, and Congress dissolved into its normal routine of garrulous inactivity. Intended by Jefferson to be a prelude to war, the Embargo proved instead to be a safety valve that kept the peace.

Jefferson himself soon recognized this and evidently decided to make a virtue of it. By the spring of 1808, he was defending the Embargo as a weapon of peaceable coercion, an effort to win recognition of American rights by halting the flow of goods to both European belligerents. The disruption of American exports to the West Indies, Madison thought, would be particularly damaging because those islands were almost totally dependent on American foodstuffs. With its West Indian colonies in ruins, Britain would almost certainly come to terms.

In addition, Jefferson and Madison both realized that an incidental result of the Embargo would be the encouragement of American manufactures. The Embargo made them realize, so Madison informed William Pinkney, "that we are less unripe for manufacturing establishments than had been supposed." The experience, he added, was a warning to the nation "to lessen our dependence for supplies on foreign nations."

As an experiment in pacifism, the Embargo certainly had grand potential, and it might have worked had it lasted long enough. Within a year there were food riots in northern England, and textile mills in Lancashire stood idle for lack of raw cotton. British business classes were just beginning to put pressure on the government to remove the orders-in-council when the Embargo was repealed. Commercial retaliation as a diplomatic weapon required time to take full effect. Time the United States did not have because it suffered more under the Embargo than England did.

The sudden stoppage of all ocean commerce not only brought stagnation to the seaports, where ships rotted at the wharves, but it also brought a virtual halt to the nation's internal commerce. Because of the inadequate road system and the comparative cheapness of water borne freight, coasting schooners, hopping from port to port, carried most of the interstate shipments in the eastern part of the country. Yet even these had to be confined to port, lest they sneak off to the West Indies or Europe. Federalist New England opposed the policy from the beginning because it sacrificed its trade for a visionary scheme that had little prospect of success. Eastern merchants were willing to risk an occasional British seizure, and cared nothing for a handful of impressed sailors, because enormous profits could be made in their neutral trade. Faced with widespread evasion of the law, the government tightened its grip. The Enforcement Act passed in 1808 gave customs officials extensive powers of search and seizure in enforcing the law. Indeed, such arbitrary powers may well have infringed on the Fourth Amendment's protection against unreasonable searches and seizures, but the issue was never tested in the courts. Ironically, the possibility of a constitutional problem never occurred to either Jefferson or Madison. With equal vigor the administration ordered the army into action to suppress a flourishing overland trade between New England and Canada.

The South supported the Embargo out of loyalty to the president, but it actually suffered more than any other region. In both New England and the middle states smuggling relieved some of the economic impact of the Embargo, and a number of merchants shifted their capital investments to manufacturing, just as Madison had anticipated. In the North, the distress was largely confined to the importing merchants; the average citizen felt the squeeze but little. The South, on the other hand, was utterly dependent on a foreign market for its staples, and its plantation economy was subject to high fixed costs. Even when their output was rotting on the wharves, the slave labor force had to be fed and clothed.

By the time Congress returned in December 1808, opposition to the Embargo could be heard in every corner of the continent. The Enforcement Act, giving customs officials broad powers of search and seizure, severely strained Republican party loyalty. A few weeks later the defenders of the Embargo succumbed, and Congress voted to terminate it on March 3, 1809, Jefferson's last day in office. Total submission was unthinkable; however, and the nation still seemed unprepared for war, so Congress replaced the Embargo with a nonintercourse law, which prohibited commerce with Britain and France only and reopened relations with the rest of the world. In order to give the executive diplomatic leverage, it further provided that the president might restore trade with either European belligerent once it agreed to respect American rights.

The Road to War

James Madison had long been considered Jefferson's logical successor, and his election in 1808 was almost a foregone conclusion. Northern opposition to the Embargo, however, gave new life to the Federalist party. Although their candidate, Charles Cotesworth Pinckney, was a relic from the 1790s, the party was coming under younger, more imaginative leadership. Though they never succeeded in refurbishing the Federalists' popular image, these new leaders did develop strong local organizations in several states. The result was that, while Pinckney was soundly defeated in the presidential contest, the Federalists made substantial gains in Congress. They recaptured the Massachusetts delegation, which had been drifting into the Jeffersonian camp since 1804, and they made important gains in New York and New Jersey. Republicans still controlled both houses, but they could no longer afford to squabble among themselves.

Unhappily, they failed to realize it. During the election campaign Monroe mysteriously appeared on the stage as a potential third-party candidate. He was put forth by the Old Republicans, John Randolph and John Taylor of Caroline, on the grounds that he was a purer Republican than Madison (Monroe had been an Antifederalist in 1788). It was also a measure of opposition to the Embargo, for the Old Republicans felt that commercial retaliation catered to northern merchants at the expense of the South (even though New England merchants did not see it that way). Monroe, still smarting from the summary rejection of his treaty, cooperated with this intrigue, but made no effort to win public support. He picked up a few hundred Federalist votes in Virginia, but no electoral votes.

The disarray within the Virginia "dynasty" gave an opportunity for dissident Republicans in Congress to make trouble. One faction, dubbed "the invisibles," was led by Maryland Senator Samuel Smith, a wealthy merchant from Baltimore, and by Senator William B. Giles from Virginia. Hoping to win a voice in the new administration, they opened fire on its strongest member, Albert Gallatin. They got support from Senate Federalists, who were always willing to muddy Republican waters, and in order to secure confirmation of Gallatin's reappointment to the Treasury, Madison had to name the senator's younger brother, Robert Smith, to the State Department. Smith, however, turned out to be totally incompetent, and Madison was soon forced to take charge personally of diplomatic negotiations. In 1811, he fired Smith and replaced him with Monroe, who had insinuated himself back into the party fold. But the disunity of the administration continued right into the war. Madison lacked Jefferson's knack for consensual decision-making.

If Madison was dismayed over the internal brawling that wracked his party, he could at least take comfort in a sudden thaw in Anglo-American relations. Alarmed at the belligerence of America's reaction to the *Chesapeake* incident, British foreign minister George Canning authorized his minister in Washington, David Erskine, to offer reparations for the *Chesapeake* and a revocation of the orders-in-council, provided the president restored full commercial relations first. In contrast to his predecessors among British envoys, Erskine was a friendly young man with an American wife, and he was quite anxious to restore Anglo-American goodwill. He considered the matter of timing—that is, which side gave in first—inconsequential, and shortly after the inauguration he informed the president that his government was willing to abandon the orders-in-council. To Madison it was clearly a victory for the policy of economic coercion, and he promptly announced that, since Britain had agreed to respect American rights, the Nonintercourse Act would be suspended in June. Northern merchants joyfully readied their vessels.

In the meantime Canning came under heavy pressure in Parliament to retain the orders-in-council and adopt a firmer stance toward the United States. On the pretext that Erskine had violated his instructions by agreeing to a revocation of the orders prior to a restoration of commercial intercourse, Canning disavowed the Erskine agreement and recalled his ambassador. To replace Erskine in Washington, Canning chose a notoriously hardheaded diplomat, Francis James Jackson, who had earned a reputation for "gunboat diplomacy" by delivering an unacceptable ultimatum to the neutral Danes shortly before the British fleet bombarded Copenhagen in 1806. "Copenhagen" Jackson arrived in the fall of 1809 armed with instructions that accused the United States of bad faith, reopened the *Chesapeake* issue, and refused to discuss the orders-in-council until the United States gave in first. Madison soon discovered that Jackson had nothing new to offer, and in November he told the British minister to submit all further communications in writing. Such a procedure would also enable him to keep watch on his inept secretary of state. Assuming that this meant a break in relations, Jackson angrily departed for New England where he was widely entertained by the Federalists. He remained there for several months sending back reports to England that the president did not have the support of the American people.

The result of this diplomatic fiasco was a climate of mutual suspicion in which war sentiment steadily gained ground. Feeling that the gentle Erskine had been tricked, the British became convinced of Madison's duplicity; on the other hand, the American people were confused and bewildered by the contradictory British actions. Sending to the United States a man like "Copenhagen" Jackson was evidence to many that the British were spoiling for a fight. By the winter of 1809, a number of prominent Republican newspapers, such as the Richmond *Enquirer* and the Philadelphia *Aurora,* were calling for war. In Congress a small band of belligerents demanded increased military preparations and the convoy of American merchant vessels to protect them from British depredations.

The majority of Republicans in Congress, however, were not yet willing to abandon the system of commercial retaliation. The Nonintercourse Act was due to expire in the spring of 1810, and the House of Representatives accordingly appointed a select committee, headed by Nathaniel Macon of North Carolina, to devise a replacement. In January, Macon's committee reported a bill that was essentially a navigation act; it proposed to admit British and French goods provided they were carried in American ships. The idea was to keep up the semblance of commercial retaliation, but at the same time restore the importation of European goods to permit the bankrupt Treasury to earn some revenue from customs duties. The bill thus bore the handprint of Albert Gallatin. Passed by the House, Macon's bill was scuttled by the anti-Gallatin "invisibles" in the Senate.

Macon's committee accordingly went back to work, and in April it produced a new measure, which naturally became known as Macon's Bill Number Two. This act, which was mild enough to slip through both Houses, reversed the previous Nonintercourse Act. It repealed all measures of commercial retaliation, thereby restoring complete freedom of trade, and then it provided that should either England or France come to terms on American rights, the president was authorized to reinstate nonintercourse against the other. Macon's Bill represented the nadir of commercial retaliation, for it abandoned all restrictions on trade and laid American rights on the bargaining table, prostituted to the highest bidder.

Napoleon immediately sensed the opportunity presented by Macon's Bill. Lacking a navy to enforce his decrees on the high seas, he had little to lose by revoking them and much to gain from American gratitude. On August 5, 1810, the French foreign minister, the Duc de Cadore, presented a letter to the American minister in Paris announcing that Napoleon's decrees, insofar as they affected the United States, would be revoked the following November, "it being understood that the United States would revoke the nonintercourse act" and enforce her rights against England. There was the same problem of timing as in the earlier Erskine agreement, for Napoleon insisted that the United States cut off trade with England as a prior condition. President Madison nonetheless decided to accept the bargain because it gave him an opportunity to play off one European belligerent against the other. Restoration of trade with France would put increased pressure on England to modify the orders-in-council. In November, he issued a proclamation under the provisions of Macon's Bill announcing that the French decrees were revoked and that further trade with England would be discontinued, as of February 1, 1811. As it turned out, Napoleon deceived him, and France continued to seize American ships throughout the winter. The British, for their part, remained adamant, demanding proof that Napoleon had actually revoked his decrees. The main effect of Macon's Bill and Napoleon's sly maneuver, then, was to direct American anger at Britain. The nation had chosen its enemy.

These diplomatic maneuvers in the winter of 1810–11 occurred during the biennial congressional elections. This was the first opportunity for American voters to express their views since the repeal of the Embargo, and, at first blush, it seemed an electoral revolution. The House of Representatives experienced the largest turnover since the government began, involving more than a third of the membership. But the election was not a clear mandate for war. Much of the turnover appeared in northern delegations, where even Republicans were generally opposed to war and Federalists became apoplectic at the thought. The change in Congress was not in numbers but in quality, for the election brought onto the political stage a host of young, able Republicans—Henry Clay and Richard M. Johnson from Kentucky, Felix Grundy of Tennessee, and John C. Calhoun of South Carolina—who would dominate American politics for the next generation. Mostly in their late twenties or early thirties, these new men were too young to recall the political battles of the 1790s. They had little use for Jeffersonian doctrines of limited government, and they were impatient with the nation's pacifistic response to humiliation abroad. Though they numbered but a small fraction of the House, these young Republican nationalists were able to give voice to the growing sense of frustration among Americans; at long last they could provide the leadership that Congress so desperately needed. Even before the Twelfth Congress assembled in November 1811, events in the West gave a new push to American belligerence.

8

"Mr. Madison's War"

GOVERNOR WILLIAM HENRY HARRISON WATCHED THOUGHTFULLY as the band of Shawnee disappeared down the Wabash River, their warpaint and headdresses gleaming in the late summer sun. The year was 1811, and Harrison had just had a stormy interview with Tecumseh, a Shawnee who considered himself the spokesman for all the Ohio tribes. Tecumseh had organized a Native American alliance to resist further encroachments upon their land. After warning Harrison that another land cession would mean war, Tecumseh was departing for the South, where he hoped to persuade the Creeks and Cherokees to join his loose confederacy. His absence, Harrison decided, offered an excellent opportunity to nip the Native American resistance movement in the bud, and he began laying plans for an attack on Tecumseh's headquarters, the Prophet's Town on Tippecanoe Creek, some 150 miles up the Wabash from Vincennes. Such a sneak attack might be ethically dubious, but ethical rules were often suspended when white met red on the American frontier.

Governor Harrison was something of a novelty in the ragamuffin society of the Indiana Territory. For one thing he had a pedigree and a family coat of arms. His birthplace was the luxurious mansion of Berkeley plantation just below Richmond on the James River. His father, Benjamin Harrison, was a signer of the Declaration of Independence and had served as governor of Virginia after the Revolution. Young William Henry had been well grounded in the classics at Hampden-Sydney College, and he had no intention of losing his educational polish in the rough environment of Indiana. His plantation Grouseland at Vincennes housed the finest collection of Greek and Latin writers west of the mountains, and the governor laced his official correspondence with classical references and Latin citations. Indeed, Daniel Webster, to whom befell the job of editing "Old Tippecanoe's" inaugural address in 1841 boasted that he eradicated seventeen Roman proconsuls "dead as smelts" in one day.

But when it came to land acquisition classical-minded Virginians were just as greedy as any westerners. Harrison proved a willing agent for Jefferson's land policies, and both were under constant pressure from land-hungry frontiersmen. After Anthony Wayne's victory at Fallen Timbers in 1794 and the Indian cession of Ohio at Greenville, settlers poured into the region. The Land

Act of 1800, sponsored in Congress by Harrison as delegate from the Northwest Territory, was a further stimulus. It retained the comparatively high minimum price of two dollars an acre, set in 1796, but it lowered the minimum tract that could be purchased from 640 to 320 acres. Most important, though, it permitted a settler to buy on credit with only a 25 percent down payment. The government's earlier insistence on selling large tracts of land for cash had served only the interests of speculators, who were able to subdivide the tracts into farm-sized parcels and offer them to settlers on credit. After 1800, farmers were better able to deal directly with the government, and they flocked to the federal land offices in such numbers that Congress in 1804 reduced the minimum tract to 160 acres and doubled the number of land offices.

The government struggled rigorously to keep up with the tide of people. In 1800, the Indiana Territory was split off, and Ohio achieved statehood three years later. Native American cessions, the erection of territorial governments, and the rush of whites, all followed one another in such a confused jumble of pressures that no one was sure which came first. Harrison's Indiana empire gave birth to the Michigan Territory in 1805 and the Illinois Territory in 1809.

Jefferson's policy was to control and protect the tribes by careful federal supervision of their trade, while simultaneously obtaining the cession of their lands by treaty. Then he hoped by various expedients to persuade them to take up farming and thus ultimately incorporate them into Anglo-American society. The president informed one federal Indian agent that "the ultimate point of rest and happiness for them is to let our settlements and theirs meet and blend together and to intermix, and become one people." For a time after the purchase of Louisiana, Jefferson toyed with the idea of removing the Native Americans to his vacant empire west of the Mississippi, but when he broached the idea to delegations of visiting chiefs, it was received with understandable coolness. Unwilling to use coercion, Jefferson returned to his original idea of amalgamation.

The Native Americans had little interest in such a policy, preferring instead to keep their lands, their customs, and their tribal identity. It was soon apparent that white frontiersmen were equally opposed to it, for it meant sharing land with their red brethren. The Cherokees in Georgia and Tennessee were an early test for Jefferson's amalgamation theory, for they were already a comparatively settled agricultural people. A few of them even owned plantations and slaves. Like the Iroquois in the North, they prospered in the eighteenth century as middlemen in the fur and skin trade. After 1760, they remained at peace, adjusting to the advance of the frontier as best they could. Thus the government had no occasion, during or after the Revolution, to send in punitive expeditions to burn their towns and demand land cessions, as it did in the Northwest. As a result, the Cherokees remained in possession of a substantial part of northern Georgia, and when the state ceded its western claims (over Alabama and Mississippi) to the federal government in 1802, one of the conditions was that the federal government extinguish the Native American title.

The process of assimilation proved tedious and costly, though several million acres were obtained from Cherokees and Creeks by the end of Jefferson's administration. In the meantime, the European demand for cotton and high wartime prices whetted southern appetites for land. Georgians had no intention of assimilating Native Americans like immigrants; before long they were satisfied with nothing less than removal. When removal did come, during Andrew Jackson's presidency, Georgia and Alabama farmers moved in and confiscated their houses and even their furnishings. Some families departed for Oklahoma with only the clothing on their backs. Racial bias and greed doomed Jefferson's policy from the start.

It may well be that, given the attitudes of most Americans towards the tribes, the only alternative to Jefferson's policy of assimilation was destruction. Jefferson himself considered his concept to be one of "pure morality," but he was willing to tolerate a certain amount of deception in its implementation. Indeed, he even suggested privately to his secretary of war that it might be well if the Native Americans were encouraged to run into debt, for it would make them more amenable to selling their lands. Jefferson apparently felt Native American leaders were not always aware of their own best interests; and, if devious methods sometimes had to be used to bring them to agreement—the end justified the means. However, in the hands of a man like William Henry Harrison, whose avarice was tempered by neither justice nor humanitarianism, deception became part of the system. And whatever Jefferson's theoretical approach, he must bear the responsibility, for Governor Harrison was a Virginian, a Republican, and Jefferson's appointee.

In 1802, Harrison sought the first adjustment of the Greenville line. He summoned representatives of the Kickapoo and Delaware tribes to Vincennes and demanded that the line be extended west across southern Indiana. The excuse was that the lands along the Ohio River had been purchased from the tribes by the Wabash Land Company during the Revolution, though the company was no longer in existence. When the Native Americans refused, Harrison informed them that the lands already belonged to the United States and would be occupied by force if necessary. This threat, together with some bribes distributed among the chiefs, brought the desired cession. In the next few years these tactics became standard procedure for Harrison. He summoned annual conferences, some to discuss Native American grievances against white squatters; others to obtain punishment for alleged tribal misdeeds. The occasion did not matter, for each conference ended up with a land cession, obtained by a mixture of liquor, bribery, and the threat of force.

In 1803, the small and debilitated Kaskaskia tribe surrendered its title to the southern half of the Illinois Territory, and the following year the Sac and Fox gave up the rest of it, from the Rock River north to the Wisconsin River. When the tribes objected to this pressure, Harrison summoned representatives from all the tribes to Grouseland, filled their ears with Latin quotations and their stomachs with whiskey, and extracted another two million acres. By 1807, when Governor William Hull of Michigan Territory secured a gigantic cession in the Detroit area, the federal government had obtained control of southern Indiana, most of Illinois, southern Wisconsin, and eastern Michigan. In each case the price was a few thousand dollars in annual payments, to be divided up among the tribes affected.

By 1820, when the Native American cessions in the Northwest Territory were pretty well completed, the government had obtained about 190 million acres and paid the tribes about $2.5 million. Since the land was sold at auction with a minimum price of two dollars an acre, the government eventually made a profit of around $300 million. Since land sales were the major source of federal revenue under the Jeffersonians, Native Americans, in effect, financed the war debts left from both the Revolution and the War of 1812. Therein lay Jefferson's moral culpability. It was not possible to halt the advance of the frontier, and it was probably not politically feasible to leave the Indians in possession of large chunks of land in the eastern states. But he could have put restraints on agents like Harrison, and he could have paid the Indians a fair price for the land.

"The Greatest Indian"

Harrison's land policies met increasing resistance, however. The Ohio tribes had been retreating before the advance of white civilization for decades, but now they were encountering fierce enemies to the West—the Sioux across the Mississippi and the Chippewa in Wisconsin. They could move no farther; it was time to make a stand. All they needed was unity and leadership, and Tecumseh offered both. In the nomadic tribal culture, which lacked a written language, there were certain requisites for leadership, and Tecumseh possessed them all. In his early forties, he was a magnificent specimen of manhood. He stood five feet ten inches, which was about average among the Shawnees, but his carriage gave observers the impression of much greater height. He never allowed his picture to be painted, for portraiture was a whiteman's craft, but many who met him left written descriptions. His most remarkable feature was his face. He had heavy eyebrows, penetrating eyes, and glistening white teeth. His teeth attracted attention because most white men had badly stained teeth from chewing or smoking tobacco. He also dressed plainly, considering his rank and stature, in a suit of unadorned buckskin. His one concession to decoration was the feather of a white crane, which he wore in his hair on ceremonial occasions.

Besides his appearance, the feature that attracted most attention was his abstinence. Tecumseh practiced what he preached—that the Native American could survive only if he abjured every aspect of European culture, especially whiskey. And he was quite right; liquor was almost a disease among many tribes. There were some abstinent Native Americans, like Tecumseh, but there is no record of any temperate drinkers among them. Tecumseh's impressive bearing and stern code were prime qualities for leadership, but the crucial element was his oratory. In a society that lacked a written language, the art of persuasion was the art of speaking, and the tribal school where Tecumseh received his formal education trained him well. He also had a marvelous memory—even though he refused to sign the Greenville Treaty, he knew every clause by heart. These were among the qualities that made for leadership among the tribes, and Tecumseh, in addition, was able to attract followers because of his radical stance. His refusal to acquiesce in Wayne's terms at Greenville attracted much attention; he reinforced his position by settling in Greenville right on the treaty line. He remained there for two years until the influx of settlers began to suffocate him, whereupon he moved to the White River in central Indiana.

In the decade after Fallen Timbers, Tecumseh used his oratorical powers to defend individual Native Americans accused of crimes, to plead Indian grievances before territorial officials, and most of all to promote the idea of Indian unity. Most tribal confederations were religious as well as political, beginning with the great mystic Hiawatha, who brought the Iroquois nations together about the time of Columbus. Tecumseh's religious cement came from his brother, the Prophet. Laulewasika, or "Loud Mouth," lived a rather shiftless and dissolute life until 1805 when he had a series of revelations, apparently influenced by frontier evangelists. He adopted Tecumseh's ethical system, which stressed abstinence from liquor and rigid adherence to Native Amrican customs and dress. Adopting the techniques of the frontier camp meeting revivalists he roared and wept through his sermons, preaching an amalgam of millenialism and red supremacy. Converts began drifting into his camp on the White River until the place became crowded. Then, in 1806, another revelation induced him to move back to Greenville and build a meetinghouse right in the heart of white man's country.

Tecumseh and the Prophet were a powerful combination, and Governor Harrison soon began to fret. From his capital at Vincennes he sent runners in the spring of 1806 to all the Indiana tribes with a message designed to cast doubt on the Prophet's pretensions: "If he really is a prophet, ask him to cause the sun to stand still, the moon to alter its course, the rivers to cease to flow, or the dead to rise from their graves. If he does these things, you may then believe he has been sent from God." The governor should have known Native Americans better. The woodland tribes of the Northwest lived in a world of miracles; spirits soughed in the pines and barked in the thunder. For an enterprising mystic miracles were no problem, and the Prophet had guile enough to take advantage of the opportunity. He promptly announced that on June 16, 1806, at Greenville, Ohio, he would cause the sun to darken, and he sent his own runners out to gather a throng to witness the occasion.

Harrison later claimed that the British must have told the Prophet about the coming eclipse. But the governor was wont to blame the British whenever his own policies got him into trouble. There is no evidence that Tecumseh and his brother had any contact with British agents in Canada; indeed, Tecumseh was still smarting over the British betrayal at Fallen Timbers. Actually, any well-informed denizen of the woods was aware of the approaching event. Astronomers from Harvard College were setting up telescopes at Springfield, Illinois, and the federal government had an observatory at Burlington, Iowa. These preparations alerted the Prophet, and he merely took personal charge of the event. At 11:32 a.m. of the appointed day he pointed his finger at the sun, which promptly went dark; then with some mysterious incantations he persuaded the Great Spirit to remove his hand from the sun. It was quite a spectacle, witnessed by hundreds of believers.

What happened over the next two years was an evangelical revival and a bloody purge. The Prophet's fame spread the length of the Mississippi. Converts appeared in every tribe, even without a visitation from the seer himself.

The Chippewas built a log tabernacle in his name on the shores of Lake Superior, and the Osage on the faraway Missouri River obeyed his arbitrary injunction to kill their dogs and throw away their medicine pouches. Doubters and dissenters mysteriously died or disappeared. In many tribes the older chiefs and sachems who counseled cooperation with the whites were replaced by younger men infused with the Prophet's zeal and who looked to Tecumseh for leadership. What had started as a religious revival was taking on the characteristics of a holy war.

As converts gathered around the two brothers, their meetinghouse at Greenville became crowded, and they came constantly under white surveillance. It was time to move again; in the spring of 1808, they relocated back to central Indiana and built a new village on Tippecanoe Creek, which they named Prophet's Town. The site was given them by the Potawatomis, and when the Miamis objected that the land was really theirs, Tecumseh informed them that all tribal land was held in common. This was the concept on which he would build his edifice of tribal unity. God created the Old World for whites and the New World for Indians, he told his followers. Although he recognized that it would be impractical for the whites to return to Europe, he thought the Ohio River at least ought to be the boundary between the two cultures. Pending such a settlement, Native Americans must maintain their tribal integrity, avoiding any taint of white ways, and make no more land cessions, even if that meant war.

These were the doctrines that he preached as he toured the villages of the Sac and Fox, the Winnebagoes, and the Menominees in Illinois and Wisconsin during the fall of 1808. Everywhere he received pledges of support if war became necessary. On his return to Prophet's Town the Wyandottes, regarded as the best fighters in the region, pledged their support. Then, in 1809, Tecumseh made a long swing through the South, from the Osage of Missouri, where his mother and sister had taken residence, to the Seminoles of Florida. The southern tribes were friendly but as yet unwilling to commit themselves to either confederation or war. Their distance from Ohio and the difficulties of communication seemed insuperable obstacles.

Governor Harrison chafed at Tecumseh's apparent success and sent detailed reports on his activities to President Jefferson, but he did not interrupt his schedule of land procurement. In the summer of 1809, he called an immense council at Fort Wayne. Representatives from all the northwestern tribes were invited except for the Shawnees and Tecumseh. There he demanded the cession of the central third of Indiana, including the whole lower Wabash Valley. The tribal delegates resisted mightily, for these were the last good hunting grounds east of the Mississippi. It required extensive feasting and several barrels of whiskey (Harrison told President Jefferson it was wine) before the delegates, many of them minor chiefs with no authority, came to terms. About three million acres came into government hands for $10,000 in annuities, to be divided among the tribes on a fixed ratio. The new boundary line between settler and Indian was drawn in a way that all could understand. It ran southeast from the point where Raccoon Creek flowed into the Wabash (between Terre Haute and Vincennes) toward the point where the sun was located at ten o'clock in the morning. The time of the year was not specified, but one might presume that Harrison would pick the summer solstice if the issue were raised.

Harrison's excuse for not inviting Shawnees to the conference was that they were a nomadic tribe without title to specific real estate, and he ignored Tecumseh because he spoke for no particular tribe. Whatever the rationale, it was a calculated insult, and Tecumseh, who might well have torpedoed the conference, was understandably outraged at the result. He promptly paddled down to Vincennes with an entourage of three hundred warriors in battle dress and told Harrison that occupation of the territory would mean war. He also informed the astonished governor that he planned to kill every chief who signed the treaty, and with the echoes of the Prophet's purge still reverberating in the forest, few could doubt that he meant it.

Indeed, it seems likely that Tecumseh would have declared war instantly if he had been able to count on British help. British influence had evaporated in the region south of the Great Lakes after Fallen Timbers and the surrender of Detroit. But it began to revive as Anglo-American relations deteriorated after 1806. British Indian agents at Fort Malden at the mouth of the Detroit River gave the Indians some supplies, mostly food and blankets and enough arms and ammunition for hunting. But Whitehall was preoccupied with Napoleon, and its agents in Canada had no authority to stir up trouble with the United States. Their mission was to keep a hand in the Great Lakes fur trade and use the Indians as a buffer against any American designs on Canada. Thus when Tecumseh journeyed to Malden in 1810 to plea for help, he got nowhere. The British agents told him that war would mean the destruction of the tribes and a further extension of the frontier.

Without British logistical support Tecumseh had no choice but to abandon his plans for war, but his threat at least prevented Harrison from occupying the Fort Wayne cession. In the summer of 1811, Tecumseh decided on another tour of the South, and he took care to stop by at Vincennes to acquaint the governor with his plans. A three-day council ended in verbal stalemate, and Tecumseh swept off down the Wabash and the Ohio.

Over the next six months he carried his crusade from Missouri to Alabama, but with only limited success. Across Tennessee and Alabama he carried on a running debate with sachems of the huge Creek confederacy, leaving colored batons, or "Red Sticks," among his converts as a means of communication when the uprising began. He had less success among the Cherokees, who were making a concerted effort to adapt to the white frontier. In desperation he took a leaf from the Prophet's notebook and told the assembled warriors that when he reached home he would stamp his foot and the whole earth would tremble. Actually, there was no way he could have foreseen the great earthquake that rocked the eastern half of the country in December 1811. That one was pure luck. On the way home he stopped again in Missouri to see his mother. He finally arrived at Prophet's Town in March 1812, and found it burned to the ground. Harrison had struck in his absence.

The governor actually began to plan his raid during Tecumseh's visit the previous summer. No sooner did Tecumseh depart than Harrison issued a call for Kentucky and Indiana militia. With an ill-disciplined force of nine hundred he marched up the Wabash in September. By November 5, he was camped near the mouth of Tippecanoe Creek, a few miles from Prophet's Town. Though under Tecumseh's orders to avoid war, the impulsive Prophet could not resist Harrison's provocation. After an all-night orgy of rituals and dancing, he attacked at dawn with fewer than five hundred warriors. Such a light and premature attack was doomed to failure, and it foredoomed all Tecumseh's plans. When Tecumseh returned, he almost executed his brother on the spot, but instead ordered him banished. The Prophet lived out his days among the buffalo-hunting tribes of the Great Plains.

Harrison was prepared for an attack and drove it back after a two-hour fight, each side suffering about 40 dead and 150 wounded. He evidently felt the battle inconclusive, however, for he spent the next two days erecting breastworks and preparing for another assault. When scouts informed him that the Indians had disappeared, he moved into the deserted village, burned it to the ground, and returned to Vincennes claiming a great victory. In Prophet's Town was a cache of British-made firearms, but so impulsive was the Indian attack that the guns had not even been unpacked. The discovery, nevertheless, was tangible evidence that confirmed the Americans' long-held suspicion of British intrigues. Word that the British were behind Tecumseh's confederacy spread like wildfire across the West, fanning the flames of war. British meddling among the Indiana tribes exactly paralleled the insults to American sovereignty and national pride on the high seas. It was the final outrage.

The Coming of War

The Twelfth Congress assembled in Washington on the very day of the battle of Tippecanoe. The mood was one of frustration and belligerence. Commercial retaliation had failed; war seemed the only alternative. Seizing the initiative, young Republican nationalists elected Henry Clay Speaker of the House. Although it was Clay's first day in the House, he had previously served a partial term in the Senate, and his views on war were well-known. A year earlier he had reached the conclusion that the weakness of American foreign policy, as exhibited by Macon's Bill Number Two, was a sign of national degeneration. He fumed that Americans had become a nation of moneygrubbers, too busy pursuing profit to defend their honor. "Are we to be governed by the low groveling parsimony of the counting room?" he roared at the Senate. If Americans failed to defend their rights, he predicted, "we forfeit the respect of the world, and what is infinitely worse, of ourselves." He pictured war as "the combined energies of a free people . . . wreaking a noble and manful vengeance upon a foreign foe." Here at last was a man capable of articulating American frustration. Installed as speaker of the House, he promptly loaded all the key committees with fellow war hawks.

In his annual message, the president recounted the wrongs suffered at the hands of Britain and encouraged military preparations, though, befitting his philosophy, he left the ultimate decision of peace or war up to Congress. In December 1811, John C. Calhoun reported for the Foreign Relations Committee a series of resolutions to increase the standing army, fit out the navy, and arm the militia. The resolutions occasioned a prolonged debate, but in the end they passed by top-heavy majorities. Then Congress became bogged down in prolonged attention to the details of war preparations. For the next three months, the war hawks struggled to overcome the ancient Republican suspicions of debts and taxes, armies and navies.

In April 1812, the administration boosted flagging war sentiment in Congress by requesting a thirty-day embargo on American shipping, intended as a prelude to war. Thereafter events moved rapidly. On May 22, the packet sloop *Hornet* docked in New York with long-awaited dispatches from Britain. The new British foreign minister, Viscount Castlereagh, was well informed of American military preparations by his minister in Washington, Augustus J. Foster, but Foster's accurate reports were drowned out by "intelligence static" from New England which indicated that Americans would not fight in the end. Castlereagh's dispatches thus contained nothing but a restatement of the British position. Nothing was said about impressment; the orders-in-council would be revoked only if the United States gave in first; and the entire dispute was blamed on the United States for accepting Napoleon's word on the repeal of his decrees. Assuming this to be the final communication from Britain, Madison sent his war message to Congress on June 1.

In outlining his reasons for going to war, Madison put impressment at the head of the list. This was a surprise to the British, for little had been said of impressment in the diplomatic exchanges since the *Chesapeake* affair. Nonetheless, it was the oldest of the American grievances, and Madison considered it the most important incursion on American pride and sovereignty. The president dwelled next on the paper blockades, orders-in-council, and unwarranted seizure of American ships. "Our commerce," he pointed out, "has been plundered in every sea, the great staples of our country have been cut off from their legitimate markets, and a destructive blow aimed at our agricultural and maritime interests." The assault on America's neutral rights involved more than a few merchants and their seamen; it was an attack on the nation as a whole. As a final note, he mentioned the British intrigues among the Indians of the Northwest. West, as well as East, was the victim of British aggression; it was time to strike back. On June 3, Calhoun introduced a war resolution, along with a lengthy report calling for a rejuvention of the American spirit.

The House passed the declaration a week later by a vote of seventy-nine to forty-nine. It was largely a sectional vote, for three-fourths of the opposition came from New England and New York, while three-fourths of the majority came from the South and Pennsylvania. But, more than that, it was a party vote—nearly all Republicans supported the war, Federalists unanimously opposed it. In the Senate a few Republicans wanted to delay the declaration until the nation was militarily prepared, but in the end war was approved by a similar party-line vote. Across the country came a collective sigh of relief that action was at last at hand. "We are beginning now to hold up our heads and boast that we are Americans," William Wirt wrote Monroe from Virginia. "There is not a man here who is not an inch taller since congress has done its duty."

The supreme irony was Parliament's simultaneous repeal of the orders-in-

council. Opposition to the orders had been rising ever since the Embargo, and by the spring of 1812 the tottering structure of British commercial regulations was upheld only by the intransigence of its architect, Prime Minister Spencer Perceval. The assassination of Perceval in May 1812, and the induction of a new cabinet under the moderate Earl of Liverpool doomed the orders. Parliament repealed them in June, and news of the repeal crossed the American declaration of war in midocean. Electronic communications might well have prevented war, but the injury to American pride ran deep. When news of the repeal reached the United States, the military commander on the Niagara frontier, General Henry Dearborn, negotiated a truce with the governor-general of Canada on the assumption that the cause for war had been removed. President Madison instantly repudiated Dearborn's initiative and ordered a resumption of the fighting on the grounds that the problem of impressment remained unresolved.

Snatching Defeat from the Jaws of Victory: 1812

Even though the United States had the military initiative, the war began inauspiciously. Madison was a brilliant diplomat and a profound political philosopher, but he was a poor administrator. Lacking both the public address to excite patriotism and the private companionability that would encourage unity, he failed to provide the spark of decisive leadership so essential in wartime. He was, moreover, a poor judge of men, and he surrounded himself with weak and inefficient commanders. Secretary of War William Eustis, a Massachusetts Republican who owed his appointment to Madison's desire for geographical balance in the cabinet, was a total incompetent, and his generals were little better. In the West, an army under the general supervision of James Wilkinson could hardly be regarded as a military threat to anybody, though Eustis did have the sense to keep Wilkinson in New Orleans and away from the front. In the East, General Dearborn, who commanded in the New York-New England theater, was aged and listless, inclined to direct the war from comfortable quarters in Albany. He was, moreover, uncertain as to whether his command extended as far west as Niagara, and Eustis never clarified the situation.

The strategy worked out between Madison and his generals was reasonable enough. It involved a combined attack on Upper Canada (Ontario) from Detroit on the west and the Niagara River on the east. Defended by only a handful of troops, Upper Canada could not resist both assaults, and the territory could then be held hostage pending peace negotiations. At Detroit, General William Hull commanded an army of 2,200; he was opposed by a miniscule British-Canadian army of 250 across the river, supported by perhaps 1,000 Native Americans under Tecumseh. The one trump the British possessed was leadership, for the Canadian General Issac Brock, commanding at Malden, was one of the ablest military leaders to emerge during the war.

By contrast, Hull, who had seen military service during the Revolution, was old, indecisive, and irresolute. His fellow officers had a low opinion of him, which extended to the ranks when, during a parade at Detroit, Hull lost control of his horse, lost his balance and his hat, and frantically clutched the mane of the frightened animal to save himself. In a society where horsemanship and physical strength were essential to leadership no one could survive the ridicule that would follow such an incident.

With orders to take the offensive, Hull crossed the river unopposed on July 12. He thereupon issued a flamboyant proclamation offering the Canadians the blessings of American liberty and sent Lieutenant Lewis Cass to probe the defenses at Malden. Cass reported that they were inconsiderable, but Hull refused to move forward, sending instead to Indiana for reinforcements. Hull dallied for three weeks while his men became increasingly restless, and then disaster struck. In early August, a supply column was surprised by Indians at the Raisin River and massacred; simultaneously word arrived of the British capture of Fort Michillimackinac at the straits between Lake Huron and Lake Michigan. Dreading Native American attack in his rear, Hull retreated across the river to Detroit.

He then became preoccupied with his isolation. Though he could ill afford the troops, he sent Cass with four hundred men to the Raisin River to try opening communications with Ohio. Brock stationed himself across the river from Detroit, and on August 15 demanded that Hull surrender to avoid a "war of extermination." Hull's behavior became increasingly erratic, perhaps because of liquor or narcotics. His speech became slurred, he drooled incessantly, and took to crouching in corners of the fort. On August 16, without consulting anyone, Hull surrendered Detroit. Not a shot had been fired in anger. The collapse of Hull's campaign, coupled with the Native American capture of Fort Dearborn (Chicago) at the foot of Lake Michigan, rolled back the American frontier to Fort Wayne, Indiana, and exposed the entire Northwest to tribal raids.

The Niagara offensive in the fall of 1812 experienced little more success. Dearborn's spurious truce with the Canadian governor delayed the attack, and by the time he was ready to move, the energetic Brock had raced back from Detroit to take command on the Canadian side of the river. While Dearborn remained in Albany buried in paperwork, command on the Niagara River devolved upon a New York Federalist, Stephen Van Renssalaer. The War Department had apparently chosen Van Rensselaer in order to gain support among

New York Federalists. What it accomplished instead was the politization of the army because nearly all the militia under Van Rensselaer's command were Republicans. To make matters worse Dearborn sent General Alexander Smyth, a pompous Virginian, to Niagara and ordered him to cooperate with Van Rensselaer, without making it clear who was in actual command.

After lengthy preparations Van Rensselaer in October was ready to cross the river with a thousand men. Though the crossing was delayed briefly when an over-eager officer rowed across with all the oars, Van Rensselaer eventually got his force across the river and assaulted the British-Canadian positions on Queenston Heights. In a brief but valiant skirmish, the British were driven from the heights, and General Brock was killed. The British then launched a counterattack, and Van Rensselaer called for reinforcements. To his amazement the rearguard of his army at Buffalo refused to cross the river on the grounds that it had not enlisted for foreign duty. Van Rensselaer then escaped to the American side, leaving the rest of his army to surrender.

Van Rensselaer resigned his command on October 16, convinced that he had been betrayed, and Smyth took over. Smyth spent November in repeated efforts to get his army across the Niagara River and attack Fort Erie, which lay across the river from Buffalo. Each time he got his army into boats, his officers called off the assault because the men lacked food, arms, ammunition, and clothing. After the second false start on November 29, Smyth terminated the campaign and sent the militia home. Smyth publicly blamed his officers for the fiasco, which induced one of them, ex-Congressman Peter B. Porter (whose district had been western New York) to challenge him to a duel. Smyth accepted, convinced that Porter and his friends had created the outcry against him because they stood to lose money on unfulfilled army contracts. The duel was a harmless affair, as both shots missed, and that ended the fighting for 1812.

Victories at Sea

In the meantime, the tiny American navy was giving a good account of itself through the autumn of 1812. The nation entered the war with seven frigates (all but one built by the Federalists in 1798–99) and a handful of brigs and sloops. The ships were well-constructed, made of durable live oak from the tidal swamps of Georgia, and three of them carried heavier armament (forty-four guns) than any British frigate afloat (the British standard was thirty-eight guns). The crews were generally well-trained, and the navy, despite the slights it received at the hands of the Jeffersonians, possessed a proud tradition that dated from the Revolution.

The *Constitution* under Captain Isaac Hull was the first to put to sea after the declaration of war. Departing from Boston in July 1812, it immediately ran into a British squadron. There ensued one of the epic chases in naval history, carried on in frustratingly light winds. Hull threw everything movable overboard while his ship drifted a few miles from the becalmed British; he finally got away by putting out his small boats and rowing the *Constitution* to New York. Refitted in New York, Hull again took to sea, and on August 12 he encountered the *Guerriere,* a British "thirty-eight" which had been menacing the American coast for a year, searching merchant vessels and impressing sailors. Both vessels were spoiling for a fight and hammered at each other at close quarters. In twenty-five minutes the *Guerriere* was a floating hulk, 50 percent of its crew dead or wounded. Unable to take the sinking vessel as a prize, Hull set it afire and sailed off.

The other important ship-to-ship duel was won by the *United States,* a sister ship of the *Constitution,* commanded by thirty-three-year-old Stephen Decatur. Ordered across the Atlantic to prey on British commerce, Decatur ran into the *Macedonian,* a thirty-eight-gun frigate, off the Madeiras on October 25. The British vessel carried the standard armament, which meant a broadside of carronades, short, stubby cannon that threw a heavy ball a short distance; but the *United States,* equipped for raiding purposes, was armed with long guns, which fired a light shot over a great distance. Decatur took full advantage of this disparity by standing off a hundred yards to leeward of the British vessel and pounding it with his deadly accurate long-range cannon. In an hour the masts and rigging of the *Macedonian* were shot away, and Decatur was closing in for the kill when the British ship struck its colors. A prize crew was put aboard, and the *Macedonian* was sailed home to be incorporated into the American navy.

The clear superiority in number of guns and weight of broadside possessed by both the *United States* and the *Constitution* did not provide a clear test of relative seamanship. More important in that regard were the minor ship duels fought by the American brigs and sloops. Eight of these were fought around the world, from the Atlantic to the East Indies, and the Americans lost only one. In each case the vessels were relatively equal; the speed and accuracy of American firepower made the difference.

The only important ship duel lost by the United States in the war involved the unlucky *Chesapeake.* A standard "thirty-eight" like the British frigates, the *Chesapeake* was fitted out for sea duty in Boston in the spring of 1813. The commander, James Lawrence, had a difficult time obtaining a crew because most of the experienced sailors preferred more lucrative duty aboard privateers. Blockading the harbor was the British frigate *Shannon,* which finally sent in a challenge to come out and fight. Such challenges were not uncommon, for the ship duels of 1812–13 were fought with all the ceremony and attention to honor of medieval tournaments. Despite his green crew, most of whom had never fired a cannon, Lawrence sailed out to do battle in May 1813. The two ships fought at close range for three hours until they finally ran together and fouled the rigging. Mortally wounded by a musket ball, Lawrence issued his last order: "Don't give up the ship. Sink her first!" Refusing to surrender, the *Chesapeake* was finally taken by a British boarding party. Both ships were wrecked; Americans suffered 186 casualties, the British 52.

Romantic as the naval duels seemed, they had relatively little impact on the outcome of the war. By early 1813, British squadrons blockaded the entire American coast south of New England, and American warships were essentially kept in port for the duration of the fighting. Privately owned warships which preyed on British commerce for profit, in the end, did far more damage. Built for speed, rather than fighting, the brigs and schooners turned out by Baltimore and Philadelphia shipwrights were the fastest ships in the world. Some five hundred of these privateers managed to capture over two thousand British merchant vessels (though many of them were recaptured by the Royal Navy) in the course of the war. No body of water was safe from these lightning marauders; British insurance rates even in the English Channel and the Irish Sea were triple what they had been in peacetime.

Recovery of the West: 1813

During the winter of 1812–13 the administration took stock of itself. It was clear that the invasions of Canada had been frustrated, not so much by the superiority of British-Canadian resistance, as by the inability of the War Department to assemble, train, and supply an army. Getting rid of Eustis was easy enough; finding a replacement was more difficult. Utilizing a New Yorker was essential since the cooperation of New York was essential, regardless of whether the target of the eastern campaign was Niagara or Montreal. Madison's favor ultimately fell upon John Armstrong, the former minister to France and relative of the Livingston clan. Armstrong had some flaws, among them an evil temper and unbridled political ambition. But his influence in New York outweighed these; and, in any case, he could hardly pursue his political ambitions without first bringing some military successes to the administration as a whole.

Armstrong first turned his attention to the West. During the winter of 1812–13 William Henry Harrison, in his capacity as a general of Kentucky militia, had led an army of Kentucky volunteers into northwestern Ohio in an effort to recapture Detroit. He managed to erect an advance outpost called Fort Meigs on the Maumee River, but his campaign thereafter bogged down in mud and ice. Armstrong had no high regard for Harrison's military abilities, but he realized his popularity in the West. He accordingly offered Harrison one of the six major generalships that had been created by Congress, which would at least make him accountable to the War Department, rather than the politicians of Kentucky. He then ordered Harrison to hold fast at Fort Meigs while the government built a fleet at Presque Isle at the eastern end of Lake Erie.

Armstrong recognized that the key to the recovery of Detroit and a possible invasion of Upper Canada from the west in 1813 was naval control of Lake Erie. At the outset of the war, the British claimed nominal control of the lake with a few small transport vessels maintained at Fort Malden. In the spring of 1813, Oliver Hazard Perry was dispatched to Presque Isle (present-day Erie, Pennsylvania) with orders to construct a fleet of ships. An outstanding leader, Perry displayed uncommon energy and initiative in overcoming obstacles. He combed western Pennsylvania for carpenters and shipwrights, and he imported sailors from New England to man the vessels. He managed to create a fleet of ships in six months and was ready to sail in early September. Perry's activities had stimulated some frantic British shipbuilding, and the two fleets that met at Put-in Bay (Sandusky, Ohio) on September 10, 1813, were about equal. Perry's fleet was led by two brigs, the *Lawrence* and the *Niagara*, each of twenty guns,

and a variety of smaller vessels which brought his total armament to fifty-four guns. The British fleet, also led by two brigs, had sixty-three guns.

Sighting the British fleet at Put-in Bay, Perry dashed in with the *Lawrence* and engaged the two largest British ships. He received some aid from his lesser vessels, but the commander of the *Niagara,* for some unaccountable reason, held off from the battle. His ship sinking under him, Perry took to a small boat and rowed through a storm of shot to the *Niagara.* He then moved in with a fresh ship, and the badly damaged British surrendered. Perry sent a triumphant message to William Henry Harrison, who was poised at the Maumee River with an army of 4,500: "We have met the enemy and they are ours: two ships, two brigs, one schooner, and one sloop."

Harrison's army consisted almost entirely of Kentucky volunteers and mounted riflemen. Perry transported it to Malden, and the outnumbered British evacuated Detroit without a fight. Tecumseh, whose warriors had ravaged the Indiana frontier for the past year, was disgusted. He had worked well with the energetic Brock, but he considered the new British commander, Henry Proctor, an incompetent coward. Even with Tecumseh's thousand warriors, the British were outnumbered by two to one, and Proctor retreated eastward along the Thames River. Finally Tecumseh insisted that he make a stand, threatening to kill him otherwise. Proctor selected a defensive position between the river and a swamp and lined his eight hundred British regulars across the road in European fashion. The Battle of the Thames took place on October 5, and it was over in less than an hour. A cavalry charge by Colonel Richard M. Johnson's mounted riflemen smashed through the British line, and after some fierce hand-to-hand combat, the Indians scattered into the woods. Tecumseh died in the battle, but his body was never found. (Richard M. Johnson would eventually reach the vice presidency in 1837 as "the man who killed Tecumseh.") Long before, General Proctor had taken to his carriage and was racing eastward to safety. The combined naval and military victories of this brilliantly executed campaign permanently secured the Northwest and the upper lakes.

Politics and War: The East in 1813

Although the focus of fighting in 1812 had been along the Niagara River, the Madison administration recognized that victories there would not seriously threaten the British hold on Canada. Canada could be taken only by an attack on Montreal, either by way of Lake Champlain or by way of the St. Lawrence River from Lake Ontario. However, when the British reinforced their naval base at Kingston on the northern end of Lake Ontario in March 1813, Secretary Armstrong gave up on that idea. The operation would take too long, and Armstrong needed a quick victory. In fact, he needed one before May 3, which was when the New York State elections were scheduled to take place. The people of western New York were thoroughly disenchanted after the comic-opera campaign of 1812; and, Armstrong feared a Federalist victory in the state, which would have been a political, as well as a military disaster. Armstrong accordingly decided to make a quick amphibious thrust at York (present-day Toronto), the capital of Upper Canada. The army would then repair to the Niagara River, seizing Fort George and Fort Erie.

An American fleet under Isaac Chauncey, based at Sackett's Harbor, New York, maintained a tenuous control of Lake Ontario, largely due to the unwillingness of the British at Kingston to come out and fight. On April 27, after waiting for two weeks for ice to clear, Chauncey ferried a raiding force of 1,600 under Zebulon Pike across the lake to York. Meeting little resistance, the raiding force burned the government buildings and some of the city. The hapless Canadians found some consolation when the city's powder magazine exploded killing Pike and three hundred of his men. A month later young Winfield Scott captured Fort George on the Canadian side of the Niagara River, and the British retaliated by raiding Sackett's Harbor. The New York election, in the meantime, was a victory for the Republicans.

General Dearborn resigned in July 1813; and, Armstrong replaced him with an old friend of his, General James Wilkinson (Armstrong and Wilkinson had both been aides to General Gates during the Revolution). The unfortunate choice of Wilkinson ended any chance of serious fighting in the east for the remainder of 1813. Ordered by Armstrong to launch an attack down the St. Lawrence River toward Montreal, Wilkinson demanded permission to surrender in case he got into difficulty. When that request was refused, he conducted a halfhearted probe down the river, was defeated at Chrysler's Farm by an outnumbered enemy, and resigned.

Jackson and Horseshoe Bend

Paralleling Harrison's recovery of the Northwest in the fall of 1813 was the bloody suppression of an Indian uprising in the South. Tecumseh had made a number of converts on his southern tour, especially among the Creeks; and when the war started his "Red Sticks" began raiding frontier settlements. The Creeks were unhappy with white incursions on their Alabama lands, and soon the whole tribe was at war. In August 1813, they captured Fort Mims at the junction of the Alabama and Tombigbee rivers and massacred the inhabitants. The story told at the time was that between 400 and 600 men, women, and children had lost their lives, although recent estimates have lowered the death toll to about 250. Either way, it was the worst massacre of white civilians in the history of the frontier.

To suppress the uprising, two armies of frontier militia were formed, one in Tennessee under General Andrew Jackson, and one in Georgia under General John Coffee. Jackson marched into Alabama, building forts as he went to protect his supply line. His campaign stalled in December, however, when he ran out of supplies and his troops' enlistments expired. More personally committed to victory than any other general in the war, Jackson refused to let his men go home, contending that no one had a right to leave an army camped in enemy country. He threatened to shoot any man that left. The soldiers slipped away anyway, and by January 1814, Jackson was down to 130 men.

That same month the War Department authorized the governor of Tennessee to raise a new force of volunteers, and it sent west additional regulars. By March, Jackson's army was up to 3,500, and he was ready to take the offensive. Solving his discipline problems by executing a militaman for refusing to obey orders, Jackson penetrated ever deeper into Creek country. He pushed on even after the Creeks defeated and turned back Coffee's army of Georgians.

Jackson encountered the main body of Creeks holed up in a strongly defended village in a horseshoe-shaped bend of the Tallapoosa River. While one detachment of Jackson's army stole the Indians' canoes to prevent any escape and another burned the town, Jackson assaulted and carried the main barricade. The Creeks refused to surrender, and 550 were killed; the rest escaped to the security of Spanish Florida. Fort Mims was avenged. Jackson then imposed a peace treaty on the defeated tribe, forcing it to surrender many of its remaining claims in Georgia, as well as three-fifths of Alabama. Except for future troubles with the Creeks and their cousins, the Seminoles in Florida, the Battle of Horseshoe Bend terminated further Native American resistance to white settlement east of the Mississippi River.

The Campaign of 1814

The summer of 1814 was the low point of the war for the United States. Napoleon was defeated that spring and exiled to the island of Elba, thus freeing Wellington's magnificent army of Peninsula veterans for service in North America. Although the "Iron Duke" himself refused to serve in America, his army reinforced British garrisons in Canada, while a separate force prepared for an invasion of Louisiana.

In December 1813, a British army reoccupied the positions taken by the Americans the previous spring on the Niagara River and then invaded western New York, laying waste Buffalo and other towns along the river. Secretary Armstrong was immediately innundated with delegations and petitions from New York Republicans demanding protection and retaliation. And once more

Armstrong's attention was diverted from Montreal, the heart of British North America.

To replace Wilkinson as commander in New York, Armstrong chose Jacob Brown, one of the happiest nominations of the war. In his ability to train, discipline, and motivate soldiers Brown was equalled only by Andrew Jackson. Brown also agreed with Armstrong that, because of poor roads and problems of supply, the Niagara frontier was the only realistic way of carrying the war to the enemy. Early in July he crossed the Niagara River, captured Fort Erie, and started northward along the river. An army of British regulars and Canadian militia, equal in size to Brown's, made its stand at Chippewa Creek, just above Niagara Falls. On July 5, Brown attacked in time-honored Continental style—a volley of musket fire followed by a bayonet charge. Brown's diligent attention to training and discipline paid off; both sides suffered heavy casualties, but the British retreated from the field. The exclamation of the surprised British General Phineas Riall, "Those are Regulars, by God!" echoes across the years at the United States Military Academy, which also commemorates the grey uniforms worn at the Battle of Chippewa.

Because an advance deeper into Canada would require naval assistance and a waterborne supply line, Brown asked Commodore Chauncey to join him at Fort George on July 10. The proud Commodore, however, refused to take orders from an army general and stayed at Sackett's Harbor. Deciding that he could not risk an assault on Fort George unassisted, Brown withdrew back toward Chippewa, followed by a newly reinforced British army. They met again on July 25 at Lundy's Lane, close enough to Niagara Falls to hear the thunder of the water. Again, two lines of infantry seventy yards apart battled muzzle to muzzle until dark when the British retired from the field. The bloodiest engagement of the war, Lundy's Lane was a standoff, each side suffering over nine hundred casualties. Although the Americans were left with the field and a technical victory, the long-run advantage lay with the British. Brown was injured in the battle, and his successor in command decided against any further offensive moves. He retired to Fort Erie; the British followed and laid the fort under siege. Brown himself escaped, but his army was forced to surrender. That ended the contest on the Niagara battlefront—bloody and fruitless fighting that ravaged the countryside and left a legacy of bitterness for years to come.

The Madison administration was further distracted that summer by the activities of a British naval squadron under Sir George Cockburn operating in the Chesapeake. Since mid-1813 Cockburn had made a nuisance of himself raiding towns along the Virginia coast and burning plantations. Following the defeat of Napoleon, the British government decided to punish the United States for having started the war, and it sent Cockburn an army of veterans from the European war, enough to enable him to attack the American capital, Washington, D. C.

Rumors reached Washington in June of Britain's hardening attitude, and Madison became concerned for the security of the capital. He summoned a cabinet meeting where it was decided to create a special military district, embracing Washington and Baltimore. At Madison's insistence, the district was placed under the command of Brigadier General William Winder of Maryland. The choice was purely political. Maryland would have to supply most of the troops for the district, and Winder, though a Federalist and an opponent of the war, was the nephew of the state's governor. Unfortunately, neither Winder nor Armstrong thought the British would actually attack the city. Washington lacked strategic importance, and the British had moved freely around the Chesapeake for a year without menacing it. Winder accepted enlistments of Maryland volunteers, but he made no effort to erect defenses around the nation's capital.

To sail up the Potomac would alert the capital city and give the defense time to prepare, so Cockburn instead sailed up the Patuxent River and landed an army of 4,500 regulars at the village of Nottingham, Maryland. From there he planned an overland march on the city's rear. Maryland farmers alerted the government to the British landing, and Secretary of State James Monroe offered his services to General Winder as a scout. Monroe set out on horseback with a spyglass but took the wrong road and missed the British. Madison initially thought the British would march on Baltimore, but by August 22, two days after the British began their march, he was making arrangements for the government to evacuate Washington.

The British route took them through Bladensburg at the eastern corner of the federal district, and there Winder chose to make his stand. By this time he had recruited a mixed force of regulars and volunteers, including navy yard workers and naval artillerists. The force numbered nearly seven thousand, which gave Winder a numerical advantage over the British. The advantage was lost, however, because the American force was ill-trained and poorly led. Winder himself had been thrown from his horse while trying to scout the British and was in bed until the eve of the battle.

Winder placed his men on a low hill astride the road that connected Bladensburg with the capital. President Madison (sporting pearl-handled dueling pistols), Secretary Armstrong, and Secretary Monroe were all present, issuing orders, some of which conflicted with General Winder's. The British attack on the morning of August 24 was preceded by a barrage of Congreve rockets, a novel, noisy, but relatively harmless weapon. The rockets panicked the raw American militia, who fled from the field without firing a shot, carrying General Winder and the government with them. The only bright spot on the bleakest day in American military annals was a rearguard defense by five hundred sailors under Commodore Joshua Barney, who manned the naval artillery on the hill. Barney's sailors forced the British to launch three charges, and took five hundred casualties before succumbing to the British assault.

While the American government scattered in all directions (Madison ended up in Leesburg, Virginia), the British occupied Washington, retiring three days later after burning the Capitol and several public buildings. Cockburn then sailed into Baltimore and bombarded Fort McHenry at the entrance to the harbor. The fort held out, saving the city; the only notable result was the poem written by Francis Scott Key, a Maryland Federalist who had gone aboard the British flagship to appeal for the release of several hostages.

Secretary Armstrong bore the brunt of the public anger for the failure to defend Washington. Even before the British moved on Baltimore President

Madison asked Monroe to assume direction of the defense of the military district. Feeling threatened by "military usurpation" and "political faction," Armstrong sent Madison his resignation on September 4. The President asked Monroe to serve as temporary secretary of war until he found a permanent replacement. Monroe was no more able than Armstrong, but he was luckier. Two brilliant military victories in the fall and winter of 1814–15 revived the nation's wounded pride and enabled the government to reach a satisfactory peace agreement.

From Lake Champlain to New Orleans

When the fighting ended at Niagara in stalemate in the summer of 1814, the British dusted off the classic campaign strategy of 1777—an invasion of the New York frontier by the Lake Champlain-Hudson River waterway. In September 1814, a magnificent army of 15,000 veterans of the European wars invaded upper New York under the command of the governor general of Canada, Sir George Prevost. The key to the campaign, however, was naval control of Lake Champlain. Anticipating the British move, President Madison had sent Lieutenant Thomas Macdonough to build a fleet on the lake. Macdonough obtained carpenters, shipwrights, and sailors from Boston, and by the end of the summer he had two brigs, a schooner, and a sloop. The British also supplemented the vessels they had captured the previous year and possessed a squadron about equal to Macdonough's. When Prevost laid siege to Plattsburg, New York, Macdonough anchored his tiny fleet in Plattsburg Bay and awaited the British squadron.

The Battle of Lake Champlain, September 11, 1814, was unique in that both fleets were at anchor. The British captain, George Downie, sailed his thirty-six-gun brig *Confiance* into the harbor and anchored it next to Macdonough's twenty-six-gun flagship, *Saratoga.* The other vessels paired off in similar fashion and blasted each other for two hours. In mid-battle Macdonough, who had thoughtfully provided his ships with additional anchors and ropes, wore his vessel around so the *Saratoga* could bring to bear a new and undamaged broadside of cannons, and the British surrendered. Prevost then abandoned the siege of Plattsburg and returned to Montreal, perhaps remembering the fate of Burgoyne, isolated in the New York wilderness in 1777. The naval victory not only terminated the invasion threat, but it also had a tremendous effect on the peace negotiations then beginning at Ghent, Belgium. The British demand for territorial concessions, which had delayed the negotiations for a year, was now hopeless.

Or nearly hopeless. There was one more British thrust to be parried. In addition to sending red-coated veterans to Canada and the Chesapeake, the Liverpool ministry sent an expedition to seize New Orleans. What exactly they planned to do with it is not clear, but if they had succeeded New Orleans and perhaps all of Louisiana would have been on the the bargaining table at Ghent. As it was, they not only failed, but their defeat occurred after the peace treaty was signed. Thus the War of 1812 ended as it had begun, with an ironic twist of timing.

Supplied with an army of nearly ten thousand veterans by September 1814, Admiral Sir Alexander Cochrane, the British naval commander on the American station, made plans for an assault on New Orleans. Recognizing that the Mississippi River was difficult to ascend, he decided to seize Mobile first and then proceed overland to New Orleans. The job of defending the Gulf Coast belonged to Andrew Jackson, who had been promoted to command the Seventh District (the territory south of the Ohio River) after his victory over the Creeks. He had two regiments of infantry in his district and several thousand Tennessee and Kentucky militia. After learning of the reinforcements sent to Cochrane, Secretary Monroe decided that New Orleans was the British target and ordered Jackson to hasten there.

Jackson, still in Alabama wringing land cessions from the Creeks, thought it was more likely that the British would land in Pensacola or Mobile where they could join forces with the remnant Creeks who had fled into Spanish Florida. He accordingly concentrated his forces at Mobile, and his theory appeared to be confirmed when the British appeared at the entrance to Mobile Bay on September 16. A British attack on Fort Bowyer at the mouth of the bay was beaten off, and the British sailed to Pensacola. Jackson warned the Spanish governor there not to violate Spain's neutrality by letting the British land. The governor replied tartly that the United States had not hesitated to violate Spanish neutrality when it suited American interests. Enraged at this lack of cooperation, Jackson stormed and captured Pensacola on November 7, but the British escaped in their ships. Actually Jackson's actions did induce Admiral Cockrane to abandon his plan to seize Mobile, and he proceeded to New Orleans by water, through Mississippi Sound and Lake Borgne, a brackish body of water that penetrated almost to the rear gate of New Orleans. Jackson, who had been ignoring Monroe's entreaties all fall, departed for New Orleans at last on November 21, and the campaign now became something of a race to see which army would reach the city first.

By avoiding the tortuous trip up the Mississippi River, Cochrane hoped to achieve surprise, but he dissipated his advantage by taking a week to ferry his infantry and artillery from Lake Borgne up a drainage canal to the riverbank below the city. Jackson, who arrived in the city on the first of December, utilized the time to mobilize the local population. The governor of Louisiana had organized a troop of free blacks in the city, and Jackson incorporated them in his army. He also procured the services of Jean Laffite and his pirates from nearby Bayou Barataria by promising them amnesty. The pirates, of course, were experienced gunners and skilled fighters.

Warned by a sugar planter of the British arrival, Jackson raided their camp on the night of the twenty-third. Though beaten back, he made the British move cautiously thereafter and won time to prepare a defensive position of his own. The site he chose was a drainage canal about eight miles south of the city, which ran from a wooded swamp to the river. His flanks were thus protected by the swamp and the river, and he threw up earthworks along the canal. The British

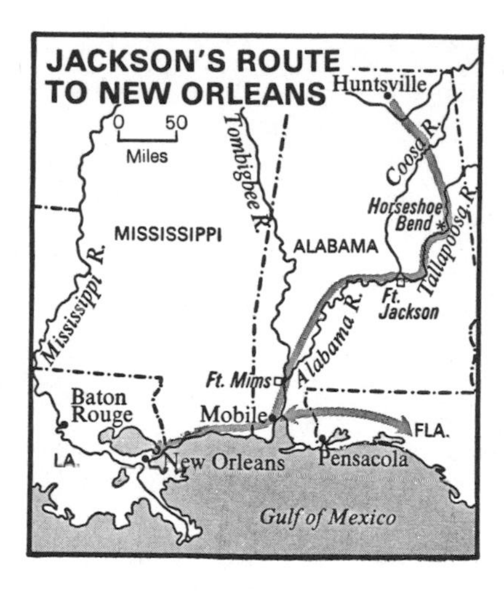

were forced to build redoubts of their own and drag up artillery from their ships.

A second battle on New Year's Day 1815, was primarily an artillery duel, won by Jackson's ignoble allies, the pirates of Barataria. A week later the British prepared their final assault, an infantry charge. But Jackson had spent the time well; his army of frontier riflemen stood four ranks deep behind sugar casks and cotton bales. The British charge on January 8 was a slaughter. Three British regiments were decimated, losing more than two thousand dead and wounded, including their commanding General Sir Edward Pakenham. Jackson's casualties were an astounding seven killed, six wounded. A fortnight later, January 18, the British retired to their ships. They were not yet ready to give up, however. On February 11, they attacked and captured Fort Bowyer on Mobile point. Three days later, on learning that a treaty had been signed, the British commander suspended further military operations and sailed for home.

Although the peace treaty had been signed by the time the Battle of New Orleans was fought, it was not ratified by both sides until February. Had Jackson been defeated and the British gained possession of Louisiana, there is reason to suspect that they might have demanded an adjustment of the peace settlement. As it was, Jackson's victory confirmed the *status quo ante bellum,* which formed the general basis for the Treaty of Ghent.

The Peace of Christmas Eve

Diplomatic negotiations for an end to hostilities were initiated almost as soon as the war broke out. When news of the American declaration of war reached Europe, Czar Alexander of Russia, who desperately needed British aid in repelling Napoleon's march on Moscow, offered to mediate the Anglo-American dispute. John Quincy Adams, the American minister in St. Petersburg, transmitted the offer to Washington, but his message did not arrive until April 1813.

By that time the United States had retreated from the belligerence displayed the previous summer when Madison terminated Dearborn's truce in order to secure satisfaction on impressments. The Northwest was lost, efforts to invade Canada across the Niagara frontier had failed miserably, and a tightening British blockade was strangling the economy. Without even waiting to see whether the British would accept the Russian offer, Madison sent Albert Gallatin and moderate Federalist James A. Bayard to join Adams in St. Petersburg. Madison hated to lose Gallatin, but the Russians had demanded a high-ranking cabinet member in the delegation as a sign of American sincerity. Gallatin, tired of the bickering within the cabinet and the carping from the "invisibles" in the Senate, was happy to go.

Gallatin and Bayard were instructed only to secure a specific renunciation of impressment and an agreement on the rights of neutrals. After arriving in Russia, the American envoys were forced to mark time until January 1814, when the British at last rejected the czar's offer of mediation. Bayard and Gallatin then went to London, hoping to initiate talks, but they found the British flushed with victory over Napoleon and disposed to teach the United States a lesson. The only thing Gallatin accomplished was an agreement to open discussion later in the summer at Ghent, Belgium.

As Wellington's veterans flowed to North America in the summer of 1814, the Madison administration, its treasury empty, decided to abandon its demands for a settlement on impressment and neutral rights. It also beefed up the negotiating team, sending to Ghent two men with a domestic political constituency, Henry Clay and Jonathan Russell. In point of sheer ability the American delegation far outweighed anything Britain could muster from its diplomatic corps, but the Americans were hampered by internal dissension. Friction developed from the opposite personalities of the puritanical Adams, champion of the eastern fisheries, and the fun-loving Clay, guardian of the interests of the West. Adams meticulously noted in his diary every occasion when he arose before dawn to read his Bible and encountered Clay just getting to bed after an all-night poker session. The sour Jonathan Russell, moreover, generally irritated everyone. Only Gallatin held the delegation together by a combination of wisdom, leadership, and tact.

When they arrived at Ghent in August 1814, the British commissioners presented their demands: territorial cessions in Maine and northern New York, rewards for their Native American allies in the form of a permanent tribal dominion in the Northwest, and concessions in regard to the Newfoundland fisheries. Such "extravagant pretensions" as Bayard called them, were not intended to provide a serious basis for negotiations; rather, the British hoped to stall for time while their armies, reinforced by veterans from Europe, gobbled up slices of American territory. In September, with one army invading northern New York and another preparing to depart to New Orleans, the British offered to settle on the basis of *uti possidetis* (that is, retaining all conquests made at the time of the signing of the treaty), while abandoning the demand for an Indian buffer state. The Americans countered with an offer of *status quo ante bellum,* which meant a return to the prewar boundaries and a restoration of conquests. When news of the British failure at Lake Champlain arrived in October, it was evident that the two sides were not far apart. Since neither had made any conquests, *uti possidetis* was virtually the same as *ante bellum.*

The British diplomatic position in Europe, moreover, was deteriorating rapidly. The Congress meeting at Vienna to frame a peace settlement for Europe had degenerated into petty bickering. Russia was looming as a new power in the East, and France was refusing to submit quietly to defeat (Napoleon returned triumphantly from Elba the following spring). In this situation Foreign Minister Castlereagh began to regret having sent some of the best British regiments to North America. He sought to retrieve his diplomatic leverage by asking Wellington himself to take command in Canada, but the "Iron Duke" declined, pointing out that military success in America was unlikely without naval control of the Great Lakes. To attempt to build a navy on the Great Lakes and mount a new military campaign in 1815 would require additional taxes and further strain the depleted British treasury. It did not seem worth it merely to gain a few acres of land in North America, and on November 18 the ministry voted to terminate the war on the basis of *status quo ante bellum.*

The American commissioners leaped at the offer, and the treaty was signed on Christmas Eve 1814. It was simply a mutual agreement to end hostilities. Neither side gained in territory; impressment, for which the United States had been fighting since the repeal of the orders-in-council, was not even mentioned. With the war in Europe ended, the whole question of neutral rights was obsolete. But the United States had in no sense surrendered its stand, and, indeed, it had vindicated its rights by fighting for them. Militarily the war was a draw, and both sides agreed that further hostilities were futile. Lingering disagreements could be worked out in time, and the settlements reached just a few years later with regard to naval arms limitations on the Great Lakes and joint occupation of the Oregon country demonstrated the sensibility of this approach.

The Hartford Convention

For the United States, the peace settlement came none too soon. At the very moment that the commissioners were inking their signatures to the treaty, a Federalist convention assembled at Hartford, Connecticut, to discuss the nature and future of the American union. The Hartford Convention was the culmination of Federalist discontent, simmering since the time of the Embargo and brought into the open by the war. Federalists had long been convinced that Jefferson and his cohorts were leading the nation down the crooked path to anarchy and atheism. The tacit alliance with Napoleon and the declaration of war against the one nation in the world that stood for order, stability, and morality confirmed their worst suspicions.

Throughout the war, Federalist governors in Vermont, Massachusetts, Connecticut, and Rhode Island wavered between patriotism and partisanship. They were unwilling to undermine openly the nation's war effort, but they did refuse various requests for cooperation. They rejected all efforts by the federal government to take command of the state militias, and, on occasion, they refused to permit their militia to serve in neighboring states. These partial measures did not satisfy many rank and file Federalists who were toying with the idea of secession and a separate peace. In October 1814, the Massachusetts Assembly issued a call for a convention of New England states to meet at Hartford, Connecticut, to discuss "a radical reform of the national compact." The convention would have power only to "advise and suggest" a course of action; but, Republicans assumed that New England's secession from the Union was the true object. President Madison, when he learned of New England's "sedition," was reported to have been "miserably shattered and woe-be-gone."

In truth, though, the convention had been promoted by moderate Federalists, who had no wish to divide the Union. The concept of a political convention, though it originated in the constitution-making of the revolutionary years, had evolved into a party mechanism. Since 1808, both parties had periodically experimented with state conventions to reach agreement on nominations and party principles. It was thus a major step in the development of the machinery of modern democratic government. In 1814, moderate New England Federalists seized upon it as a way to keep control of their party, and the tactic worked. The Massachusetts assembly deliberately excluded men of "impetuous temperament and fiery earnestness" and named a slate of twelve moderate Federalists, headed by young Harrison Gray Otis. When the convention met in December 1814, moderates were able to capitalize on the traditional Federalist fear of radical change and social upheaval. The Hartford Convention thus turned out to be nothing more than a harmless safety valve for Federalist discontent.

After some debate, the meeting adopted a report asserting the right of each state to "interpose its authority" for the protection of its citizens (an echo of Madison's Virginia Resolutions of 1798) and suggesting that each state take care of its own military defense. Extremist Otis then headed a three-man delegation to carry the report to Washington. They arrived in mid-February, a few days after news of the Treaty of Ghent. Realizing that their recommendations were now irrelevant, they departed hastily without even seeing the president.

Despite the efforts of its moderate leaders, the Federalist party was finished as a viable institution. It never overcame the stigma of disloyalty in a national emergency, and its concepts of energetic government were already being absorbed by young Republican nationalists. Rufus King, who ran against James Monroe in 1816, was the party's last presidential candidate. The nation's first two-party system dissolved, and the Republicans dominated the political scene for the next decade. Yet the war was a triumph, not only for Republican partisans and policies, but for the nation as a whole. Americans survived their ordeal by fire and emerged with a new feeling of pride and unity—in that sense it was truly a "second war for independence."

Changing of the Guard

James Monroe, who succeeded Madison in 1817, was the last president to wear the male costume associated with the eighteenth century—the three-cornered hat, ruffled shirt, knee breeches, stockings, and buckled shoes. His outmoded dress was symbolic, for in a real sense he was the last of the revolutionary generation. The unseemly squabble for the office which took place on his retirement represented a new generation playing the political game under new rules.

The war brought to the fore a new breed of politicians who had scant respect for the old verities. Men like Henry Clay and John C. Calhoun received their political baptism in the Twelfth Congress leading the movement for war. The humiliations suffered at the hands of the European belligerents showed the weakness in the old Republican doctrines of unobtrusive, frugal government, and the difficulties that the government experienced in fighting the war only confirmed it. Without the Bank of the United States (whose charter Congress let expire in 1811), the Treasury was helpless, and the nation stumbled through the conflict on a highly inflated paper currency. Without a national network of roads, the government could neither move its armies nor keep them supplied. Thus the war exposed the need for more energetic government; and, when peace came the young nationalists in Congress set to work fostering manufactures, revitalizing the federal bank, and encouraging the construction of transportation facilities. For a generation the nation had been intensely concerned with its place in the world—breaking the bonds of empire and then establishing a stable, respected political system. After 1815, foreign affairs were almost ignored, except insofar as they involved continental expansion. The next generation became preoccupied instead with internal problems—with industrial development, with settlement of the frontier, and with the menacing sectional controversy.

Severe problems still beset American society—problems of prejudice, of discrimination, of injustice—problems which would still await solution a century and a half later. But even so, the generation which surrendered its authority in the years after 1815 could look back with some satisfaction. The experiment in republican government—a source of concern to both Washington and Jefferson in their inaugural addresses—had been made to work.

Some Suggested Readings

The American Landscape in 1760

Nearly all the description in the Introduction was taken from the accounts of travelers who toured America in the middle decades of the eighteenth century. Since the fictionalized account was set in the year 1760, the most useful relation of actual events was *Burnaby's Travels Through North America,* with Introduction and Notes by Rufus Rockwell Wilson (1904). Andrew Burnaby was an Anglican clergyman who toured the colonies from Virginia to Massachusetts in 1759–60. His account is particularly good for its description of the countryside and is full of sidelights on crops, farm animals, and the weather. Of equal value was the account of Dr. Alexander Hamilton, an Annapolis physician who journeyed to New England and back to Maryland in 1744. Carl Bridenbaugh has annotated the most recent edition under the title *Gentleman's Progress: The Itinerarium of Dr. Alexander Hamilton, 1744* (1948). The doctor was an acute observer of people, and his story sparkles with amusing anecdotes. A Swedish visitor provided one of the best descriptions of the American landscape. His journal has been published as *The America of 1750: Peter Kalm's Travels in North America,* revised from the original Swedish and edited by Adolph B. Benson (2 vols., 1937). Kalm was a botanist who toured the length of the continent, including Canada. His narrative is marvelously detailed with long digressions on American plants and animals.

The description of plantation life in Virginia was taken from the *Journal and Letters of Philip Vickers Fithian, 1773–1774,* edited by Hunter D. Farish (1957). Fithian was a Princeton graduate who served as a tutor to the Carter children at Nomini Hall in Virginia's Northern Neck, and his portrayal of life among the tobacco gentry is unequalled. The description of Mount Airy is from the author's own observation with special thanks to the Tayloe family for their hospitality. Charles Woodmason's journal, *The Carolina Back County on the Eve of the Revolution* (edited by Richard J. Hooker, 1953) offers a colorful tour of the southern hinterland. Newton D. Mereness, editor, *Travels in the American Colonies* (1916), contains a number of minor journals, and Anne Grant's *Memoirs of an American Lady* (1916) has a good description of Albany in the mid-eighteenth century.

There are also some secondary sources that present a view of life in the American colonies. William C. Langdon, *Everyday Things in American Life, 1607–1776* (1946) is not as comprehensive as its title suggests, but it has good descriptions of German farms in Pennsylvania, iron furnaces and glass works in New England, and the Moravian settlement at Bethlehem. Carl Bridenbaugh focuses on the emergence of cities in his *Cities in Revolt: Urban Life in America, 1743–1776* (1955) and *Rebels and Gentlemen: Philadelphia in the Age of Franklin* (1942). An extremely useful portrait of the frontier is Solon J. Buck and Elizabeth H. Buck, *The Planting of Civilization in Western Pennsylvania* (1939).

Finally, the modern reader should be warned that one cannot tour the American colonies, even in an imaginary way, without frequent recourse to Jedidiah Morse, *The American Geography* (1789) and *The American Gazetteer* (1797). Although much of Morse's statistical data, on population and trade, for instance, dates from the period after the Revolution, he offers a wealth of information—on roads and ferries, distances between towns, variations in the landscape, and agricultural practices—that is valid for the colonial period.

England's Atlantic Community

The best overview of the British Empire in the eighteenth century, with its complex network of trade patterns and cultural cross-fertilization, is Michael Kraus, *The Atlantic Civilization: Eighteenth Century Origins* (1949). "What distinguished Americans from other peoples?" is a question asked by Daniel J. Boorstin, and his search for an answer in *The Americans: The Colonial Experience* (1958) provides a fascinating, suggestive view of colonial life and institutions.

An excellent overview of the imperial economy is John J. McCusker and Russell R. Menard, *The Economy of British America, 1607–1789* (1985). For detailed statistics on wealth distribution, income, and economic growth the reader should consult Alice Hanson Jones's monumental study, *Wealth of a Nation To Be: The American Colonies on the Eve of the Revolution* (1980). Among the better monographs on particular segments of the Atlantic trading community are Frederick B. Tolles, *Meeting House and Counting House: The Quaker Merchants of Colonial Philadelphia* (1948); James B. Hedges, *The Browns of Providence Plantations* (1952); and William T. Baxter, *The House of Hancock: Business in Boston, 1724–1775* (1945). These works all focus on the mercantile elite; Carl Bridenbaugh, *The Colonial Craftsman* (1955) is an introduction to the workingman. The lot of the white servant is discussed in Abbott E. Smith, *Colonists in Bondage: White Servitude and Convict Labor in America, 1607–1776* (1947). Winthrop D. Jordan's *White over Black: American Attitudes toward the Negro, 1550–1812* (1968) is a splendid account of the origins of slavery and racial prejudice in the American colonies. It is supplemented by Peter H. Wood's *Black Majority: Negroes in Colonial South Carolina from 1670 through the Stono Rebellion* (1974) and by Edmund S. Morgan *American Slavery, American Freedom: The Ordeal of Colonial*

Virginia (1975). Allan Kulikoff, *Tobacco and Slaves: The Development of Southern Culture in the Chesapeake, 1680–1800* (1986) and Mechal Sobel, *The World They Made Together: Black and White Values in 18th Century Virginia* (1987) explore the interaction between planters and slaves.

The colonial "climate of opinion," as Carl L. Becker called it, has received much attention from historians. Becker's *Heavenly City of the Eighteenth Century Philosophers* (1932) and his *Declaration of Independence* (1942) are classics. Louis B. Wright, *The Cultural Life of the American Colonies, 1607–1763* (1957) is a good general survey. Perry Miller, *The New England Mind: From Colony to Province* (1953) is much admired by historians, but the nonprofessional reader will find Samuel Eliot Morison's *Intellectual Life of Colonial New England* (2nd ed., 1956) smoother sailing. Jack P. Greene, *Pursuits of Happiness: Social Development of Early Modern British Colonies and the Formation of American Culture* (1988) is an important synthesis that plays down the importance of New England in the shaping of American culture.

The standard treatment of the "age of reason" is Henry F. May, *The Enlightenment in America* (1976). Recent studies of the impact of the Great Awakening on society and politics include Rhys Isaac, *The Transformation of Virginia, 1740–1790* (1982) and Patricia U. Bonomi, *Under the Cope of Heaven: Religion, Society, and Politics in Colonial America* (1986).

The Imperial Challenge, 1763–1774

The most comprehensive study of the American colonies in the mid-eighteenth century is Lawrence H. Gipson's *The British Empire before the American Revolution* (14 vols., 1936–1968). Gipson devoted much of his life to the subject, and the reader who does not want to do the same might consult his more manageable work, *The Coming of the Revolution, 1763–1775* (1954). Gipson views the colonies from the standpoint of the empire as a whole, and although this approach lends a needed perspective, it does not satisfactorily explain the movement for American independence. A more recent work, which describes in vivid detail both the evolution of British policies and the American reaction, is Merrill Jensen, *The Founding of a Nation: A History of the American Revolution, 1763–1776* (1968).

Neither Gipson nor Jensen was much concerned with interpretation, with explaining the "why" of the American Revolution. But the question has evoked a great deal of disagreement among other scholars. Historians writing in the early part of this century argued that the Revolution was caused in part by class conflict, that the key element in overthrowing British rule was the "lower orders" of society who were organized and manipulated by "popular" leaders. This interpretation has been revived and phrased in a somehwhat more sophisticated manner by Gary B. Nash in *The Urban Crucible: Social Change, Political Consciousness, and the Origins of the American Revolution* (1979). Another elderly interpretation, once thought to be hopelessly dated—that Virginians were motivated in part by the debts they owed to British merchants—has been given new life by T. H. Breen in *Tobacco Culture: The Mentality of the Great Tidewater Planters on the Eve of the Revolution* (1985).

Despite these excursions into the economic origins of the Revolution, interest in its intellectual origins has remained strong, largely due to the continuing influence of Bernard Bailyn. In *The Origins of American Politics* (1967), Bailyn argued that Americans possessed a well-developed theory of republicanism, gleaned from English and continental writers, and the Revolution was a natural and ideologically coherent response to British threats to American liberty. His student, Gordon S. Wood, enlarged on this idea by examining the ideology of the revolutionary leaders in *The Creation of the American Republic, 1776–1787* (1969). Similarly, Jack P. Greene examined the often violent evolution of representative institutions in *The Quest for Power: The Lower Houses of Assembly in the Southern Royal Colonies, 1689–1776* (1963). The most recent and—as befits its author—most stimulating excursion into this field is Edmund Morgan, *Inventing the People: The Rise of Popular Sovereignty in England and America* (1988).

The Triumph of Independence, 1774–1783

The best account of the military contest is Christopher Ward, *The War of the Revolution* (2 vols., 1952). A considerably shorter narrative is John R. Alden's *American Revolution, 1775–1783* (1954), in which some attention is devoted to political and diplomatic events. The works of Lynn Montross can be especially recommended for their combination of fast-paced narrative and sound scholarship. His account of the army is entitled *Rag, Tag, and Bobtail* (1952), and his *Reluctant Rebels* (1950) tells the story of the Continental Congress. Volumes IV and V of Douglas Southall Freeman's biography of *George Washington* (7 vols., 1948–1957) are a fascinating story told from the point of view of the commander in chief. Relations between the army and the Continental Congress are explored by Jonathan Gregory Rossie in *The Politics of Command in the American Revolution* (1975). The treason of Benedict Arnold, one of the most dramatic events of the war, is brilliantly narrated by James T. Flexner in *The Traitor and the Spy* (1953).

For many years the standard history of the Loyalists was Claude H. Van Tyne, *The Loyalists in the American Revolution* (1902). The most glaring defect in Van Tyne's work was his failure to explain why certain men became Loyalists while others joined the revolutionary cause. William H. Nelson tried to remedy this by examining Loyalist literature in *The American Tory* (1961), but his analysis was confined to the rhetoric of the articulate few. The problems of who were the Loyalists and how many there were are explored in Wallace Brown, *The King's Friends: The Composition and Motives of American Loyalist Claimants* (1966). Brown, however, relied solely on the claims for compensation filed with the British government after the war. The definitive study of the Loyalists thus remains to be done.

The war in the West is a story all its own. Jack Sosin, *Whitehall and the Wilderness: the Middle West in British Colonial Policy, 1760–1775* (1961) discusses the role of the West in the coming of the Revolution. Thomas P. Abernethy, *Western Lands and the American Revolution* (1937), unravels the terribly complicated story of the land speculators and their influence on both British and American policies. The casual reader who wants nothing more than a good story should pick up the works of Dale Van Every: *Forth to the Wilderness* (1961), *A Company of Heroes* (1962), and *Ark of Empire* (1963).

Samuel F. Bemis's classic *Diplomacy of the American Revolution* (1935) has been replaced by Jonathan R. Dull, *A Diplomatic History of the American Revolution* (1985). Detailed accounts of the peace negotiations can be found in Richard B. Morris, *The Peacemakers: The Great Powers and American Independence* (1965) and James H. Hutson, *John Adams and the Diplomacy of the Revolution* (1980).

From Many, One

The most recent exploration of the social changes that accompanied the War for Independence is Edward Countryman, *The American Revolution* (1985). Countryman emphasizes in particular the impact of the Revolution on artisans, blacks, and women. Merrill D. Peterson, in his excellent biography, *Thomas Jefferson and the New Nation* (1970), devotes a chapter to Jefferson's role in revolutionary reform, and David Freeman Hawke traces Dr. Benjamin Rush's efforts to improve American society in *Benjamin Rush, Revolutionary Gadfly* (1971).

The impact of the Revolution on women and the family has been examined by Mary Beth Norton in *Liberty's Daughters: The Revolutionary Experience of American Women, 1750—1800* (1980). Nancy Cott provides the follow-up story of the feminine experience in the early republic: *Bonds of Womanhood: Women's Sphere in New England, 1780–1815* (1977). Joan M. Jensen, *Loosening the Bonds: Mid-Atlantic Farm Women* (1986) portrays the lives of rural women in Pennsylvania and Delaware during this period. Paul C. Nagel focused on some of the most interesting women of the age in *The Adams Women: Abigail and Louisa Adams, Their Sisters and Daughters* (1987).

New insights as to the Revolution's impact on African Americans can be found in Jeffrey J. Crow, *The Black Experience in Revolutionary North Carolina* (1977), Ira Berlin and Ron Hoffman, eds. *Slavery and Freedom in the Age of the American Revolution* (1983), and Gary B. Nash, *Forging Freedom: Formation of Philadelphia's Black Community, 1720–1840* (1988) as well as his succinct and controversial *Race and Revolution* (1990).

The standard authority on the Confederation period is Merrill Jensen, *The New Nation* (1950). The work destroyed the old notion that the 1780s were a "critical period," and pointed instead to the substantial amount of political and economic progress that occurred prior to the Constitution. In a recent contribution to the New American Nation Series, Richard B. Morris has updated Jensen's work and modified his conclusions in some ways in *Forging of the Union, 1781–1789* (1987).

Jack N. Rakove has provided a thoughtful study of the politics of the Continental Congress in *The Beginnings of National Politics: An Interpretive History of the Continental Congress* (1979). The origins of political parties in the Confederation period have been examined by Jackson T. Main, *Political Parties before the Constitution* (1973) and by Norman K. Risjord, *Chesapeake Politics, 1780–1800* (1978). Peter S. Onuf's *Statehood and Union: A History of the Northwest Ordinance* (1987) is a nice piece of scholarship; and Charlene Bangs Bickford's and Kenneth R. Bowling's *Birth of the Nation* (1989) is a fine short history of the accomplishments of the first federal Congress.

The recent bicentennial inspired a plethora of books describing the writing and ratification of the Constitution. None of them, however, achieves the level of Catherine Drinker Bowen's *Miracle at Philadelphia* (1966) for narrative power and graceful writing. The question of who supported the Constitution and why has stirred intense and continuing historical debate. In 1913, Charles A. Beard suggested in *An Economic Interpretation of the Constitution* that the document was written by men who had an economic interest in strong government. Many of them, Beard pointed out, held large amounts of public securities which would rise dramatically in value under a government with power to tax and pay its debts. Though not accepted in all its details, Beard's interpretation remained historical dogma until Forrest McDonald's *We the People: The Economic Origins of the Constitution* (1958) demonstrated that securities were only one of many forms of property held by those who wrote the Constitution, and that ownership of securities had little or no influence in the state ratifying conventions. In 1985, Forrest McDonald supplemented this work with a study of the political thought of the Founding Fathers in *Novus Ordo Seclorum: The Intellectual Origins of the Constitution.* Calvin S. Jillson subjected the voting in the federal Convention to sophisticated roll call analysis in *Constitution-Making: Conflict and Consensus in the Federal Convention of 1787* (1988). For a comparative view of ratification in the states see the sprightly collection, *The Constitution and the States* (1988) edited by Patrick T. Conley and John P. Kaminski. *The Selling of the Constitutional Convention, A History of News Coverage* (1990) by John K. Alexander ably shows how the press "prepared the minds of their readers" for the Constitution.

The Search for National Identity

Russell B. Nye, *The Cultural Life of the New Nation, 1776–1830* (1960), summarizes American progress in a wide variety of fields, from science and medicine to religion and the fine arts. Unfortunately, the scope is so broad that the story often degenerates into a catalog of names. More focused on the revolutionary period is Kenneth Silverman, *Cultural History of the American Revolution* (1976). Joseph J. Ellis, *After the Revolution: Profiles of Early American Culture* (1979) takes a biographical approach to the subject. John C. Greene, *American Science in the Age of Jefferson* (1984) is the latest statement on that subject. A good analysis of the thinking of one of the leading cultural nationalists of the period is Richard J. Moss, *Noah Webster* (1985).

Curtis P. Nettels, *The Emergence of a National Economy, 1775–1815* (1962) is comprehensive but dull. The thesis suggested by the title, that an interdependent national market developed in these years when the nation had neither factories nor interstate transportation facilities, is also open to serious question. A better and more comprehensive study is John J. McCusker and Russell R. Menard, *The Economy of British America, 1607–1789* (1985). Thomas Doerflinger, *A Vigorous Spirit of Enterprise: Merchants and Economic Development in Revolutionary Philadelphia* (1986) is an important study. Barbara M. Tucker, *Samuel Slater and the Origins of the American Textile Industry, 1790–1860* (1984) offers a cultural history of American industrialization.

Like most of his other works, Perry Miller's *Life of the Mind in America from the Revolution to the Civil War* (1965) is openly admired by intellectual historians and studiously avoided by almost everyone else. The dilettante is better advised to try Daniel J. Boorstin's *The Americans: The National Experience* (1965) for a melange of anecdotal material wrapped in a provocative thesis. Van Wyck Brooks offers a charming survey of early American literature in *The World of Washington Irving* (1944). The major religious movements of the early national period are treated in Conrad Wright, *The Beginnings of Unitarianism in America* (1955), C. A. Johnson, *The Frontier Camp Meeting* (1955), and John Boles, *Religion in Antebellum Kentucky* (1976).

The most scholarly and complete study of early American architecture is William H. Pierson, Jr., *American Buildings and their Architects: The Colonial and Neo-Classical Styles* (1970). Wayne Andrew's *Architecture, Ambition, and Americans* (1964) is an interesting attempt to relate architecture and home furnishings to the political and social atmosphere of each period of American history. There are a number of competent studies of early American painting, but the most readable are those by James T. Flexner, *American Painting: First Flowers of the Wilderness* (1957), and *America's Old Masters* (1939).

The Federal Experiment

Noble E. Cunningham, Jr., *The Jeffersonian Republicans: Formation of Party Organization, 1789–1800* (1956) probably remains the best descriptive study of the beginnings of the Jeffersonian party, although this writer disagrees with Cunningham's view that the parties of the 1790s had no connection with the factions that divided over the Constitution (see Norman K. Risjord, *Chesapeake Politics, 1780–1800*). There have been a number of computer-assisted quantitative studies of the origins of political parties in the 1790s, the most recent and most sophisticated of which is John F. Hoadley, *Origins of American Parties, 1789–1803* (1986). Historians have recently made considerable progress in explaining the motivations of common people in choosing party affiliation. In *Chants Democratic: New York City and the Rise of The American Working Class, 1788–1850* (1984), Sean Wilentz presented a convincing argument as to why urban artisans became Jeffersonian Republicans; Thomas P. Slaughter, *The Whiskey Rebellion: Frontier Epilogue to the American Revolution* (1986) presents an equally convincing argument for the frontier.

Other recent scholarship has been directed at party ideology. Lance Banning, *The Jeffersonian Persuasion: Evolution of a Party Ideology* (1978) remains useful, but the most exciting new direction has been taken by Joyce Appleby in her *Capitalism and a New Social Order: The Republican Vision of the 1790s* (1984). Appleby argued that the Jeffersonian vision of a nation of independent entrepreneurs pointed the way to the free enterprise capitalism and self-made gospel of the nineteenth century. John R. Nelson, Jr., *Liberty and Property: Political Economy and Policymaking in the New Nation, 1789–1812* (1987) and Stephen Watts, *The Republic Reborn: War and the Making of Liberal America, 1790–1820* (1987) have enlarged upon this thesis and filled in some of the details.

The best survey of foreign affairs between the Revolution and the War of 1812 is Paul A. Varg, *Foreign Policies of the Founding Fathers* (1963). Albert H. Bowman, *The Struggle for Neutrality: Franco-American Diplomacy during the Federalist Era* (1974) focuses on the sometimes stormy relationship with France. On British relations, see Charles R. Ritcheson, *Aftermath of Revolution: British Policy Toward the United States, 1783–1795* (1969) and Bradford Perkins, *The First Rapprochement, England and the United States, 1795–1805* (1959). Jerald A. Combs, *The Jay Treaty: Political Background of the Founding Fathers* (1973) focuses on that climactic event. A provocative essay on the intellectual origins of American foreign policy is Felix Gilbert's *To the Farewell Address: Ideas of Early American Foreign Policy* (1961).

Francis S. Philbrick's *The Rise of the West, 1754–1830* (1965) provides an overview of the West in this period. Wiley Sword, *President Washington's Indian War: The Struggle for the Old Northwest, 1790–1795* (1985) blends thorough scholarship with fast-paced narrative. Collin Calloway, *Crown and Calumet: British Indian Relations, 1783–1815* (1987) investigates the British side and presents interesting insights into Native American social and political organization. Glenn Tucker's *Tecumseh, Vision of Glory* (1956) is a nicely written biography of "the greatest Indian."

Page Smith's *John Adams* (2 vols., 1962) is a fine, sympathetic study of the second president. Stephen Kurtz, *The Presidency of John Adams* (1957) focuses specifically on Adams's term as president. James Morton Smith's *Freedom's Fetters* (1956) tells the story of the alien and sedition laws and the judicial proceedings that resulted.

The election of 1800 has never been singled out for scholarly treatment. Cunningham's *Jeffersonian Republicans* describes the party apparatus that was mobilized for the occasion. The best accounts of the backstairs intrigues are in Irving Brant, *James Madison, Secretary of State, 1800–1809* (1953), and Morton Borden, *The Federalism of James A. Bayard* (1955).

Jefferson's "Empire for Liberty"

The classic statement of the Jeffersonian period is by Henry Adams, *History of the United States During the Administrations of Thomas Jefferson and James Madison* (9 vols., 1889–91). For the reader with leisure to spend, Henry Adams is still a rewarding experience. Recent research has altered some of his conclusions and challenged some of his views, however. Adams's biggest shortcoming was his unfriendly view of the two presidents who are the main figures in the story. He dismisses both as shallow thinkers and inept administrators. A number of recent works have sought to demonstrate Jefferson's genuine abilities as a politician and administrator. The best of these by far is Noble E. Cunningham, Jr., *The Process of Government under Jefferson* (1978). Irving Brant, *James Madison, The President, 1809–1812* (1956) and *James Madison, Commander in Chief* (1961) attempted to do the same service for Madison, though occasionally his brief is overstated. Marshall Smelser, *The Democratic Republic, 1801–1815* (1968) is a balanced survey that ably utilized the scholarship available at the time. Ralph Ketcham's *Presidents Above Party: The First American Presidency, 1789–1829* (1984) is an interesting, but in the end unconvincing, argument that all the presidents prior to Andrew Jackson viewed themselves as spokesmen for the nation, independent of political parties.

Among the many monographs dealing with particular events of the Jefferson and Madison administrations, the best are: Richard E. Ellis, *The Jeffersonian Crisis: Courts and Politics in the Young Republic* (1971), George Dangerfield, *Chancellor Robert R. Livingston of New York* (1960), especially for the Louisiana Purchase; David Lavender, *The Way to the Western Sea: Lewis and Clark Across the Continent* (1988), Thomas P. Abernethy, *The Burr Conspiracy* (1954), and James M. Banner, *To the Hartford Convention: The Federalists and the Origins of Party Politics in Massachusetts, 1789–1815* (1970).

"Mr. Madison's War"

The events leading to the War of 1812 are ably chronicled in Bradford Perkins, *Prologue to War: England and the United States, 1805–1812* (1961), and Reginald Horsman, *Causes of the War of 1812* (1962). Perkins' study is particularly useful for its account of the British view of things. Clifford L. Egan, *Neither Peace nor War: Franco-American Relations, 1803–1812* (1983) tells the other diplomatic story. Harry Coles, *The War of 1812* (1965) and Reginald Horsman, *The War of 1812* (1969) are both fast-paced surveys of the fighting. J. C. A. Stagg, *Mr. Madison's War: Politics, Diplomacy, and Warfare in the Early American Republic, 1783–1830* (1983) provides important insights into President Madison's thinking during the events that led up to the war; Stagg also found a close connection between politics and military strategy during the war. The best account of the peace negotiations is Bradford Perkins, *Castlereagh and Adams: England and the United States, 1812–1823* (1964).

Index

Adam, Robert, 202, 204
Adams, Abigail, 180, 241–42
Adams, John, 48, 117, 158
  and Boston Massacre, 76
  on Church of England, 102
  in First Continental Congress, 89
  and Massachusetts constitution, 135, 136
  opposes Stamp Act, 66
  as peace commissioner, 127
  as president, 230–32, 234–36, 242, 248
  as presidential candidate, 228–29, 236–39
  in Second Continental Congress, 97, 99, 99
  as vice president, 208–09
  views of on government, 132–33
Adams, John Quincy, 295–96
Adams, Samuel, 59, 88, 93, 117, 158, 177, 215–16
  and Boston Tea Party, 84–85
  establishes committee of correspondence, 81
  in First Continental Congress, 89
  leads Sons of Liberty, 66, 74–75
  and Massachusetts politics, 70
  and moral reform, 184
  and the federal Constitution, 169–70
Addison, Joseph, 45, 197
Adet, Pierre, 229
Administration of Justice Act (1774), 86
African Americans
  free blacks after Revolution, 179
  importation of, 32
  in New York City, 8
  in revolutionary America, 177–80
  See also Slavery
The Age of Reason (1794), 48, 194
Agriculture, 3, 6, 8, 15–17, 18, 21–22
  cotton, 26, 190–91
  indigo, 24–25, 31–32, 147
  rice, 24–25, 31–32, 33, 147, 190
  tobacco, 18, 20, 22, 31, 60, 147–48, 190
Aitkin, Edward, 57
Akwright, Richard, 192
Alamance Creek, Battle of, 78
Albany, N.Y., 7
Alexander (Tsar of Russia), 295
Alexandria, Va., 18
Alien and Sedition Acts, 232–34, 243
  See also Kentucky Resolutions; Virginia Resolutions
Allen, Ethan, 48, 94, 109
Allen, William, 101
Amendments to Constitution
  Eleventh, 247
  Fourth, 269–70
  proposed by New York ratifying convention, 172
  and second convention movement, 169
The American Crisis (1776), 107–08
The American Dictionary (1828), 197
American Philosophical Society, 38, 41
American Revolution, 125–27
  nature of, 132–33
  See also Loyalists
American Spelling Book (1783), 197
Andover Theological Seminary, 194
André, John, 122
Anglicans. *See* Church of England
Annapolis, 20
  women in during Revolution, 181
Annapolis Convention, 157
Antifederalists, 165–72, 209, 211
Anti-nationalists, 140
Architecture
  colonial, 44
  post-revolutionary, 200–05
Arminianism, 48, 53, 194
Arminius, Jacob, 48
Armstrong, John
  as minister to France, 260
  and Newburgh Conspiracy, 146
  as secretary of war, 287, 289, 290–91, 292–93
Army, British
  and Boston Massacre, 74–76
  in colonies, 57–58
Army, Continental
  Baron von Stueben trains, 119–20

blacks in during Revolution, 177
colonial militia drills in 1774, 92–93
demobilization of after Revolution, 145–47
effectiveness of, 125
formation of, 95
pensions for, 145–47
Washington takes command of, 95–96
weapons and tactics during 1770s, 103–04
women accompany during Revolution, 121–22
See also Militia; Navy
Arnold, Benedict, 94, 115–16, 126
and Canadian campaign, 109–11
treason of, 122
Articles of Confederation
adopted, 137–40
efforts to strengthen, 139, 154–58
and the West, 141–45
U.S. under, 145–49
Arts
colonial, 43–44
in early republic, 203–05
revolutionary, 199–200
Assumption of state debts, 213
Astronomy, 39–40, 278–81
Aurora (Philadelphia), 272

Bache, Richard, 141
Backcountry. *See* Frontier
Backus, Isaac, 53
Balanced government, 133
Baltimore, Md., 292
Bank of Massachusetts, 149
Bank of North America, 128, 139, 149, 159, 191
Bank of the United States, 214, 246, 299
Bank of New York, 149
Banneker, Benjamin, 179
Baptist Church, 18, 51–52, 53–54, 194–95
Barbary Coast War, 251–53
Barlow, Joel, 198
Barney, Joshua, 292
Barre, Isaac, 65
Barton, Benjamin Smith, 196
Bartram, John, 38
Baton Rouge, La., 261
Bayard, James A., 296
Beaumarchais, Pierre, 117–18
Beccaria, Cesare, 185
Benezet, Anthony, 178
Bennington, Vt., 115
Berlin Decree, 266
Bernard, Francis, 59, 72, 74
Bethlehem, Pa., 9–10
Beverley, Robert, 44
Bill of rights, 133
added to Constitution, 211
lack of in Constitution criticized, 164
in Northwest Ordinance, 144–45
Bladensburg, Battle of, 292
Blair, John, 159
Bland, Richard, 63
Bland, Theodorick, 171
Blennerhassett, Herman, 262–63
Blue Jacket (Shawnee chief), 222
Board of War, 119
Boone, Daniel, 80, 189, 219
Boorhaave, Hermann, 41
Boston, 3–6, 34, 35–36
British troops in and massacre, 74–76
nonimportation in, 76
opposition to Stamp Act in, 65–67
opposition to writs of assistance in, 59
port closed, 85–86
siege of, 94–95
Boston Alms House, 4
Boston Evening Post, 73
Boston Gazette, 71, 76
Boston Manufacturing Company, 193
Boston Massacre, 74–76
Boston News Letter, 45
Boston Port Act (1774), 85–86
Boston Tea Party, 83–85
Botany, 38–39
Botetourt, Lord, 80
Bouquet, Henry, 57
Bowditch, Nathaniel, 195–96
Bowdoin, James, 152–53, 153
"Boy with a Squirrel," 44
Boylston, Zabdiel, 43
Braddock, Edward, 57
Brandywine Creek, Battle of, 112
Brant, Joseph, 115
Breed's Hill, Battle of, 95
Brock, Isaac, 284–85
Brooklyn Heights, Battle of, 106–07
Brown, Charles Brockden, 198
Brown, Jacob, 291
Brown, Moses, 193
Brown, Nicholas, 29, 30
Brown University, 53
Brunswick, N.C., 24
Buckingham County, Va., 176–77
Buffalo, N.Y., 290
Bulfinch, Charles, 201–02
Bull, William, 85
Bunker Hill, 95
Burgoyne, John, 94, 111–12
and Saratoga campaign, 114–16
Burke, Edmund, 75, 83–84, 86
Burlington, N.J., 11
Burr, Aaron
conspiracy of, 261–64
and election of 1796, 228–29
and election of 1800, 238–39
Business organizations, 191
Bute, John Stuart, Earl of, 61, 75
Byrd, William II, 39, 44, 45

Cabinet meetings, 252
Cadore, Duc de, 272
Calhoun, John C., 273, 281–82, 299
Cambridge, Mass., 5
Camden, Battle of, 123–24
Camp Meetings, 194–95
Canada
U.S. invasion of during 1775–76, 109–11
and War of 1812, 283–85, 287–89
Cane Ridge, Ky., revival, 195
Canning, George, 271
Capital, U.S.
British burn, 292
construction of, 201–02
permanent location of, 213, 241
Caramelli, Hamet, 252–53
Carlton, Sir Guy, 105, 109–11
Carpenter's Hall, 90
Carroll, Charles, of Carrollton, 138
Carter, Robert, 19
Cass, Lewis, 284
Castlereagh, Viscount, 282, 297
Catesby, Mark, 38–39
Census of 1790, 174

Channing, William Ellery, 194
Charleston, S.C., 25, 32, 67, 85, 123, 127, 180
Charleston Library Society, 45
Chase, Samuel, 250–51
Chauncey, Isaac, 289, 291
Cherokees, 17, 57, 80, 275–76, 280
Chesapeake (ship), 268, 271, 286
China
  American trade with, 148–49
Chippewa Creek, Battle of, 291
Chippewa Indians, 220, 279
Chisholm v. *Georgia* (1793), 247
Christianity as Old as the Creation (1730), 48
Christmas
  observed in colonies, 14
Chrysler's Farm, Battle of, 289
Church of England, 14, 21, 23, 52–53, 60–61, 101–02
Cincinnati, Society of the, 147
Cities
  in colonial America, 34–36
  See also individual cities
Civil Liberties
  and Alien and Sedition Acts, 232–33
  and enforcement of Embargo Act, 269–70
Claiborne, William C. C., 261
Clark, Daniel, 261
Clark, George Rogers, 122–23, 220
Clark, William, 257
Clatsop Indians, 257
Clay, Henry, 262, 263, 273, 281, 296, 299
Clinton, George, 140, 155, 215–16, 217, 261
  as Antifederalist, 169, 172
Clinton, Sir Henry, 94, 116, 120–21, 123, 126, 127
Cochrane, Sir Alexander, 294
Cockburn, Sir George, 291–92
Coercive Acts (1774), 85–87, 88
Coffee, John, 290
Coinage Act (1792), 214
Coke, Sir Edward, 37, 38
Colden, Cadwallader, 40–41, 42, 48
Colleges, 5, 14, 23, 47, 53, 184, 188, 194
Collinson, Peter, 38–39, 40
The Colonel Dismounted (1764), 63
The Columbiad (1807), 198
Columbia River, 257
Committee of Secret Correspondence, 117
Committees of correspondence
  created in colonies, 82–83
  established in Massachusetts, 81
Committees of Safety, 91–92, 100
Common Sense, 97–98
Concord, Battle of, 93
Concord coach, 191
Conestoga wagon, 15, 190
Confiance (ship), 293
Congregational Church, 50–52
Congress, Confederation
  asks for additional powers, 154–55
  considers Constitution, 165
  and demobilization of army, 145–47
  responds to Shays's Rebellion, 153
  and the economy, 147–48
Congress, First Continental, 88–89, 89–91, 91–92
Congress, Second Continental, 94–95, 98–100, 117–18
Congress, U.S.
  declares war in 1812, 281–82
Connecticut, 28–29, 66, 89, 97
Connecticut Compromise, 163
Connecticut River Valley, 6
The Conquest of Canaan (1785), 197
Constitution (ship), 285–86
Constitution, U.S.
  drafting of, 158–64
  ratification of, 164–73
Constitutional Convention, 158–64
  and slavery, 178
Constitutionalist party (in Pennsylvania), 134, 166–67
Constitutions
  state revolutionary, 133–37
Continental Association, 91–92
Convention of 1800, 235
Conway, Thomas, 119
Copley, John Singleton, 43–44, 199
Cornstalk (Shawnee chief), 80, 219
Cornwallis, Charles Lord, 107, 108, 112, 123–25, 125–27
Corporations, 191
Cotton, 26, 28, 190, 199
Courts, Colonial
  and Regulators, 77
  vice admiralty, 62, 67, 72
Courts, U.S.
  creation of, 210
  enforce Alien and Sedition Acts, 231–33
  Republican assault on, 247–51
Cowpens, Battle of, 125
Creeks, 220, 275–76, 280, 289–90
Creek War of 1813–14, 289–90
Creoles, 261
Crevecoeur, St. Jean de, 1
Crimes and Punishments, 185, 187
Cult of Domesticity, 182–83
Cumberland Road, 247
Currency Act (1764), 62–63
Customs Commissioners, Board of, 72
Cutler, Manasseh, 144

Dalton, John, 196
Dane, Nathan, 165–72
Dartmouth (ship), 84–85
Dartmouth, William Legge, Earl of, 83, 85, 86
Daughters of Liberty, 73
Davenport, James, 54
Davie, William R., 235
Davies, Samuel, 53
Dawes, William, 93
Deane, Silas, 90, 117–18, 119
Dearborn, Henry, 283, 283, 284
Debts
  in colonial America, 31, 60, 64
  debtor relief during 1780s, 149–52
  Gallatin's plan for paying national, 245–47

and Peace of Paris of 1783, 130
and Regulators, 78
relief of, 159
Debts, U.S.
Hamilton's plans for paying, 211–14
Decatur, Stephen, 252, 286
Declaration of Independence, 99–100
Declaratory Act (1766), 69
Deism, 47–48, 193–94
Delaware, 135
Delaware Indians, 79–80, 219, 220, 276
Democracy
defined, 132
Jeffersonian, 234, 242–44
and state constitutions, 136–37
and the federal Constitution, 172–73
Democratic societies, 218
Denmark
and American Revolution, 129
Department of Foreign Affairs, 141
Depressions, 36, 147–48, 152
Detroit, 218, 284, 287
Dickinson, John, 94, 98, 99, 101, 137
at Constitutional Convention, 159, 160–61
"Letters from a Farmer in Pennsylvania" (1768), 71
Dickinson College, 184
Digges, Edward, 22
Directory (French), 230–32, 235
Divorce, 182
Dorchester, Lord, 221
Dorchester Heights, 96
Douglas, David, 20
Downie, George, 293
Dryden, John, 68
Duane, James, 91, 101
Dudingston, William, 82
Duer, William, 215
Dulaney, Daniel, 17
Dunmore, John Murray, Earl of, 80, 97, 177, 219
Dutch, 7–8, 9
Loyalist strength among, 102
Dwight, Timothy, 197

East India Company, 83, 84, 149
Eaton, William, 252–53
Economy
of American colonies, 2–3, 28–34
depression and growth during 1780s, 147–48, 152
and Gallatin's financial policies, 246–47
growth of during Revolution, 128
and Hamilton's financial policies, 211–16
of U.S. in 1790, 188–94
Eden, Robert, 97
Edinburgh University, 36–37, 42
Education
in colonial America, 13–14
Jefferson's plan for in Virginia, 187–88
and transatlantic interchange of ideas, 36–43
of women, 184–85
See also Colleges
Edwards, Jonathan, 50–51
Elections
of 1788, 209
of 1792, 215–16
of 1796, 228–29
of 1800, 236–39
of 1804, 361–62
of 1808, 270–71
of 1810, 273
Elements of Botany, 196
Eleventh Amendment, 247
Elliot, Matthew, 102
Ellsworth, Oliver, 210, 235
Embargo (1812), 282
Embargo Act (1807), 268–70
The Empress of China (ship), 148
Enforcement Act (1808), 270
Enlightenment, 36–43, 46–48
Enquirere (Richmond), 272
Entail, 186
Episcopal Church. *See* Church of England
Erskine, David, 271
An Essay on Human Understanding (1690), 46–47
Essex (ship), 267
Eustis, William, 283
Evans, Oliver, 192
Evening Gazette (Charleston), 33
Excise taxes, 213–14
Experiments and Observations on Electricity (1751), 39

Fairfax, Lord, 19
Fallen Timbers, Battle of, 221–22
Farewell Address, 228
Farming. *See* Agriculture
Father Abraham's Speech, 27
Fauchet, Jean Antoine Joseph, Baron, 228
Fauquier, Francis, 67
Federalist, The, 161, 172, 208
Federalist party, 240
in 1780s, 155, 165–72, 209
and Alien and Sedition Acts, 232–33
divided over Quasi War, 234–36, 241–42
and election of 1800, 237–39
and election of 1808, 270
and Hartford Convention, 297–98
and Judiciary Act of 1801, 248
oppose Embargo, 269–70
opposes Louisiana Purchase, 255–56
oppose War of 1812, 273, 282
and presidential election of 1796, 228–29
Federal style (architecture), 202–03, 204
Ferguson, Patrick, 124
Fishing, 29–30, 130
Flatboats, 191
Florida, 258–61
as U.S. southern boundary, 130
See also Pensacola, Fla.
Food and drink
in Albany, N.Y., 7
in Newport, R.I., 2–3
in New York City, 8
in North Carolina, 24
in Pennsylvania, 10, 15
in Virginia, 21–22
Forbes Road, 189
Fort Dearborn (Chicago), 223, 284
Fort Erie, 285, 289, 291
Fort George, 289, 291
Fort Greenville, 222
Fort Jackson, Treaty of, 290
Fort Malden, 221, 280, 284, 287
Fort McHenry, 292

Fort Miami, 222
Fort Michillimackinas, 284
Fort Mims, 290
Fort Ninety-Six, 125
Fort Stanwix, Battle of, 115
Fort Stanwix, Treaty (1765), 79–80, 219
Fort St. Johns, 109
Fort Ticonderoga, 94, 111, 114
Fort Washington (Cincinnati), 221
Fort Wayne, 223, 284
Treaty of, 279–80
Foster, Augustus J., 282
Fourth Amendment, 269–70
Fox, Charles James, 129, 267
France
Adams negotiates peace with, 234–36
American alliance with, 116–19, 216–18
and American neutral rights, 264–70, 272–73
and Peace of Paris of 1783, 129–31
and presidential election of 1796, 229
sells Louisiana to U.S., 254–56
trade agreement with in 1786, 148
U.S. trade with, 191
and victory at Yorktown, 126–27
and XYZ affair, 230–32
Franklin, Benjamin, 27–28
as civic leader, 13–14
as inventor, 41
as peace commissioner, 127, 129, 130
as postmaster general, 141
as scientist, 38, 39
at Constitutional Convention, 159, 163
deist, 48
and Hutchinson letters, 82
and negotiations with France, 117–18
on painting, 43
in Paris, 118
resigns as colonial agent, 84
in Second Continental Congress, 94, 99
and Stamp Act, 63, 66–67, 69
and the West, 79, 80, 138
Franklin, State of (Tennessee), 141
Franklin, William, 79, 100
Freeman's Farm, Battle of, 115–16
French Revolution
and U.S. foreign policy, 216–18
Freneau, Philip, 198, 215–16
Fries, John, 237, 250
Frontier
in 1790, 189
as alternative for discontented, 175–76
British and Indians in Northwest, 218–23, 274–81
British policy toward, 56–58, 78–81
and Burr Conspiracy, 261–64
exploration of Meriwether Lewis, 256–57
and Louisiana Purchase, 253–66
Loyalists on, 102
Regulators in Carolinas, 76–78
settlement of Great Valley, 15–17
and Shays's Rebellion, 152–54
territorial government for, 142–45
in War of 1812, 284, 289–90
western lands ceded, 138–39, 141
Whisky Rebellion on, 223–25
Furniture design, 204–05
Fur trade, 148–49

Gadsden, Christopher, 67, 89
Gage, Thomas, 74, 93, 95
Gallatin, Albert
as secretary of treasury, 245–47, 268, 271, 272
in Congress, 242
and Treaty of Ghent, 296
and Whisky Rebellion, 224–25
Galloway, Joseph, 66–67, 67, 89, 89–91, 94
Galvez, Bernardo de, 118
Garden, Alexander, 33, 42
Gardoqui, Don Diego de, 158
Garrick, David, 51
Gaspee (ship), 82
Gates, Horatio, 114–16, 119, 123–24
General Magazine and Historical Chronicle for all the British Plantations in America, 45
Genêt, Edmond, 217–18
The Genuine Information, 168
George I, 42
George III, 68–69, 75, 104–05, 112
Georgia
agricultural problems in, 190
description of, 25–26
independence of, 134–35
Indians in, 220, 275–76
invaded by British army, 123
and Stamp Act, 68
and western lands, 142
Georgian architecture, 200, 202
Germain, Lord George, 112, 126
Germans, 11–12, 15–17, 102
Germantown, Battle of, 113–14
Gerry, Elbridge, 162, 164, 231, 235
Giles, William B., 271
Gilpin, Thomas, 41
Girard, Stephen, 226
Girty, Simon, 102
Glasgow, 18
Godoy, Prince, 230
Gooch, William, 62
Gothic novel, 198
Government
in colonial America, 2, 9
independent income for colonial governors, 71
nature of in state constitutions, 134–36
rise of colonial assemblies, 54–55, 62
state governments formed, 97, 132–33
for territories, 142–45, 178–79
Grafton, Duke of, 75
Graham, John, 263
The Grammatical Institute, 197
Granville District, N.C., 77
Grasse, Admiral de, 127
Grayson, William, 165–72
Great Awakening, 49–54
Great Britain
and American neutral rights, 264–73, 282–83

army carries off slaves, 177–78
attempts to tax colonies, 61–74
difficulties faced by during Revolution, 104–05
frontier policies of during 1750s and 1760s, 56–58
frontier policy of during 1770s, 78–81
and Hamiltonian finance and foreign policy, 216–17
and Indians in Northwest, 280–81
and Jay Treaty, 225–27
and Northwest post, 218–23
postwar regulation of American trade, 148
riots in during 1782, 129
Tea Act and coercion, 83–87
and Treaty of Ghent, 295–97
and War of 1812, 283–95
and writs of assistance, 58–59
Great Valley of Virginia, 14–17
Greek architecture, 201–02, 203
Greene, Nathanael, 94, 107, 112, 124–28
Green Mountain Boys, 94, 115
Greenville, Treaty of, 277–78
Grenville, George, 61–63, 68, 70, 71, 74
Grundy, Felix, 273
Guerriere (ship), 286
Guilford Courthouse, Battle of, 125

Half-Way Covenant, 50
Halifax, N.C., 23
Hamilton, Alexander, 146
as nationalist, 140, 155, 156, 157
as secretary of treasury, 210, 212–14, 216–17, 224, 228
at Constitutional Convention, 159, 162
at Yorktown, 127
death of, 262
and slavery, 178
and split in Federalist party, 234, 238–39
and *The Federalist*, 172
Hancock, John, 93, 94, 140, 158
as governor of Massachusetts, 152
as revolutionary, 36, 72–73
and federal Constitution, 169–70
Harlem Heights, Battle of, 107
Harmar, Joseph, 220–21
Harrington, James, 132
Harrison, Benjamin, 274
Harrison, Peter, 2–3, 201
Harrison, William Henry
and Battle of Thames, 287–88
and Tippecanoe, 274, 278–81
and U.S. Indian policy, 274–81
Hartford Convention, 297–98
Hartford Wits, 197
Harvard College, 5, 194
Hazard, Ebenezer, 141
Henderson, Richard, 81
Henderson, Thomas, 156
Henry, John, 60
Henry, Patrick, 53, 73, 97, 177, 228
and Articles of Confederation, 140
as Antifederalist, 169, 170–72
as anti-nationalist, 158–59
as governor of Virginia, 122
in First Continental Congress, 89, 90
and navigation of Mississippi River, 158
opposes Stamp Act, 64–65
and Parson's Cause, 60–61
reads law, 37
and religious freedom, 187
in Virginia politics, 155
Henry, Rev. Patrick, 52
Hessians, 105, 108, 113–14, 174
Hiawatha (Iroquois prophet), 278
Hillsborough, Earl of, 70, 72, 74, 79, 82
History and Present State of Virginia (1705), 44
A History of New England with Particular Reference to the Denomination of Christians Called Baptists, 53
History of the Colony of Massachusetts Bay (1764), 44
History of the Five Nations (1727), 40
Hoban, James, 201
Holland
and American Revolution, 129
Holland Land Company, 189
Holston Valley, 141
Home furnishings
in early republic, 203–05
Hopkins, Stephen, 48
delegate to First Continental Congress, 89
Hopkinson, Francis, 44, 205
Hornet (ship), 282
Horseshoe Bend, Battle of, 290
House of Baring, 246
Howe, Sir William, 94, 95
New York campaign, 105–09
Philadelphia campaign, 112–14
Hudson River, 7
Hull, Isaac, 285–86
Hull, William, 276, 284
Humphreys, David, 153–54
Hunter, Robert, 40
Hus, John, 9
Hutchinson, Thomas
as governor of Massachusetts, 75, 81, 83, 84
as historian, 44
house burnt, 66
as lieutenant governor of Massachusetts, 59
as Loyalist, 101
and Massachusetts politics, 70

Illinois Land Company, 138
Illinois Territory, 275, 276
Immigration, 9, 11–12, 15–17, 175
Impeachment, 249–51
Impost amendment, 139, 154–55
Impressment of seamen, 265, 282
Indentured servitude, 176
Independence Hall, 90
Indiana Land Company, 79, 138
Indiana Territory, 256, 275
Indian Policy

British before Revolution, 57–58
Jeffersonian, 274–81
and Tippecanoe, 277–81
U.S. in 1790s, 218–23
Indians. *See* Native Americans
Indigo, 24, 26–27, 31–32, 35, 147, 156
Industrial Revolution, 192–93
Innoculations, 42–43
Inns and ordinaries
in Albany, N.Y., 7
in Boston, 3
in New York City, 8
in Pennsylvania, 10, 11
in Virginia, 23
Inns of Court, 37
Institutes of the Laws of England, 37
Internal improvements, 247
"Intolerable Acts" (1774), 85–87
Iron mining and smelting, 6, 30, 192
Iroquois, 79–80, 115, 122, 219, 278
Irving, Washington, 198–99

Jackson, Andrew
and Battle of New Orleans, 293–95
and Burr Conspiracy, 262
and Creek War, 289–90
and Indian removal, 276
Jackson, Francis James, 271–72
Jamestown, Va., 22, 23
Jay, John
as chief justice, 210
in First Continental Congress, 91
and Jay Treaty, 225–27
and Mississippi River navigation, 158
as nationalist, 140
as peace commissioner, 127
as secretary for foreign affairs, 141
on Shays's Rebellion, 153
on slavery, 178
and *The Federalist*, 172
Jay Treaty, 225–27
Jefferson, Martha Wayles, 181
Jefferson, Patsy, 182
Jefferson, Thomas, 73, 156
as architect, 201
on boardinghouse life, 241
and Burr Conspiracy, 261–64
on Constitutional Convention, 158
drafts Declaration of Independence, 99
and exploration of Louisiana Purchase, 256–58
foreign policy of, 251–56, 258–61, 264–70
inaugural address of, 242–44
on Indians, 218, 274–77
and Jay Treaty, 225–26
and Kentucky Resolutions, 243–45
and legal training, 37, 38
on marriage of daughter, 182
as minister to France, 148
and Northwest Territory, 142–43
as president, 244–47, 250–51
as presidential candidate, 228–29, 236–39
and Republican party, 215–16
as scientist, 195
in Second Continental Congress, 94
as secretary of state, 210, 213, 216–17, 227
as secular reformer, 185–88
on Shays's Rebellion, 154
and slavery, 32, 178–79, 188
Summary View, 89
and the Enlightenment, 47–48
as vice president, 242
views of on government, 132–33
as war governor of Virginia, 126
Johnson, Gabriel, 62
Johnson, Richard M., 273, 288
Johnson, Samuel, 48, 51
Johnson, Sir William, 57, 79
Joint stock companies, 191
Judicial review, 248–49
Judiciary Act of 1789, 210, 247–48
Judiciary Act of 1801, 248
Judiciary Act of 1802, 248
Junto Club, 45
Kalb, Baron de, 119, 123–24
Kaskaskia, Ill., 122–23
Kaskaskia Indians, 276
Keelboats, 191
Kentucky, 79–80, 143, 189
Kentucky Resolutions (1798), 243–45, 298
Key, Francis Scott, 205, 292
Kickapoo Indians, 276
Kilpatrick, James, 43
King, Rufus, 140, 159, 178, 298
King's Mountain, Battle of, 124–25
Kip's Bay, Battle of, 107
Knickerbocker's History of New York (1809), 199
Knox, Henry, 181–82, 228
in Continental Army, 96
as secretary of war, 141, 153, 210, 218–19
and Society of the Cincinnati, 147
Knox, Lucy Flucker, 181–82
Kosciusko, Thaddeus, 114, 115, 119

Ladder chair, 205
Lady and Gentleman's Pocket Magazine of Literature and Polite Amusement, 183
Lafayette, Marquis de, 119, 121, 126
Laffite, Jean, 294
Lake Champlain, Battle of
in 1776, 111
in 1814, 293
Lake Erie, Battle of, 287–88
Lamb, John, 66, 88
Lancaster, Pa., 15
Lancaster, Treaty of, 219
Lancaster Pike, 190
Land Act (1800), 274–75
Lansing, John, Jr., 159, 162
La Petite Democrate (ship), 217
Latrobe, Benjamin H., 201–02
Laurens, Henry, 97
Lavoisier, Antonie Laurent, 196
Lawrence (ship), 287–88
Lawrence, James, 286
Lawyers, 37–38, 153
League of Armed Neutrality, 129
Leander (ship), 267
Leclerc, Victor Emmanuel, 254–55
Ledyard, John, 256

Lee, Arthur, 117–18
Lee, Charles, 120–21
Lee, Henry (Light Horse Harry), 125, 206, 224
Lee, Richard Henry, 73, 117, 158
as antinationalist, 140
favors independence, 99
and Federal Constitution, 165
in First Continental Congress, 89
and religious freedom, 187
resolution for independence, 137
L'Enfant, Pierre Charles, 179
Leni Lenape, 219
Leopard (ship), 268
L'Espirit des Lois (1748), 133
Letters from a Federal Farmer, 168–69
Letters of a Westchester Farmer, 102
Lewis, Andrew, 80
Lewis and Clark Expedition, 256–57
Lexington, Battle of, 93
Liberty (ship), 72
Libraries, 14, 45
Library Company of Philadelphia, 14, 45
Life of George Washington, 207
Lincoln, Benjamin, 123, 139, 153
Linnaeus, Carolus, 38, 40, 42
Literature
colonial, 44
revolutionary, 197–99
Little Turtle (Miami chief), 221–22
Liverpool, Robert Jenkinson, Earl of, 283
Livingston, Robert R.
and Articles of Confederation, 137
as secretary for foreign affairs, 139
favors independence, 98
and Louisiana Purchase, 254–55, 259
and Republican party, 215–16
in Second Continental Congress, 99
Locke, John, 38, 46–47, 51, 99
Logan, George, 39
Logan, James, 45
Long Island, Battle of, 107
Lord Dunmore's War, 80, 219
Louisiana Purchase, 253–66
Creoles in, 261
exploration of, 256–58
L'Ouverture, Toussaint, 254–55
Loyalists, 101–03
and Continental Association, 91–92
and evacuation of Philadelphia, 120
fight with British in South, 124
and Peace of Paris of 1783, 130
property of redistributed, 177
Loyal Nine, 66
Lundy's Lane, Battle of, 291

McClurg, James, 159
McCready, James, 194–95
Macdonough, Thomas, 293
McDougall, Alexander, 66
Macedonian (ship), 286
McGillivray, Alexander, 220
McHenry, James, 228, 241–42
McIntyre, Samuel, 204
Mackintosh, Ebenezer, 65
Macon, Nathaniel, 272
Macon's Bill Number Two (1810), 272–73
Madison, James
at Constitutional Convention, 159, 161
and coming of War of 1812, 270–73, 281–83
in Congress, 209, 211, 212–14, 242
and Jay Treaty, 226
and Jeffersonian reform in Virginia, 186–87
as nationalist, 140, 155–56, 157, 158
on paper money, 152
and Republican party, 215–16
on republics, 208
as secretary of state, 254, 267–68, 269–70
and *The Federalist*, 172
and Virginia Resolutions, 234
war message in 1812, 282
as war president, 283, 291–93, 296
and West Florida, 259–61
works for ratification of Constitution, 171
Magnalia Christi Americana (1702), 44
Mandan Indians, 257
Marbury, William, 248–49
Marbury v. *Madison* (1803), 248–49
Marietta, Ohio, 189
Marion, Francis, 123, 125
Marlboro, Md., 20
Marshall, David, 53
Marshall, John
as biographer of Washington, 206
as chief justice, 242, 248–49
and Burr Conspiracy, 263–64
and federal Constitution, 171
and XYZ affair, 231, 235
Martin, Luther, 168
Maryland, 97, 190
description of, 20
disputed boundary with Virginia, 156–57
and ratification of Articles of Confederation, 138–39
ratifies Constitution, 170
state constitution, 135–36
Mason, George, 48, 133, 156, 159, 164, 171
Massachusetts
abolishes slavery, 178
calls Continental Congress, 88
colonial charter revoked, 86
constitution for, 134, 135, 136, 184
description of, 3–6
elects delegates to First Continental Congress, 89
opposes Stamp Act, 65–67
opposes tea tax, 81
opposes Townshend taxes, 72
politics in, 69–70
provincial congress of, 94
ratifies Constitution, 169–70
Shays's Rebellion in, 152–54
and writs of assistance, 58–59
Massachusetts Government Act (1774), 86

Mather, Cotton, 39, 42–43, 44, 45
Maury, James, 60, 63
Medicine
colonial, 13, 41–42
revolutionary, 196–97
Mennonites, 178, 205
Menominee Indians, 279
Mercer, George, 67
Merry, Alexander, 244
Merry, Anthony, 262
Methodism, 49, 194–95
Mexican Association, 261
M'Fingall (1776), 198
Miami Indians, 220, 279
Michigan Territory, 275, 276
Milan Decree, 266
Militia, 92–93
Mint, 214
Minutemen, 93
Mississippi River
as U.S. western boundary, 127, 129–30
exploring headwaters of, 258
and Louisiana Purchase, 253–66
navigation of during 1780s, 158
and Pinckney Treaty, 230
Missouri River, 257
Mitchill, Samuel Latham, 196
Mobile, Ala., 294
Mobs
in Great Britain during 1782, 129
oppose Stamp Act, 65–67
oppose Townshend duties, 72–73
Shays's Rebellion, 152–54
Molasses, 28
Molasses Act (1732), 62
Monmouth, N.J., Battle of, 120–21
Monroe, James, 267–68
as Antifederalist, 171
as end of era, 298–99
in Confederation Congress, 155
and election of 1808, 270–71
and Louisiana Purchase, 255, 259
and War of 1812, 292–93
Montagu, Lady Mary Worley, 42
Montesquieu, Charles, Baron de, 133
Montgomery, Richard, 109–11
Monticello, 201
Montreal
Americans capture in 1775, 109–10
Moore's Creek, Battle of, 78, 98
Moravians, 9–10
Morgan, Daniel, 57, 111, 115, 116, 125
Morris, Gouverneur, 159, 164, 169
Morris, Robert, 117
as land speculator, 138
as merchant, 148
as nationalist, 140
as superintendent of Finance, 128, 139, 145–46
at Constitutional Convention, 159
in debtor's prison, 176
opposes paper money, 159
Morris, Samuel, 52
Morristown, N.J., 107–08, 108–09, 121
Mount Airy (plantation), 21–22
Mount Vernon, 19
Mount Vernon Conference, 156–57
Murray, William Vans, 235
Music, 44

Napoleon
and American neutral rights, 265–68, 272–73
assumes power, 235
exiled to Elba, 290
sells Louisiana to U.S., 254–56
and West Florida, 259–60
Nashville, Tenn., 189
National Gazette (Philadelphia), 198, 215–16
Nationalism
as government policy, 251–53
symbols of, 206–07
Nationalists, 140
National Road, 247
Native Americans, 17
British policy toward, 57–58
description of, 16, 22
resistance in Northwest, 218–23, 274–81, 277–81
in Revolution, 115
and Treaty of Fort Stanwix, 79–80
and Treaty of Ghent, 296
Natural History of Carolina, Florida, and the Bahama Islands, 39
Naturalization, 175
Naturalization Act (1798), 232, 243
Naval stores, 24
Navy
in War of 1812, 285–87, 287–88, 293–95
Neutrality Proclamation of 1793, 217
Neutral rights, 225–27, 264–73, 282–83
Neville, John, 223–24
The New American Practical Navigator (1802), 195
New Brunswick, N.J., 9
Newburgh Conspiracy, 146–47
New Hampshire, 97, 135
ratifies Constitution, 170
New Jersey, 100, 150–51, 178
description of, 9, 11
New Jersey Plan, 162
New Lights, 51–52, 53, 67
New Orleans
Battle of, 293–95
trade through, 253–54
U.S. attempts to buy, 254–55
Newport, R.I., 2–3, 151
Newspapers, 45
Newton, Sir Isaac, 39, 46, 51–52
New York
culture in, 198–99
and Declaration of Independence, 100
description of, 7–9
and election of 1800, 238
elects delegates to First Continental Congress, 89
emancipation in, 178
frontier in 1790, 189
and impost, 155
Loyalists in, 101
opposes Stamp Act, 66
opposes Townshend taxes, 73
paper money in, 159
politics in during War of 1812, 289
protests Quartering Act, 74
ratifies Constitution, 172
resists Tea Act, 85

second convention movement in, 169
state constitution, 135–36
turnpikes in, 190
New York City
description of, 8, 30
imports of, 76
population of, 34
and Revolution, 74, 105–09, 127, 131
New York City, Treaty of, 220
New York Society for Promoting Manumission, 178
Nez Perce Indians, 257
Niagara, 218, 287–88
as theater of war, 284–85, 289, 290–91
Nicholas, Wilson Cary, 233
Nicholson, Joseph H., 250
Nomini Hall (plantation), 19
Nonimportation
as response to Townshend taxes, 71–72, 72–74, 76
Nonimportation Act of 1806, 267
Nonintercourse, Resolution of 1794, 226
Nonintercourse Act of 1809, 272
Nootka Sound, 148–49
North, Frederick Lord, 75, 83–84, 85–86, 95, 105, 129
North Bridge (Boston), 93
The North Britain, 68
North Carolina
constitution of 1776, 135
Continental Association enforced in, 92
description of, 23–24
and federal Constitution, 170, 172
fighting in during Revolution, 125
Loyalists in, 102
opposes Townshend taxes, 78
Regulators in, 77–78
votes for independence, 98
western lands of, 138–39, 141–42
Northwest Ordinance (1787), 144–45, 178–79
Northwest Territory
British and Indians in, 218–23
Clark's campaign in, 122–23
Indians in, 274–81
land sales in, 144
territorial government for, 142–45
Notes on Virginia (1785), 179, 188, 195
Nullification, 233–34

Oceana (1656), 132
Of Civil Government, Two Treatises (1691), 46–47
Office of Foreign Affairs, 139
Ohio, 143, 145, 275
Ohio Company, 144
Old Lights, 53
Old Republicans, 268, 270
Oliver, Andrew, 65–66, 81
Orders-in-council
and Jay Treaty, 225–26
of July 1783, 148, 150, 152, 154
and War of 1812, 265–66, 271, 282–83
Ordinance of 1784, 142–43
Ordinance of 1785, 144
Orleans Territory, 256, 261
Ormonde (1799), 198
Osage Indians, 279
Osborn, Sarah, 52
Oswald, Richard, 129
Oswego, 218
Otis, Harrison Gray, 298
Otis, James, Jr., 59, 66, 67, 70, 74–76
Otis, James, Sr., 59
Ottawa Indians, 220

Packet service, 28
Paine, Thomas, 105
The Age of Reason, 48, 194
The American Crisis, 107–08
Common Sense, 97–98
Painting
colonial, 43–44
revolutionary, 199–200
Pakenham, Sir Edward, 295
Palladio, Andrea, 200–01
Pamunkey Indians, 22
Paper money, 62–63, 64, 128, 138, 147, 149–50
Parson's Cause, 60–61
Passenger pigeons, 3
Paterson, William, 159, 162
Pawtucket, R.I., 193
Paxton Boys, 66
Peace of Paris (1783), 129–31
Peale, Charles Willson, 43, 199–200
Peale, Rembrandt, 200
Pendleton, Edmund, 140, 171
Penitentiaries, 185
Penn, Thomas, 66
Penn, William, 11, 218
Pennsylvania
constitution of 1776, 134
description of, 9–15
and election of 1800, 237
elects delegates to First Continental Congress, 89
frontier in, 57, 79–81, 189
opposes Stamp Act, 66–67
paper money in, 159
politics in, 67, 69
ratifies federal Constitution, 166–68
turnpikes in, 190
Whisky Rebellion in, 223–25
Pennsylvania Gazette, 13, 180
Pensacola, Fla., 118, 294
Perceval, Spencer, 283
Perry, Oliver Hazard, 287–88
Perth Amboy, 9, 150
Philadelphia
as cultural center, 198
British evacuate, 120
colonial growth of, 34
description of, 11–14
nonimportation in, 76
trade of, 30–31
women in, 180–81
workingmen in, 35
Philadelphia (ship), 252–53
Philadelphia, College of, 14, 184
Philadelphia Academy of Fine Arts, 200
Philadelphia Young Ladies Academy, 184
Philosophes, 132
Phyfe, Duncan, 204
Pickens, Andrew, 123, 125
Pickering, John, 250
Pickering, Timothy, 228, 231, 235
Pike, Zebulon Montgomery, 258, 289
Pinckney, Charles Cotesworth, 159, 229, 231, 238, 270
Pinckney, Thomas, 228–29, 230
Pinckney Treaty, 230
Pine Barren Act (1786), 159

Pinkney, William, 267–68
Pitt, William, Earl of Chatham, 58, 69, 70, 75
Pitt, William, the younger, 226
Plantae Coldenghamiae, 41
Plattsburg Bay, Battle of, 293
Point Pleasant, Battle of, 80
Political parties
  accepted in America, 239–40
Pontiac's conspiracy, 57
Poor Richard's Almanac, 27
Pope, Alexander, 45, 197
Pope's Day, 35, 66
Population of U.S., 174
Porter, Peter B., 285
Potawtomi Indians, 279
Potomac Company, 156
Potomac River, 156–57
Poverty
  in colonial cities, 4, 34–38
  in North Carolina, 24
Preble, Edward, 252–53
Presbyterian Church, 49–50, 194–95
Presbyterian party (in Pennsylvania), 67, 69
Presque Isle, Pa., 287
Prevost, Sir George, 293
Price, Richard, 38
Priestly, Joseph, 38, 195
Primogeniture, 186
Principia Mathematica (1686), 39, 46
Principles of Action in Matter (1746), 40
Printing, colonial, 44–45
Privy Council
  and Boston Tea Party, 85
  denounces Franklin, 84
  and Parson's Cause, 60
Proclamation Line of 1763, 58, 79
Proctor, Henry, 288
Prophet, 278–81
Prophet's Town, 279–81
Proposals Relating to the Education of Youth in Pennsylvania, 13–14
Providence, R.I., 151
Pulaski, Count Casimir, 119
Punishment for crimes, 185, 187
Put-In-Bay, Battle of, 287–88
Putnam, Israel, 94, 95
Putnam, Rufus, 144

Quaker party (in Pennsylvania), 66–67
Quakers, 9, 11–13, 52, 178, 179
Quartering Act (1765), 74, 86
Quasi War (with France), 241–42
Quebec
  American attack on, 110–11
Quebec Act (1774), 81
Queenston Heights, Battle of, 285
Quincy, Josiah, 76

Ramsey, David, 182–83, 206
Randolph, Edmund, 156, 210, 227–28
  at Constitutional Convention, 159, 161, 164, 171
  and federal Constitution, 169
Randolph, John, of Roanoke, 169, 179, 250–51, 260, 263, 267, 268, 270
Randolph, Thomas Mann, 182
Raritan River, 9
Rasin River Massacre, 284
Read, George, 160
Red Sticks, 280, 289–90
Redwood Library, 2, 45, 201
Reed, Esther DeBerdt, 181
Reeve, Tapping, 37
Reform
  in post-revolutionary America, 183–88
Regulating Act (1773), 83
Regulators
  in North Carolina, 77–78
  in South Carolina, 76–77
Religion
  in colonial America, 2, 9, 9–10, 14, 21, 47–48, 52–53
  impact of Revolution on, 132
  and politics of 1780s, 140
  revivals in, 49–54, 194–95
  in the early republic, 193–95
  Virginia Statute for freedom of, 187
Report on a National Bank, 214
Report on Manufactures, 214–15
Reports on Public Credit, 211–14
Republicanism
  and creation of state governments, 132–33
Republican party (in Pennsylvania), 134
Republican party (Jeffersonians), 242
  and Alien and Sedition Acts, 232–44
  assault on courts, 247–51
  in elections, 228–29, 236–39
  ideology of, 242–44, 244–47
  origins of, 215–16
  strength among merchants, 226
  supports Louisiana Purchase, 255–56
  supports War of 1812, 273, 282
Revenue Act (1764), 36, 62
Revere, Paul, 85, 90, 93, 170
Revivals, 49–54
"Revolution of 1800," 236–39
Reynolds, Sir Joshua, 43, 44
Rhoads, Samuel, 13
Rhode Island
  and burning of *Gaspee*, 82
  description and government of, 2–3
  elects delegates to First Continental Congress, 89
  and federal Constitution, 170, 172
  and federal impost, 139–40, 154
  forms state government, 97
  opposes Stamp Act, 66
  paper money in, 151
  trade of, 28–29, 30
Rhode Island College, 53
Riall, Phineas, 291
Rice, 24–25, 26–27, 31–32, 33, 35–36, 37, 147, 156, 190, 199
Riots. *See* Mobs
Rittenhouse, David, 40
Robinson, John, 64, 65
Rochambeau, Comte de, 127
Rockingham, Marquis of, 69, 70, 83–84, 129
Roderique Hortalez and Company, 117
Rome, as symbol, 201, 205–06
Romney (ship), 72
Royal African Company, 28

Royal Society, 40, 42, 43
Rule of 1756, 226, 266–67
Rum industry, 29
Rush, Benjamin, 155, 173, 184–85, 196–97
Russell, Jonathan, 296
Russia
and American Revolution, 128–29
Rutledge, Edward, 91, 99, 137, 140
Rutledge, John, 89, 159

Sacajawea, 257
Sac and Fox Indians, 276, 279
Sackett's Harbor, 289
St. Clair, Arthur, 114, 221
St. Leger, Barry, 115
St. Tammany, Society of, 220–21
San Ildefonso, Treaty of, 254
San Lorenzo, Treaty of, 230
Santo Domingo, 254–55
Saratoga (ship), 293
Saratoga, Battle of, 115–16
Savannah, Ga., 26, 123
Schuyler, Philip, 109, 114
Science
colonial, 38–43
revolutionary, 195–97
Scots, 102
Scots-Irish, 15–17, 49
Scott, Winfield, 289
Seabury, Samuel, 91–92, 102
Sea Island cotton, 26
Sears, Isaac, 66, 88
Second Great Awakening, 194–95
Sectionalism
in Constitutional Convention, 162
and navigation of Mississippi River, 158
Sedition Act (1798), 232–33, 243
Seminoles, 279
The Sentiments of an American Woman (1780), 181
Separation of powers, 133, 136
Sevier, John, 141
Shakers, 205
Shannon (ship), 286
Sharpe, Horatio, 62
Shawnee Indians, 79–80, 80, 219–20, 274, 277–81
Shays, Daniel, 153
Shays's Rebellion, 152–54
Shelburne, William Petty Fitzmaurice, Earl of, 75, 79, 129
Shelley, Mary, 198
Shenandoah Valley, 16–17
Sherman, Roger, 89, 99, 159, 163
Shipbuilding, 29, 192
Shippen, Peggy, 122
Shirley (plantation), 44
Shirley, William, 62
Sickle cell, 33
Sierra Leone, 178
Sioux Indians, 257
The Sketchbook (1819–20), 199
Slater, Samuel, 192–93
Slavery
in colonies, 8, 18, 23, 26, 32–34
and Constitution, 162
elderly in, 20–21
Jefferson on, 188
opposition to, 178–79
and Peace of Paris of 1783, 130
and plantation life, 21–22
prohibited in Northwest Territory, 142–43, 144–45
in revolutionary America, 177–80
Slave trade, 28, 32
Small, William, 47
Smallpox inoculations, 42–43
Smith, Adam, 103, 236, 243, 246
Smith, Melancton, 165–72
Smith, Samuel, 226, 271
Smith, William, 14, 48
Smyth, Alexander, 285
Society
in colonial America, 4, 34–38
impact of Revolution on, 132
and Regulators in Carolinas, 76–78
U.S. as bourgeois republic in 1790, 175–77
in Virginia in 1790, 176–77
Society for Establishing Useful Manufactures, 215
Society for the Propagation of the Gospel, 102
Society of Friends. *See* Quakers
Sons of Liberty, 65–67, 68, 74–75, 76, 85
South Carolina
British operations in, 123
cotton cultivation in, 190
description of, 24–25
economy of, 31–32
elects delegates to First Continental Congress, 89
nonimportation in, 76
opposes Stamp Act, 67
paper money in, 159
ratifies Constitution, 170
Regulators in, 76–77
slavery in, 33–34
state constitution of, 135–36
Spain, 261
in American Revolution, 118–19
attitude of toward U.S., 131
cedes Louisiana to France, 253–54
closes Mississippi River, 158, 255
and Pike's explorations, 258
and Pinckney Treaty, 230
and West Florida, 258–61
Spectator, 45
Speculators
and the national debt, 211–12
in western lands, 17, 138
Stagecoaches, 191
Stamp Act (1765), 63–70
Congress, 67–68
riots, 65–67
Star Chamber, 82
Stark, John, 94
State Department, 210
Staten Island, 8
Stearns, Shubal, 53
Steele, Richard, 197
Stiles, Ezra, 197
Stoddard, Solomon, 50
Stono Rebellion, 34
Stony Point, 121
Strickland, William, 203
Stuart, Gilbert, 200
Stuart, John, 79
Stueben, William Augustus, Baron von, 119–20
Suffering traders, 79
Suffolk Resolves, 90
Suffrage, 244
for free blacks, 179
Jefferson on, 185–86
in Northwest Ordinance, 145

in state constitutions, 134–36
Sugar Act (1764), 36, 62
Sullivan, John, 122
A Summary View of the Rights of British America (1774), 89
Sumter, Thomas, 123
Supreme Court, U.S., 247
created, 210
judicial review by, 248–49
The Surrender of Cornwallis, 199
Swift, Jonathan, 45
Symbols of American nationalism, 206–07

Talleyrand, 231, 234–36, 259
Tariff of 1789, 209
Tariffs, 214–15
Tarleton, Banastre, 125, 126
Taxes
and depression in New England, 148
Gallatin's plan, 246
levied by Congress, 209
protective tariffs, 214–15
and Shays's Rebellion, 152–54
on whisky, 213–14, 223–25
Tayloe, John, 20, 21–22
Taylor, John, of Caroline, 233, 270
Tea
Boston Tea Party, 84–85
Tea Act (1773), 75–76, 81, 84
Tecumseh, 223, 274, 277–81, 284
death of, 288
Tennent, Gilbert, 49–50, 51, 54
Tennent, William, 49–50
Tennessee, 141, 143, 189
Territories
government and statehood for, 142–45
Territory Southwest of the River Ohio, 142
Tertium Quids, 260
Textile manufacturing, 192–93
Thames, Battle of, 288
Thomson, Charles, 41, 88, 90
Thornton, William, 201
Thoughts on the Cause of the Present Discontents (1770), 75
Tindal, Matthew, 48
Tippecanoc, Battle of, 274
Tobacco, 18, 20, 22, 24, 31, 35, 60, 147–48, 156–57, 190, 199
Tories. *See* Loyalists
Townshend, Charles, 70–71, 75
Townshend taxes, 70–74, 75–76, 78
Trade
after Revolution, 148, 148–49
before War of 1812, 266–67
carrying trade and Jay Treaty, 225–27
colonial, 18, 25, 26, 28–34, 58
through New Orleans, 253–54
U.S. foreign in 1790, 191
See also Orders-in-council
Trafalgar, Battle of, 265
Transportation, 190–91
National Road, 247
Transylvania, 81
Travels in New England and New York (1821–22), 197
Treason, 264
Treasury Department, 209–10
Treaty of Fort Greenville, 222–23
Treaty of Ghent, 296–97
Treaty of Paris of 1763, 56
Treaty of Paris of 1783, 129–31
Trenton, Battle of, 108
Triangular trade, 28–34
Tripolitan War, 251–53
Trumbull, John, 198
Trumbull, Jonathan, 43, 199
Tryon, Sir William, 78
Tryon Palace, 78
Turnpike era, 190
Two Million Act (1806), 260
Two-Penny Act (1758), 60
Tyler, John, 157
Tyler, Moses Coit, 86

Unitarian Church, 48, 194
United States (ship), 286
United States Military Academy, 245

Valcour Island, Battle of, 111
Valley Forge, Pa., 114, 119–20
Vandalia, 80
Van Renssalaer, Stephen, 284–85
Vergennes, Charles Gravier, Comte de, 117–18, 130–31
Vermont, 178
Vice Admiralty courts, 62, 67, 72
Vincennes, Ind., 122–23, 274
A Vindication of the Rights of a Woman (1792), 183
Virginia
agriculture in, 190
constitution of 1776, 135, 185–86
creates committee of correspondence, 82
debtor relief in, 159
Virginia Declaration of Rights (1776), 133
description of, 16–19, 21–24
disputed boundary with Maryland, 156–57
fighting in during Revolution, 125–27
forces Lord Dunmore to flee, 97
frontier expansion in, 79–81
Jeffersonian reform in, 185–88
opposes Stamp Act, 67
opposes Townshend taxes, 73
Parson's Cause in, 60–61
planter debt in, 31
ratifies Constitution, 170–72
religion in, 52–53
resists Stamp Act, 64–65
second convention movement in, 169
selects delegates to First Continental Congress, 89
slavery in, 32–35
society in, 176–77
turnpikes in, 190
votes for independence, 98
western lands of, 138–39
Virginia Plan (1787), 161
Virginia Resolution (1798), 243–45, 298
Virginia Statute for Religious Freedom (1786), 156, 187

Wabash Land Company, 138
Walker, Quork, 178
Wampum, 8–9
Ward, Artemas, 94

War Department, 139, 210
War of 1812
  campaigns of, 283–95
  causes of, 264–73, 281–83
  peace treaty ending, 295–97
Warren, Joseph, 66, 93, 95
Warren, Mercy Otis, 206
Warville, Brissot de, 179
Washington, D.C.
  agreement to establish, 213
  as new capital, 241–42
  British burn, 292
  buildings in, 201–02
Washington, George, 48, 73, 116
  as commander in chief, 95, 96
  at Constitutional Convention, 159, 160
  death of, 197
  defends New York City, 105–09
  elected president, 208–09
  Farewell Address, 228
  in First Continental Congress, 89
  in French and Indian War, 57
  inaugural address of, 208
  at Morristown, 121
  as nationalist in 1780s, 156
  as national symbol, 206–07
  as planter, 19
  as president, 214, 216–17, 220, 224–25, 227–28
  attacks Trenton, 108
  selects capital site, 241
  on Shays's Rebellion, 154
  Stuart portrait of, 200
  and the Newburgh Conspiracy, 146
  at Valley Forge, 119–20
  and Virginia ratification, 171
  and western settlement, 143
  on women, 121–22
  at Yorktown, 126–27
Washington, Martha, 181
Wayne, Anthony, 114, 121, 221–22
Wealth of Nations (1776), 103, 236, 243
Webster, Daniel, 274
Webster, Noah, 197
Weems, Parson Mason Locke, 206–07
Wellington, Duke of, 290, 297
Wentworth, Benning, 62
Wesley, Charles, 49
Wesley, John, 49, 51
West. *See* frontier
West, Benjamin, 43, 44, 199
Western lands
  cession by states, 141
  government for, 142–45
  and ratification of Articles of Confederation, 138–39
  sales of, 144
Western Reserve, 141
West Florida, 258–61
West Indies
  Americans excluded from after Revolution, 148
  and colonial trade, 28–29, 30, 58
  and Franco-American treaties of 1778, 118
  and Jay Treaty, 225–27
  U.S. trade with blocked, 266–67
  See also Orders-in-council
Westover (plantation), 44
West Point
  Arnold's treason, 122
  military academy, 245
Whaling, 30
Wharton, Samuel, 80
Whisky
  taxes on, 213–14, 223–25
Whisky Rebellion, 223–25
White Plains, N.Y., 107
Whitfield, George, 51, 52, 53, 54
Wieland (1798), 198
Wilderness Road, 80, 189, 219
Wilkes, John, 68, 75, 105
Wilkinson, Eliza, 180
Wilkinson, James, 258, 261–64, 283, 289, 291
William and Mary, College of, 23, 37, 47, 188
Williams, Roger, 53, 218
Williamsburg, 22–23
Willing, Thomas, 246
Wilmington, N.C., 24
Wilson, James, 99, 138, 159
Winchester, Va., 17
Winder, William, 292
Windsor chair, 204–05
Winnebago Indians, 279
Winthrop, John IV, 39–40
Wirt, William, 282
Wisconsin, 145
Wolcott, Oliver, 228
Wollstonecraft, Mary, 183
Women
  and Continental Army, 121–22
  education of, 184–85
  in post-revolutionary America, 180–83
  in revivals, 51–52
  in revolutionary America, 73, 92, 181
Woolman, John, 178
Workingmen, colonial, 35–36
Wren, Christopher, 5
Writs of assistance, 58–59
Wyandot Indians, 220, 279
Wythe, George, 37, 48, 159, 171

XYZ Affair, 230–32

Yale University, 197
Yates, Robert, 159, 162
York (Toronto), 289
York, Pa., 113
Yorkshire Association, 129
Yorktown, campaign of, 126–27
Yusef, Pasha, 252–53

Zenger Case, 232
Zinzendorf, Count Nicholas Ludwig von, 10